SIXTH EDITI

CORNERST NE

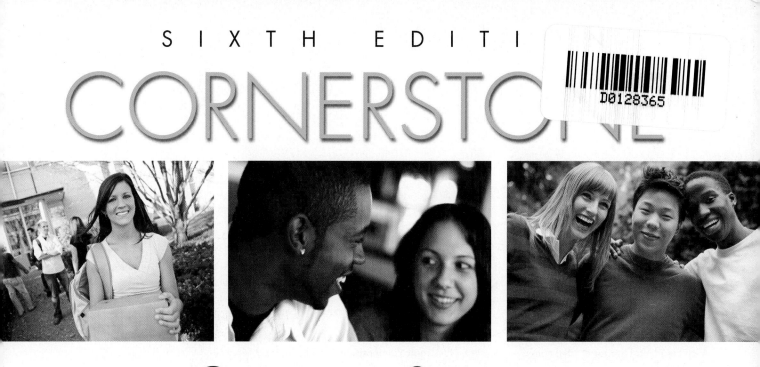

Creating Success
Through Positive Change

ROBERT M. SHERFIELD
College of Southern Nevada

PATRICIA G. MOODY
University of South Carolina

Boston ● Columbus ● Indianapolis ● New York ● San Francisco ● Upper Saddle River
Amsterdam ● Cape Town ● Dubai ● London ● Madrid ● Milan ● Munich ● Paris ● Montreal ● Toronto
Delhi ● Mexico City ● Sao Paulo ● Sydney ● Hong Kong ● Seoul ● Singapore ● Taipei ● Tokyo

Executive Editor: Sande Johnson
Development Editor: Jennifer Gessner
Editorial Assistant: Clara Ciminelli
Vice President, Director of Marketing:
    Quinn Perkson
Marketing Manager: Amy Judd
Production Editor: Janet Domingo

Editorial Production Service: Elm Street
    Publishing Services
Manufacturing Buyer: Megan Cochran
Electronic Composition: Integra Software Services
    Pvt. Ltd.
Interior Design: Carol Somberg
Cover Designer: Linda Knowles

For related titles and support materials, visit our online catalog at www.pearsonhighered.com

Library of Congress Cataloging-in-Publication Data

Sherfield, Robert M.
Cornerstone : creating success through positive change / Robert M. Sherfield, Patricia G. Moody. — 6th ed.
    p. cm.
Previously published under title: Cornerstone : your foundation for discovering your
potential, learning actively, and living well.
    Includes bibliographical references and Index.
    ISBN-13: 978-0-13-700757-8
    ISBN-10: 0-13-700757-4
    1. College student orientation—United States.   2. Study skills—United States.   3. College
students—United States—Life skills guides.   I. Moody, Patricia G.   II. Title.
LB2343.32.S53 2011
378.1'98—dc22
                                                                            2009042101

Printed in the United States of America

Credits appear on page 383, which constitutes an extension of the copyright page.

10 9 8 7 6 5 4 3 CKV 13 12 11

www.pearsonhighered.com

ISBN 13: 978-0-13-700757-8
ISBN 10:   0-13-700757-4

Dedication

We would like to dedicate this book to the **many teachers** throughout our lives who taught us about life, responsibility, and our role in the world. We carry you with us every day.

Louise Lymas	Neely Beaty	Beverly Jordan
Kitty Carson	Betty Griffin	Dick Smith
Steve Brannon	Frank Jackson	Dr. Harvey Jeffreys
Dr. Marilyn Kameen	Dr. Lars Bjork	Ann Wenz
Phil Lynn	Dr. Howard Jackson	Dr. Leonard Maiden
Mary Alice Roughton	Dr. Marilyn Neidig	Audrey Fulford

TABLE OF CONTENTS

PART ONE
CHANGING YOUR THOUGHTS

CHAPTER 1
CHANGE

ADJUSTING TO THE CULTURE OF COLLEGE, NURTURING CHANGE, AND SETTING GOALS, *page 2*

CHAPTER 2
ENGAGE

DEVELOPING YOUR PERSONAL AND ACADEMIC MOTIVATION, *page 28*

CHAPTER 3
PERSIST

USING THE TOOLS OF SELF-MANAGEMENT TO STAY IN COLLEGE, *page 50*

CHAPTER 4
COMMUNICATE

IMPROVING YOUR INTERPERSONAL COMMUNICATION AND CONFLICT MANAGEMENT SKILLS, *page 72*

CHAPTER 5
THINK

EXPANDING YOUR APTITUDE FOR CRITICAL THINKING, EMOTIONAL INTELLIGENCE, AND INFORMATION LITERACY SKILLS,
page 94

PART TWO
CHANGING YOUR PERFORMANCE

CHAPTER 6
PRIORITIZE

PLANNING YOUR TIME AND REDUCING STRESS,
page 124

CHAPTER 7
LEARN

USING YOUR DOMINANT INTELLIGENCE, PREFERRED LEARNING STYLE, AND UNIQUE PERSONALITY TYPE TO BECOME AN ACTIVE LEARNER,
page 156

CHAPTER 8
READ

BUILDING YOUR READING AND COMPREHENSION SKILLS,
page 184

/CHAPTER 9
RECORD

CULTIVATING YOUR LISTENING SKILLS AND DEVELOPING A NOTE-TAKING SYSTEM THAT WORKS FOR YOU, *page 210*

/CHAPTER 10
UNDERSTAND

EMPOWERING YOUR MEMORY, STUDYING EFFECTIVELY, AND TAKING TESTS WITH CONFIDENCE, *page 236*

PART THREE
CHANGING YOUR LIFE

/CHAPTER 11
PROSPER

MANAGING YOUR MONEY AND YOUR DEBTS WISELY, *page 264*

Robert M. Sherfield, Ph.D.

Robert Sherfield has been teaching public speaking, theatre, and student success and working with first-year orientation programs for over 25 years. Currently, he is a professor at the College of Southern Nevada, teaching student success, professional communication, public speaking, and drama.

An award-winning educator, Robb was named **Educator of the Year** at the College of Southern Nevada. He twice received the **Distinguished Teacher of the Year Award** from the University of South Carolina Union, and has received numerous other awards and nominations for outstanding classroom instruction and advisement.

Robb's extensive work with student success programs includes experience with the design and implementation of these programs—including one program that was presented at the International Conference on the First-Year Experience in Newcastle upon Tyne, England. He has conducted faculty development keynotes and workshops at over 350 institutions of higher education across the United States. He has spoken in 46 states and several foreign countries.

In addition to his co-authorship of *Cornerstone, Opening Doors to Career Success* (Prentice Hall, 2009), he has authored or co-authored *Solving the Professional Development Puzzle: 101 Solutions for Career and Life Planning* (Prentice Hall, 2009), *Cornerstone: Discovering Your Potential, Learning Actively, and Living Well* (Prentice Hall, 2008), *Roadways to Success* (Prentice Hall, 2001), the trade book *365 Things I Learned in College* (Allyn & Bacon, 1996), *Capstone: Succeeding Beyond College* (Prentice Hall, 2001), *Case Studies for the First Year: An Odyssey into Critical Thinking and Problem Solving* (Prentice Hall, 2004), *The Everything® Self-Esteem Book* (Adams Media, 2004), and *Cornerstone: Building On Your Best for Career Success* (Prentice Hall, 2006)

Robb's interest in student success began with his own first year in college. Low SAT scores and a dismal high school ranking denied him entrance into college. With the help of a success program, Robb was granted entrance into college, and went on to earn five college degrees, including a doctorate. He has always been interested in the social, academic, and cultural development of students and sees this book as his way to help students enter the world of work and establishing lasting, rewarding careers. Visit www.robertsherfield.com.

Patricia G. Moody, Ph.D.

Patricia G. Moody is Dean Emerita of the College of Hospitality, Retail and Sport Management at the University of South Carolina, where she served on the faculty and in administration for over 30 years. An award-winning educator, Pat was honored as **Distinguished Educator of the Year** at her college and as **Collegiate Teacher of the Year** by the National Business Education Association. She was also a top-five finalist for the **Amoco Teaching Award** at the University of South Carolina. She received the prestigious **John Robert Gregg Award**, the highest honor in her field of over 100,000 educators.

Pat has co-authored many texts and simulations including: *Solving the Professional Development Puzzle: 101 Solutions for Career and Life Planning, Cornerstone: Discovering Your Potential, Learning Actively, and Living Well, 365 Things I Learned in College, Capstone: Succeeding Beyond College, Case Studies for the First Year: An Odyssey into Critical Thinking and Problem Solving,* and *Cornerstone: Opening Doors to Career Success.*

A nationally known motivational speaker, consultant, and author, Pat has spoken in most states, has been invited to speak in several foreign countries, and frequently keynotes national and regional conventions. She has presented her signature, motivational keynote address, *"Fly Like an Eagle"* to tens of thousands of people, from Olympic athletes to corporate executives to high school students.

As the Dean of her college, Dr. Moody led international trips to build relationships and establish joint research projects in hospitality. Under her direction, faculty members in her college began a landmark study of Chinese Tourists. Pat now travels the country delivering workshops, keynotes, and presentations on topics such as Managing Change, Working in the New Global Community, The Future of the Future, Student Motivation, and Emotional Intelligence. She also serves as a personal coach for business executives.

Filled with stories of inspiration and activities with immediate impact, this book is founded on the hope that comes with education, goal-setting, and determination. *Cornerstone* motivates students by concentrating on concrete academic and personal strategies which will help them navigate the personal and professional changes they face. Using the overriding theme of change and utilizing Bloom's Taxonomy and SQ3R throughout, it is a text that actually uses reading and critical thinking strategies rather than just talking about them. The sixth edition reflects a deeper focus on self-responsibility, active learning (which is reinforced by its interactive design), and building academic and personal success through positive change. Thoroughly updated, *Cornerstone* now includes a new chapter on Interpersonal Communication (with information on communicating effectively in the digital age), updated and expanded information on money and debt management, and a stronger focus on self-engagement and personal responsibility. A totally revised chapter on critical thinking now uses a "Critical Thinking Wheel" to assist students in understanding and using critical thinking more effectively. The sixth edition also boasts a new and exciting section on "HOW we learn," and "HOW to learn" in the learning styles chapter. *Cornerstone* also now extensively covers the ever-popular and timely topic of information literacy and how to apply the concepts to every class. The final chapter on planning for a career and your future now includes information on writing a winning resume, cover letter, and interviewing with confidence and assertiveness.

NEW TO THIS EDITION:

▶ **10 ESSENTIAL CORNERSTONES**—focuses on the 10 most important aspects of one's personal and professional life. These 10 Essential Cornerstones show up throughout the text to help students apply them to everyday situations at school and work.

▶ **ETHICAL BEHAVIOR**—A new section and diagram on the Six Ethical Questions asks students to review his or her thoughts and actions on ethical behavior to ensure successful transitions.

▶ **HOW TO APPROACH CHANGE IN YOUR LIFE**—a six-step process that allows students to implement change into their lives in a practical and concrete fashion.

▶ **INTERPERSONAL COMMUNICATION**—a totally new chapter on interpersonal communication, self-disclosure, getting along with others, and communicating in the digital age.

▶ **SELF-DISCIPLINE AND PROCRASTINATION**—new information on self-discipline as related to time management and a new section on simplifying your life, saying no, and a new focus on beating procrastination.

▶ **MONEY AND DEBT MANAGEMENT**—totally updated and revised information to reflect today's "new" economy. Includes a new economic readiness assessment that asks students to estimate next semester's costs. New information on loans and how much it costs to repay them. New section called "The Big IF's" offers tips for *if* you have to buy a car; *if* you have to purchase furniture; *if* you have to cut your food expenses; *if* you have to watch how much you spend on family; and *if* you need to cut your fuel costs.

▶ **THE WRITING LADDER**—Totally revised chapter on writing and speaking and includes a new, easy to use, Writing Ladder to help students with the college writing process.

▶ **SUCCESS STICKERS**—*Cornerstone* will include a sheet of success stickers so that students can tag important information throughout the text to reread, study for a test, mark a great quote, or just tag information he or she finds informative and interesting.

ACKNOWLEDGMENTS AND GRATITUDE

We would like to thank the following individuals at **The College of Southern Nevada** for their support:

Dr. Michael Richards, President
Dr. Darren Divine, Interim Vice President for Academic Affairs
Professor Rose Hawkins, Interim Dean, School of Arts and Letters
Professor John Ziebell, Department Chair—English
Professor Kathy Baker, Assistant Chair—English

We would like to thank individuals at the University of South Carolina, and faculty members at the College of Hospitality, Retail and Sport Management.

Our fondest gratitude to the following **colleagues and friends** who recommended individuals for the features, *Why Read This Chapter . . . from My Perspective* and *from Ordinary To Extraordinary—Real People. Real Lives. Real Change.*

Elaine Richardson, Clemson University
Melanie Deffendall, Delgado Community College
Al Dornbach, ITT Technical Institute, Bensalem, PA
Doug Paddock, Louisville Technical College
Bill Rinkenbaugh, Butler Community College
Lea Redmond, Art Institute of Philadelphia
Tim Quezada , El Paso Community College
Arthur Webb, Oklahoma State University-Stillwater
David Housel, Houston Community College
Nancy Stiller, University of Arizona-Tucson
Kathy Nelson, University of Nevada, Las Vegas
Brian Maitland, Pittsburgh Technical Institute
JoAnne Credle, Northern Virginia Community College
Wistar Withers, Northern Virginia Community College
Cheryl Rohrbaugh, Northern Virginia Community College
Charlie Dy, Northern Virginia Community College
Everett Vann Eberhardt, Northern Virginia Community College
Antionette Payne, Pearson Education
Wendy DiLeonardo, Pearson Education

To the **amazing individuals** who shared their life stories with us for the feature, *From Ordinary to Extraordinary: Real People. Real Lives. Real Change.*

Bill Clayton
Lydia Hausler Lebovic
Dino Gonzalez, M.D.
Vivian Wong
Dr. Wayne A. Jones
Maureen Riopelle
Chef Odette Smith-Ransome
Sylvia Eberhardt

Catherine Schleigh
H.P. Rama
Leo G. Borges
Ricky Britner
Matthew Karres
Mark Jones

To **the marvellous students** who shared their advice and experiences for *Why Read This Chapter . . . from My Perspective:*

Crystal Johnson, College of Southern Nevada, Nevada
Brannon Sulka, Clemson University, South Carolina
Stacy Seals, Delgado Community College, Louisiana
Martin Cram, Butler Community College, Kansas
Eric Despinis, ITT Technical Institute, Pennsylvania
Sakinah Pendergrass, The Art Institute of Philadelphia, Pennsylvania
Thomas Paddock, Louisville Technical Institute, Kentucky
Griffin Jones, Point Park University, Pennsylvania
Fernando Machado, El Paso Community College, Texas
Melissa Von Aschen, University of Oklahoma-Stillwater, Oklahoma
Acacia Jamison, University of South Carolina, South Carolina
Priscilla Renew, Houston Community College, Texas
Kendra Hernandez, University of Arizona-Tucson, Arizona
Alyssa Bucchianeri, University of Nevada, Las Vegas

Our wonderful and insightful reviewers for the Sixth Edition:

Kristina Leonard, Daytona Beach College
Kim Long, Valencia Community College
Taunya Paul, York Technical College
Charlie L. Dy, Northern Virginia Community College
Gary H. Wanamamker, Ph. D., Houston Community College
Jo Ann Jenkins, Moraine Valley Community College
Judith Lynch, Kansas State University
Timothy J. Quezada, El Paso Community College
Cathy Hall, Indiana University NW
Beverly J. Slaughter, Brevard Community College
Peg Adams, Northern Kentucky University
Sheryl Duquette, Erie Community College
Melanie Deffendall, Delgado Community College
Arthur Webb, Oklahoma State University
Stephanie Young, Butler Community College
Tara Wertz, MTI College
Diana Clennan, College of Southern Nevada
Jennifer Huss-Basquiat, College of Southern Nevada
Wayne A. Jones of Virginia State University

Reviewers for Previous Editions whom we recognize with deep appreciation.

Barbara Auris, Montgomery County Community College; Betty Fortune, Houston Community College; Joel V. McGee, Texas A & M University; Jan Norton, University of Wisconsin–OshKosh; Todd Phillips, East Central College, Christian M. Blum, Bryan and Stratton College; James Briski, Katherine Gibbs School; Pela Selene Terry, Art Institute of NYC; Christina Donnelly, York Technical College; Connie Egelman, Nassau Community College; Amy Hickman, Collins College; Beth Humes, Pennsylvania Culinary Institute; Kim Joyce, Art Institute of Philadelphia; Lawrence Ludwig, Sanford-Brown College; Bethany Marcus, ECPI College of Technology; Kate Saywer, Pittsburg Technical Institute; Patricia Sell, National College of Business and Technology; Janis Stiewing, PIMA Medical Institute; June Sullivan, Florida Metropolitan University; Fred Amador, Phoenix College; Kathy Bryan, Daytona Beach Community College; Dorothy Chase, Community College of Southern Nevada; JoAnn Credle, Northern Virginia Community College; Betty Fortune, Houston Community College; Doroteo Franco Jr., El Paso Community College; Cynthia Garrard, Massasoit Community College; Joel Jessen, Eastfield College; Peter Johnston, Massasoit Community College; Steve Konowalow, Community College of Southern Nevada; Janet Lindner, Midlands Technical College; Carmen McNeil, Solano College; Joan O'Connor, New York Institute of Technology; Mary Pepe, Valencia Community College; Bennie Perdue, Miami-Dade Community College; Ginny Peterson-Tennant, Miami-Dade Community College; Anna E. Ward, Miami-Dade Community College; Wistar M. Withers, Northern Virginia Community College; and Marie Zander, New York Institute of Technology; Joanne Bassett, Shelby State Community College; Sandra M. Bovain-Lowe, Cumberland Community College; Carol Brooks, GMI Engineering and Management Institute; Elaine H. Byrd, Utah Valley State College; Janet Cutshall, Sussex County Community College; Deborah Daiek, Wayne State University; David DeFrain, Central Missouri State University; Leslie L. Duckworth, Florida Community College at Jacksonville; Marnell Hayes, Lake City Community College; Elzora Holland, University of Michigan, Ann Arbor; Earlyn G. Jordan, Fayetteville State University; John Lowry-King, Eastern New Mexico University; Charlene Latimer; Michael Laven, University of Southwestern Louisiana; Judith Lynch, Kansas State University; Susan Magun-Jackson, The University of Memphis; Charles William Martin, California State University, San Bernardino; Jeffrey A. Miller; Ronald W. Johnsrud, Lake City Community College; Joseph R. Krzyzanowski, Albuquerque TVI; Ellen Oppenberg, Glendale Community College; Lee Pelton, Charles S. Mott Community College; Robert Rozzelle, Wichita State University; Penny Schempp, Western Iowa Community College; Betty Smith, University of Nebraska at Kearney; James Stepp, University of Maine at Presque Isle; Charles Washington, Indiana University–Purdue University; and Katherine A. Wenen-Nesbit, Chippewa Valley Technical College.

Our Creative and Supportive Team at Pearson

Without the support and encouragement of the following people at Pearson, this book would not be possible. Our sincere thanks to:

Susan Badger   Nancy Forsyth   Sande Johnson
Amy Judd   Quinn Perkson   Janet Domingo

Your constant belief in us over the years has been a most cherished gift. We are lucky to know you and are better people because of you. Thank you!

We also thank the following friends at Pearson for their support, dedication and exceptional work: Jenny Gessner, Clara Ciminelli, Antionette Payne, Walt Kirby, Debbie Ogilvie, Alan Hensley, Pam Jeffries, Barbara Donlon, Cathy Bennett, Meredith Chandler, Jeff McIlroy, Matt Mesaros, Connie James, Wendy DiLeonardo, Dave Gessell, Eric Hackanson, Deborah Wilson, Eric Weiss, Julie Morel, Julie Hilderbrand, Dana Dodge, Andrea Iorio, and Richard Rowe.

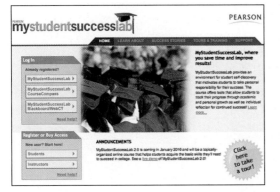

MyStudentSuccessLab is an online solution designed to help students acquire the skills they need to succeed. They will have access to peer-led video presentations and develop core skills through interactive exercises and projects that provide academic, life, and career skills that will transfer to ANY course.

It can accompany any Student Success text, or be sold as a stand-alone course offering. Often students try to learn material without applying the information. To become a successful learner, they must consistently apply techniques to their daily activities.

MyStudentSuccessLab provides students with opportunities to become successful learners:

Connect:
• Engage with real students through video interviews on key issues.

Practice:
• Three skill-building exercises per topic provide interactive experience and practice.

Personalize:
• Apply what is learned to your life.
• Create a personal project that will be graded and can be posted to your portfolio.
• Journal online and set short- and long-term goals.

JAMES
freshman

Resources
• Tools to use: Plagiarism Guide, Dictionary, Calculators, and a Multimedia index of Interactive case studies and activities.

Text-Specific Study Plan
• Chapter Objectives provide clear expectations.
• Practice Tests for each chapter of your text assess your current understanding.
  - Completion of each practice test generates a study plan that is unique to you.
• Enrichment activities identify strengths and weaknesses, provide immediate feedback, and link to additional media.
• Flashcards help you study and review.

Assessments
• Includes Career Assessment tool, Learning Styles, and Personality Styles.

BEGIN

THE GOAL OF CORNERSTONE AND OUR COMMITMENT TO YOU

Talent alone won't make you a success. Neither will being in the right place at the right time, unless you are ready. The most important question is: 'Are you ready?'

—Johnny Carson

If you look at the figure printed here you will see the Chinese symbol (verb) for "*to change*." It is made up of two symbols—the first means *to transform* or to be flexible. The second means *to do* or *to deliver*. In its purest form, the symbol means to *deliver transformation*. That is what *Cornerstone* is all about, helping you deliver or bring about transformation, positive change if you will,  to your life. It is about helping you discover ways to change your thoughts, change your performance, and change your life.

Our goal in writing *Cornerstone* is to help you discover your academic, social, and personal strengths so that you can build on them and to provide **concrete and useful tools** that will help you make the changes that might be necessary for your success. We believe that in helping you identify and transform areas that have challenged you in the past, you can *discover your true potential, learn more actively, and have the career you want and deserve*.

Cornerstone: Creating Success through Positive Change is devoted to three specific areas where positive change can help you become the individual you would like to be. The book is divided into three parts:

Changing Your Thoughts

Changing Your Performance

Changing Your Life

PART ONE, Changing Your Thoughts, addresses a broad spectrum of topics that begins with a focus on change as it relates to becoming a college student in a different culture and setting than you may have known before. In this section, you will be introduced to tools of self-management as they relate to college life. You will be exposed to a variety of new terms, ideas, and thoughts—all of which begin your journey of change. You will learn to enhance your communication skills, improve your self-concept, and manage conflict, all valuable tools on the road to change. You will become more adept at critical thinking and problem solving as you study this section. When you have completed this section, you should notice a difference in the way you approach tasks and think about subjects, challenges, and people.

PART TWO, Changing Your Performance, focuses on you and how you physically and mentally manage yourself. You will begin this part of the journey to change by learning to manage your time and control the inherent stress that accompanies being a college student. You will realize that you have a dominant intelligence, learning style, and personality type and how to use them to your advantage. Even though you have been reading for some time, you will be shown strategies to improve both your speed and comprehension since reading is a major part of college studies. You will be shown several note-taking systems designed to improve your ability to record what your professors are teaching. Finally, you will be taught strategies for empowering your memory, learning to study more effectively, and taking tests with confidence. When you complete this section, you should be able to perform most tasks more effectively and confidently.

PART THREE, Changing Your Life, is a culmination of the journey you have embarked on as a first-year student. This section is designed to round out your total personal profile and springboard you to success as you move into a different realm. Many college students do well on the topics covered in the first two sections and fall short when they arrive to this point. To be the complete successful college student, you need to address all these areas because they are significant to the changes you need to embrace. You will learn to manage your money and your debts wisely. So many college students are burdened with astronomical college debts when they graduate; our desire is for you to have accumulated as little debt as possible at the same time you are taking advantage of all that college has to offer. You will study the important emerging topic of information literacy and improve your writing and speaking skills. On this important journey to change, you will be shown how to immerse yourself in many categories of diversity while you learn to celebrate all kinds of people. You will be taught to be responsible for your own wellness and how to exercise personal responsibility. Finally, you will be introduced to techniques for planning your professional career in the face of dramatic global changes. When you finish this section, you should be prepared to move through the next few years of college and beyond with confidence and optimism.

We know that your **time is valuable** and that you are pulled in countless directions with work, family, school, previous obligations, and many other tasks. For this reason, we have tried to provide only the most concrete, useful strategies and ideas to help you succeed in this class and beyond.

We have spent over 55 years collectively gathering the information, advice, suggestions, and activities on the following pages. This advice and these activities have come from trial and error, colleagues, former students, instructors across the United States, and solid research. We hope that you will enjoy them, learn from them, and most of all, use them to change your life and move closer to your dreams.

Let the journey to positive change begin!

Robb *Pat*

Robb and Pat

SQ3R

What Is It and Why Do I Need to Know It?

You may be asking, "*What does SQ3R mean and what could it possibly have to do with me, my text, this course, and my success?*" The answer: *SQ3R* (**S = Scan, Q = Question, 3 R = Read, Recite, Review**) is one of the most successful and widely used learning and study tools ever introduced.

This simple, yet highly effective mnemonic (memory trick) asks that *before you actually read the chapter*, you look over the contents, check out the figures and photos, look at section headings, and review any graphs or charts. This is called **scanning**. Step two, **question**, asks that you jot down questions that you think you will need to answer about the chapter's content in order to master the material. These questions might come from charts or figures, but most commonly, they come from the chapter's section headings. Examine the example below of a section heading from: *Criminal Justice, A Brief Introduction,* 6th Edition by Frank Schmalleger (Prentice Hall, 2006).

(1) *What are the categories of crime?*
(2) *Why do they matter?*
(3) *What is crime typology?* or
(4) *When are categories of crime most often used?*

reported data.[64] Crimes that result from an anomalous event, but which are excluded from reported data, highlight the arbitrary nature of the data-collection process itself.

Special Categories of Crime

crime typology

A classification of crimes along a particular dimension, such as legal categories, offender motivation, victim behavior, or the characteristics of individual offenders.

A **crime typology** is a classification scheme that is useful in the study and description of criminal behavior. All crime typologies have an underlying logic, and the system of classification that derives from any particular typology may be based on legal criteria, offender motivation, victim behavior, the characteristics of individual offenders, or the like. Criminologists Terance D. Miethe and Richard C. McCorkle note that crime typologies "are designed primarily to simplify social reality by identifying homogeneous groups of crime behaviors that are different from other clusters of crime behaviors."[65] Hence one common but simple typology contains only two categories of crime: violent and property. In fact, many crime typologies contain overlapping or nonexclusive categories—just as violent crimes may involve property offenses, and property offenses may lead to violent crimes. Thus no one typology is likely to capture all of the nuances of criminal offending.

After writing these questions from the section heading, you will read this section and then answer those questions. This technique gives you more focus and purpose for your reading. Each chapter in *Cornerstone* begins with this technique through a feature called **Scan & Question**.

We included this feature in *Cornerstone* to help you become a more active reader with greater comprehension skills in all of your other classes. This technique is fully discussed in Chapter 8 of this text.

BLOOM'S TAXONOMY

What Are All of Those Little Triangles Throughout My Book?

Another feature that you will notice in your text is small triangles throughout followed by questions pertaining to the content. These triangles help you recognize which of the six levels of learning is being used from Bloom's Taxonomy. A quick reference chart of Bloom's Taxonomy (Revised) is on the inside front cover of this text and on page xxi.

Bloom's Taxonomy (also called Levels of Thinking and Learning) is simply a way of explaining the stages at which we all acquire information. These levels, explained in detail on the next page, progress from simple learning and thinking (levels 1, 2, 3) to more complex learning and thinking (levels 4, 5, 6). In addition to having questions from Bloom's Taxonomy throughout your text, each chapter will end with an exercise called *Knowledge in Bloom*. This chapter-end activity is included to help you process and apply the information from the chapter.

So, Why Use Bloom in the *Cornerstone* Text?

Bloom's Taxonomy is important to us all because it helps us determine the level at which we understand important information. For example, it is important to be able to answer questions at Level 1 such as:

▶ *Abraham Lincoln was the _____ President of the United States.*

or

▶ *Abraham Lincoln's wife's name was _____ Lincoln.*

However, it is also important to be able to answer questions at levels 5 and 6 such as:

▶ *Based on your knowledge of the Civil War era, predict what would have happened to the United States without the Emancipation Proclamation. Justify your answer.*

or

▶ *Summarize the main events that led to President Lincoln's assassination.*

As you can clearly see, there is a great difference between these levels of learning. The higher the level, the more information and knowledge you need to be able to understand and respond to the question or problem.

The chapter-end activity, **Knowledge in Bloom,** will help you process and demonstrate your knowledge at different levels. This is important because you will have professors who **teach and test** at levels 1, 2, and 3 and those who **teach and test** at levels 4, 5, and 6. Learning to process and demonstrate your knowledge at every level can assist you in:

- doing well in other classes by providing a foundation for effective studying/learning,
- learning to solve problems more thoroughly,
- predicting exam questions,
- learning how to critically evaluate and assess ideas and issues,
- learning to thoroughly and objectively research topics for papers and presentations, and
- testing your own reading comprehension.

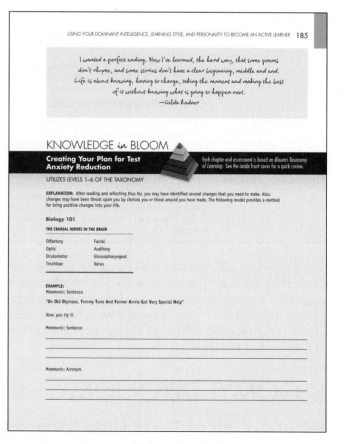

Examine the following chart for Bloom's Taxonomy (Levels of Thinking and Learning).

BLOOM'S TAXONOMY (Revised)
Examining the Levels of Thinking and Learning

LEVELS OF *THINKING AND LEARNING*.	WHAT **SKILLS** YOU SHOULD HAVE AT THIS LEVEL.	**EXAMPLES** OF *QUESTIONS* OR *ACTIVITIES* YOU MIGHT ANTICIPATE OR *PRODUCTS* YOU MAY HAVE TO GENERATE
1—REMEMBERING This level is based on simple recall of information. This type of knowledge usually comes from being told or from basic reading. It is the "lowest" or most simple type of learning.	write, list, label, name, state, define, describe, identify, recognize, recall, draw, select, locate, recite, quote, order, state, reproduce, match, tell, and the five standards, who, what, when, where, and how	What is . . . , When did . . . , Why did . . . , Who were . . . , Describe the . . . , Which of the following . . . , Define the . . . , Name the . . . , Identify who . . . , Describe what happened after . . . **SAMPLE:** What are the six levels of learning in Bloom's Taxonomy?
2—UNDERSTANDING This level determines your grasp or comprehension level of the information presented. It asks, "Do you understand the meaning?" and "Can you explain the ideas or concepts?"	summarize, describe, interpret, contrast, predict, associate, distinguish, estimate, differentiate, discuss, extend, convert, explain, generalize, give examples, rewrite, restate, classify, translate, paraphrase, illustrate, visualize, retell	How would you contrast . . . , Explain why the . . . , Summarize the main . . . , What facts show . . . , Predict the outcome of . . . , Restate the story in your own words . . . , prepare a flow chart to illustrate . . . **SAMPLE:** Explain why Bloom's Taxonomy is being used in *Cornerstone* and describe its importance.
3—APPLYING This level asks you to "use" the information you have by solving, showing, or applying that information in "real-world" or workplace situations. Can you use the information in a new way?	apply, demonstrate, discover, modify, operate, predict, solve, draw, dramatize, model, sketch, paint, produce, prepare, make, calculate, record, compute, manipulate, modify, use, employ	How could you use . . . , How could you solve . . . , What approach would you take . . . , Write an essay to explain why . . . , Prepare a timeline of . . . , Predict what would happen if . . . **SAMPLE:** Prepare a plan to show how you could use Bloom's Taxonomy to get a better grade in your history class?
4—ANALYZING This level asks you to "take apart" the information for clarification, classification, and prioritizing. It also asks you to recognize what is "not" said, i.e., . . . hidden meanings and unstated assumptions. This level requires that you distinguish between facts and inferences.	break down, distinguish, infer, arrange, prioritize, order, divide, categorize, appraise, test, examine, separate, deduce, choose, compare/contrast, detect, group, sequence, scrutinize, connect, outlines, research, point out	How is ___ related to ___?, What conclusions can be drawn . . . , What is the relationship between . . . , Categorize the main . . . , Based on X, why is Y . . . , What were the motives behind . . . , What was the turning point in . . . , Write a survey to find out if . . . **SAMPLE:** What assumptions can be made about the rest of the term if your history teacher's first two exams included 20 questions, all from level six?
5—EVALUATING This level of thinking and learning asks you to make personal judgments about the value of issues, ideas, policies, and evidence based on your complete understanding of the information AND based on stated judging criteria. Basically, it asks that you justify a decision, idea, or belief that you have formulated.	decide, rank, test, measure, recommend, defend, conclude, appraise, assess, judge, predict, rate, select, critique, justify, estimate, validate, measure, discriminate, probe, award, rank, reject, grade, convince, weigh, support	Defend your position about . . . , How would you have handled "X"? Why? Debate the issue of . . . , Prepare a paper or speech to present your ideas of . . . , What is your opinion of . . . , How would you rate . . . , What judgment could you make . . . , Justify your opinion of . . . , Based on your research, convince the reader of your paper or speech that . . . , What criteria would you use to assess the . . . **SAMPLE:** Assess how effective Bloom's Taxonomy was when used to study for your history exam. Recommend two ways to improve the use of Bloom's for the next test.
6—CREATING This level asks you to integrate your previous knowledge with your new knowledge and come up with new ideas, plans, and solutions. It also asks you to be able to predict outcomes based on what you have learned. This level asks you to be innovative and creative.	compose, combine, compile, create, design, generate, construct, revise, write, rewrite, tell, role play, formulate, invent, develop, modify, arrange, rearrange, prepare, assemble, set-up, forecast, imagine, act, improvise, propose, substitute, integrate, incorporate	Design a plan to . . . , Write a speech or paper that . . . , Create a marketing plan that . . . , Devise a way to . . . , Compose a mnemonic that . . . , Generate a list of questions that . . . , Propose a solution to . . . , Revise the story of . . . **SAMPLE:** Write two possible test questions from each level of Bloom's Taxonomy from Chapter 1 of *Cornerstone*.

STICKERS FOR SUCCESS

What Are These Stickers in the Front of My Book?

In the back of this text, you will find a sheet of peel off stickers to help you "tag" pages and content that (1) you need to study for a quiz, (2) review for mastery, (3) seek help with, or (4) mark as important. We have also included a row of blank stickers for your personal use (5). We encourage you to use them to help you locate information easily. The tabs include:

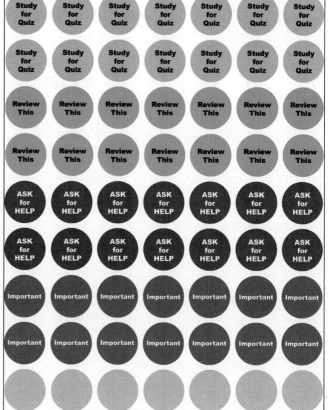

Study for Quiz Use to tag information that your instructor tells you will be on the test.

Review This Use to identify key terms, definitions, or difficult material that you need to revisit.

ASK for HELP Use to remind you to ask questions about the content you may not understand.

Important Use to tag important information.

Create your own tab to mark important quotes, charts, or other material you would like to reference quickly.

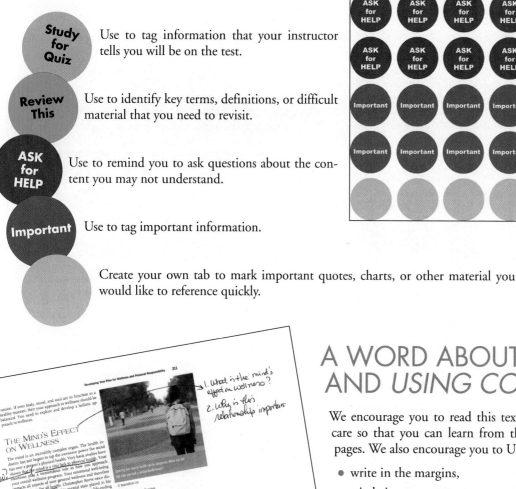

A WORD ABOUT *READING* AND *USING CORNERSTONE*

We encourage you to read this text (and every text) with great care so you can learn from the ideas presented within its pages. We also encourage you to USE this book –

- write in the margins,
- circle important terms,
- highlight key phrases,
- jot down word definitions in the margins,
- dog-ear the pages, and
- write questions that you have in the white spaces provided.

By treating this book like your "foundation to success," you will begin to see remarkable progress in your study practices, reading comprehension, and learning skills. Review the example from another *Cornerstone* text.

CORNERSTONE

CHAPTER 1
CHANGE

ADJUSTING TO
THE CULTURE
OF COLLEGE,
NURTURING
CHANGE,
AND SETTING
YOUR GOALS

"The greatest reward of an education is to be able to face the world with an open mind, a caring heart, and a willing soul."

—R. M. Sherfield

WHY READ THIS CHAPTER?

What's in it for me?

Why? Because this chapter, indeed this whole book and course in which you are enrolled, is about helping you become the best college student, thinker, citizen, leader, and lifelong learner that you can possibly be. The information in this chapter is included to help you understand some of the basic truths about college life and academic survival. Quite simply, this chapter was written to help you learn how to adjust to college life, discover your potential, build on your strengths, and bring about positive change in your life through self-analysis, reflection, and goal setting. By reading this chapter and working through the activities, you will begin to see how important change is to your life, your growth, and your future, and more importantly, how to bring about that positive change.

By carefully reading this chapter and taking the information provided seriously, you will be able to:

1. Understand the relationship between your education and the new world economy.
2. Identify and apply the Ten Essential Cornerstones for Success in a Changing World.
3. Understand the basic truths about how college can help you beyond the classroom.
4. Understand the differences among high school, college, and career.
5. Understand why change is important and how to bring about change through goal setting.

WHY read this stuff on positive change? *WHY* will a chapter on change and goal setting help me in college, at work, with my friends, and beyond? *WHY* spend my time reading something that I'm not sure will help me at all? *WHY* is it important to understand the "Culture of College"?

CHAPTER 1 / CHANGE

"When it comes to the future, there are three kinds of people: those who let it happen, those who make it happen, and those who wonder what happened."

—John Richardson, Jr.

WHY READ THIS CHAPTER?

. . . FROM MY PERSPECTIVE

NAME: Mark
INSTITUTION: Spartanburg Methodist College, Spartanburg, SC
MAJOR: Associate of Arts—Theatre and Speech
AGE: 18

Change has been a major part of my life, and learning how to transform myself was a very important tool that helped me succeed in my first year of college. A major change in my life was learning how to overcome years of self-defeating behaviors, a horrible academic background, a negative attitude, and terrible study skills. I quickly learned that my success depended on my becoming an open-minded person who knew how to set goals, work to achieve those goals, develop self-motivation skills, and study effectively. These were not easy steps for me after 12 years of failure and disappointment.

I am the son of textile workers. Both of my parents worked in a cotton mill for over 30 years. My hometown is in the rural south about 35 miles from the nearest metropolitan area. I attended a small high school and was never a good student. Because of my poor performance through the years, working full time, and family commitments, I decided to attend a community college and then transfer to a four-year college.

I barely finished high school with a D– average and my SAT scores and class rank were so bad that I was denied entrance to a community college. The college granted me provisional acceptance with the stipulation that I enroll in, and successfully complete, a summer preparatory program. I graduated high school on a Friday night and began my college studies the very next Monday morning enrolled in the prep program. I never realized what lay ahead. I never realized how my life was about to change forever. I never realized at that point how much I would have to change.

My first class that semester was English. Professor Brannon walked in, handed out the syllabus, called the roll, and began to lecture. Lord Byron was the topic for the day. The class ended and after an hour's break, I headed across campus for history. Professor Wilkerson entered with a dust storm behind her. She went over the syllabus, and before we had a chance to blink, she was involved in the first lecture. "The cradle of civilization," she began, "was Mesopotamia."

We all scurried to find notebooks and pens to begin taking notes. I could not believe I was already behind on the first day. "Who teaches on the first day?" I thought.

One minute before class ended, she closed her book, looked directly at us, and said, "You are in history now. You elected to take this class and you will follow my rules. You are not to be late, you are to come to this class prepared, and you are to do your homework assignments. If you do what I ask you to do, read what I've assigned to you, and do your homework activities, you will learn more about Western civilization than you ever thought possible. If you don't keep up with me, you won't know if you are in Egypt, Mesopotamia, or pure Hell! Now get out!"

On the 30-mile trip home, my mind was filled with new thoughts . . . *Lord Byron, Mesopotamia, professors who talked too fast, tuition, parking, and the size of the library*. I knew that something was different, *something had changed in me*. I couldn't put my finger on it. It would be years before I realized that the change had not been my classes, not my schedule, not the people, not the professors—but me; *I had changed*. In one day, I had tasted something intoxicating, something that was addictive. *I had tasted a new world*.

I had to go to work that afternoon at the mill, and even my job and my coworkers had changed. I had always known that I did not want to spend the rest of my life in the factory, but this day the feeling was stronger. My job was not enough, my family was not enough, the farm on which I had been raised was not enough anymore. *There was a new light in me, and I knew that because of that one day in college, I would never be the same.* It was like tasting Godiva chocolate for the first time—Hershey's kisses were no longer enough. It was like seeing the ocean for the first time and knowing that the millpond would never be the same. *I couldn't go back. What I'd known before was simply no longer enough.*

My name is Robert **Mark** Sherfield, and 34 years later, as I coauthor your *Cornerstone* text, I am still addicted to that new world. College changed my life, and I am still changing—with every day I live, every new book I read, every new class I teach, every new person I meet, and every new place to which I travel, I am changing. I wish the same for you.

SCAN & QUESTION

In the preface of this book (page xix), you read about the **SQ3R Study Method**. Right now, take a few moments, **scan this chapter**, and on page 27, write **five of your own questions** that you think will be important to your mastery of this material. In addition to the two questions below, you will find five questions from your authors. Use one of your **"Study for Quiz"** stickers to flag this page for easy reference.

EXAMPLES:

▶ **What are the six basic truths about the culture of college?** (from page 11)

▶ **Why must goals be measurable?** (from page 21)

THE TIMES . . . THEY ARE A-CHANGIN'

What Is the Relationship Between Your Education and the New World Economy?

Composer, singer, and activist Bob Dylan once wrote, ***"The times, they are a-changin'."*** Truer words have never been spoken—especially for anyone living at this moment. This is not your daddy's economy. It is not your mama's workplace, and it certainly is not your grandfather's job market. To glide over this simple truth *could be the most costly decision of your life.*

"New world economy," you might say, *"who cares about a world economy?"*

"China? Who cares about the fluctuating but growing economy in China, Russia, Dubai, or India? I live in Kansas and I'm worried about America's future."

"An iPhone? A Blackberry? A podcast? Twittering? I can't even afford my bus ticket this month," you may be thinking.

While you may not be alone in thinking, ***"This does not matter to me,"*** you would be very wrong and exceptionally foolish to think that today's world affairs do not concern **you**, your **education**, and your **future**. Yes, it may be true that you are simply trying to get a degree in medical assisting to work in a small doctor's office in Spokane, Washington—or to obtain a degree in criminal justice to work at the local police department in Union, South Carolina—or to earn a degree in education so that you can teach first grade in Stockton, California. However, no certificate, no degree, no job, and certainly no person will be exempt from the changes and challenges of "the new world economy."

"So, where does this leave ME?" you might be asking. It leaves you in an exciting, vulnerable, challenging, scary, and wonderful place. We did NOT include this information to scare you or to turn you off, but rather to give you a jolt, to open your eyes to the world in which you live and the workforce for which you are preparing. We included it to encourage you to use ***every tool*** available, ***every resource*** possible, ***every connection*** imaginable, and ***every ethical, moral, and legal means*** possible to prepare yourself for this ever-changing world in which you live today. The present and the future may not be as rosy as you had hoped, but the future is here, and it is yours. However, you must know this: If you make strategic changes in your life now, you can have a much brighter future. No workplace will be immune from the changes facing our world today, and your very survival depends on your being prepared and knowing how to quickly adapt to and change in a variety of situations.

In his book *The 2010 Meltdown* (2005), Edward Gordon writes, *"Simply stated, today in America, there are just too many people trained for the wrong jobs. Many jobs have become unnecessary, technically obsolete . . . or worse yet, the job/career aspirations of too many current and future workers are at serious odds with the changing needs of the U.S. labor market"* (p. 17).

However, all is not lost to you or your future. People who are well-skilled, possess superb oral and written communication skills, know how to solve problems, have the capacity to change, and can work well with others will *be in high demand* for many years to come.

What Employers Are Saying

According to the report *College Learning for the New Global Century* (2008), "Employers want college graduates to acquire versatile knowledge and skills. Fully sixty-three percent of employers believe that too many recent college graduates do not have the skills they need to succeed in the global economy and a majority of employers believe that only half or fewer recent graduates have the skills or knowledge needed to advance or to be promoted in their companies." Skills listed as vitally important to employers include:

computer literacy	attention to detail
accuracy	tact
self-confidence	character
humor	the ability to learn new skills quickly

Whether we like it or not, a massive transformation is going on all around us in this country, as well as all over the world. Thriving in the coming years is going to be more difficult than in the past and will require certain new and different abilities and attitudes for us to be successful. You will need to learn and acquire the skills that will make you competitive, give you an edge, and help you master a life filled with changes and challenges. Many of these skills are outlined in the **Ten Essential Cornerstones for Success in a Changing World** (Figure 1.1). These skills will be needed for your success, personal independence, and growth in the new millennium. Study them carefully, as you will see them throughout the text and be asked to reflect upon each one.

By learning to develop these enduring skills, you will be able to carry them with you on your first job, your 10th job, and well into your future. By learning how to change and reinvent yourself with the times and demands of the world, you will position yourself to become—AND remain— competitive.

Why is it important to learn as much as possible about technology?

1.1   *Ten Essential Cornerstones for Success in a Changing World*

PASSION—The ability to show the world a person who is passionate about his or her mission and who has aligned his or her goals with his or her education, talents, experiences, and skills. A person who cares not only about his or her own success, but also about the world and his or her surroundings—a person who possesses *Civic Literacy* and sees himself or herself as "a citizen of the world."

MOTIVATION—The ability to find the *inner strength and personal drive* to get up each day and face the world with an "I can, I will" attitude. The ability to develop a strong personal value and belief system that motivates you when the going gets tough. The ability to know who you are and to never let anyone steal your identity or erode your personal ethics.

KNOWLEDGE—The ability to become *highly skilled in a profession* or craft that will enable you to make a good living for yourself and your family in a rapidly changing workplace and to use lifelong learning to maintain your marketable skill sets. The ability to master important academic information beyond that of your major field in areas such as math, science, psychology, history, technology, economics, and communication and to practically apply that information in an evolving and highly technical work environment.

RESOURCEFULNESS—The ability to apply *information literacy*—to know WHERE to find information and the resources that will help you be successful in your academic studies and your chosen profession, and HOW to evaluate that information to determine if it is useful and accurate. The ability to look for and to seek new opportunities, options, and outcomes. The ability to imagine, integrate, and implement new ways of solving old problems.

CREATIVITY—The ability to use *creativity and innovation* in solving problems, which will enable you to anticipate new and emerging issues and to communicate and use what you know and what you have learned and discovered to answer critical questions and solve complex and demanding problems.

ADAPTABILITY—The ability to make good choices based on future opportunities and a changing workplace and to constantly *reinvent yourself* as change brings about necessity and opportunity. The ability to work effectively in a climate of changing priorities and uncertainty.

OPEN-MINDEDNESS—The ability to *accept and appreciate a highly diverse workplace* and the inherent differences and cultures that will be commonplace. The ability to listen to others with whom you disagree or with whom you may have little in common and to learn from them and their experiences. The ability to learn a new language, even if your mastery is only at a primitive, broken, conversational level. The ability to conduct yourself in a respectable and professional manner.

COMMUNICATION—The ability to develop and maintain healthy, *supportive personal and professional relationships* and to build a solid network of well-connected professionals who can help you and who YOU can help in return.

ACCOUNTABILITY—The ability to *accept responsibility and be accountable* for all aspects of your future including your psychological well-being, your spiritual well-being, your relationships, your health, your finances, and your overall survival skills. Basically, you must develop a plan for the future that states, "If this fails, I'll do this," or "If this job is phased out, I'll do this," or "If this resource is gone, I'll use this," or "If this person won't help me, this one will."

VISION—The ability to guide your career path in a new global economy and to understand and take advantage of the inherent impact of worldwide competition—even if you live in a small town and work for a small "mom and pop" company. The ability to *"see" what is coming* and prepare for the changes, adapt to circumstances, and grow with grace and style.

THE M & M THEORY

What Have Your Money and Your Mama Got to Do with It?

What is the M & M Theory? It is quite simple really. We all pay attention to and try to protect the things that matter most to us. Your "**m**oney and your **m**ama" are symbolic of what you care about. Most people care deeply about what happens to their families, their income, their friends, their careers, and the environment, and most people do care and are concerned about world events and what is happening around them.

However, in the hustle and bustle of finding day care, studying for classes, working a full-time job, cleaning the house, helping the kids with homework, and trying to prepare a meal from time to time, we may lose sight of some of the most important things in our lives. Try to keep this thought in mind: **Your EDUCATION is important, too.** In fact, it is of paramount importance to your future on many levels—culturally, socially, intellectually, and in preparing you for the future. Your education is a part of the M & M Theory because it involves your money—the future financial health of you and your family.

According to one of the leading research sources in higher education, *The Chronicle of Higher Education* (August 29, 2008, p. 18), first-year students have a variety of thoughts regarding a college education and money. Of the 272,000 students who responded to the survey, 74% said that *"being very well-off financially"* was an essential or very important objective; 66% responded that *"the chief benefit of a college education is that it increases one's earning power."* Another interesting finding was that 79% of those responding to the survey stated that they believed that *"through hard work, everybody can succeed in American society."*

How can your friends, classmates and peers help you achieve your goals?

According to the U.S. Census Bureau in their annual report *Education and Training Pay* (2007), people with college degrees can earn considerably more than those who do not have a degree. For a complete look at the earning power of U.S. citizens age 25 and older, look at the Education, Pay, and Unemployment chart in Figure 1.2.

By focusing on money in this section, we do not mean to suggest that the only reason to attend college is to make more money. As a matter of fact, we feel that it is a secondary reason. Many people *without college degrees* earn huge salaries each year. However, as the data in Figure 1.2 suggests, those with college degrees traditionally **earn MORE** money and **experience LESS**

FIGURE 1.2 *Education, Pay, and Unemployment Statistics of Full-Time Workers, 25 and Over*

Unemployment Rate	Degree	Mean Earnings
1.35%	Professional Degree	$122,480
1.40%	Doctorate Degree	$108,563
1.85%	Master's Degree	$80,407
2.20%	Bachelor's Degree	$66,133
3.15%	Associate Degree	$47,196
3.85%	Some College, No Degree	$44,488
4.35%	High School Graduate	$37,424
7.40%	Less than High School Graduate	$28,539

Source: Department of the Census, Department of Labor, 2007.

unemployment. Basically, college should make the road to financial security easier, but college should also be a place where you learn to make decisions about your values, your character, and your future. College can also be a place where you make decisions about the changes that need to occur in your life so that you can effectively manage and prosper in an ever-changing world.

COLLEGE AND YOU

Why Is It the Partnership of a Lifetime?

What can college do for you? The list will certainly vary depending on whom you ask, but basically, college can help you develop in the areas listed below. As you read through the list, place a checkmark beside the statements that most accurately reflect which skills you hope to gain from attending college. If there are other skills that you desire to achieve from your college experience, write them at the end of the list.

_____ Grow more self-sufficient and self-confident
_____ Establish and strengthen your personal identity
_____ Understand more about the global world in which you live
_____ Become a more involved citizen in social and political issues
_____ Become more open-minded
_____ Learn to manage your emotions and reactions more effectively
_____ Understand the value of thinking, analyzing, and problem solving
_____ Expand and use your ethical and moral thinking and reasoning skills
_____ Develop commanding computer and information literacy skills
_____ Manage your personal resources such as time and money

How can your college classes help you grow, change, and prosper?

_____ Become more proficient in written, oral, nonverbal, and technical communication
_____ Grow more understanding and accepting of different cultures
_____ Become a lifelong learner
_____ Become more financially independent
_____ Enter a career field that you enjoy

_____ _____

_____ _____

Which skill is THE most important to you? _____

Discuss how you think this skill will help you in your college classes, in your profession, and in your personal life. _____

_____

2

BLOOM LEVEL 2
QUESTION

The Chronicle of Higher Education's annual report mentioned earlier on first-year students does not list *"I want to change"* as one of the reasons for attending college. However, you are going to experience changes in your attitudes, your values, your actions, and your intellectual character. You are going to notice changes in old relationships and even in the relationships with your family members. Many of the changes will be positive and rewarding. Sure, there will be a few changes that test your nature and temperament, but that is why this chapter is included in this book—to help you understand how to navigate difficult changes and create positive changes in your life by goal setting, planning, hard work, and persistence.

THE CULTURE OF COLLEGE

What Are the Basic Truths about College Success?

> "Forget mistakes. Forget failures. Forget everything except what you're going to do now . . . and do it."
> —Will Durant

In your lifetime, you will experience many things that influence and alter your views, goals, and livelihood. These may include travel, relationships, and personal victories or setbacks. However, few experiences will have a greater influence than your college experience. College can mean hopes realized, dreams fulfilled, and the breaking down of social and economic walls. To get the most from your college experience and to lay a path to success, it will be important for you to look at your expectations and the vast differences among high school, jobs you may have held, and the culture of college. This section will introduce you to some of the changes you can expect and give you a brief introduction into the "culture of college."

Basic Truth #1

SUCCESS IS ABOUT CHOICES, SACRIFICES, AND CHANGE

Life is a series of choices. Hard choices. Easy choices. Right choices. Wrong choices. Nevertheless, the quality of *your life* is determined by the *choices you make* and your willingness to evaluate your life and determine if changes are in order. You will have many important and hard choices in the near future such as deciding whether to devote your time to studying or partying; whether to ask for help in classes that challenge you or give up and drop out; whether to get involved in campus life or "go it alone"; and/or whether to make the sacrifices needed for your future success or take the easy road. Those choices will determine the quality of your future. Some of the choices that you make will force you to step beyond your comfort zone—to move to places that may frighten you or make you uncomfortable. That's OK. That's good. In fact, that's very good.

So what is a **Comfort Zone?** It sounds cozy, doesn't it? Warm and fuzzy. However, do not let the term fool you. A comfort zone is not necessarily a happy and comfortable place. It is simply a place where you are familiar with your surroundings and don't have to work too hard. It is where you feel confident of your abilities, but it is also a place where your growth stops. *It can be a prison and staying there is a cop-out.* Successful people who have won personal and professional victories know that moving beyond one's comfort zone helps in nurturing change, reaching one's potential, and creating opportunities for positive growth.

What sacrifices do you think you'll need to make in your personal life to be academically successful?

Basic Truth #2

HIGHER EDUCATION IS A TWO-WAY STREET

Perhaps the first thing that you will notice about higher education is that you have to **give** in order to **receive**. Not only do you have expectations of your institution and instructors, but your institution and instructors have expectations—great expectations—of you. To be successful, you will need to accept substantially more responsibility for your education than you may have in the past. By attending your college of choice, you have agreed to become a part of its community, values, and policies. You now have the responsibility to stand by its code of academic and moral conduct, and you also have the responsibility to give your very best to every class and organization in which you are involved. And, you have a responsibility to YOURSELF to approach this new world with an

THINKING for CHANGE: An Activity for Critical Reflection

After the first week of classes, Devon was very disheartened about the difficulty of the classes for which he was registered. He had not thought that he was going to have so much reading or homework, and he never thought the instructors would be so demanding. He had never been strong at math, but he was just floored at how difficult his beginning math course had become. He failed his first test. He passed his first essay in English, but only with a grade of C. He seriously considered dropping out. It was just too much. It was more than he had expected.

Devon knew, however, that he had to succeed. He looked at his current financial situation, his dead-end job, and his desire to work in the health profession. Dropping out would never get him there. Dropping out would never make him a better, more prepared person. Dropping out would never afford him the opportunity to provide a better life for his family. However, Devon felt that he was just too far behind to catch up. He was at a loss as to what to do.

Pretend that Devon is enrolled at your institution. In your own words, what would you suggest that Devon do at this point? List at least two things that he could do to ensure his success and that would help him change his mind about dropping out. Think about what services are offered and what people might be of assistance to him.

1. _____

_____

2. _____

_____

open mind, curiosity and enthusiasm. In return, your institution will be responsible for helping you reach your fullest potential and live the life you desire.

So, what are your thoughts at the moment? Respond to the following questions honestly and personally.

1. Thus far, I think my most rewarding class is _____ taught by Mr./Mrs./Ms./Dr. _____

2. I believe this because _____

_____

_____

3. To date, I've learned that he or she expects me to _____

_____

4. To meet this expectation, how will my academic habits have to change?

_____

_____

BLOOM LEVEL 3 QUESTION

Basic Truth #3

YOU'RE IN CHARGE HERE—IT'S ALL ABOUT SELF-MOTIVATION AND SELF-RESPONSIBILITY

ONE person and ONLY one person has the power to determine your thoughts and the direction of your future. It is YOU! You will decide the direction of your future. You are NOT a victim and you will not be treated as a victim at this institution. You will not be allowed to use "Victim Excuses" or employ the "Victim Mentality." This is all about you and your desire to change your life. Higher education is not about others doing the work, but rather about you finding internal motivation and accepting responsibility for your actions, your decisions, your choices, and yourself. It is

FIGURE **1.3** *Victim and Winner Chart*

The VICTIM	The WINNER
The victim blames others for his or her problems.	The winner accepts responsibility for what happens in his or her life.
The victim procrastinates and makes excuses for not doing a good job.	The winner thinks ahead and plans for success.
The victim sees adversity as a permanent obstacle.	The winner sees adversity as a way to get stronger.
The victim constantly complains and has a negative mentality about most things.	The winner has an optimistic attitude and is pleasant to be with most of the time.
The victim does just enough to get by and is happy with poor grades and mediocre accomplishments.	The winner works hard to raise his or her level of achievement and constantly seeks to improve.
The victim lets life happen without trying to make things happen.	The winner has a plan and sets goals and works every day to make positive things happen.
The victim is always late and often absent and always has an excuse.	The winner is on time, prepared, and rarely ever negligent regarding his or her responsibilities.
The victim hangs out with negative people who are troublemakers and party animals and have low ambition and a poor work ethic.	The winner surrounds himself or herself with people who are working hard to make something of themselves and who are encouraging and motivating.

not about making excuses and blaming others. *You are in charge here.* This is YOUR education, and no one else will be responsible for acquiring the knowledge and skills you will need to survive and thrive. No one else will be able to "give you" personal motivation.

Regardless of your circumstances, that **late paper** for English is not your husband's fault. That **missed lab report** is not your child's problem. Your **tardiness** is not your mother's mistake. That **unread chapter** is not your partner's liability. Likewise, that **98 you scored** on your Drug Calculation Test is yours. That **A you got** on your paper about the criminal justice system is yours. That **B+ you got** on your first math test is yours. This is about YOU! Your life. Your future. Your attitude is going to greatly affect your possibility of success.

Consider the preceding chart (Figure 1.3) describing the differences between a "Victim" and a "Winner."

1. Name one person available to you (personally or professionally) who can offer you support, encourage you, and to whom you can turn when things get tough. _____

   _____

2. Why do you respect and/or admire this person enough to ask him or her for help? _____

   _____

3. Generate a list of three questions you would like to ask this person about his or her life, how he or she "made it," and how he or she overcame adversity.

   1. _____

   2. _____

   3. _____

BLOOM LEVEL 6 QUESTION

Basic Truth #4

SELF-MANAGEMENT WILL BE YOUR KEY TO SUCCESS

A major change coming your way involves the workload for your courses and the choices YOU will need to make regarding your schedule and time. You may be assigned a significant amount of reading as homework; in fact, the amount of reading that college classes demand is usually a shock to many students. Although you may have only two or three classes in one day, the basic guideline is that for every hour spent in class, a minimum of 2–3 hours should be spent in review and preparation for the next class.

QUICK MATH: If you are taking five classes and are in class for 15 hours per week, you need to spend 30 hours studying; this makes a 45-hour week—5 hours more than a normal workweek for most people! "Not I," you may say, and you may be right. It all depends on how wisely you use your time, how difficult the work is, and how strong your academic background is. We will discuss time management and study techniques later in this text.

Basic Truth #5

THIS IS NOT HIGH SCHOOL

It sounds so simple, but this is perhaps the most universal and important truth discussed here: College is very different from high school OR the world of work and perhaps one of the most different places you'll ever encounter. The expectations for four different areas are outlined on the following chart (Figure 1.4). Review each area carefully and consider your past experiences as you study the differences.

Basic Truth #6

ELIMINATING THE "THIS ISN'T HARVARD SYNDROME" WILL BE ESSENTIAL TO YOUR SUCCESS

Some students enter college with little or no perception of how much work is involved or how much effort it is going to take to be successful. They do not think that the local community college or state university they are attending could possibly be **"that difficult."** Many even perceive their college or university to be less rigorous than it actually is. *"It's only Maple State University,"* or *"It's just Trion Technical College,"* some might reason. They do not think that the college they are attending has the academic standards of a Harvard, a Yale, or a Stanford University. The truth is that your college education is what *YOU make of it.* When you graduate and you are interviewing for a job, the name of your institution may hold some weight, but your skills, your passion, your experiences, your knowledge, and your thinking abilities will be the paramount "tipping point."

True, you may not be at Harvard or Yale, but the rigor of your programs, the amount of reading required, the level of math skills needed, and the degree to which critical thinking, communication, and information literacy skills will be required may surprise you. We thus think that it is important for you to dispel the **"This Isn't Harvard Syndrome"** as quickly as possible so that you can prepare yourself for the coursework and requirements ahead and make the most of your college experience.

What is the most surprising thing you have learned about your institution's curriculum thus far?

You've probably already attended a few of your classes and received syllabi from those classes as you read this. Examine the syllabi of two of your current classes. What surprises you the most about what is going to be required of you this semester? Enter your response in the chart on page 17. By embracing these truths about college life, learning, self-motivation, and education in general, you will have taken some very important steps toward your success.

FIGURE 1.4 *A Guide to Understanding Expectations*

	HIGH SCHOOL	COLLEGE	WORK
PUNCTUALITY AND ATTENDANCE	**Expectations:** • State law requires a certain number of days you must attend • The hours in the day are managed for you • There may be some leeway in project dates **Penalties:** • You may get detention • You may not graduate • You may be considered a truant • Your grades may suffer	**Expectations:** • Attendance and participation in class are strictly enforced by many professors • Most professors will not give you an extension on due dates • You decide your own schedule and plan your own day **Penalties:** • You may not be admitted to class if you are late • You may fail the assignment if it is late • Repeated tardiness is some times counted as an absence • Most professors do not take late assignments	**Expectations:** • You are expected to be at work and on time on a daily basis **Penalties:** • Your salary and promotions may depend on your daily attendance and punctuality • You will most likely be fired for abusing either
TEAMWORK AND PARTICIPATION	**Expectations:** • Most teamwork is assigned and carried out in class • You may be able to choose teams with your friends • Your grade may reflect your participation **Penalties:** • If you don't participate, you may get a poor grade • You may jeopardize the grade of the entire team	**Expectations:** • Many professors require teamwork and cooperative learning teams or learning communities • Your grade will depend on your participation • Your grade may depend on your entire team's performance • You will probably have to work on the project outside of class **Penalties:** • Lack of participation and cooperation will probably cost you a good grade • Your team members will likely report you to the professor if you do not participate and their grades suffer as a result	**Expectations:** • You will be expected to participate fully in any assigned task • You will be expected to rely on coworkers to help solve problems and increase profits • You will be required to attend and participate in meetings and sharing sessions • You will be required to participate in formal teams and possess the ability to work with a diverse workforce **Penalties:** • You will be tagged" as a non-team player • Your lack of participation and teamwork will cost you raises and promotions • You will most likely be terminated

(continued)

1.4   *A Guide to Understanding Expectations (continued)*

	HIGH SCHOOL	COLLEGE	WORK
PERSONAL RESPONSIBILITY AND ATTITUDE	**Expectations:** • Teachers may coach you and try to motivate you • You are required by law to be in high school regardless of your attitude or responsibility level **Penalties:** • You may be reprimanded for certain attitudes • If your attitude prevents you from participating you may fail the class	**Expectations:** • You are responsible for your own learning • Professors will assist you, but there is little "hand holding" or personal coaching for motivation • College did not choose you, you chose it and you will be expected to hold this attitude toward your work **Penalties:** • You may fail the class if your attitude and motivation prevent you from participating	**Expectations:** • You are hired to do certain tasks and the company or institution fully expects this of you • You are expected to be positive and self-motivated • You are expected to model good behavior and uphold the company's work standards **Penalties:** • You will be passed over for promotions and raises • You may be reprimanded • You may be terminated
ETHICS AND CREDIBILITY	**Expectations:** • You are expected to turn in your own work • You are expected to avoid plagiarism • You are expected to write your own papers • Poor ethical decisions in high school may result in detention or suspension **Penalties:** • You may get detention or suspension • You will probably fail the project	**Expectations:** • You are expected to turn in your own work • You are expected to avoid plagiarism • You are expected to write your own papers • You are expected to conduct research and complete projects based on college and societal standards **Penalties:** • Poor ethical decisions may land you in front of a student ethics committee or a faculty ethics committee or result in expulsion from the college • You will fail the project • You will fail the class • You may face deportation if your visa is dependent on your student status	**Expectations:** • You will be required to carry out your job in accordance with company policies, laws, and moral standards • You will be expected to use adult vision and standards **Penalties:** • Poor ethical decisions may cause you to be severely reprimanded, terminated, or in some cases could even result in a prison sentence

Activity

CLASS	SURPRISING REQUIREMENT	YOUR PLAN FOR SUCCESS
#1		
#2		

CREATING SUCCESS THROUGH POSITIVE CHANGE

How Can You Bring Change to Your Daily Life?

Why is change so important to you and your future? Quite simply, change that you direct creates opportunities for you to grow and prosper in ways you may have never imagined. It allows you to become and remain competitive. It allows you to actively live in a world that is fluid and unpredictable. There are several things you need to know about creating success in your life through positive change. Consider the following ideas:

How can surrounding yourself with positive, upbeat, optimistic people help you with personal change?

1. **Change is a skill.** Change is a LEARNED SKILL that any willing person can engage in. Period. Public speaking is a skill. Learning how to drive a car is a skill, and just like those activities, change is a skill, too. You'll need to familiarize yourself with the tools and skills discussed below to bring positive change to your life.

2. **Change takes time.** Change does not happen immediately at the snap of your fingers. If you've ever taken piano, guitar, or drum lessons, you know it takes time to learn how to play an instrument because it is a skill—just like change. You did not learn to play overnight just as you won't learn everything about math or history or nursing in one semester. Often, change is a slow, systematic series of events that eventually lead you to your desired end.

3. **Change requires an "attitude adjustment."** As corny or hokey as the following example may sound, a recent contestant on *America's Got Talent* was being interviewed about her chances of success on the show. Queen Emily was an African-American single mother working full time. She had given up her dream of being a professional singer years earlier to raise her children. She stated that before her audition, she stood and looked in the mirror crying. Her only thought was, *"My time has passed; this is never going to happen for me. Never!"* Then she looked herself in the eyes and said, *"Why NOT me? I'm talented. I'm good at performing, and I KNOW I can sing. **WHY NOT ME?**"* Her attitude adjustment was the key to her being able to change her life. She auditioned for the show, surpassed thousands of contestants, and was invited to Los Angeles as one of five finalists. She now performs in a major show in Las Vegas, Nevada.

"The key to change . . . is to let go of fear."
—Rosanne Cash

From Ordinary to Extraordinary

REAL PEOPLE | REAL LIVES | REAL CHANGE

BILL CLAYTON
ACE Certified Personal Trainer / Post-Rehabilitation Specialist
Owner/Operator, Clayton Personal Fitness – Las Vegas, NV

"I was..." Those are powerful words. For example, *I was* the manager of the gardening department of a major retail chain. *I was* an employee in a shop that prints and mails inserts and flyers. *I was* a rock band drummer for several bands. *I was* a crystal meth addict. Yes . . . *I was!*

It seems strange to write that now, but the term, "I was...." is impossible to erase. My friends and clients often ask me how I managed to go from the life of a meth addict to a personal trainer. The journey was a strange one and often difficult.

I began playing the drums when I was six years old and by the time I was eight, I had my first "garage band." Writing and playing music were my only passions. They were my life. After high school, I worked many odd jobs, but my love of performing never waned.

In my 20's, I had a band that steadily played gigs and I was living the life of a rocker. We traveled. We sang. We partied. We traveled some more and we partied some more . . . and more. Before I really realized what was happening with me, I had become

My friends and clients often ask me how I managed to go from the life of a meth addict to a personal trainer.

addicted to meth. It was my life. I hung around people who used with me and they became my family. I met Kathy, the woman I would eventually marry, while performing with my band. She and I hit it off even though she knew of my addiction. One evening after we were married, Kathy and I were talking and she mentioned that she would like to have children one day. I wanted children, too. At that moment, the strangest thing came to my mind. I thought, "If she gets pregnant, I'll stop doing meth." How could I be so messed up that I would work to abolish my addiction for a child not yet born, BUT I would not consider trying to stop *just for ME*? That was my wake-up call. I knew I had to change my life. I was 29 years old.

I was one of the lucky ones. I was able to stop "cold turkey" on my own. I know that others are not so lucky. I began to look at my life and tried to determine what I wanted to do. I had to seriously evaluate every aspect of who and what I was. I knew that I had to set goals to get my life back on track.

I had been in a life-threatening motorcycle accident years earlier and remembered the great care I received from my physical therapist. So, I began to look at PT programs and that is when I found the Personal Trainer Program at our local college. Something about this was very attractive to me. Again, I was lucky. I happened to find my passion and my life's vocation without much struggle.

Today, after working through my addiction, surviving a divorce, and mourning the death of my mom, I can say without a doubt that I am one of the luckiest people on earth. Because I was willing to change and stay committed to finding a better life, I own my own gym, hold certifications from every major fitness and rehabilitation organization in America, and count each day as a true gift.

EXTRAORDINARY REFLECTION

Read the following statement and respond to it in your online journal or class notebook.

Mr. Clayton mentions that he was one of the "lucky ones." What role do you think luck plays in one's success? Is there a difference among luck, readiness, and action? If so, what is it?

18

4. **Change demands action.** While circumstances and desire may drive the need for change in your life, don't lose sight of the fact that ultimately, change is an action. It is something you must do—mentally, physically, spiritually, and intellectually. Just as Queen Emily in the previous example knew, without action by her, her life was not going to change.

5. **Change is about working toward something, not running away from something.** If you want true, lasting, meaningful change in your life, you have to think about it as working toward good, positive, useful things, not as running away from bad, negative, unpleasant things. "Working toward" is *positive and internal*. "Running away from" is *negative and external*. Try to work **toward a goal** and not **run from a problem**.

6. **Change is about letting go and holding on.** As with any new endeavor, you will have to decide what is working in your life and what is not. By doing so, you can decide what you need to hold onto and what you finally need to let go of. You will want to hold onto the positive strengths and talents you have while letting go of the negative, destructive attitudes that you may have held in the past.

ELIMINATING ROADBLOCKS TO YOUR SUCCESS

What Should You Do if Your Fears and Self-Talk Try to Derail Your Efforts to Change?

Try as you might, sometimes harmful emotions, fear of the unknown, and that nagging little voice inside your head (negative self-talk) can cause you problems. Negative self-talk usually appears when you are afraid, uneasy, hurt, angry, depressed, or lonely. By the time you read this, you may have experienced these feelings. When you experience change, your body, mind, and soul typically go through a process of physical and emotional change as well. Learning to recognize these symptoms of change in order to control them can help you control the stress that can accompany change.

LISTEN TO YOURSELF FOR A FEW DAYS. Are you more of an optimist or a pessimist? Do you hear yourself whining, complaining, griping, and finding fault with everything and everybody around you? Do you blame others for things that are wrong in your life? Do you blame your bad grades on your professors? Do you feel that someone else is responsible for your unhappiness? If these thoughts or comments are in your head, you are suffering from the *"I CAN'T Syndrome"* (**I**rritated, **C**ontaminated, **A**ngry, **N**egative **T**houghts). This pessimistic condition can negatively influence every aspect of your life, from your self-esteem to your motivation level to your academic performance, your relationships, and your career success.

If you want to eliminate *I CAN'T* from your life, consider the following tips:

- ☑ Think about the many positive aspects of your life and show gratitude for them.
- ☑ Work every day to find the good in people, places, and things.
- ☑ Eliminate negative thoughts that enter your mind before you begin your day.
- ☑ Discover what is holding you back and what you need to push yourself forward.
- ☑ Visualize your success—visualize yourself actually being who and what you want to be.
- ☑ Locate and observe positive, optimistic people and things in your life.

DID YOU KNOW?

ABRAHAM LINCOLN was born on February 12, 1809, in Hardin, Kentucky, to two uneducated farmers. They lived in a one-room log cabin. His mother died when he was 10 years old, just a few years after his father had moved the family to Illinois.

He was raised in great poverty and had only 18 months of formal schooling. He studied very hard on his own and learned to read, write, and do mathematical problems. He went on to become a lawyer. One of his law partners once said of him, *"His ambition was a great engine that knew no rest."*

He lost the love of his life when he was 26, suffered a nervous breakdown at age 27, failed in business twice, lost eight elections, and suffered the death of three children all BEFORE he became our president and changed the course of our nation. On Good Friday, April 14, 1865, Lincoln was assassinated at Ford's Theatre in Washington, D.C., by John Wilkes Booth. (Adapted from whitehouse.gov)

"You gain strength, experience, and confidence by every experience where you stop to look fear in the face. You must do the thing you think you cannot."
—Eleanor Roosevelt

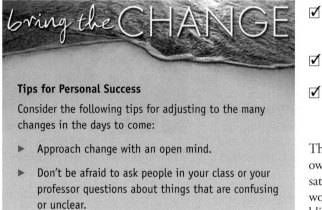

Tips for Personal Success

Consider the following tips for adjusting to the many changes in the days to come:

► Approach change with an open mind.

► Don't be afraid to ask people in your class or your professor questions about things that are confusing or unclear.

► If you are not technologically savvy, find out what other resources are available to you.

Now it is your turn. Create a list of at least three more tips that you would offer a fellow classmate to assist him or her in bringing about positive change in his or her life.

1. _____

2. _____

3. _____

☑ Make a list of who helps you, supports you, and helps you feel positive—then make a point to be around them more often.

☑ Take responsibility for your own actions and their consequences.

☑ Force yourself to find five positive things a day for which to be thankful.

You've seen the differences between an optimist and a pessimist. They are both everywhere—at work, at school, and maybe in your own family. Think of the optimist for a moment. You've probably sat next to him or her in one of your classes or seen him or her at work—the person who always seems to be happy, motivated, bubbling with personality, organized, and ready for whatever comes his or her way. Optimists greet people as they enter the room, respond in class, volunteer for projects, and have a presence about them that is positive and lively. You may even look at an optimist out of the corner of your eye and wonder, "What is he on?"

Positive, upbeat, and motivated people are easy to spot. You can see their attitude in the way they walk, the way they carry themselves, the way they approach people, and the way they treat others.

Be wary, however, of *"the others,"* the ones you need to avoid. Whiners. Degraders. Attackers. Manipulators. Pessimists. Backstabbers. Abusers. Cowards. Two-faced racists, sexists, ageists, and people who are homophobic or ethnocentric. These people carry around an aura so negative that it can almost be seen as a dark cloud above them. They degrade others because they do not like themselves. They find fault with everything because their own lives are a mess. They do nothing and then attack you for being motivated and trying to improve your life. We call them ***contaminated people***. Contaminated people are unhappy with who they are. To make themselves feel better, they try to tear down people who are the opposite of what they are. They belittle positive actions and try to make others' lives as miserable as their own.

Sure, everyone has bad days and bad stretches in his or her life. ***This is not the person*** we are talking about here. With contaminated people, being negative and trying to bring you down is epidemic in their lives. It is the way they operate all the time. It is constant. Having a bad day and complaining is normal for some people at various times, but contaminated people see life (and you) as negative and bad on an hourly and daily basis.

BUILDING A NEW YOU

How Can You Change Your Life Through Goal Setting?

Positive change can be brought about in several ways, but the most effective way is through goal setting and having a "change plan." Think about what you really want or need to change in your life. More importantly, think about why you want "this thing" and what it is going to mean to your life. By thinking about what you want, what needs to change, and where you want to be, goals become easier to achieve.

Characteristics of Attainable Goals

The following characteristics will help you in your quest to bring about change through effective goal setting. Goals should be:

► **Reasonable**   Your goal should be a challenge for you, but also within reason based on your abilities.

▶ **Believable**   To achieve a goal, you must really believe it is within your capacity to achieve it.

▶ **Measurable**   Your goal needs to be concrete and measurable in some way.
Avoid such terms as "earn a lot" or "lose some weight."

▶ **Adaptable**   Your goals may need to be adapted to changing circumstances in your life.

▶ **Controllable**   Your goals should be within your own control; they should not depend on the whims and opinions of anyone else.

▶ **Desirable**   To attain a difficult goal, you must want it very badly. You should never work toward something just because *someone else* wants it.

ESSENTIAL CORNERSTONE

Vision:
How can having a clear vision of your future and what you want help you become a more optimistic person?

Social Networking Moment:
Share your response to this Essential Cornerstone with peers in your social network. Choose two responses from your peers and respond to their postings.

How to Write Your Goals to Bring about Positive Change

"I will pass my next math test with a B or better" is an example of a short-term goal. *"I will purchase my first home in 7 to 10 years"* is probably a long-term goal. During college, more of your goals may be short term than long term, but you can certainly begin setting both. Goals can be lofty and soaring, but great goals can also be as simple as *"I will spend two hours at the park with my children tomorrow afternoon."*

Well-written, exciting, and effective goals include:

▶ a goal statement with a target date,
▶ action steps,
▶ a narrative statement,
▶ an "I deserve it" statement, and
▶ a personal signature.

The **goal statement** should be specific and measurable; that is, it should entail some tangible evidence of the goal's achievement and have a **target date** and a timeline for accomplishing your goal. Your goal statement MUST also use an action verb. An example of a goal statement with an action verb and target date is: *"I will lose 10 pounds in six weeks"* or *"I am going to* join a campus club by the fifth week of this term." These are much more powerful statements than: "I am thinking about joining a club" or "I wanna have a new car."

After you write the goal statement, you'll need to create **specific action steps** that explain exactly what you are going to do to reach your goal. There is no certain number of steps; it all depends on your goal and your personal commitment. An example of action steps for weight loss might be: (1) I WILL join the campus health center, (2) I WILL meet with a personal trainer on campus, (3) I WILL set an appointment with a nutrition counselor in the health center, (4) I WILL . . .

The next step is to write a **narrative statement** about what your goal accomplishment will mean to you and how your life will change after you reach this goal. For example, if

What exactly is it going to take to achieve your biggest, most important goals?

your goal is to lose 30 pounds, paint a "verbal picture" of how your life is going to look once this goal has been reached. Your verbal picture may include statements such as: "I'll be able to wear nicer clothes." "I'll feel better." "I'll be able to ride my bicycle again." "My self-esteem will be stronger." If your goals don't offer you significant rewards, you are not likely to stick to your plan.

Next, write two reasons why you deserve this goal. This is called your **"I Deserve It Statement."** It may seem simple, but this is a complex issue. Many people do not follow through on their goals because deep down, they don't feel they deserve them. The narrative statement helps you understand how your life will look once the goal is met, but your "I deserve it statement" asks you to consider *why* you deserve this goal.

Finally, **sign your goal statement.** This is an imperative step in that your signature shows that you are making a personal commitment to see this goal to fruition. This is your name. Use it with pride. Use the goal sheet on page 23 to build your goals.

CHANGING IDEAS TO Reality

REFLECTIONS ON CHANGE AND GOAL SETTING

The transition from one place to another is seldom easy, even when the change is one you want. Entering college has given you the opportunity to assume new roles, develop new friendships, meet new people, work under different circumstances, and perhaps adjust your lifestyle. It is an opportunity to improve who you are at this moment or to build an entirely new person. College helps you do this. Going to college gives you the opportunity to reflect on your strengths and consider areas where you might need to change. These changes form the very essence of the college experience; they create wonderful new experiences and help you discover who you really are and what you have to offer the world.

As you reflect upon this chapter, keep the following pointers in mind:

▶ Evaluate your reason(s) for attending college and what it means to your life.

▶ Use goal setting to help you direct changes in your life.

▶ Don't just let change happen; get involved in your own life and learning.

▶ Focus on the positive by eliminating your negative self-talk.

▶ Keep your sense of humor.

▶ Be courageous by facing your fears, before they derail you.

"A possibility was born the day you were born, and it will live as long as you live."

—R. Burak

My Personal Goal

To help you get started, use this goal-setting sheet as a template for this and future goals.

Name _____

Goal Statement (with action verb and target date) _____

_____

_____

Action Steps (concrete things you plan to do to reach your goal)

1. _____

2. _____

3. _____

4. _____

5. _____

Narrative Statement (how your life will look when you reach your goal) _____

_____

_____

_____

_____

_____

I deserve this goal because:

1. _____

_____

2. _____

_____

I hereby make this commitment to myself.

_____   _____
My Signature   Date

KNOWLEDGE *in* BLOOM

Bringing Positive Change to Your Life

Each chapter-end assessment is based on *Bloom's Taxonomy of Learning.* See the inside front cover for a quick review.

UTILIZES LEVELS 1–6 OF THE TAXONOMY

EXPLANATION: After reading and reflecting thus far, you may have identified several changes that you need to make in your academic or personal life. Also, changes may have been thrust upon you by choices you or those around you have made. The following model provides a method for bringing positive changes into your life and/or reshaping the changes over which you had little control.

PROCESS: Based on Bloom's Taxonomy, the **Change Implementation Model** asks you to consider questions and recommends actions at each level of learning. The chart moves from less difficult questions (Levels 1, 2, 3) to more challenging questions (Levels 4, 5, 6). To begin the change process in your life, follow the steps in this chapter-end activity.

Step 1: Review the steps of the **Change Implementation Model** based on **Bloom's Taxonomy**.

LEVEL 1—REMEMBER	*Describe* one behavior, belief, or action that you need to change in your life. Also, *list* the possible obstacles that you might encounter.
LEVEL 2—UNDERSTAND	*Explain* why this change needs to occur in order for you to be successful. Also, *give two examples* of the options available to you at college, at home, or in the community for making the desired change.
LEVEL 3—APPLY	*Using* the information from Levels 1 and 2, *show* your plan (action steps) to overcome the obstacles listed above.
LEVEL 4—ANALYZE	*Compare* your current action steps to the steps you have previously taken to overcome obstacles and enact change. What conclusions can be drawn from this comparison?
LEVEL 5—EVALUATE	Pretend that someone very close to you asks what you are doing with this plan and why. Write a detailed paragraph *justifying* what you are doing, why you need to do it, and how it is going to positively affect your life.
LEVEL 6—CREATE	Based on the information you have gathered above from investigation and reflection, *design your plan* to bring about this change in your life. Consider using the goal-setting format illustrated in this chapter to create a plan and action steps that are truly unique to you.

Step 2: After studying the change model above, read the following fictional scenario in which you encounter difficulty in Accounting 101.

You enter your Accounting 101 class eager to take the first course in your major field. You are shocked to find that the professor begins lecturing on the first day. Not only is the material difficult to understand, so is the professor, whose first language is not English.

For homework, the professor assigns two chapters to read per class, but the lectures are not based on material found in the textbook. You try to study as you had in high school but now you feel overwhelmed and isolated. The material is much harder.

After three weeks and a failed first test, you notice that the students who passed the test have formed study groups, something that you once thought only the brightest students did.

Using the **Change Implementation Model,** you decide to make positive changes in your study habits. As an example, plans for change are shown in Step 3.

Step 3: Review this EXAMPLE and determine how you might use the **Change Implementation Model** to enact changes to save your grade in Accounting 101.

LEVEL 1—REMEMBERING

Identify one behavior, belief, or action that you need to change in your life. Also, *list* the possible obstacles that you might encounter.

If I could, I would change my study habits in accounting and become stronger in my math skills.

Obstacles: fear of change, shyness, pride, and time constraints

LEVEL 2—UNDERSTANDING

Explain why this change needs to occur in order for you to be successful. Also, *give two examples* of the options available to you at your college, home, or in the community for making the desired change.

Why change is needed: Weak math skills are causing me to fail accounting.

Campus: tutoring center and math lab

Professor's office hours

Community: Aunt works in accounting office

LEVEL 3—APPLYING

Using the information from Levels 1 and 2, *show* your plan (action steps) to overcome the obstacles listed above.

Step 1—I will join a study group.

Step 2—I will make an appointment for tutoring in the math lab.

Step 3—I will talk to my advisor about services available.

Step 4—I will plan at least five hours per week to study for my accounting class.

Step 5—I will seek help from my aunt who is an accountant.

LEVEL 4—ANALYZING

Compare your current action steps to the steps you have previously taken to overcome obstacles and enact change. What conclusions can be drawn from this comparison?

Past: I took notes in class, looked them over before a test.

New: Join study group, go to tutoring center and math lab

New: Talk with advisor

New: Meet with my aunt for advice and assistance

Conclusion: In taking personal responsibility for my education, taking calculated risks to bring about change, and asking for help, I'm more likely to pass accounting.

LEVEL 5—EVALUATING

Pretend that someone very close to you asks what you are doing with this plan and why. Write a detailed paragraph justifying what you are doing, why you need to do it, and how it is going to positively affect your life.

I am working so hard to pass accounting because I want this degree and I want the knowledge of how to run my own business. If I don't change my habits, I will not pass accounting and I will not have this degree. Without this degree, I will most likely have to work in low-paying jobs for the rest of my life. By asking for help, spending more time studying, and spending more time around people who have some of the same interests, I can develop the skills to graduate, start my own business, and help my family out financially.

LEVEL 6—CREATING

Based on the information you have gathered above from investigation and reflection, *design your plan* to bring about this change in your life. Consider using the goal-setting format illustrated in this chapter to create a plan and action steps that are truly unique to you.

Goal: I WILL get involved with a study group, schedule a tutor, and spend at least five hours per week studying for accounting. I will do this by the ***end of this week***.

Action Steps:

Step 1—I will join a study group/get an accounting tutor.

Step 2—I will talk to my advisor about services available.

Step 3—I will study five hours per week for accounting class.

Step 4—I will work w/ my boss to design a plan for more study time.

Step 5—I will meet with my aunt once a week to get her help.

Narrative Statement: Basically, by getting involved and not trying to do this alone, I will begin to enjoy college more and do better in my classes.

I DESERVE this goal because I have the courage to ask for help and the intelligence to put my pride aside and seek assistance. I deserve to learn this material so that I can successfully run my own business.

Step 4: After studying the **Change Implementation** example, focus on a few things that you might want to change about your own academic life such as study habits, motivation level, financial or time management, or your attitude. Now, choose **one** of the major changes you wish to incorporate into your life from the list. Using the Change Implementation Model, devise a strategy to effect this change.

LEVEL 1—REMEMBERING

Identify one behavior, belief, or action that you need to change in your life. Also, *list* the possible obstacles that you might encounter.

LEVEL 2—UNDERSTANDING

Explain why this change needs to occur in order for you to be successful. Also, *give two examples* of the options available to you at college, at home, or in the community for making the desired change.

LEVEL 3—APPLYING

Using the information from Levels 1 and 2, *show* your plan (action steps) to overcome the obstacles listed above.

LEVEL 4—ANALYZING

Compare your current action steps to the steps you have previously taken to overcome obstacles and enact change. What conclusions can be drawn from this comparison?

LEVEL 5—EVALUATING

Pretend that someone very close to you asks what you are doing with this plan and why. Write a detailed paragraph justifying what you are doing, why you need to do it, and how it is going to positively affect your life.

LEVEL 6—CREATING

Based on the information you have gathered above from investigation and reflection, *design your plan* to bring about this change in your life. Consider using the goal-setting format illustrated in this chapter to create a plan and action steps that are truly unique to you.

SQ3R *Mastery* STUDY SHEET

EXAMPLE QUESTION *(from page 11)* What are the six basic truths about the culture of college?	**ANSWER:**
EXAMPLE QUESTION *(from page 21)* Why must goals be measurable?	**ANSWER:**
AUTHOR QUESTION *(from page 11)* Why is it important to know and understand the basic "truths" about college success?	**ANSWER:**
AUTHOR QUESTION *(from page 14)* What is the "This Isn't Harvard" syndrome?	**ANSWER:**
AUTHOR QUESTION *(from page 17)* Why does change take time?	**ANSWER:**
AUTHOR QUESTION *(from page 19)* Explain the "I can't" syndrome (from page 19).	**ANSWER:**
AUTHOR QUESTION *(from page 21)* What is a narrative statement?	**ANSWER:**
YOUR QUESTION *(from page ____)*	**ANSWER:**
YOUR QUESTION *(from page ____)*	**ANSWER:**
YOUR QUESTION *(from page ____)*	**ANSWER:**
YOUR QUESTION *(from page ____)*	**ANSWER:**
YOUR QUESTION *(from page ____)*	**ANSWER:**

Finally, after answering these questions, recite this chapter's major points in your mind. Consider the following general questions to help you master this material.

▶ What was it about?
▶ What does it mean?
▶ What was the most important thing I learned? Why?
▶ What were the key points to remember?

CHAPTER 2
ENGAGE

DEVELOPING YOUR PERSONAL AND ACADEMIC MOTIVATION

"To be successful you need to find something to hold on to, something to motivate you, something to inspire you."

—Tony Dorsett

PART ONE CHANGING YOUR THOUGHTS

WHY READ THIS CHAPTER?

What's in it for me?

WHY is personal motivation so vital to my success? WHY is overcoming doubts and fears important to my personal success in college and later? WHY is self-esteem important to my personal motivation? WHY does visualization contribute to what I accomplish?

Why? Because your success depends, to a great extent, on personal motivation and learned optimism. First, you have to decide what you want in life, learn to grow from past failures, put challenges aside, and focus on who you are becoming. You have to physically, mentally, and emotionally engage in motivating yourself to accomplish your goals and dreams. No one can do that for you. Right now—and for the next few years of college—you are literally laying the foundation for the person you will become. You are deciding to excel or to just get by. You are deciding to pay the price to graduate with a college degree or to become a dropout. You are deciding to either take control of your life or let life control you. Developing a passion for learning and personal development can be a critical tool for expanding your internal motivation and drive.

By carefully reading this chapter and taking the information provided seriously, you will be able to:

1. Understand the difference between internal and external motivation.
2. Discuss the relationships between internal motivation and Maslow's Hierarchy of Basic Needs.
3. Define, discuss, and use the Cornerstones of Personal and Professional Success.
4. Identify your values and use them to develop a strong and enduring "Guiding Life Statement."
5. Build healthier self-esteem and understand the impact of self-esteem on your values, motivation, and attitude.

CHAPTER 2 / ENGAGE

"The moment you begin to do what you really want to do, your life becomes a totally different kind of life."

—B. Fuller

... FROM MY PERSPECTIVE

NAME: Crystal Johnson
INSTITUTION: The College of Southern Nevada, Las Vegas, NV
MAJOR: Gerontology
AGE: 26

To an outsider, it might seem like I have every reason to just sit down, put my head in the sand, and never look up again. However, nothing could be further from the truth. I am a 26-year-old returning college student raising two children, working a full-time job, juggling home and family issues, and studying during every free moment. Why do I keep coming to class and giving it my best? Because my mother taught me years ago that if you can visualize it, you can become it. If you can see what you want in your heart, with faith, belief, and hard work, you can achieve it in your life.

I have suffered great loss. When I was younger, my father died of prostate cancer. Shortly afterward, my mother died of heart disease. As a teenager, I was left to raise my two siblings. A few years later, my brother was killed in a car accident. At times, it seemed as if it was more than I could bear. But I kept remembering the words of my mother: "If you can visualize it, you can do it." When I'm asked what keeps me motivated, I simply state one of my personal mottos: "I do not have time to feel sorry for myself, and I don't have time for you to feel sorry for me either."

After my sister grew up, I decided to return to college. When I requested my transcripts from attending earlier, I noticed that my grades were very good. I was shocked at how well I had done. I knew I could do it again. I moved to Las Vegas in search of a better life, found a job as a public school bus driver, and began my college career again. It is my dream to work with and care for the elderly. I have found that once again, I love learning, I love reading, and I love growing. When things get crazy and hectic, I simply take a breath, focus, visualize my future, and say to myself, "I WILL NOT quit! I WILL NOT quit!"

The advice, information, and activities in Chapter 2, "Engage," can help you learn how to become a more motivated person and how to use creative, positive visualization in your life and how to develop a set of goals and values that will help you endure during hard times. I invite you to remember the words of my mother: *"If you can visualize it, you can do it."*

SCAN & QUESTION

In the preface of this book (page xix), you read about the **SQ3R Study Method**. Right now, take a few moments, **scan this chapter**, and on page 49, write **five questions** that you think will be important to your mastery of this material. In addition to the two questions below, you will find five questions from your authors. Use one of your "**Study for Quiz**" stickers to flag this page for easy reference.

EXAMPLES:

▶ **What is the difference between internal and external motivation?** (from page 32)

▶ **How can overcoming self-defeating behaviors help you become a better student?** (from page 36)

THE POWER AND PASSION OF MOTIVATION

What Is the Difference Between Internal and External Motivation?

Motivation can change your life! *Read that statement again. Motivation can change your life!* Ask any successful businessperson. Ask your favorite athlete or actor. Ask your classmates who pass every exam, project, or paper with an A. It is their burning desire—their aspiration to succeed, to live an exceptional life, and reach their goals—that changed their lives and got them to where they are today. Motivation is a force that can transform your attitude, alter the course of your performance, intensify your actions, and illuminate your future. Motivation can help you live a life that reflects your true potential. Motivation can help you live a life beyond your grandest dreams.

How can doing something you love and enjoy increase your motivation level?

If you have a need or desire to change your motivation level or attitude toward personal and academic success, there are steps you can take to help you with this goal. Some of the steps described in this chapter will be easy to implement *and* others will greatly challenge you, but taken seriously, each step can assist you in discovering who you really are and what you want in life, and help you find the motivation you need to change. No one can do this for you.

There are two types of motivation: **external and internal**. *External motivation* is the weaker of the two because, as the term suggests, *external forces or people* are causing you to do something. You do not own it. External motivators may be things or people such as your parents, spouse, or partner pushing you to complete your degree; your supervisor telling you to do "x, y, or z" or you will be fired; or even your professors giving you an exam to make sure you have read Chapter 2. You may do the things asked of you, but your reason for doing them is external. You did not necessarily choose to do them on your own.

Internal motivation, on the other hand, is uniquely yours. It is *energy* inside of you—pushing YOU to go after what YOU want. Internal motivation is a strong and driving force because you own it. There are no external forces or people telling you that you must do something—the motivation comes from your desire *to be something, to have something, to attain a goal that you truly desire*, or *to solve a problem*. Successful people live in the world of internal motivation or find ways to convert external motivation into internal motivation.

A simple example of this conversion may be that your current degree requires you to take classes for which you cannot understand their value or purpose. You may ask yourself, *"Why would a theater major have to take two classes in college algebra?"* The class is hard, math is not your thing, the chapters are frustrating and difficult to read, and math has little to do with your interests, career goals, or overall life plan. The challenge for you is to find an internal reason to move forward—a rationale for how math is going to help you, now and in the future. This is called *internalizing*. Perhaps you want to own your own theater, which is a business and which will require the use of math. Internalizing the content of this math class and its requirements can motivate you to do well.

By converting this external motivation (a requirement for your degree) into internal motivation (something that can help you run your business), the math class will become easier and more relevant because you have found a way to link it to your success, your goals, your money, your health, your family, or your overall life plan.

By internalizing, you see that good math skills can help you land a work-study job in the theater scene shop. You find that good math skills can help you create an effective personal budget and help you save money. You find that the more you learn about the logic and process

FIGURE

2.1   *Seeing the Importance*

Think about a class that is required for your degree that seems to have no relevance to you or your career field. (You may have to look at your college catalog to check your degree requirements.) What courses do you think you are going to have to work hard to convert? One example is given below. We have also provided space for you to do several conversions, too.

MY MAJOR IS THEATER/ACTING	HOW CAN THIS CLASS HELP ME IN MY CHOSEN PROFESSION?
Seemingly irrelevant Class #1 HISTORY	✓ A class in history can help me understand the historical and social context in which the plays I'm studying were written. ✓ A class in history can help me understand more about scene design and period costumes.

MY MAJOR IS _____	HOW CAN THIS CLASS HELP ME IN MY CHOSEN PROFESSION?
Seemingly irrelevant Class #1 _____	_____ _____
Seemingly irrelevant Class #2 _____	_____ _____

of math, the easier it is to solve problems and think more critically, thus helping you perform better in other classes. By silencing your negative self-talk about math (*"I hate math," "Math is so stupid," "I'm going to fail this class"*), you are able to internalize the rewards of the class and own the outcome. You have made a conversion. Consider the exercise in Figure 2.1.

THE NEED TO BE MORE

What Is the Relationship Between Motivation and Maslow?

One important way to think about motivation is to consider the work of Abraham Maslow, a renowned psychologist who in 1943 introduced ***The Hierarchy of Basic Needs*** in his land-mark paper, ***A Theory of Human Motivation***. His basic premise is that EVERY human being is motivated by a set of basic needs and that we will do whatever it takes to have these things in our lives. The bottom four levels are what he calls deficiency needs, and they include things such as food, air, water, security, family, health, sexual intimacy, self-esteem, achievement, and respect from others. The top level is called a psychological need, and it involves self-actualization, personal growth, and fulfillment. See Figure 2.2.

Self-actualization, the top level, is perhaps the most obscure and abstract to understand, but it is the most important when it comes to motivation. Maslow suggests that we all have a basic, driving desire to matter, to have a life in which we are doing what we were meant to do. Self-actualization can also be described as living at our "peak" and being fully ourselves. The renowned psychologist, author, and speaker Dr. Wayne Dyer describes self-actualization as meaning: *"You MUST be what you CAN be."* By this he suggests that if you know you are living a life that is "less" than the life you know you are capable of living, true happiness will never be yours.

If, indeed, self-actualization is a basic need in us all, then the theory holds that we all have a burning desire to do our best work, to live a life that matters, and to reach our fullest potential— "to be what we can be." It means that we want to be fulfilled in our lives and experience personal growth. For example, if you are taking a class that you do not really enjoy and don't know why you have to take, you may not be putting your best "self" forward. Doing this may seem to be OK, but deep down inside, you know that you could, and SHOULD, do better. You know that

FIGURE

2.2   *Maslow's Hierarchy of Basic Needs*

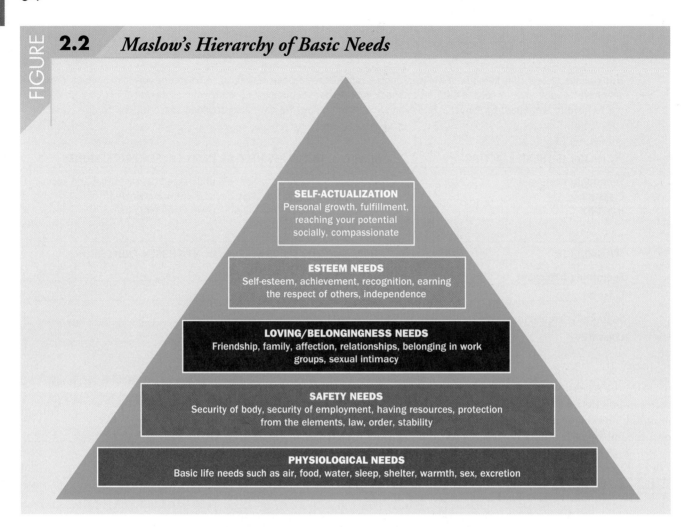

SELF-ACTUALIZATION
Personal growth, fulfillment, reaching your potential socially, compassionate

ESTEEM NEEDS
Self-esteem, achievement, recognition, earning the respect of others, independence

LOVING/BELONGINGNESS NEEDS
Friendship, family, affection, relationships, belonging in work groups, sexual intimacy

SAFETY NEEDS
Security of body, security of employment, having resources, protection from the elements, law, order, stability

PHYSIOLOGICAL NEEDS
Basic life needs such as air, food, water, sleep, shelter, warmth, sex, excretion

you are not living up to your full potential or fulfilling your purpose in class, at college, or in life. You know in your heart that you are not living at your peak, and this will begin to gnaw at you until it affects other areas of your life.

"Watch your thoughts, they become words. Watch your words, they become actions. Watch your actions, they become habits. Watch your habits, they become character. Watch your character, it becomes your destiny."

—Frank Outlaw

ACHIEVING YOUR POTENTIAL AND INCREASING YOUR MOTIVATION

What Are the Cornerstones of Personal and Professional Success?

"I am a winner."
"I fail at everything I do."

"I am a dedicated person."
"I don't really care about anything."

"I can't wait for my day to start."
"I hate getting up in the morning."

As you can see by the two different perspectives in each set your attitude and perspective on how you approach life, relationships, problems, and goals can mean the difference between being a motivated, inspired, and successful person and being a weary, frightened, and unsuccessful person.

The reason that we have included the following Eight-Point Plan in this chapter is to help you see that by focusing on you—by becoming a person who knows where you're going, what you want, and what you have to offer—your motivation and passion for learning and growing will flourish. By knowing more about yourself, you can then establish a clearer vision of your true potential. Take your time and read each point carefully. Consider the questions asked and complete the chapter activities to assist you with your motivation plan.

Point #1

DEVELOP A NEW ATTITUDE

Your attitude—new or old, good or bad—belongs to you. As you learned in Chapter 1, change and growth may require a shift in attitude and actions. If your attitude needs changing, no one else can change it for you. Now is the perfect time to begin changing your attitude if it needs an adjustment because small changes in the way you approach life can mean major changes to your success throughout your college career.

Just as some people embrace the attitude of ***learned helplessness*** (i.e., letting your past and the people in your family or personal community and their failures dictate your future), you can just as easily embrace the attitude of learned optimism. A ***pessimist*** finds bad news in most situations; he or she lives in a world that has a cloud overhead all the time. ***Optimists***, on the other hand, can handle bad news and difficult challenges because they have a positive way of viewing the world. Optimists learn how to determine why things "went wrong" and can adjust and fix the underlying problem.

People actually create their own success, reach their goals, and become successful by embracing a positive outlook on life. Conversely, a great deal of personal misery and failure is caused by adopting a bad attitude and by embracing negative feelings and ***self-defeating behaviors***. Take the assessment in Figure 2.3 to determine your current attitudes. Afterward select one of the self-defeating habits that you checked. On the lines below, state exactly what your behavior is and why you think you are experiencing this problem.

_____

_____

_____

Develop five action steps to help you change your attitude and overcome this self-defeating behavior.

1. _____
2. _____
3. _____
4. _____
5. _____

Do you think that surrounding yourself with optimistic, motivated people will help you succeed? Why or why not?

BLOOM LEVEL 1
QUESTION

FIGURE

2.3   *Is My Behavior Self-Defeating?*

Review the checklist below of typical self-defeating habits that can be changed by adapting the right attitude. Place a check by the ones that relate to you and your behavior:

☐ I am frequently depressed, lonely, sad, frustrated, worried, or frightened.

☐ I spend a lot of time with people who aren't very motivated to excel in college.

☐ I waste a lot of time watching TV, playing video games, texting, scanning Facebook, etc. . . .

☐ I get very uptight and negative when I have to take a test.

☐ I am more worried about associating with friends than I am about my grades.

☐ I spend money that I shouldn't spend and charge things on my credit card that I can't afford.

☐ I eat too much junk food when I get stressed.

☐ I don't exercise properly.

☐ I procrastinate a lot and I lose my temper quickly when I am under pressure.

☐ I tend to give up easily when things get hard.

☐ I am having trouble with my living arrangement.

☐ I have trouble making it through the day without some form of stimulant such as coffee, cigarettes, drugs, or alcohol.

☐ I daydream in some of my classes.

☐ I turn in my assignments late and make up excuses as to why.

☐ I seem to daydream a lot about how things used to be.

☐ I cut class when I feel depressed or unprepared.

☐ I don't feel comfortable talking to my advisor and professors.

☐ I don't feel like I am making many friends here and I often feel lonely and discouraged.

☐ I do not participate in any co- or extra-curricular activities.

☐ I spend a lot of my time doing nothing.

☐ I hate my job.

☐ Some of my classes suck and I cut them often.

If you checked off five or more statements on this chart, you may be experiencing self-defeating behavior. You will need to consider carefully how to eliminate these behaviors from your life as you work on a personal attitude adjustment.

"NEVER leave well enough alone. If it ain't broke, fix it; take fast and make it faster; take smart and make it smarter; take good and make it great."

—Cigna Advertisement

Point #2

MAKE EXCELLENCE A HABIT

As you work to change some of your habits and to become a highly motivated person, one practice you need to embrace is excellence in everything you do. The average person is happy doing just enough to get by. Those who excel and succeed demand excellence from themselves in everything they do. If you don't think excellence matters, consider these points: Would you want a doctor who cheated his or her way through medical school to operate on you or your child? Would you want a pilot who hadn't performed very well on the simulated crash test to fly your plane? Would you want to cross the bridge every day that was designed by an engineer who cheated his way through design class? ***Excellence matters!***

Figure 2.4 illustrates the importance of excellence in several real-life situations.

FIGURE

2.4   *Is 99.9% Good Enough?*

If it was good enough then:

- 12 newborns would be given to the wrong parents in the United States every day.
- 7 people would be buried in the WRONG graves or cremated incorrectly daily in the United States.
- 292 book *titles* published in the United States would be shipped with the wrong covers on them this year.
- 400 entries in *Webster's Dictionary* would be misspelled.
- 1,200,000 credit cards held in the United States would have incorrect cardholder information on the black magnetic strip on the back of the card.
- 79,000 drug prescriptions would be written incorrectly this year in the United States.
- 32,000 of the Library of Congress' BOOKS would be filed on the shelves incorrectly.

EXCELLENCE MATTERS!

Point #3

OVERCOME YOUR DOUBTS AND FEARS

Success is a great motivator, but so is fear. Actually, fear probably motivates more people than anything else. Unfortunately, fear motivates most people to hold back, to doubt themselves, to stay in their comfort zones, and to accomplish much less than they could without the fear.

Your own personal fears may be some of the biggest obstacles to reaching your potential. If you are afraid, you are not alone; everyone has fears. Isn't it interesting that *our fears are learned?* As an infant, you had only **two fears**: a fear of falling and a fear of loud noises. As you got older, you added to your list of fears. And, if you are like most people, you may have let your fears dominate parts of your life, saying things to yourself like: *"What if I try and fail?" "What if people laugh at me for thinking I can do this?"* or *"What if someone finds out that this is my dream?"* You have two choices where fear is concerned: You can let fear dominate your life, or you can focus on those things you really want to accomplish, put your fears behind you, and *"go for it."*

Dr. Robert Schuller, minister, motivational speaker, and author, once asked, **"What would you attempt to do if you could not fail?"** This is an important question for anyone, especially someone who is trying to increase his or her motivation level. In the spaces below, work through this idea by answering the questions truthfully. We have adapted and expanded this question for the purpose of this exercise.

> *"People BECOME who they are. Even Beethoven BECAME Beethoven."*
> —Randy Newman

1. What would you attempt to do or what would your college major be if you could not fail?

_____

_____

_____

2. Beyond the answers, *"I'm afraid"* or *"Fear,"* WHY are you not doing this "thing"?_____

_____

_____

_____

3. If you did this "thing" and were successful at "it," how would your life change? Be specific.

_____

BLOOM LEVEL 6 QUESTION

When faced with adversity, what techniques have you used in the past to survive and "move on?"

"If you fall down or if you're knocked down, try to land on your back because if you can LOOK up, you can GET up."
—Les Brown

ESSENTIAL CORNERSTONE

Motivation:
How can increasing your internal motivation help you put your past adversities and failures into perspective?

Social Networking Moment:
Share your response to this Essential Cornerstone with peers in your social network. Choose two responses from your peers and respond to their postings.

Consider using the goal sheet in Chapter 1 as a template to develop an entire goal strategy to bring this "thing" to fruition in your life.

Point #4

PUT ADVERSITY AND FAILURE INTO PERSPECTIVE

Thomas Edison was once asked how it felt to fail over 1,000 times at making the light bulb work. He responded, *"I have NEVER failed at making the light bulb work. I successfully identified over 1000 ways that it would not work."* Edison looked on his unsuccessful attempts to create the electric light bulb positively. He saw them as eliminating ways that it would not work, not as failure. Failure is just a temporary by-product of the success that lies ahead if you persevere. A part of being motivated is learning to deal with failure and setbacks. Most people compile a string of failures before they have great success.

Have you ever given up on something too quickly, or gotten discouraged and quit? That feeling is quite different from the feeling you have after completing a goal and getting an adrenaline rush from success. Can you think of a time when you were unfair to yourself because you didn't stay with something long enough? Completing a goal feels much different than giving up. Have you ever stopped doing something you really loved because somebody laughed at you or teased you about it? Doing what brings you joy in the face of adversity gives you a feeling much different than the one you have after caving in to peer pressure.

Overcoming failure and learning from mistakes make victory much more rewarding. Motivated people know that losing and making mistakes are necessary aspects of winning: The difference between winning and losing is the ability to get up, stand tall, and try again. Winning is getting up one more time than you are knocked down. A successful person is successful because he or she hung on *just one moment longer* than the person who gave up.

Point #5

IDENTIFY AND CLARIFY WHAT YOU VALUE IN LIFE

If you have been highly motivated to accomplish a goal in the past, this achievement was probably tied to something you valued a great deal. Since most of what you do in life centers on what is truly important to you, you need to identify and then clarify what you value in your life—what really matters to you.

Values, self-esteem, motivation, and goal setting are all mixed up together, making it difficult to separate one from the others. The things you work to accomplish are directly connected to the things you value. Therefore, your ATTITUDE and ACTIONS are tied to your VALUES. If you value an attitude or belief, your actions will be centered on these ideals. If you love to spend time with your friends and this is valuable to you, then you will make the time for this on a regular basis. Why? Because your friendships are a fundamental part of your value system. You like spending time with your friends and get pleasure from it, so you are motivated by it and you do it. It is that simple. Our values influence our actions. It is, once again, tied to Maslow's Hierarchy of Basic Needs.

Many of our values are in our unconscious mind. They were put there by things we've heard, items we've read, music we've listened to, TV shows we've watched, and actions we've seen others do. We may not even know that we value something until it is threatened or removed. Until you clarify what it is that YOU really value, you may be working to accomplish goals or pursuing career choices that someone else values, not you. By having vague or poorly clarified values, you may be working toward something, believing in something, or acting in a way that is not really who you are. This can cause you to wander aimlessly and become frustrated, eventually destroying your motivation level and self-esteem. Values bring direction to your life and help you stay motivated.

Below, you will find a wide and varied list of items. Read them over carefully and circle the ones you truly value. Be careful and selective. DO NOT just randomly circle words. As a criterion for each word you circle, ask yourself, "Can I defend why *I value* this in my life?" and "Is this truly something I value or something I was told to value and have never questioned why?" If you value something that is not on the list, add it in the spaces at the bottom.

> "Our souls are not hungry for fame, comfort, wealth, or power. These rewards create almost as many problems as they solve. Our souls are hungry for meaning, for the sense that we have figured out a way to live so that our lives matter."
> —H. Kushner

Honesty	Affection	Punctuality	Respect
Frankness	Open-Mindedness	Reliability	Trustworthiness
Sincerity	Wit/Humor	Spontaneity	Devotion
Frugality	Justice	Creativity	Caring
Spirituality	Friendliness	Energy	Intellect
Attentiveness	Conversational	Money	Security
Fine Dining	Beauty	Devotion	Enthusiasm
Positivism	Commitment	Foresightedness	Giving
Organization	Learning	Listening	Success
Control	Comfort	Knowledge	Courage
Athletic Ability	Thoughtfulness	Independence	Partying
Safety	Fun	Excitement	Speaking
Love	Friendship	Writing	Teamwork
Reading	Family	Dependability	Walks
Time Alone	Time w/Friends	Phone Calls	Integrity
Exercise	Problem Solving	Empowerment	Tolerance
Service to Others	Modesty	Strength	Power
Imagination	Self-Esteem	Food	Change
Winning	Goals	Risk Taking	Optimism
Self-Improvement	Forgiveness	Fairness	Direction in Life
Successful Career	Motivation	Trust	Mentoring
Working	Hobbies	Books	Stability

_____   _____   _____   _____
_____   _____   _____   _____
_____   _____   _____   _____
_____   _____   _____   _____

Now that you have circled or written what you value, choose the five items that you value the most. In other words, if you were allowed to value ONLY five things in life, what five would you list below? In the space to the right of each value, rank them from 1 to 5 (1 being the most important to you, your life, your relationships, your actions, your education, and your career).

THINKING for CHANGE: An Activity for Critical Reflection

Your friend Jamal is struggling with staying motivated during his first semester at college. He didn't have to study much in high school and still pulled good grades, but he has been overwhelmed with the amount of work his college professors are assigning. He knows he is not doing his best work, but he can't seem to get motivated to excel. You know he is capable because he participated in your study group several times before he stopped coming.

Lately, Jamal tells you he has been waking up during the night very stressed out and afraid that he is going to flunk out. His parents will be devastated if this happens because he is a first-generation college student, and they have sacrificed so much

to send him to college. His fears gnaw at him all the time.

Sometimes he can see himself going home and telling his parents that he is failing. He visualizes how embarrassed he would be telling them and his friends that he has failed. One of his professors has told him that he has a bad attitude. He spent a long time this afternoon talking to you about his lack of motivation and how he is thinking of dropping out.

What advice and motivational tips would you offer Jamal to help him get on the right track?

1. _____

2. _____

Take your time and give serious consideration to this activity, as you will need to refer back to this exercise later in this chapter.

	LIST	RANK
▶	_____	____
▶	_____	____
▶	_____	____
▶	_____	____
▶	_____	____

Now, look at YOUR #1. Where did this value originate?

_____

_____

"Your character is determined by how you treat people who can do you no good and how you treat people who can't fight back."
—Abigail Van Buren

Defend why this is the one thing you value more in life than anything else.

_____

_____

_____

How does this one value motivate you?

_____

_____

_____

Point #6

TAKE PRIDE IN YOUR NAME AND PERSONAL CHARACTER

"My name?" you may ask. *"What does my name have to do with anything?"* The answer: At the end of the day, the end of the month, the end of your career, and the end of your life, your name and your character are all that you have. Taking pride in developing your character and protecting your good name can be a powerful motivational force.

Imagine for a moment that you are working with a group of students on a project for your psychology class. The project is to receive a major grade, and you and your group will present your findings to 300 psychology students at a campus forum. Your group works hard and when you present the project, your group receives a standing ovation and earns an A. The name of each individual group member is read aloud as you stand to be recognized. Your name and project are also posted in a showcase. You are proud. Your hard work paid off. Your name now carries weight in the psychology department, with your peers, and among the psychology faculty. It feels good.

Conversely, imagine that your group slacks off; the project is poorly prepared and received by the audience and your professor. Your group earns an F on the project. Your name is associated with this project, and your name and grade are posted with every other group's. Your group is the only group to receive an F. It doesn't feel good.

Basically, it comes down to this: Every time you make a choice, every time you complete a project, and every time you encounter another person, your actions define your character and your name. People admire and respect you when you make an honorable and moral choice, especially if it is a difficult decision. Both your character and your name are exclusively yours, and you are responsible for their well-being. When you care passionately about your reputation and character, your life is governed by protecting your name. Your actions, beliefs, and decisions are all tied to this one belief: "My name and my reputation matter and I will do nothing to bring shame or embarrassment to my name."

What negative effects can damaging your name and reputation have on your overall success?

Point #7

DEVELOP A STRONG, PERSONAL "GUIDING STATEMENT"

You're wearing a T-shirt to class. It is not your normal, run-of-the-mill T-shirt, however. No, you designed this T-shirt for everyone to see and read. It is white with bright red letters. On the front of the T-shirt is written your ***personal guiding statement***—the words by which you live—the words that govern your life. What would your T-shirt say? Perhaps you would use the golden rule, "Do unto others. . . . " It might be an adaptation of the Nike® slogan, "Just Do It," or it might be something more profound such as, "I live my life to serve others and to try to make others' lives better," or "Be a blessing," or "Live, Love, Laugh."

Whatever your guiding statement, it must be yours. It can't be your parents' or your professor's or your best friend's statement. It must be based on something you value and it must be strong enough to motivate you in hard, tough times. Your guiding statement must be so powerful that it will literally "guide you" when you are ethically challenged, broke, alone, angry,

Tips for Personal Success

Assume you are 90 years old and on your deathbed. You are thinking back over your life. Most likely you would think about certain people and events that have transpired. Perhaps you might want people to say or write the following about you:

▶ She was kind to people.

▶ He spent quality time with his children.

▶ She was a wonderful friend.

▶ He was always a giving person.

Now it is your turn. Create a list of at least three things that you hope to have people say or write about you upon your death.

1. _____

2. _____

3. _____

hurt, sad, or feeling vindictive. It is a statement that will guide you in relationships with family, friends, spouses, partners, or would-be love interests. It is a statement that gives direction to your DAILY actions. Think about how different your life would be if you woke up each morning and LIVED your guiding statement to the fullest.

One of the best places to start working on your guiding statement is to look back at those things you circled as valuable to you on page 39 of this chapter. If you value something, it may appear in your guiding statement. For example, if you circled the words *Respect, Giving*, and *Optimistic* among those you value, this is a basis for your statement. A guiding statement based on these words might read:

"I will live my life as a positive, upbeat, motivated person who respects others and enjoys giving to others on a daily basis."

If your circled words included *Integrity, Truth*, and *Fairness*, your statement may read:

"My integrity is the most important thing in my life and I will never act in any way that compromises my integrity. I will be truthful, fair, and honest in all my endeavors."

More simply, your guiding statement may read something like:
"Be reliable," "Live optimistically," or *"Never give up."*

In the space below, transfer the most important words from the values list on page 39 and then work to develop your guiding statement.

The most important values were:

_____ _____ _____

_____ _____ _____

_____ _____ _____

Using these words, draft your Guiding Statement (Take your time and be sincere. You will need this statement later in the chapter.)

_____

_____

_____

_____

ESSENTIAL CORNERSTONE

Passion:
How can having passion help you determine your values?

Social Networking Moment:
Share your response to this Essential Cornerstone with peers in your social network. Choose two responses from your peers and respond to their postings.

Point #8

MAKE A COMMITMENT TO STRENGTHEN YOUR SELF-ESTEEM
If you were asked to name all the areas of your life that are impacted by self-esteem, what would you say? The correct answer is, "Everything." Every area of your life is affected by your self-esteem.

Self-esteem and self-understanding are two of the most important components of your personal makeup! To be truly motivated, you have to know yourself and love yourself! Many people who are in therapy are there simply because they cannot accept the fact that they are OK. Self-esteem is a powerful force in your life and is the source of your joy, your productivity, and your ability to have good relationships with others.

You might think of self-esteem as a photograph of yourself that you keep locked in your mind. It is a collective product—the culmination of everyone with whom you have associated, everywhere you've traveled, and all of the experiences you have had. William James, the first major psychologist to study self-esteem, defined it as *"the sum total of all a person can call their own*: the *Material Me* (all that you have), the *Social Me* (recognition and acceptance from others), and the *Spiritual Me* (your innermost thoughts and desires)."

Stanley Coopersmith, noted psychologist and developer of the most widely used self-esteem inventory in America, defined self-esteem as *"a personal judgment of worthiness."* Psychologist and author Nathanial Branden defines self-esteem as *"confidence in our ability to cope with the basic challenges of life."* And finally, psychologist Charles Cooley called it *"the looking glass."* Perhaps in everyday terms, we can define healthy self-esteem as "I know who I am, I accept who I am, I am OK, and I'm going to make it."

Self-esteem has five basic characteristics based on Maslow's Hierarchy of Basic Needs. They are:

- ▶ A sense of **security** (I am safe and have the basics of life, food, water, etc. . . .)
- ▶ A sense of **identity** (I know who I am and where I'm going.)
- ▶ A sense of **belonging** (I know how to love and I am loved.)
- ▶ A sense of **purpose** (I know why I'm here and what I am going to do with my life.)
- ▶ A sense of **personal competence** (I have the ability to achieve my goals and grow.)

These characteristics are considered key to a person's ability to approach life with motivation, confidence, self-direction, and the desire to achieve outstanding accomplishments.

How can actively participating in class help build your self-esteem?

Tips to Enhance Your Self-Esteem

TAKE CONTROL OF YOUR OWN LIFE. If you let other people rule your life, you will always have unhealthy self-esteem. Get involved in the decisions that shape your life. Seize control—don't let life just happen to you!

ADOPT THE IDEA THAT YOU ARE RESPONSIBLE FOR YOU. The day you take responsibility for yourself and for what happens to you is the day you start to develop healthier self-esteem. When you can admit your mistakes and celebrate your successes knowing you did it your way, loving and respecting yourself become much easier.

REFUSE TO ALLOW FRIENDS AND FAMILY TO TEAR YOU DOWN. Combat negativity by admitting your mistakes and shortcomings to yourself (without dwelling on them) and by making up your mind that you are going to overcome them. By doing this, you are taking negative power away from anyone who would use your mistakes to hurt you.

CONTROL WHAT YOU SAY TO YOURSELF. "Self-talk" is important to your self-esteem and to your ability to motivate yourself positively. If you

"To every person there comes that special moment when he is tapped on the shoulder to do a very special thing unique to him. What a tragedy if that moment finds him unprepared for the work that would be his finest hour."
—Winston Churchill

From Ordinary to Extraordinary

REAL PEOPLE | REAL LIVES | REAL CHANGE

LYDIA HAUSLER LEBOVIC
Jewish Holocaust Survivor
Auschwitz Concentration/Extermination Camp
Auschwitz, Poland, 1944

"Sweet Sixteen." Isn't that the moment of joy for so many female teens today? It is a milestone date when childhood passes and young adulthood arrives. One can legally drive and in many states, "Sweet Sixteen" signifies the age of consent.

My "Sweet Sixteen" was very different. Yes, I was dating, had a somewhat rebellious relationship with my mother, and socialized with friends, but in the countryside around me, World War II raged. In 1944 when I was 16, my family and I were ordered to pack 20 pounds of personal belongings and told that we were being taken to "the Ghetto," a holding area for Jews in my hometown of Uzhorod, Czechoslovakia, now a part of Ukraine. I understood that the

> *Little did I know at that point that those shoved to the right would be put to work and those shoved to the left would be dead by the evening.*

situation was not good and that things were changing, but I had no real idea of how my life would forever be altered in the coming weeks, months, and years.

After two weeks in "the Ghetto," my family, friends, neighbors, and I were ordered onto cattle cars—60 to 80 per car—and told that we were being taken to Hungary to work in the corn and wheat fields. So there, in the darkness of night, our journey began—young, old, weak, strong, nursing mothers, and babies—all in the same cattle car with no water and only two buckets to use for a bathroom.

After two days of travel, the train stopped and the doors of the cattle car opened. My mother recognized that we were not in southern Hungary, but

rather on the Hungary/Poland border in the north. She took us aside in the car and told us of her suspicion—that we were being taken to Auschwitz concentration camp. After another two days on the train, we arrived at Auschwitz in the early dawn hours.

The doors of the cattle cars opened and the men were quickly separated from the women and the children from the adults. We were put into lines of five and marched forward. In front of every line was an SS officer. Quickly, I was pushed to the right and my mother and sister were pushed to the left. Little did I know at that point that those shoved to the right would be put to work and those shoved to the left would be dead by the evening. I never saw my mother or sister again after that moment. I never said goodbye. I was "Sweet Sixteen."

After the separation, my group was taken to a very large building and told to undress. We were completely shaven, sponged from head to toe with a bleach-like substance, showered, and given a uniform. We were then marched to the barracks where we would sleep 12–14 to a bed with 600 to 800 people per barrack. The black and white photo was taken as we marched toward the barracks from the shower facility and now hangs in the National Holocaust Museum in Washington, D.C.

Some of the Jewish girls who had been in the camp for a while were considered "foremen." I remember approaching one such female. I asked her, "When do I get to see my mother and my sister?"

She took me by the arm and pointed me toward the billowing chimney of the crematory. *"You see that smoke? You see that ash? You smell that flesh burning? That's your mother. That's your sister."* She walked away. I did not believe her at the time, but she was absolutely right. This realization remains the most distressing of all events in my life—past and present—that my mother and sister died in such a horrific manner. Gassed and cremated.

I remained in Auschwitz until I was shipped to the labor camp, Bergen-Belsen, in Germany. We were liberated on April 15, 1945. Upon liberation, I began working for the British Red Cross. Later that year, I was reunited with a friend of my brother and we were married in November of 1945. We moved to Chile in 1947 and then to Los Angeles, CA, in 1963.

I now travel the nation speaking about the events of my life and delivering the message, "NEVER AGAIN." I write this essay to you for many reasons, but specifically to let you know this: The Holocaust did not ruin me. They did not destroy me. They did not destroy my belief in love. They did not destroy my faith in people. They did not destroy my religion or values. The events made me a stronger, more compassionate person. I went on to become a loving wife and mother, a successful businesswoman, and eventually a devoted grandmother. *I refused to be ruined.* I encourage you to use the adversity in your life to make you stronger, more compassionate, more caring, and more helpful to mankind.

EXTRAORDINARY REFLECTION

Read the following statement and respond in your online journal or class notebook.

Mrs. Lebovic suffered the death of family members during the Holocaust, but she makes the statement, *"The Holocaust did not ruin me. They did not destroy me. They did not destroy my belief in love. . . . I refused to be ruined."* How can adversity in your live, like that in Mrs. Lebovic's, make you a stronger and more motivated person?

allow negative self-talk into your life, it will rule your self-esteem. Think positive thoughts and surround yourself with positive, upbeat, motivated, happy people.

TAKE CALCULATED RISKS. If you are going to grow to your fullest potential, you will have to learn to take some calculated risks and step out of your comfort zone. While you should never take foolhardy risks that might endanger your life or lose everything you have, you must constantly be willing to push yourself.

STOP COMPARING YOURSELF TO OTHER PEOPLE. You may never be able to "beat" some people at certain things. Does it really matter? You only have to "beat yourself" to get better. If you constantly tell yourself that you are not "as handsome as Bill" or "as smart as Mary" or "as athletic as Jack," your inner voice will begin to believe these statements, and your motivation and self-esteem will suffer. Everyone has certain strengths and talents to offer to the world.

KEEP YOUR PROMISES AND BE LOYAL TO FRIENDS, FAMILY, AND YOURSELF. If you have ever had someone break a promise to you, you know how it feels to have your loyalty betrayed. The most outstanding feature of your character is your ability to be loyal, to keep your promises, and to do what you have agreed to do. Few things can make you feel better about yourself than being loyal and keeping your word.

WIN WITH GRACE—LOSE WITH CLASS. Everyone loves a winner, but everyone also loves a person who can lose with class and dignity. On the other hand, no one loves a bragging winner or a moaning loser. If you are engaged in sports, debate, acting, art shows, or academic competitions, you will encounter winning and losing. Remember, whether you win or lose, *if you're involved and active*, you're already in the top 10% of the population. You're already more of a winner than most because you showed up and participated.

BE A GIVER. Author, speaker, and teacher Leo Buscaglia states: *"You want to make yourself the most brilliant, the most talented, the most fabulous person that you can possibly be so that you can give it all away. The only reason we have anything is to be able to give it away."* By giving to other people and sharing your talents and strengths, you begin to live on a level where kindness, selflessness, and others' needs gently collide. Whatever you want in this life, give it away and it will come back to you.

CHANGING IDEAS TO *Reality*

REFLECTIONS ON MOTIVATION AND SELF-ESTEEM

Motivation can change your life. Healthy self-esteem can change your life. *You* can change your life. This chapter has been about self-discovery and defining what you value, what role your attitude plays in your motivation, and how to surround yourself with positive, optimistic people. By focusing on YOU and determining what is important to your college studies, your career, your relationships, and your personal life, you can develop a vision of your future. If you can see your future, *really see it*, then you are more likely to be motivated to achieve it. Remember, we are motivated by what we value. As you continue on in the semester and work toward personal and professional motivation, consider the following ideas:

▶ Convert external motivators into internal motivation.
▶ Use the power of positive thinking and surround yourself with positive people.
▶ Step outside your comfort zone.

► Use your values to drive your life statement.
► Clear up your past by forgiving those who may have hurt you.
► Do one thing every day to strengthen your self-esteem.
► Turn negative thoughts into positive energy.
► Don't give in to defeat.
► View adversity as a stepping stone to strength.
► Picture yourself as optimistic and motivated.

Good luck to you as you begin developing the motivation and positive attitude you need to be successful in your studies and beyond.

> *"The thing always happens that you believe in; and the belief in a thing makes it happen."*
> —Frank Lloyd Wright

KNOWLEDGE *in* BLOOM

Using and Evaluating Your Guiding Statement

Each chapter-end assessment is based on *Bloom's Taxonomy of Learning.* See the inside front cover for a quick review.

UTILIZES LEVELS 3 AND 6 OF THE TAXONOMY

PROCESS: Now that you have developed your guiding statement, consider how *it can be used to guide you* in the following situations:

Guiding Statement as written on page 42 of this chapter:

_____

_____

_____

_____

HOW WILL YOUR GUIDING STATEMENT HELP . . .

If you have a disagreement with your supervisor at work. _____

_____

_____

_____

_____

If your class paper or project receives a failing grade from your professor. _____

_____

_____

_____

_____

If you are having a disagreement with someone for whom you care deeply (friend, spouse, partner, parent, work associate, etc. . . .).

_____
_____
_____
_____
_____
_____
_____
_____
_____
_____
_____

If you see that someone is struggling and having a hard time "making it". _____

_____
_____
_____
_____
_____
_____
_____
_____
_____
_____
_____

Now that you have had a chance to apply your guiding statement to several simulations, on a scale of 1 to 10 (1 being not effective at all and 10 being very effective), how would you rate its effectiveness to you and to those involved? Why? Discuss. _____

_____
_____
_____
_____
_____
_____
_____
_____
_____
_____
_____

SQ3R *Mastery* Study Sheet

EXAMPLE QUESTION *(from page 32)* What is the difference between internal and external motivation?	**ANSWER:**
EXAMPLE QUESTION *(from pages 35–36)* How can overcoming self-defeating behaviors help you become a better student?	**ANSWER:**
AUTHOR QUESTION *(from page 36)* Why does striving for excellence matter?	**ANSWER:**
AUTHOR QUESTION *(from page 38)* How can identifying your values help you stay motivated?	**ANSWER:**
AUTHOR QUESTION *(from page 41)* Discuss how "character" plays a role in your motivation level.	**ANSWER:**
AUTHOR QUESTION *(from page 42)* Explain how self-esteem plays a role in one's motivation.	**ANSWER:**
AUTHOR QUESTION *(from page 46)* Why is loyalty important to self-esteem?	**ANSWER:**
YOUR QUESTION *(from page ____)*	**ANSWER:**
YOUR QUESTION *(from page ____)*	**ANSWER:**
YOUR QUESTION *(from page ____)*	**ANSWER:**
YOUR QUESTION *(from page ____)*	**ANSWER:**
YOUR QUESTION *(from page ____)*	**ANSWER:**

Finally, after answering these questions, recite this chapter's major points in your mind.
Consider the following general questions to help you master this material.

- ▶ What was it about?
- ▶ What does it mean?
- ▶ What was the most important thing I learned? Why?
- ▶ What were the key points to remember?

CHAPTER 3
PERSIST

USING THE TOOLS OF SELF-MANAGEMENT TO STAY IN COLLEGE

"I know the price of success: dedication, hard work, and constant devotion to the things you want to see happen."

—Frank Lloyd Wright

WHY READ THIS CHAPTER?

What's in it for Me?

Why? Because dropping out of college is a very common event! However, you and your future do not have to become casualties. Over 40% of the people who begin college never complete their degrees. Many leave because they made serious and irreparable mistakes early in their first year. Some leave because they could not manage their money and didn't know how to look for scholarships and other funding sources. And still others leave because they simply could not figure out how "the system" works, and frustration, anger, disappointment, and fear got the best of them. DON'T be led to believe that you have to be one of these students. You do not! The information shared in this chapter **will help you** maneuver through college with greater ease.

By carefully reading this chapter and taking the information provided seriously, you will be able to:

1. Understand your college's policies, procedures, and professors.
2. Define personal responsibility and your role in the grading process.
3. Use civility, personal decorum, self-management, and ethics to guide future plans.
4. Understand personal integrity and avoid plagiarism and cheating.
5. Find and use academic, cultural, campus, and personal success centers.

WHY is it important to know how to work with my professors, advisors, and counselors? WHY is information on ethics and academic integrity important? WHY do I need to know anything about the services offered on my campus? WHY is persistence important?

CHAPTER 3 / PERSIST

"The very first step toward success in any endeavor is to become interested in it."

—William Osler

WHY READ THIS CHAPTER?

. . . FROM MY PERSPECTIVE

NAME: Brannon Sulka
INSTITUTION: Clemson University, Clemson, SC
MAJOR: History
AGE: 19

Being in college is very different from being in high school and the transition can be quite difficult for a lot of people, myself included. Knowing how to "stick with it" is going to be a monumental asset to you. Persistence means *pushing on*—even when times get tough and you feel like giving up. While in college, if you don't learn how to face challenges, deal with them head-on, take care of your body and mind, and tell yourself, "I am not going to quit," the rest of your life may be very difficult. Your future may not hold all of the things you want and need. That is what this chapter is all about: learning how to hold on, learning how to push yourself, learning where to go for assistance, and never being afraid to ask for help.

I am not only a full-time student, but I am also an athlete. Practice as an athlete is extremely physical, mentally grueling, and at times, not very fun. But just like studying something that you don't want to study or writing a paper you don't want to write, it's what has to be done in order to succeed. That's why persistence is vitally important when it comes to doing well in college. I have learned that you not only have to push yourself to do things to improve, you have to push yourself to do the "right" things. When you are faced with a difficult assignment or something that seems beyond your ability, you can't just give up or turn in work that is not your best. You have to find it within yourself to overcome procrastination, draw from your inner motivation, and stay positive.

When I'm practicing on the field and my joints begin to hurt and I'm tired and weary, these are the moments when I don't think I can go on. However, when these times arise, I think about "the finish line." I think about winning. I think about doing my very best and before I know it, I'm engaged in the activity and nothing can stop me. Recently, for example, by pushing myself harder and further, I ran my best race ever. I trusted my coach's advice, pressed on, and set a new personal record. There is no greater feeling in the world than overcoming obstacles and achieving your best. This is true of your academic work as well. In college, you'll be required to read more, study more, take more tests, and write more papers, but if you do your best, never give up, and face your challenges with a positive attitude, you will be successful. The information in this chapter can help you learn to develop an attitude of persistence and winning.

In the preface of this book (page xix), you read about the **SQ3R Study Method.** Right now, take a few moments, **scan this chapter**, and on page 71 write **five questions** that you think will be important to your mastery of this material. In addition to the two questions below, you will find five questions from your authors. Use one of your **"Study for Quiz"** stickers to flag this page for easy reference.

EXAMPLES:

▶ **What is academic integrity and why is it so important to my success?** (from page 59)

▶ **How do I learn to accept criticism from my professors?** (from page 56)

How does it feel to be at the top of your game? How can you develop a positive attitude to do your best?

TO BE SUCCESSFUL, YOU HAVE TO LAST

How Can I Make It and Persist in College?

Have you ever faced adversity and heavy odds when attempting to do something? Most everyone has. If you are one of the people who has refused to let adversity hold you back, faced your fears, and continued with the project at hand, then you know how it feels to survive. You know how it feels to reach a goal when the odds were not in your favor. You know the feeling of winning. You know the value of persistence.

Conversely, have you ever given up on something in the past and regretted it later? Do you ever think back and ask yourself, "What would my life be like if only I had done this or that?" Have you ever made a decision or acted in a way that cost you dearly? If you have, then you know how difficult it can be to begin new projects or face the future with motivation. You know the feeling of defeat. Know this, however: Defeat DOES NOT have to be a part of your life. It may be a part of your journey, but it does not have to be a permanent part of your life.

So, what is ***persistence***? The word itself means that you are going to stay—that you have found a way to stick it out, found a way to make it work, and found a way *to not give up*. That is what this chapter is all about—giving you the tools to discover how your college works and what tools you will need to be successful. Self-management is about taking initiative and not waiting for someone to tell you how "it" works and not waiting until something goes wrong. Self-management is about investigating and researching ways to be successful at your college from this day forward. It is about your ability to *last during tough times*.

KNOWING THE RULES UP FRONT

Why Do I Need to Know about College Policies and Procedures?

Policies and procedures vary from institution to institution, but regardless, it is your responsibility to know what you can expect from your institution and what your institution expects from you. These policies can be found in the college catalog (traditional and online), your student handbook, or your schedule of classes, depending on your college.

FIGURE **3.1** *Understanding College Policy*

Policy Question	Response
What is the last day to drop a class without penalty?	
What is the grade appeal policy at your institution?	
What is your college's refund policy?	
What is your college's policy regarding academic suspension?	
What is your college's religious holiday policy?	
What is your college's policy for placement testing?	
What is your college's policy on academic probation?	
What is your college's academic residency policy?	

A few universal college policies include:

▶ All students are subject to the Federal Privacy Act of 1974 (this ensures your privacy, even from your parents).

▶ Most institutions require placement tests (these are different from admission tests). They are used to properly place you in the correct English, math, international language, reading, and/or vocabulary classes.

▶ Most colleges adhere to a strict drop/add date. Always check your schedule of classes for this information.

▶ Most colleges have an attendance policy for classroom instruction.

▶ Most colleges have a strict refund policy.

▶ Almost every college in the United Sates has an academic dishonesty policy.

Colleges do not put these policies and procedures in place to punish you or to make things harder; rather, they are designed to ensure that all students are treated fairly and equitably. Some of the policies are also mandated by the federal government in order for the college to be allowed to receive federal monies. By reviewing your college's catalog, schedule of classes, or student handbook, you can familiarize yourself with your institution's specific guidelines. Use these documents to complete the exercise in Figure 3.1.

THE COLLEGE PROFESSOR

Nutty or Nurturing?

The college teaching profession is like no other profession on earth. There are certain rights and privileges that come with this profession that are not granted to any other career; however, there are also demands that no other profession faces. Unlike high school teachers, college professors are charged with much more than just classroom instruction. Many are required to research, write articles and books, attend and present at academic conferences, advise students, and keep current in their ever-changing fields of study.

The Freedom to Teach and Learn

Professors are granted something called *academic freedom*. Most high school teachers do not have this privilege. Academic freedom means that a professor has the right to teach controversial issues, topics, subjects, pieces of literature, scientific theories, religious tenets, and political

points of view *without* the threat of termination. However, this does not mean that a faculty member has the right to push a personal agenda. Teaching information that is related to the course is different from spending an hour talking about his or her political or religious agenda.

You may not have been able to read Mart Crawley's *The Boys in the Band* in your high school drama class because of its homosexual content, but you would be able to study it uncensored in a college literature or drama class. You may have never engaged in a discussion on the "existence of God" in high school, but this may very well be a topic of debate in your logic, religion, sociology, or critical thinking class. This is the right of the college professor—to teach and guide in an unobstructed atmosphere free from parental, administrative, trustee, religious, political, and public pressure.

I CAN'T BELIEVE YOU GAVE ME AN F

What Is <u>Your</u> Role in *Earning* Grades?

There will be times when you are disappointed with a grade that *you earn* from a professor. And yes, you do *earn* an A or an F; professors *do not give A's or F's*. What do you do? Threaten? Sue? Become argumentative? Those techniques usually cost you more than they gain for you.

First, remember that the grade assigned by a professor is seldom changeable. If you made a less-than-satisfactory grade, there are several things that you need to do. First, be truthful with yourself and examine the amount of time you spent on the assignment.

Review the requirements for the assignment. Ask yourself:

▶ Did I miss something or omit some aspect of the project?
▶ Did I take an improper or completely wrong focus?
▶ Did I turn the project in late?
▶ Did I document my sources correctly?
▶ Did I really give it my very best?

Answering these important questions, and the ones listed in Figure 3.2 can help you determine the extent of your personal responsibility and preparation for success.

FIGURE **3.2** *Do I Practice Personal Responsibility?*

Think about a grade or project on which you scored lower than you would have liked or expected. Answer these questions truthfully to determine your role in the grading process. Place a check mark beside the questions that truly reflect your effort. If you have not yet turned in a project or taken an exam, consider these questions as a "check list" to success.

☐ I attend class regularly.
☐ I participate in class discussions and group work.
☐ I ask pointed and direct questions in class.
☐ I read my assignments, do my homework, and come to class prepared.
☐ I work with a study group.
☐ I have all of the supplies I need to be successful in this class (text, workbook, calculator, highlighters, etc.).
☐ I visit my professor during office hours to ask questions and seek clarification.

(continued)

FIGURE

3.2 *Do I Practice Personal Responsibility? (continued)*

☐ I use the academic support services on my campus (tutorial services, math lab, writing centers, communication lab, language lab, science lab, etc.).

☐ I use the library as a resource for greater understanding.

☐ I practice academic integrity.

☐ I bring my best to the class every time we meet.

Being able to answer these personal responsibility questions positively can mean the difference between success and failure with a project, assessment, or class. If you are truly concerned about the grade, talk to the professor about the assignment. Ask the professor to describe the most apparent problem with your assignment, and ask how you might improve your studying or how best to prepare for the *next* assignment.

CLASSROOM CHALLENGES

What Do I Need to Know Right Now?

The professor's first language is not English. Yes, you may have professors whose first language is not English. Universities often hire professors from around the world because of their expertise in their subjects. You may find that it is difficult to understand a professor's dialect or pronunciation from time to time. If you have a professor who is difficult to understand, remember these hints:

▶ Sit near the front of the room.

▶ Watch the professor's mouth when you can.

▶ Follow the professor's nonverbal communication patterns.

▶ Use a tape recorder if allowed.

▶ Read the material beforehand so that you will have a general understanding of what is being discussed.

▶ Ask questions when you do not understand the material.

You and your professor(s) have a disagreement. There may be times when you clash with your professor. It may be over a grade, an assigned project, a topic of discussion, a misunderstanding, or a personality issue. Above all, don't get into a verbal argument or physical confrontation. This will only make matters worse for everyone involved. If you have a disagreement, make sure that *the professor is your first point of contact*. Unless you have spoken with him or her *first* and exhausted all options with him or her, approaching the department chair, the dean, the vice president, or the president will more than likely result in your being sent directly back to the professor.

THE GOLDEN RULE— OR JUST A CROCK

Do Civility, Classroom Etiquette, and Personal Decorum Impact Success?

You may be surprised, but the way you act in (and out) of class can mean as much to your success as what you know. No one can make you do anything or act in any way that you do not want. The following tips are provided from years of research and actual conversations

ESSENTIAL CORNERSTONE

Communication:
How can learning to communicate openly and honestly with your professor and peers reduce conflict?

Social Networking Moment:
Share your response to this Essential Cornerstone with peers in your social network. Choose two responses from your peers and respond to their postings.

THINKING *for* CHANGE: An Activity for Critical Reflection

JoAnne was a very shy lady who had been out of school for 27 years. When she entered her first class, she was stunned to see so many younger people and to learn that everyone else seemed to have more in-depth computer skills than she did.

Horrified that her first assignment was to include a chart created in Microsoft Excel, she thought about dropping the class. *"How am I going to ever learn how to turn data into a chart and insert it into a document by next week?"* she thought. She even heard a classmate grumbling about dropping the class, too. Determined

that she was not going to be beaten, JoAnne decided to go to the computer lab and ask for help. Within an hour, she had learned how to make a simple chart and paste it into a document.

In your own words, what advice would you give to someone who is nervous about being in school (or back in school)? List at least two things that your classmate could do to ensure his or her success.

1. _____

2. _____

Do you think establishing a positive relationship with your advisor or counselor is really all that important? Why or why not?

"Respect your efforts, respect yourself. Self-respect leads to self-discipline. When you have both firmly under your belt, that's real power."

—Clint Eastwood

with thousands of professors teaching across the United States. You have to be the one who chooses whether or not to follow this advice.

▶ If you are late for class, enter quietly, DO NOT walk in front of the professor, don't let the door slam, don't talk on your way in, and take the seat nearest the door. Make every effort not to be late to class.

▶ Wait for the professor to dismiss class before you begin to pack your bags to leave. You may miss important information or you may cause someone else to miss important information.

▶ Do not carry on a conversation with another student while the professor or another student is talking.

▶ Don't ask your professor to "break the rules" just for you. The rules in your class syllabus are provided to everyone so that all students will be treated fairly. If you have a true, legitimate reason to ask for an extension or some other exception, talk to your professor beforehand.

▶ Do not sleep in class. If you are having problems staying awake, you should consider dropping the class and taking it at another time of day.

▶ If for any reason you must leave during class, do so quietly and quickly. It is customary to inform the professor before class begins that you will be leaving early.

▶ If you make an appointment with a professor, keep it. If you must cancel, a courtesy call is in order.

▶ If you don't know how to address your professor—that is, by Mr., Mrs., Miss., Ms., or Dr.—ask for his or her preference, or simply call him or her "Professor _____."

▶ Turn off your electronic devices (iPods, cell phones, etc.). Even if the device is off, take your earplugs out of your ears. Leaving them in is disrespectful.

▶ Be respectful of other students. Profanity and obscene language may offend some people. You can have strong, conflicting views without being offensive.

▶ Visit professors during office hours. The time before and after class may not be the most appropriate time for you or the professor. Your professor may have "back-to-back" classes and may be unable to assist you.

▶ If you act like an adult (which you are), you'll be treated as one.

Remember that respect for others on your part will afford you the opportunity to establish relationships that otherwise you might never have had. Respect begets respect.

SELF-MANAGEMENT, ETHICS, AND YOUR FUTURE

Who Are You When No One Is Looking?

Think about these questions: What if there were no rules or laws to govern your behavior? What if there were no consequences or ramifications for any of your actions? Let's pretend for a moment that you could never go to jail or face fines or be shunned for your words, actions, behaviors, or thoughts. If these statements came to pass, what would your life—or the lives of those you love—look like? This is one of the best ways to offer a practical definition of ethics. Basically, ethics is the *accepted* moral code or standard by which we all live, and that code is communicated many ways, including through our relationships with others. Codes of ethics vary from culture to culture, country to country, college to college, and group to group, but each carries with it certain "rules" by which members of that culture, country, college, or group are expected to follow.

Making professional or personal ethical decisions usually involves three factors or levels, as shown in Figure 3.3. They include: the **law**, **fairness**, and your **conscience** (Anderson and Bold, 2008). You might also consider adding three other levels: **time**, **pride**, and **publicity**.

MAKING MATURE DECISIONS

What Is the Importance of Academic and Personal Integrity?

As a college student, you will be faced with temptations that require you to make hard choices. You have probably already been forced to make decisions based on ethics. Do I cheat and make a higher grade so that I can compete with top students? Will cheating help me earn higher grades so that I get a better job? Do I copy this paper from the Internet? Who will know? Why shouldn't I buy one of the term papers that is floating around my fraternity? What if I just copy someone else's homework and not cheat on a test? What if I lie to the instructor and say I was sick so that I can get more time for a test for which I am not prepared? What if I let someone look at my paper during a test? I'm not cheating, am I? These are all ethical questions that require you to use your personal integrity to make mature decisions.

Integrity is purely and simply making decisions about what is right and wrong according to your personal code of ethics and accepted social behavior. What will you do when nobody knows but you? It is also making decisions about what is right and wrong according to your institution's standards. As a college student, you will see many people do things that you think are not right. You have to decide what is right for you and follow your values no matter what others may be doing. Just because "everyone is doing it" doesn't make it right, and it certainly doesn't make it right for you.

Even if you cheat and don't get caught, you lose. You lose respect for yourself, your self-esteem is likely to decline, and you cheat yourself of the knowledge for which you are paying.

> "Have the courage to say no. Have the courage to face the truth. Do the right thing because it is right. These are the magic keys to living your life with integrity."
> —Clement Stone

FIGURE

3.3   *Six Levels of Ethical Decision Making*

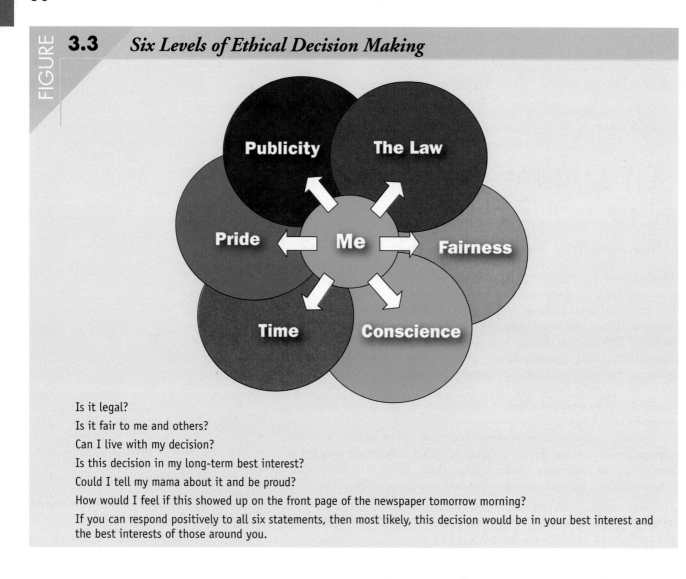

Is it legal?

Is it fair to me and others?

Can I live with my decision?

Is this decision in my long-term best interest?

Could I tell my mama about it and be proud?

How would I feel if this showed up on the front page of the newspaper tomorrow morning?

If you can respond positively to all six statements, then most likely, this decision would be in your best interest and the best interests of those around you.

"No one will question your integrity if your integrity is not questionable."
—Nathaniel Bronner, Jr.

You also lose because you damage your character and the person you hope to become. Cheating can cause you to feel guilty and stressed because you are afraid that someone might find out.

CHEATING!

What Do You Need to Know about Academic Misconduct?

It is important to know what constitutes dishonesty in an academic setting. Following is a list of offenses that most colleges consider academic misconduct.

▶ Looking at another person's test paper for answers.

▶ Giving another student answers on tests, homework, or lab projects.

▶ Using any kind of "cheat sheets" on a test or project.

▶ Using a computer, calculator, dictionary, or notes when not approved.

▶ Discussing exam questions with students who are taking the same class at another time.

▶ Plagiarizing, or using the words or works of others without giving proper credit. This includes works from the Internet!

- ▶ Stealing another student's class notes.
- ▶ Using an annotated instructor's edition of a text.
- ▶ Having tutors do your homework for you.
- ▶ Copying files from a lab computer.
- ▶ Bribing another student for answers or academic work such as papers or projects.
- ▶ Buying or acquiring papers from individuals or the Internet.
- ▶ Assisting others with dishonest acts.
- ▶ Lying about reasons you missed a test or a class.

THE DANGERS OF USING SOMEONE ELSE'S WORK AS YOUR OWN

How Can Plagiarizing Affect Your Future?

Plagiarism is a serious offense, and you should not take it lightly—your professors do not! You have no doubt already heard your professors discuss plagiarism and the ramifications of using someone else's work without proper documentation. You should strongly consider their advice and take plagiarism seriously so that you do not find yourself in trouble. Some college students seem to think that plagiarism is merely copying someone else's work or borrowing an original idea and claiming it as their own work, and, of course, these acts are included in the definition; but that terminology may not adequately reflect what a serious offense this act can be. Plagiarism includes fraud, stealing, and lying. People who would never take someone's wallet or personal identity information may carelessly "borrow" another person's words and ideas without properly documenting them, which is just as wrong as stealing someone's money.

"I would prefer to fail with honor than to win by cheating."
—Sophocles

Merriam-Webster's OnLine Dictionary defines plagiarism as:

1. to steal and pass off (the ideas or words of another) as one's own
2. to use (another's production) without crediting the source
3. to commit literary theft
4. to present as new and original an idea or product derived from an existing source.

Turnitin.com (2008) provides a solution to avoiding plagiarism: "Most cases of plagiarism can be avoided by citing sources. Simply acknowledging that certain material has been borrowed, and providing your audience with the information necessary to find that source, is usually enough to prevent plagiarism." Avoiding plagiarism just takes a little more effort, but it saves you a great many problems.

SUCCESS CENTERS AND STUDENT SERVICES ON CAMPUS

How Do They Support Student Success?

Most colleges offer you assistance for academic, social, cultural, spiritual, and physical enrichment outside the classroom. Your tuition or student activities fee may fund many of the centers on your campus. You've paid for them; you should take full advantage of their services. Some

ESSENTIAL CORNERSTONE

Adaptability:
How can learning to adapt to changing environments help you plan a smooth transfer?

Social Networking Moment:
Share your response to this Essential Cornerstone with peers in your social network. Choose two responses from your peers and respond to their postings.

college services are easier to find than others, but most are usually listed in your student handbook, college catalog, or schedule of classes. When in doubt, don't be afraid to ask your professor, advisor, or counselor if a particular service exists. It could save you time, effort, and, in many cases, money. Review Figure 3.4 for a general list of centers.

LET ME GIVE YOU A PIECE OF ADVICE

How Can You Make the Most of Your Advisor/Counselor Relationships?

Your academic advisor can be of enormous assistance to you throughout your college career. They are usually assigned to you, although a few colleges will allow you to select your own advisor. Your advisor will help you select courses for the completion of your degree. However, you are the person most responsible for registering for classes that will count toward graduation. You should know as much as your advisor does about your degree.

If you do not know why you have to take certain courses or in what sequence courses should be taken, don't leave your advisor's office until you find out. Lack of understanding of your course sequence, your college catalog, or the requirements for graduation could mean the difference between a four-year degree, a five-year degree, or no college degree at all.

Academic advisors are not usually psychological counselors. They are assigned to assist students in completing their academic programs of study. They may offer advice on personal or career matters, but they may not be trained to assist with psychological and emotional matters. However, if you are having problems not related to your academic studies, your academic advisor may be able to direct you to the professional on campus who can best help you address certain issues and problems. Your academic advisor may be the first person to contact in times of crisis.

Tips for Personal Success

Consider the following tips for making the most of your relationships with professors, advisors, and counselors:

▶ Make an effort to get to know your professor, advisor, or counselor on a personal basis. Don't avoid him or her.

▶ When you visit your professor, advisor, or counselor, have a prepared list of questions ready to ask him or her.

▶ Volunteer for projects that allow you to work closely with your professor, advisor, or counselor.

Now, it is your turn. Create a list of at least three more tips that you would offer a fellow student to assist him or her with building a positive relationship with professors, advisors, and counselors.

1. _____
2. _____
3. _____

MOVING ON

What Are the Biggest Issues Related to Transferring?

Many students enroll with the notion that they will one day transfer to another institution, perhaps after a semester, after a year, or after earning a two-year degree. First, your "Survival Guide for Transfer" is the college catalog—not only the catalog from your current institution, but also the catalog from the institution *to which you plan to transfer*. They are both helpful, but you need to be as mindful of the receiving college's requirements and policies as you are of those of your current college.

You also need to be aware that most colleges WILL NOT accept grades below a C (2.0) from another institution. Also, you will find that your future college DOES NOT transfer your grade point average (GPA). When you transfer to your future college, your GPA will start anew. This can be a double-edged sword. If you have a 4.0 at your current college, sadly, you must

FIGURE

3.4 *Campus/Community Success Centers*

CAMPUS/COMMUNITY SERVICE	HOW IT CAN HELP YOU	PHONE NUMBER AND LOCATION
Academic Advisement Center	Assists in choosing classes for each semester and offers career assessments and advice on careers.	
Computer Lab	Offers students the use of e-mail, Internet services, and other online applications, usually free of charge.	
Writing Center	Offers assistance with your writing skills. They will not rewrite your paper for you, but they can give you advice on how to strengthen your project.	
Math Center	Offers help with math problems, one-on-one or group tutoring, and study sessions.	
Tutoring or Mastery Learning Center	Offers assistance in almost any subject matter. Many colleges offer this service free of charge (or for a very nominal fee).	
Language Lab	Offers assistance with international languages or sign language.	
Library	Your college library can be the hub of your learning experience from printed materials to Internet usage to computer-assisted tutorials. Your library and librarians are vital to helping you succeed in your classes and to become information literate.	
Veteran Affairs	Offers assistance to veterans, especially with government paperwork and financial aid.	
Health Services	Some campuses offer student services for physical and mental health, complete with a nurse or physician's assistant.	
International Student Services	Assists international students with admissions, housing, cultural adjustment, and language barriers.	
Minority Student Services	Offers services and programming for minority students on campus.	
Financial Aid Office	Assists students with federal, state, and local paperwork to apply for financial aid and scholarships. They are especially helpful in assisting with your FAFSA form each year.	
Student Activities	Offers a wide variety of programming in social and cultural activities.	
Disabled Student Services	If you have a documented disability, colleges and universities across the United States are required by law to offer you "reasonable accommodations" to ensure your success (Americans with Disabilities Act, Sec. 504). Some of these accommodations include: Handicapped parking, Special testing centers, Extended time on tests and timed projects, Textbook translations and conversions, Interpreters, Note-taking services, TTY/TDD services.	

start again at the future college. However, if you had a 2.0, you get to start again at your future college. GPAs are explained later in this chapter.

Finally, and maybe *most* importantly, you need to speak with an informed, qualified TRANSFER advisor or counselor before registering for any course or degree if you plan to transfer. Your relationship with your advisor or counselor holds as much importance as your relationship with your professors and peers.

HOW TO CALCULATE YOUR GRADE POINT AVERAGE

Does 1 + 1 Really = 2?

The grade point average (GPA) is the numerical grading system used by almost every college in the nation. GPAs determine if a student is eligible for continued enrollment, financial aid, or honors. Most colleges operate under a 4.0 system. This means that:

> Each A earned is worth 4 quality points, each B is worth 3 points, each C is worth 2 points, each D is worth 1 point, and each F is worth 0 points.

For each course, the number of quality points earned is multiplied by the number of credit hours carried by the course. For example, if you are taking:

English 101 for 3 semester hours of credit earning an A (3 x 4 = 12)
Speech 101 for 3 semester hours of credit earning a C (3 x 2 = 6)
History 201 for 3 semester hours of credit earning a B (3 x 3 = 9)
Psychology 101 for 3 semester hours of credit earning a D (3 x 1 = 3)
Spanish 112 for 4 semester hours of credit earning a B (4 x 3 = 12)

then you are enrolled for 16 hours of academic credit and earned 42 quality points. Examine Figure 3.5 to see an example of this GPA calculation.

ON THE GO AND GOING ONLINE

How Do You Succeed in Distance-Education Courses?

Distance-learning classes can be great for students who may live far from campus, have transportation issues, work full time, or have families and small children. These courses have flexible hours and few, if any, class meetings. Most online classes allow you to work at your own pace, but most still have stringent deadlines for assignment submission. Do not let anyone try to tell you that these

FIGURE 3.5   *Calculating a GPA*

	GRADE	SEMESTER CREDIT		QUALITY POINTS		TOTAL POINTS
ENG 101	A	3 hours	×	4	=	12 points
SPC 101	C	3 hours	×	2	=	6 points
HIS 201	B	3 hours	×	3	=	9 points
PSY 101	D	3 hours	×	1	=	3 points
SPN 112	B	4 hours	×	3	=	12 points
		16 hours				42 Total Points

42 total points divided by 16 semester hours equals a GPA of 2.62 (or C + average).

FIGURE **3.6** *Give It a Try–Calculating Bennie's GPA*

Using the information provided below, calculate Bennie's GPA.

English 101	3 credits	Grade = A	Quality Points ____	Total ____
History 210	3 credits	Grade = C	Quality Points ____	Total ____
Art Lab 100	1 credit	Grade = A	Quality Points ____	Total ____
Math 110	4 credits	Grade = B	Quality Points ____	Total ____
French 101	3 credits	Grade = D	Quality Points ____	Total ____
Speech 101	3 credits	Grade = B	Quality Points ____	Total ____
Total	____ credits		quality points ____	Total ____

Bennie's Grade Point Average = _____

courses are easier than regular classroom offerings; they are not. Distance-learning courses are usually more difficult for the average student. You need to be a self-starter and highly motivated to complete and do well in these courses. Take the assessment in Figure 3.7 on page 68 to determine if an online class is right for you.

If you decide to take an online class, consider the following advice:

▶ If at all possible, review the course material before you register. This may help you in making the decision to enroll. Often, professors' syllabi are accessible online.

▶ Begin before the beginning! If at all possible, obtain the distance-learning materials (or at least the text) before the semester begins.

▶ Make an appointment to meet the professor as soon as possible. Some colleges will schedule a meeting or orientation for you. If it is not possible to meet, at least phone the professor and introduce yourself.

▶ Develop a schedule for completing each assignment and stick to it! Don't let time steal away from you. This is the biggest problem with online classes.

▶ Keep a copy of all work mailed, e-mailed, or delivered to the professor.

▶ Always mail, e-mail, or deliver your assignment on time—early if possible.

▶ Take full advantage of any online orientation or training sessions.

▶ Participate in class and in your groups (if you are assigned a group).

▶ If you have computer failure, have a backup plan.

▶ Log in EVERY DAY even if you do not have an assignment due.

▶ Alert your professor immediately if you have family, computer, or personal problems that will prevent you from completing an assignment on time.

▶ Work ahead if possible.

▶ Find out where to go or who to call on campus should you encounter technical problems with the learning platform or getting online.

PERSISTING IN COLLEGE

Won't You Stay for a While?

It is estimated that 30% of college students leave during the first year and that nearly 50% of the people who begin college never complete their degrees (Department of Education, 2008). The age-old "scare tactic" for first-year students, "Look to your left, look to your right—one of those people will not graduate with you," is not far from the truth. But the good news (actually, the great news) is that you do not have to become a statistic. You do not have to drop out of classes or college. You have the power to earn your degree. Sure, you may have some catching up to do or face a few challenges, but the beauty of college is that if you want help, you can get help.

From Ordinary to Extraordinary

REAL PEOPLE | REAL LIVES | REAL CHANGE

DINO J. GONZALEZ, M.D.
Board-Certified Internal Medicine and AAHIVM Certified HIV Specialist
University Medical Center Wellness Center, Las Vegas, NV

Can one person make a difference in your life? Can one person change the course of your destiny? The answer is yes! Most definitely, yes! The person who altered the course of my future was my third-grade teacher, Mrs. Allison. She was a strong African-American lady who pushed us to do our best and would not let us fail. She was hard and demanded the best from us, but she was fair and an awesome teacher. She made us bring a toothbrush from home so that we could brush our teeth after lunch. She corrected our grammar and let us know that "street English" would not fly in her classroom. She even made us do Jazzercise after lunch to teach us how to take care of our bodies. I was lucky to be under her tutelage again in the fifth grade.

Why was she so dynamic? Why did she mean so much to my life? Well, I had always been a good student in school, earning mostly A's. However, my home life was another story. I was born in 1970 in a HUD housing project in Las Vegas, Nevada, in the gang-infested 28th Street area. My mother, two brothers, and I lived in poverty. By the time I was three, my mother was bedridden and on disability due to chronic obstructive pulmonary disease, caused by a three-pack-a-day smoking habit. We were on welfare, food stamps, and the free lunch program.

As it turned out, my father never married my mother or helped support us because he was already married to another woman with children of their own. My mother did not know this until after my birth. So basically, we were on our own. Often, I felt alone in my community because I looked different. My father was Hispanic, but my mother was a blond, light-skinned Norwegian. I was not brown. I was not white. I felt like I did not have a real place in my community or in school. Mrs. Allison helped change all of that.

Because of her and a few close friends, I began to see the positive aspect of school and getting an education. I managed to stay away from the heavy gang influence that had engulfed my brothers. By the time I began high school, one of my brothers was already

> *I was born in 1970 in a HUD housing project in Las Vegas, Nevada, in the gang-infested 28th Street area.*

From Ordinary to Extraordinary

REAL PEOPLE | REAL LIVES | REAL CHANGE

in prison because of drugs and gang activity. Because of Mrs. Allison's influence, I began to surround myself with people who were positive and worked hard. I wanted to be around people who *wanted something*—who had a wider view of the world than I had.

The harder I worked and studied, the better I did. I excelled in junior high and high school and by the time I graduated, I did so with honors. I became the first person in my family to attend college. I was offered four scholarships and they paid for everything, even giving me some spare money to live on. I had been working anywhere from 20 to 30 hours per week since I was 14 years old, but I continued to work full time while attending college.

I had always loved science and the study of the human body, so I decided to major in chemistry and education. I began to develop a keen interest in infec-

tious diseases and viruses. By the time I was a junior in college, I had decided to become a doctor, so I dropped my education major and focused on biology. After graduation, I applied to medical school and was accepted into the University of Nevada School of Medicine. I completed my studies, did a three-year residency, and decided to open my own practice. I became board certified in internal medicine and as an HIV specialist. Six years later, my practice is hugely successful and I enjoy days filled with helping people maintain or regain their health. My dream of doing something real and helping others is now an everyday occurrence in my life.

My advice to you as a first-year college student is this: You have the power to make your dreams come true. *YOU can CHANGE* your life if you truly know what you want and do the work that comes with making dreams come true.

Surround yourself with upbeat, positive, smart, giving, open-minded people from whom you can learn and grow. Mrs. Allison was my inspiration. Yours is out there, too.

EXTRAORDINARY REFLECTION

Read the following statement and respond in your online journal or class notebook.

Dr. Gonzalez talks about his teacher, Mrs. Allison, and how she challenged him and changed his life. What teacher(s) can you think of that has/have dramatically altered the course of your life?

FIGURE

3.7   *Distance Education Readiness Assessment*

© Robert M. Sherfield, Ph.D., 2009.

Please answer each question truthfully to determine your readiness for online learning.

1. Do you own your own computer?	Yes	No
2. Is your computer relatively new (enough memory, CD-rom, graphics card, wireless internet, etc . . .)?	Yes	No
3. Can you type (NOT text, but type)?	Yes	No
4. Are you comfortable using a computer and web technology?	Yes	No
5. Do you have the technical requirements for online learning (Internet access, Internet browser, Adobe, Word or compatible program, PowerPoint)?	Yes	No
6. Are you highly organized?	Yes	No
7. Are you a good manager of time?	Yes	No
8. Are you highly motivated: a self-starter?	Yes	No
9. If you work full or part-time, do you feel you have at least 6-8 hours per week to spend working with each of your online classes?	Yes	No
10. If you have family issues that require a great deal of your time, do you have family support?	Yes	No
11. Do you have "down time" to spend working on your online classes?	Yes	No
12. Can you get to campus if necessary?	Yes	No
13. Do you feel comfortable chatting online with unknown persons?	Yes	No
14. Do you think you can "relate" to others in an online relationship?	Yes	No
15. Do you consider yourself as a good reader with high-level comprehension?	Yes	No
16. Can you concentrate on your work even with online distractions (e-mail, friends, etc . . .)?	Yes	No
17. Do you feel comfortable calling your professor during his or her office hours if you need to do so?	Yes	No
18. Do you think you will be able to take notes during an online chat or class session?	Yes	No
19. Are you comfortable with online terminology such as URL, listserv, Portal, Streaming Video, Podcasts, Facebook, Twitter, etc . . . ?	Yes	No
20. Are you excited about taking an online class?	Yes	No

If you answered NO to more than five of these questions, you should reconsider taking an online class at this time. To prepare for future classes, you may also want to spend time researching and becoming more familiar with the questions that you marked "NO". You can also speak with your advisor or professor about your possibility for success in his or her course. Your campus probably offers an online orientation from which you might benefit.

Below, you will find some powerful, helpful tips for persisting in college. Using even a few of them can increase your chances of obtaining your degree. Using all of them virtually ensures it!

▶ Visit your advisor or counselor frequently and establish a relationship with him or her. Take his or her advice. Ask him or her questions. Use him or her as a mentor.

▶ Register for the classes in which you place. It is unwise to register for Math 110 if you placed in Math 090 or English 101 if you placed in English 095. It will cost you money, heartache, time, and possibly a low GPA.

▶ Make use of every academic service you need that the college offers, from tutoring sessions to writing centers; these are essential tools to your success.

▶ Work hard to learn and understand your "learning style." This can help you in every class in which you enroll. Chapter 7 "Learn," will assist you with this endeavor.

▶ Work hard to develop a sense of community. Get to know a few people on campus such as a special faculty member or another student— anyone whom you can turn to for help.

▶ Join a club or organization. Research proves that students who are connected to the campus through activities drop out less.

▶ After reading Chapter 1 "Change," concentrate on setting realistic, achievable goals. Visualize your goals. Write them down. Find a picture that represents your goal and post it so that you can see your goal every day.

> *"Striving for success without hard work is like trying to harvest where you have not planted."*
> —David Bly

▶ Work hard to develop and maintain a sense of self-esteem and self-respect. The better you feel about yourself, the more likely you will reach your goals.

▶ Learn to budget your time as wisely as you budget your money. You've made a commitment to college, and it will take a commitment of time to bring your degree to fruition.

▶ If you have trouble with a professor, don't let it fester. Make an appointment to speak with the professor and work through the problem.

▶ If you feel your professor doesn't care, it may be true. Some don't. This is where you have to apply the art of self-management.

▶ Find some type of strong, internal motivation to sustain you through the tough times— and there will be tough times.

▶ Focus on the future. Yes, you're taking six classes while your friends are off partying, but in a few years, you'll have something that no party could ever offer, and something that no one can ever take away . . . your very own college degree.

▶ Move beyond mediocrity. Everyone can be average. If college were easy, everybody would have a college degree. You will need to learn to bring your best to the table for each class.

▶ Focus on your career choice. Can you do what you want to do without a college degree? That is perhaps the most important question when it comes to persistence. Can you have what you want, do what you want, be who you want without this degree?

As professors, we wish you every success imaginable. Use us as resources, contact us, ask us questions, trust us, visit us, and allow us to help you help yourself.

CHANGING IDEAS TO *Reality*

REFLECTIONS ON PERSISTENCE AND SELF-RESPONSIBILITY

College is an exciting and wonderful place. You're meeting new people, being exposed to innovative ideas, and learning new ideas. There has never been a time when the old saying, "Knowledge is power" is more true. By participating in your own learning, engaging in the art of self-management, and taking the initiative to learn about your institution, you are potentially avoiding mistakes that could cost you your education. Good for you!

Simply taking the time to familiarize yourself with the workings of your college can eliminate many of the hassles that first-year students face. By doing this, you can enjoy your experience with more energy, excitement, and optimism. As you continue on in the semester and work toward self-management, consider the following ideas:

▶ Determine what it is going to take for you to persist and succeed in college.

▶ Practice self-responsibility.

▶ Guard your ethics and integrity and display civility and personal decorum on campus.

▶ Know the policies and rules of your college.

> ▶ Establish a *relationship* with your professors, advisors, and counselors.
> ▶ Join a *campus club* and get involved.
> ▶ Determine if you have the time to take an online class.
> ▶ Make use of *student services*.

Practicing self-management can help you not only in your classes, but also as you enter the world of work. Strive to become a person who is accountable and responsible for his or her own life and learning.

> *"There is no secret to success. It is the result of preparation,*
> *hard work, and learning from failure."*
> —General Colin Powell

KNOWLEDGE *in* BLOOM

Discovering Your Campus Resources

Each chapter-end assessment is based on *Bloom's Taxonomy of Learning.* See the inside front cover for a quick review.

UTILIZES LEVEL 1 OF THE TAXONOMY

EXPLANATION: Now that you have discovered more about your campus, professors, and services available, complete the following Identification and Scavenger Hunt.

QUESTION	ANSWER	LOCATION	PHONE #
If you happen to fail a math test, where could you go on your campus to find assistance?			
If you are having trouble writing a paper, where could you go on your campus to get assistance before you turn the paper in to your professor?			
Where can you go to find out the names and meeting times of clubs and organizations on your campus?			
If you need to speak to someone about a personal health issue, stress, or overwhelming anxiety, where could you go on your campus to get help?			
You have been assigned the strange project of identifying the sculptor AND material from which *The Thinker* was cast. Where could you go for help?			
You discover that someone broke into your car while you were in class, where should you go at this point?			
If you are not really sure about your major in college or what you want to do for a career, what office on your campus can help you?			
If you read in the schedule of classes that you must have your advisor's signature to register for next semester, who is this person and where is he or she located?			
If you're thinking of taking an online class, where is the first place you could go on your campus to speak with someone about the technical requirements?			
If you want to read more about the penalties for academic dishonesty (cheating) on your campus, where could you look?			

SQ3R *Mastery* STUDY SHEET

EXAMPLE QUESTION: *(from page 60)* What is academic integrity and why is it so important to your success?	**ANSWER:**
EXAMPLE QUESTION: *(from page 56)* How do you learn to accept criticism from your professors?	**ANSWER:**
AUTHOR QUESTION: *(from page 57)* List three tips for succeeding in a class where you and the professor do not have the same first language.	**ANSWER:**
AUTHOR QUESTION: *(from page 57)* Why are civility and personal decorum important in a college classroom?	**ANSWER:**
AUTHOR QUESTION: *(from page 62)* How can you get to know your advisor or counselor better?	**ANSWER:**
AUTHOR QUESTION: *(from page 62)* What is an academic support service?	**ANSWER:**
AUTHOR QUESTION: *(from page 68)* Discuss two ways that you can persist in college.	**ANSWER:**
YOUR QUESTION: *(from page ____)*	**ANSWER:**
YOUR QUESTION: *(from page ____)*	**ANSWER:**
YOUR QUESTION: *(from page ____)*	**ANSWER:**
YOUR QUESTION: *(from page ____)*	**ANSWER:**
YOUR QUESTION: *(from page ____)*	**ANSWER:**

Finally, after answering these questions, recite this chapter's major points in your mind. Consider the following general questions to help you master this material:

▶ What was it about?
▶ What does it mean?
▶ What was the most important thing I learned? Why?
▶ What were the key points to remember?

CHAPTER 4
COMMUNICATE

IMPROVING YOUR
INTERPERSONAL
COMMUNICATION
AND CONFLICT
MANAGEMENT
SKILLS

"Words can
destroy
relationships.
What we call
each other
ultimately
becomes what we
think about each
other, and what
we think about
each other
matters."

—Jeanne S.
Kirkpatrick

WHY READ THIS CHAPTER?

What's in it for me?

WHY will interpersonal communication be important to my life and career? *WHY* is it important to understand Computer Mediated Communication? *WHY* does managing conflict really matter at this point in my life? *WHY* is it important to study relationships?

Why? Because, simply, people do not live alone. We are constantly communicating and relating to others even when we think we may not be and even when we are not trying to do so. The ability to know yourself and how to communicate with others—to understand them, to work with them, and to manage conflicts that may arise with them—are some of THE MOST valuable tools you will ever learn to use. Effective communication determines so much about the nature and quality of your life including aspects of your education, your relationships, your romances, your career, your future, your friends, your values, your ethics, and, indeed, your character. These qualities are also important because most employers name interpersonal communication skills as one of the top attributes that any potential employee should possess.

By carefully reading this chapter and taking the information provided seriously, you will be able to:

1. Identify the elements and power of the communication process.
2. Define the concept of interpersonal communication and learn the associated essential skills.
3. Discuss Computer Mediated Communication as it relates to interpersonal communication.
4. Define and discuss the role of nonverbal communication.
5. Navigate and learn how to manage conflict more effectively.

CHAPTER 4 / COMMUNICATE

"I see communication as a huge umbrella that covers and affects all that goes on between human beings."

—Joseph Adler

NAME: Stacy Seals
INSTITUTION: Delgado Community College, New Orleans, LA
MAJOR: Office Technology Administration
AGE: 18

Without communication, we would never get anything accomplished. We would not learn because we would not be able to ask questions. We would not have relationships because we would not know how to approach people. In my chosen major and profession, interpersonal communication is very important, but I can't imagine a profession where it would not be. In the field of office technology administration, communication is a vital part of everyday functions, from telephone calls to taking minutes in meetings to interacting with colleagues to supervising staff. It would be impossible to function and be successful without having superior interpersonal communication skills.

When I began my degree program at Delgado Community College, I was very shy and withdrawn. Some of this was due to my age (I was only 16), but some of this shyness came from not knowing how to communicate very well with others. I enrolled in a student success class where we were required to participate, speak up, and work in groups. At first, I was terrified, but as the semester progressed, I learned how to ask questions, comment on different topics, and participate in discussion groups. By learning how to engage in interpersonal communications more effectively, I became a better student. Also, my fears of communicating with, and in front of, others lessened. Learning to communicate better helped me improve in all of my classes as well as my relationships.

Another way that interpersonal communication has helped me is by allowing me to meet and establish friendships and relationships with other people. Once I began meeting other people, I became more open and willing to take chances. I started learning more about people and their backgrounds and families. I even started a study group for one of my classes. By learning to communicate and apply many of the techniques discussed in this chapter, I began to participate more in my own education, I learned more about others, and I began to understand the world more effectively and how to get along in it. Nothing has helped me change more than learning how to communicate with others. Improving your interpersonal communication skills will be a great tool for you, too.

SCAN & QUESTION

In the preface of this book (page xix), you read about the **SQ3R Study Method.** Right now, take a few moments, **scan this chapter,** and on page 93, write **five questions** that you think will be important to your mastery of this material. In addition to the two questions below, you will find five questions from your authors. Use one of your **"Study for Quiz"** stickers to flag this page for easy reference.

EXAMPLES:

▶ **What are the six elements of the communication process?** (from page 76)
▶ **What is self-disclosure and why is it important for healthy relationships?** (from page 82)

THE COMMUNICATION PROCESS

How Does Communication Work?

Communication is not something we do **to people**; rather, it is something that is done **between people**. Communication can take a variety of forms such as oral speech, the written word, body movements, electronic messages, and even yawns. All of these actions communicate something to another person. As you begin thinking about communication, it is paramount that you know this: If you are in the presence of another person, communication cannot be stopped.

Multiple types of communication are all around you every day. Almost every single moment of every single day of every single week, you are involved in some type of communication activity. The communication activity may be speaking, listening, or writing, but those are not the only types of communication. You also receive a great deal of information from the Internet, Webcasts, TV, billboards, music, video games, cell phones, Blackberries, and print material such as newspapers and magazine articles.

Basically, the communication process involves **SIX ELEMENTS**: the source, the message, the channel, the receiver, barriers, and feedback. Consider Figure 4.1.

Barriers (represented by the white lines in Figure 4.1) are things that can interfere with the source, the message, the channel, or the receiver. Barriers can occur anywhere within the communication process and can include things like external noise (others talking, cell phones, and traffic), internal noise (self-talk, doubt, and questioning), interference, and poor communication habits. Your emotions, past experiences, social norms, communication expectations, and prejudices can also be barriers to effective communication. Think about a time when your feelings for someone interfered with your ability to listen to him or her objectively. This would be a perfect example of a barrier. **Feedback** is the verbal and nonverbal responses given to you by the receiver.

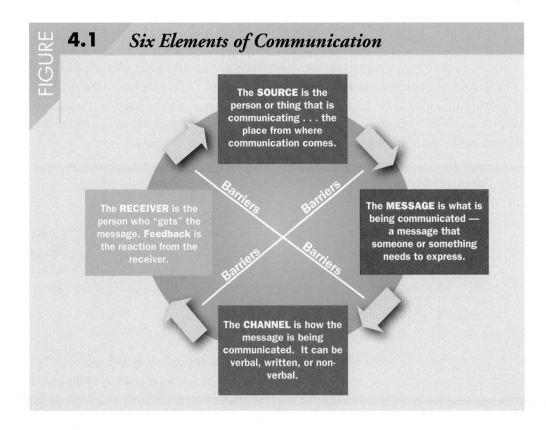

FIGURE **4.1** *Six Elements of Communication*

The **SOURCE** is the person or thing that is communicating . . . the place from where communication comes.

The **MESSAGE** is what is being communicated — a message that someone or something needs to express.

The **CHANNEL** is how the message is being communicated. It can be verbal, written, or non-verbal.

The **RECEIVER** is the person who "gets" the message. **Feedback** is the reaction from the receiver.

Barriers

FIGURE

4.2 *Interpersonal Communication Goals*

TYPE OF GOAL	EXPLANATION	EXAMPLE
Self-Presentation Goals	Goals that help us present ourselves to others in a particular fashion and help others see us as we wish to be seen.	If you want a new acquaintance or love interest to see you as a caring, compassionate person, you will use words and actions that reveal yourself as caring, trustworthy, honest, and compassionate.
Instrumental Goals	Goals that help us present information in a way that we get what we want or need from another person; to possibly win approval.	If you wanted to borrow your best friend's laptop computer, you would remind him or her that you are always careful and respect other's property.
Relationship Goals	Goals that help us build meaningful, lasting, and effective relationships with other people.	If your friend loaned you her computer, you might write a thank you note or buy a small gift as a token of your appreciation.

What Is the Role of Interpersonal Communication?

Interpersonal communication is a part of the greater communication spectrum. It is "a dynamic form of communication between two (or more) people in which the messages exchanged significantly influence their thoughts, emotions, behaviors, and relationships" (McCornack, 2007). The messages in interpersonal communication are not necessarily static like the words in a book, a written letter, or a text message; rather, they are fluid and constantly changing, potentially causing your relationships to change along with them. Texting and e-mails can be a part of interpersonal communication, and we will discuss Computer Mediated Communication later in this chapter.

Steven McCornack, in his book *Reflect and Relate* (2007), suggests that there are three interpersonal communication goals, as shown in Figure 4.2. They are: *Self-Presentation*, *Instrumental*, and *Relationship Goals*.

Take a moment and identify one way that you could use each of the interpersonal communication goals to help you succeed in college.

Self-Presentation Goal   I can use this to ——————————————————

——————————————————————————————————

Instrumental Goal   I can use this to ——————————————————

——————————————————————————————————

Relationship Goal   I can use this to ——————————————————

——————————————————————————————————

BLOOM LEVEL 3
QUESTION

Later in this chapter, we will discuss how to use interpersonal communication to your best advantage in understanding and learning from others, building lasting relationships, and dealing with eventual conflicts both in person and through technology.

THE STORY OF ONE WILD BOY

Why Is Interpersonal Communication Important?

You do NOT have a choice. If you are in the presence of another human being, you are communicating. Period! Smiling is communication. Reading a newspaper is communication.

ESSENTIAL CORNERSTONE

Communication:
How can becoming more adept at developing positive relationships help you with your career aspirations?

Social Networking Moment:
Share your response to this Essential Cornerstone with peers in your social network. Choose two responses from your peers and respond to their postings.

Entering a room where others are present with your head down and shoulders slumped is communication. Silence is communication. It is just the law of nature—if you are around one or more people, you are communicating with them. With that said, understanding the impact of your communication is paramount.

Consider this: Nothing in your life is more important than effective communication. Nothing! Your family is not. Your friends are not. Your career is not. Your religion is not. Your money is not. *"Why?"* you may ask. *"That's a harsh, drastic statement."* We make this assertion because without effective communication, you would not have a relationship with your family and friends. You would not have a career or money or even religious beliefs. Communication is that important. In fact, communication is so important that it gives us our identity. That's right. Without communication and interaction, *we would not even know that we were human beings.*

Take into account the *true story* of the Wild Boy of Aveyron. It may sound like this story was taken from *The National Enquirer,* but it was not. This story has been documented in many science, psychology, sociology, and communication texts over the years. In January of 1800, a gardener in Aveyron, France, went out one morning to collect vegetables for the day. To his surprise, he heard this unusual moaning and groaning sound. Upon further inspection, he found a "wild boy" squatting in the garden, eating vegetables as an animal might do. This boy showed no signs or behaviors associated with human beings. He appeared to be 12–14 years old, but stood just a little more than four feet tall. He had scars and burns on his body and his face showed traces of smallpox. His teeth were brown and yellow and his gums were receding. It can only be assumed that when he was an infant, he was abandoned in the woods and left to die. It has also been suggested, because of the long scar across his trachea, that someone may have tried to kill him as an infant (Lane, 1976).

When he was found in 1800, he could not speak and barely stood erect. *"He had no sense of being a human in the world. He had no sense of himself as a person related to other persons"* (Shattuck, 1980). Because of his lack of communication and contact with other humans, he had no identity, no language, no self-concept, and no idea that he was even a human being in a world of human beings. Of course, he had no religious beliefs or relationships with other human beings.

That is how **powerful** communication is in our world today—it gives us our identity. It lets us know we are HUMAN! It helps establish our place and purpose in the world.

The Sapir-Whorf Hypothesis

Much work has been done on the topics of identity, communication, and personal actions, but perhaps the most widely cited research comes from the *Sapir-Whorf Hypothesis* (1956). Edward Sapir and Benjamin Whorf researched the relationships among language, culture, and thought. Basically, their theory suggests that the language we know, hear, and speak *determines the way we interpret and understand* the world. Just as the Wild Boy of Aveyron had never heard human language, his actions suggested that he did not know he was human. The theory also suggests that as humans, we are *unconscious* of this language/action situation and live our lives accordingly without choice. At its core, the Sapir-Whorf Hypothesis suggests that because of the language we hear, our "realities" and interpretations of the world around us vary from culture to culture and from person to person.

Consider this example: In the Native American culture, there are no words for *"to own the earth."* The concept of land ownership does not exist. They do not believe that the earth can be "owned" by human beings. Think about that for a moment. If you have no concept of what it is "to own the earth," then your actions and beliefs about the earth differ greatly from those of people who think they can and do own the earth. Language, in this and many other cases, determines our thoughts and actions.

Another example comes from the Civil Rights Movement of the 1960s. We've all see the photos of fire hoses being used to "control" African-Americans who were marching for equal rights. According to the Sapir-Whorf Hypothesis, if you were raised where segregation was normal and natural and African-Americans were considered second-class citizens, this footage may not have affected you at all. In fact, you may have even thought the police who used the hoses were justified. You may have seen the photo and thought, "They deserve it." If the only language to which you have ever been exposed consists of bigotry and prejudice, then you may believe that supremacy is OK, and your thoughts and actions mirror this.

Whereas, if you were reared in an atmosphere in which you were taught that everyone is equal and that racial prejudice is shameful and disgraceful, you may see these fire hose photos as barbaric and horrific. The language we hear and live with on a daily basis determines how we think and how we act. THAT is the important lesson of the power of language and communication. It gives us our identity. It defines us.

NONVERBAL BEHAVIOR IN INTERPERSONAL COMMUNICATION

Can We Communicate Without Words?

Nonverbal communication is any and all communication other than words—and it is ever-constant. We cannot escape our body language or the body language of others. Why is it important to study nonverbal communication? Because there can be so many interpretations of a single nonverbal clue that we must understand that not every action is equal or carries the same message. We must consider everything from cultural traditions to unconscious acts in order to fully grasp what may be intended by a look, a smile, a touch, or how close we stand to someone. We must consider that many of our nonverbal clues are accidental. Think about how many interpretations there can be of a pat on the shoulder. It could mean "Congratulations" or "Welcome back" or "Way to go" or "I'm sorry" or "Hey, friend" (Lane, 2008).

Nonverbal clues mean different things to different people and cultures and can be interpreted in vastly different ways. One's facial expressions are perhaps one of the, if not THE, most telling of our nonverbal clues. "One research team found that some facial expressions such as those conveying happiness, sadness, anger, disgust, and surprise were the same in 68 to 92 percent of all cultures examined" (Beebe et al., 2008).

Proximity is also a strong nonverbal clue. Maybe you are not overly fond of the person who has approached you and you decide to keep your physical distance from him or her. Conversely, when a person approaches you that you consider to be your friend and confidant, you may move closer to him or her. The rules surely vary from culture to culture, but consider the diagram in Figure 4.3, The Classification of Spatial Zones, as described by interpersonal expert Edward T. Hall (1966). Consider Figure 4.4 describing more common nonverbal clues beyond proximity. As you study each action and example, try to determine what each action would mean to YOU based on your thoughts and cultural traditions.

Understanding nonverbal communication and the cultural clues that can accompany them can greatly enhance your ability to establish effective interpersonal relationships and avoid conflicts caused by misunderstanding. Work hard to hear the verbal message and learn to decode the nonverbal clues in conjunction with each other. This will help you establish a rich, rewarding relationships.

> "Research indicates that between 65 percent and 93 percent of the meaning of messages comes from nonverbal communication."
> —Shelley Lane

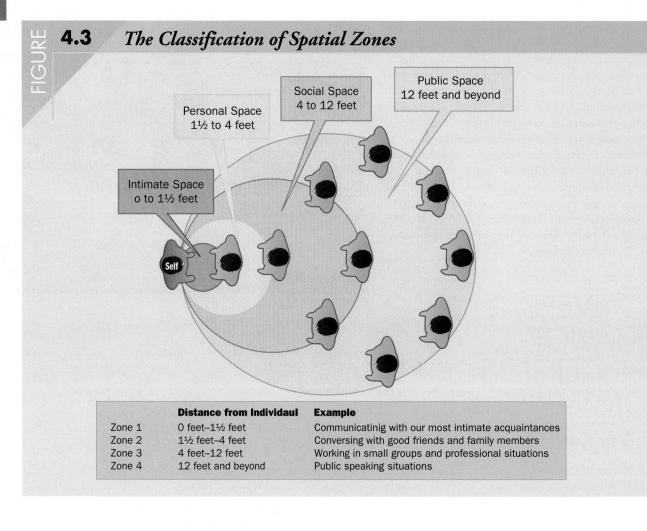

FIGURE

4.3   *The Classification of Spatial Zones*

	Distance from Individaul	Example
Zone 1	0 feet–1½ feet	Communicatinig with our most intimate acquaintances
Zone 2	1½ feet–4 feet	Conversing with good friends and family members
Zone 3	4 feet–12 feet	Working in small groups and professional situations
Zone 4	12 feet and beyond	Public speaking situations

O M G U R O T T (Oh My God, You Are Over The Top)

Why Is Studying Computer Mediated Communication Important in Today's Society?

Believe it or not, there was a time not too long ago when there was no such term as "Computer Mediated Communication (CMC)." There were no e-mails, Blackberries, iPhones, text messages, blogs, twittering, Facebooking, MySpacing, or instant messaging. OMG, YKM! No, we're not kidding you. As a matter of fact, it was not until a few years ago that the study of interpersonal communication even mentioned CMC. It was not considered to be a part of interpersonal communication at all because it was believed that interpersonal communication had to take place *in person*.

Today, it is widely considered that CMC is a vital subcategory of interpersonal communication studies. "There is some evidence that those wishing to communicate a message to someone, such as a message ending a relationship, may select a less-rich communication message—they may be more likely to send a letter or an e-mail rather than share the bad news face-to-face" (Beebe et. al., 2008). Technology has thus become an integral part of our communication strategies.

Some may ask, can CMC really be considered "interpersonal" when you are not meeting face-to-face with another person? The answer is yes. Why? Because in today's rich CMC environment, we can ***infer or imply emotions*** as we send and receive electronic communication. For example, we use symbols such as ☺ to indicate happiness or funny and ☹ to indicate sad or upset.

FIGURE **4.4** *Nonverbal Communication*

NONVERBAL ACTION	EXAMPLES	WHAT THEY COULD MEAN
Eye Contact	Looking directly at someone	_____
	Avoiding eye contact	_____
	Fixed gaze	_____
Posture	Slumping	_____
	Standing very erect	_____
	Leans forward when seated	_____
Facial Expressions	Smiling/Frowning	_____
	Squinted eyes	_____
	Blank stare	_____
Clothing/Emblems	Well dressed and pressed	_____
	Wrinkled and sloppy	_____
	"Smelly"	_____
Artifacts	Jewelry	_____
	Tattoos	_____
	Body/Facial piercings	_____
Gestures	Waving arms	_____
	Fingers pointed toward person	_____
	Crossed arms	_____
Touch	Patting someone on the back	_____
	Firm handshake	_____
	Weak handshake	_____

We use abbreviations such as LOL (for "laugh out loud"). We even SCREAM AT OTHERS when we use all capital letters in our communication. Additionally, many people have cameras connected to their computers and the sender and receiver can see each other's facial expressions on the screen. Therefore, emotions can be conveyed through CMC, although there are not as many nonverbal clues to view and interpret as in face-to-face communication (Lane, 2008).

The fact that we are not face-to-face does not seem to negatively affect our communication efforts via technology. Several studies suggest that CMC relationships differ very little from the relationships of those who meet face-to-face. Further, research also suggests that CMC relationships may even be stronger than face-to-face relationships because people using CMC ask more pointed and direct questions, reveal more about themselves, and communicate more frequently (Tidwell and Walther, 2002; Walther and Burgoon, 1992). Think about the last time you revealed something online that you may have never revealed to that person face-to-face.

There is a downside to CMC, however. For years, communication experts have worried about the effects of electronic communication on the entire communication process, especially traditional interpersonal communication. In today's technologically advanced world, we do not have to speak to anyone if we don't want to. We purchase gasoline at the pump, pay for groceries at self-checkout, use automated tellers to get money, go to Amazon or iTunes to purchase our music and books, search eBay for sale items, and e-mail others rather than pick up the phone or visit them. Social isolation is a major concern and you have to work hard to guard against becoming a *"technological recluse."*

"The information superhighway is clearly not just a road for moving data from one place to another, but a roadside where people can pass each other, occasionally meet, and decide to travel together."
—Beebe, Beebe, and Redmond

SELF-DISCLOSURE AND INTERPERSONAL COMMUNICATION

Are You Willing to Let Others into Your Life?

By understanding more about your self-concept, you can better understand how you communicate and how others communicate with you. You can also begin to understand more about the concept of self-disclosure. **Self-disclosure** is how much you are willing to share with others about your life, your goals, your dreams, your fears, and your setbacks. Often, self-disclosure determines the *quality* of your interpersonal relationships. The level of self-disclosure is up to you, and it can vary from **insignificant** facts ("I had dinner at O'Toole's last night" or "I'm a Leo") to **informational** facts ("I'm majoring in history" or "I have two children") to **highly significant** facts ("I'm fighting ovarian cancer" or "I'm going through a divorce"). True self-disclosure must present new information about the parties involved.

Self-disclosure also involves a great deal of trust from both parties involved. It takes courage to disclose things about yourself, but it also takes courage to listen to a person reveal intimate details about his or her life—and to treat this disclosure with the proper respect and trustworthiness. You should always be careful **what information** you reveal and **to whom** you reveal that information. You do not want to confide in people who may betray you or use your personal information against you. This can end up being detrimental in a variety of situations such as work, romantic encounters, and even friendships. You do not want to reveal too much, too soon.

How Much Are You Willing to Let Others Know about You?

Irwin Altman and Dalmas Taylor (1973) state that self-disclosure is "showing ourselves to others on a conscious and unconscious level." They use the analogy of an onion and ask that you think of your life as having multiple layers. As you know, an onion has layer after layer, each hidden beneath the other. The outer layer is different from the inner layers and is only the covering of what lies inside—much like our clothes are a covering for what is inside us. The skin of an onion is easily peeled away. The further you peel into the onion, though, the smaller it becomes and the more protected those inner layers are. We too have many layers and we can choose to "peel" them away or keep them all intact.

Consider Figure 4.5. What would you be willing to reveal (peel away) about yourself, and to whom would you feel comfortable revealing this information? Everyone has more than three layers, but this figure gives you a good idea of how you can peel away layers to let others know you more intimately. By self-disclosing and getting past your outer layers, you can enrich the quality of your relationships with others and also strengthen your own self-concept. You must, however, self-disclose (tell the truth to yourself) before you can ever self-disclose to others. Without personal and interpersonal self-disclosure, you cannot have mature, intimate, well-developed, sincere interpersonal relationships because your inner life remains hidden.

FIGURE **4.5** *The Third Layer*

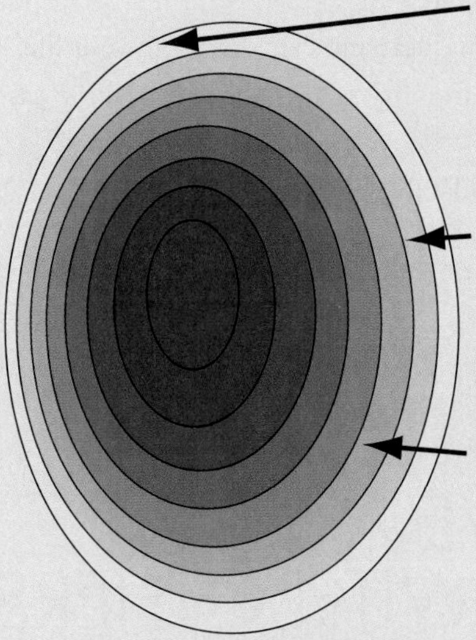

Outer (public) Layer or Insignificant fact: What would you be willing to reveal?

_____
_____
_____

To Whom? _____

Second Layer or Informational fact: What would you be willing to reveal?

_____
_____

To Whom? _____

Third Layer or Highly Significant fact: What would you be willing to reveal?

_____
_____

To Whom? _____

THE TIES THAT BIND

How Can You Strengthen Your Relationships with Friends?

Think about your best friend. How did you meet? In class? Through another person? By chance? Perhaps, fate brought you together. What was the force that brought you together and is the "glue" that holds you together? If you compare your relationships with your closest friends, you will probably recognize that honest communication, self-disclosure, and trust are paramount in these relationships. You can't choose your family, but you can, and do, choose your friends.

Sometimes, when your situation changes, your friendships do too. When you move to another area of the country, embark upon a new endeavor, or begin meeting new people, old friendships may fade. This is just another example of how life is full of constant change. Recently, a friend stated that he was having conflicts with his "best" friend. As he discussed the situation in more depth, he began to realize that this person was not really his "best" friend anymore, but rather his "oldest" friend. There is a huge difference between the two situations. While time is important in establishing friendships, time does not guarantee that friendships will last forever or that they will always be as strong and comfortable as they are right now.

So, why are friendships important? Friendships can bring a plethora of joys including comfort, understanding, a loyal confidant, and a listening ear. They give you someone to talk to about happiness and sorrow and someone to laugh with when things are funny. You can share your hopes and dreams and fears with good friends. Take a moment to list the qualities that you like in your close friends. Consider the emotional, intellectual, spiritual, and physical aspects of friendship.

_____   _____
_____   _____
_____   _____

> "The worst solitude is to be destitute of sincere friendship."
> —Francis Bacon

As a new college student, you are in the process of building a community of friends and associates. When making new friends, consider adding people to your life who:

▶ Treat you well and equally

▶ Bring new and different ideas and experiences to your life

▶ May be very different from friends you have had in the past

▶ Have ambition and courage

▶ Have healthy work habits and a strong work ethic

▶ Have pride in his or her character

▶ Enjoy college and learning new things

▶ Are outgoing and adventurous

▶ Have found their goals and mission in life

LEARNING TO LIVE AND COMMUNICATE WITH OTHERS

Why Are Intimate Relationships Important to Our Survival?

There are many types and degrees of love relationships. The love between two old friends differs tremendously from the passion of two lovers. Love can be as relaxing and comfortable as an easy chair or as tumultuous and exhilarating as any roller coaster ride. The way love is manifested in a relationship does not necessarily attest to the degree or intensity of that love.

Loving someone means caring about that person's happiness, trying to understand and be understood by that person, and giving/receiving emotional support. Some believe that if you truly love someone, you care more about that person's well-being than you do your own. Most love relationships involve intimacy to some degree. Intimacy is not synonymous with sex; it may or may not involve sexual relations. Rather, intimacy refers to the emotional openness that usually develops over time between two people who love each other. Intimacy allows people to share hopes and dreams as well as pain and sorrows.

Some of you will meet and fall in love with your life-long partner in college, and the process you will most likely use to become acquainted is dating. Because college campuses are filled with people from all walks of life, you have to be careful when you are developing a new relationship that might turn romantic. Keep the following tips in mind when you begin dating someone:

How have your friendships changed since you started college?

▶ Don't go out alone with a stranger, especially someone who is not from your campus; go out in a group until you are better acquainted with your date and, if possible, have your own transportation.

▶ Make sure someone knows the name of the person with whom you are going out, where you are going, and the approximate time you'll return; call that person if your plans change.

▶ Don't go to someone's home unless you know that person very well.

▶ If someone you date a few times becomes controlling or abusive, you need to sever that relationship immediately—it will only get worse. Good relationships have to be built on trust, and jealousy has no part in a solid, strong relationship.

CONFLICT IN RELATIONSHIPS IS INEVITABLE

Why Is It Important to Learn How You Deal with Conflict?

ESSENTIAL CORNERSTONE

Open-Mindedness:
How can being open-minded toward others help you build strong, solid friendships?

Social Networking Moment:
Share your response to this Essential Cornerstone with peers in your social network. Choose two responses from your peers and respond to their postings.

Many people intensely dislike conflict and will go to extreme measures to avoid it. On the other hand, some people seem to thrive on conflict and enjoy creating situations that put people at odds with each other. While in college, you certainly will not be sheltered from conflicts. In fact, on a college campus, where a very diverse population lives and learns together, conflict is likely to arise on a regular basis. The simple truth is, conflict is pervasive throughout our culture, and you simply cannot avoid having some confrontations with other people. Therefore, you should not try to avoid conflict; rather, you can use it to create better relationships by exploring workable solutions—hopefully win-win solutions.

"The best relationship is the one in which your love for each other exceeds your need for each other."
—Anonymous

Consider the Chinese symbol for Conflict (Figure 4.6). You will see that it is made up of two different symbols: Danger and Hidden Opportunity. Why? Because when you are engaged in a conflict, you have the potential to enter into ***dangerous*** territory. Violence, alienation, and irreparable damage could be caused. However, you also have the ***hidden opportunity*** to grow, learn, and strengthen your relationships. Just because conflict in relationships is inevitable does not mean that it has to be permanent, dangerous, or destructive. Conflict can occur in any relationship, whether it is with your parents, your girlfriend or boyfriend, your best friend, a roommate, a spouse or partner, your children, or a total stranger.

Some of the causes of ***Relationship Tensions*** include:

Jealousy	Honesty	Emotions
Dependency	Culture	Sexual orientation
Outside commitments	Opinions, values, beliefs	Perceptions
Personality traits or flaws	Affiliations	

FIGURE **4.6** *Chinese Figure for Conflict*

危
Danger

機
Hidden Opportunity

From Ordinary to Extraordinary

REAL PEOPLE | REAL LIVES | REAL CHANGE

VIVIAN WONG
Founder
Global Trading Consortium, Greenville, SC

In the early 1960s, I was a very young woman and a new wife when my husband began talking about coming to America. We dreamed of living in our own house with a yard rather than a flat as we did in China. We were working as front desk clerks in a Hong Kong hotel, when fate intervened in the person of Robert Wilson, who was in China marketing his Barbeque King grills. We told him about our dream, and he decided to help us. Many people would have never followed through, but Mr. Wilson gave us $100 and told us to get photos made and to acquire passports. He promised to work on a visa for us. It took a year for us to finally be granted a Trainee Visa, and we headed to

"We spent the first 20 years in America simply trying to earn a meager living and put food on the table."

Greenville, SC, to work for Mr. Wilson, leaving our little girl behind with her grandparents.

In South Carolina we trained and learned to sell Barbeque King grills in China. After about 10 months, we were very homesick for China so we went home. We realized after we got to Hong Kong that our hearts were really in America because now we were homesick for Greenville. Without even realizing it, Greenville and America had become our home. Mr. Wilson brought us back and this time, we brought our little girl.

In 1967 we were blessed with twin girls, and in 1968 we were given a permanent visa and U.S. citizenship. I often say, "We spent the first 20 years in

America simply trying to earn a meager living and put food on the table." We began to look around to try to figure out what kind of edge we had that we could use to start our own business in Greenville because we didn't want to work for other people the rest of our lives. In 1970, with Mr. Wilson as a partner, we opened our first business, a Chinese restaurant, after my husband had spent two years in Washington, D.C., training for restaurant ownership. We opened other restaurants in 1975, 1976, and 1988. By now, I could put food on the table, and I wanted to do something other than sell egg rolls.

I became very interested in commercial real estate and began to learn everything I could and branched out into real estate. Today I own several hotels in America, and I am starting a chain in China with my brother. This chain will be called Hotel Carolina and is aimed at business travelers. We

From Ordinary to Extraordinary

REAL PEOPLE | REAL LIVES | REAL CHANGE

found a niche that had not been tapped—a clean, reasonable, three-star hotel for business travelers who can't afford five-star accommodations. We also own and operate a large business park and foreign trade zone in Greenville, SC. We are partners and franchisees of the Medicine Shoppe, China's first American pharmacy.

I am also a partner in three banks located in Greenville, Atlanta, and Myrtle Beach. People ask me how I know how to own and manage such a disparate collection of businesses. My answer is simple: "I know how to con-nect the dots; this is what I do best." I also believe strongly in networking and communicating with partners and people who know how to get things done. I have partners all over the world in a great variety of businesses. I have developed the vision, action plans, and good teams to make things happen. I take nothing for granted!

We have been very blessed to live in America and now to open businesses in our native land. In this wonderful country, we have succeeded beyond our wildest dreams! So can you!

EXTRAORDINARY REFLECTION

Read the following statement and respond in your online journal or class notebook.

Mrs. Wong mentions how important it is to establish relationships, communicate, and network with other people. How can communication, networking, and strong relationships help you in your chosen field?

THINKING *for* CHANGE: An Activity for Critical Reflection

In a student leadership council meeting, John made the suggestion that the council sponsor a fund raiser to secure funds to send the officers to a leadership retreat. His suggestion included having all members of the council participate in raising the funds even though only the officers would get to attend. This suggestion set Barry off and he began to talk very animatedly in a loud, intimidating voice about how this would be unfair to everyone who worked and didn't get to attend the retreat. He stood up and towered over John and continued to use abusive language.

Rather than fuel Barry's argument, John remained calm and in a very quiet, controlled, but firm voice,

said, "Barry, I understand your feelings, but what you need to realize is that next year you will be an officer, and all of us will be working to send you and your team. Why don't we move to another agenda item and come back to this one after we have all had time to collect our thoughts."

In your own words, what two suggestions would you give John to further help control the situation at hand?

1. _____

2. _____

DID YOU KNOW

FLORENCE BALLARD, one of the founding members of the ultra-successful trio The Supremes (with Diana Ross and Mary Wilson), was born in the projects of Detroit in 1943. She was the eighth of 15 children. Highly talented and driven to succeed, Florence was only 16 when The Supremes was formed (as The Primettes) and at 18, they signed a recording contract with Motown Records. They became the number-one female recording group in America. However, Florence's depression and interpersonal conflicts began to cause her to miss rehearsals and some performances, and this put more strain on her already rocky relationship with Motown founder Barry Gordy. In 1963, Diana Ross was made lead singer of the group that Florence had founded and named.

Because of the constant conflicts and tumultuous relationships within the group, Florence fell into deeper depression and began abusing alcohol. In 1967, the group was renamed Diana Ross and The Supremes. Later that year, Florence was replaced by Cindy Birdsong and never performed with The

(Continued)

Dealing with Conflict

Conflict does not happen in just one form. Conflict can be personal or situational. There are several ways that people deal with issues. They include:

▶ **Blowing your lid**—This involves screaming, uncontrolled anger, hurling insults, and an unwillingness to listen.

▶ **Shunning**—This involves shutting the other person out and being unwilling to engage in any type of resolution.

▶ **Sarcasm**—This involves using stinging remarks to make the other person feel small, unimportant, or stupid.

▶ **Mocking**—This involves using past experiences of verbiage to "mock" or ridicule the other person: laughing at him or her, poking fun at him or her or the situation.

▶ **Civility**—This involves sitting down and logically, rationally discussing the issues or problems, and trying to come to a win-win solution. (Adapted from Baxter et al., 1993)

THE FACES OF CONFLICT

How Do I Deal with Negative, Nasty, Difficult People?

We've all encountered them from time to time. DIFFICULT people who are negative, angry, unhappy, destructive, argumentative, sad, depressed, and judgmental. They are the people who seem to walk around with a black cloud above their heads and seem to enjoy causing interpersonal conflict—like the negative people discussed in Chapter 1. They are likely to pop up everywhere—at work, in class, in traffic, in restaurants, and even in places of worship. They cannot be avoided. Figure 4.7 profiles the most common types of negative, difficult people. Perhaps you recognize some of them. Read the descriptions and try to develop at least two to three strategies to effectively deal with each type of difficult person. In developing your strategies, you may have to rely on others in your class for assistance, pull from your past experiences (what worked and what did not), and do some research on your own.

Learning to manage conflict and learning to work with difficult people are very important steps in developing sound communication practices and healthy relationships. If you can learn to stay calm, put yourself in the other person's shoes, and try to find mutually beneficial solutions, you will gain admiration and respect from your friends, family, peers, and colleagues. As you consider conflicts in your life and relationships, take a moment to complete the Conflict Management Assessment in Figure 4.8 to determine your awareness of issues related to conflict and managing conflict.

(Continued)

Supremes again. She later married and had three children, but financial problems and unrest in her marriage plagued her for the rest of her life. In 1976, she entered Mt. Carmel Mercy Hospital complaining of numbness in her arms and legs. The next day, at 32, one of the most successful female recording artists of all time died of a blood clot.

In 1981, the Broadway musical *Dreamgirls* opened, featuring the lead character Effie White, whose life was based on that of Florence Ballard. In 2007, Jennifer Hudson of *American Idol* won an Academy Award® for her portrayal of Effie White in the hit movie *Dreamgirls*.

FIGURE 4.7 Types of Difficult Behaviors and People

TYPES OF DIFFICULT BEHAVIORS BY DIFFICULT PEOPLE	DESCRIPTION	WHAT CAN YOU DO TO EFFECTIVELY DEAL WITH THEM?
Gossiping	They don't do a lot of work and would rather spread rumors and untruths about others to make themselves feel better.	
Manipulating	They constantly try to negotiate every aspect of life. "I'll do this for you if you do this for me."	
Showing Off	They usually talk more than they work. They know everything about every subject and are not willing to listen to anything or anybody new.	
Goofing Off	They usually do very little and what they do is incorrect. They pretend to be involved, but spend more time looking busy rather than actually being busy.	
Standing By	They do not get involved in anything or any cause but then complain because something did not go their way.	
Complaining	They produce work and be involved, but complains about everything and everybody and seems to exist under a rain cloud. Nothing is ever good enough.	
Dooming and Glooming	They are so negative they make death look like a joy ride. They are constantly thinking about the "worst-case" scenario and don't mind voicing it.	

FIGURE

4.8 *Conflict Management Assessment*

© Robert M. Sherfield, Ph.D.
Read the following questions carefully and respond according to the key below. Take your time and be honest with yourself.

1. = **NEVER** typical of the way I address conflict
2. = **SOMETIMES** typical of the way I address conflict
3. = **OFTEN** typical of the way I address conflict
4. = **ALMOST ALWAYS** typical of the way I address conflict

1. When someone verbally attacks me, I can let it go and move on.	1	2	3	4
2. I would rather resolve an issue than have to "be right" about it.	1	2	3	4
3. I try to avoid arguments and verbal confrontations at all costs.	1	2	3	4
4. Once I've had a conflict with someone, I can forget it and get along with that person just fine.	1	2	3	4
5. I look at conflicts in my relationships as positive growth opportunities.	1	2	3	4
6. When I'm in a conflict, I will try many ways to resolve it.	1	2	3	4
7. When I'm in a conflict, I try not to verbally attack or abuse the other person.	1	2	3	4
8. When I'm in a conflict, I try never to blame the other person; rather, I look at every side.	1	2	3	4
9. When I'm in a conflict, I try not to avoid the other person.	1	2	3	4
10. When I'm in a conflict, I try to talk through the issue with the other person.	1	2	3	4
11. When I'm in a conflict, I often feel empathy for the other person.	1	2	3	4
12. When I'm in a conflict, I do not try to manipulate the other person.	1	2	3	4
13. When I'm in a conflict, I try never to withhold my love or affection for that person.	1	2	3	4
14. When I'm in a conflict, I try never to attack the person; I concentrate on their actions.	1	2	3	4
15. When I'm in a conflict, I try to never insult the other person.	1	2	3	4
16. I believe in give and take when trying to resolve a conflict.	1	2	3	4
17. I understand AND USE the concept that kindness can solve more conflicts than cruelty.	1	2	3	4
18. I am able to control my defensive attitude when I'm in a conflict.	1	2	3	4
19. I keep my temper in check and do not yell and scream during conflicts.	1	2	3	4
20. I am able to accept "defeat" at the end of a conflict.	1	2	3	4

Number of 1s _____   Number of 2s _____   Number of 3s _____   Number of 4s _____

If you have more 1s, you do not handle conflict very well and have few tools for conflict management. You have a tendency to anger quickly and lose your temper during the conflict. If you have more 2s, you have a tendency to want to work through conflict, but you lack the skills to carry this tendency through. You can hold your anger and temper for a while, but eventually, it gets the best of you. If you have more 3s, you have some helpful skills in handling conflict. You tend to work very hard for a peaceful and mutually beneficial outcome for all parties. If you have more 4s, you are very adept at handling conflict and do well with mediation, negotiation, and anger management. You are approachable; people turn to you for advice about conflicts and resolutions.

STANDARDS FOR DEALING WITH DIFFICULT PEOPLE AND MANAGING CONFLICT

▶ Check your own behavior before anything else. Don't become the same type of difficult person as the ones with whom you are dealing. Fighting fire with fire will only make the flame hotter. Learn to be the "cool" one.

▶ Don't take the other person's attitude or words personally. Most of the time, they don't know you or your life.

▶ AVOID physical contact with others at any expense.

▶ If you must give criticism, do so with a positive tone and attitude.

▶ Remember that everyone is sensitive about himself or herself and his or her situation. Avoid language that will set someone off.

▶ Do not verbally attack the other person; simply state your case and your ideas.

▶ Allow the other person to save face. In other words, "Don't beat a dead horse."

▶ If you have a problem with someone or someone's actions, be specific and let him or her know before it gets out of hand. That person can't read your mind.

▶ If someone shows signs of becoming physically aggressive toward you, get help early, stay calm, talk slowly and calmly to the person, and if necessary, walk away to safety.

▶ Allow the other person to vent fully before you begin any negotiation or resolution.

▶ Try to create "win-win" situations where everyone can walk away having gained something.

▶ Determine if the conflict is a "person" conflict or a "situation" conflict.

▶ Ask the other person or people what he/she/they need/s. Try to understand the situation.

▶ Realize that *you* may very well be "in the wrong."

▶ When dealing with conflict and other people, ask yourself, "***If this were my last action on earth, would I be proud of how I acted?***"

CHANGING IDEAS TO *Reality*

REFLECTIONS ON INTERPERSONAL COMMUNICATION AND CONFLICT MANAGEMENT

In today's fast-paced, ever-changing, cell phone–addicted, text message–crazy, pay-at-the-pump, "don't have to talk to anyone unless I want to," action-packed world, it is easy to forget that communication is paramount in so many areas of your life. From building healthy and meaningful relationships with your fellow students to talking to your instructors to managing conflict, few tools will give you the power to affect change more than effective interpersonal communication skills will.

By working to improve your interpersonal communication skills, your self-concept, and your conflict management abilities, you will begin to see how the relationships in your life begin to change. They will grow from superficial, insignificant encounters to powerful, meaningful relationships where trust, honesty, and maturity are commonplace.

Remember, we are motivated by what we value. As you continue on in your studies and work toward personal and professional growth, consider the following ideas related to interpersonal communication and conflict management:

"Communication works for those
who work at it."
—John Powell

> Work every day to strengthen your interpersonal communication skills.

> Listen to people and try to understand them, especially in conflict situations.

> Use Computer Mediated Communication in conjunction with face-to-face communication.

> Strive to let people into your life by "turning off" technology from time to time.

> Work hard to understand all aspects of your own life and develop a positive sense of self.

> Peel away "layers" and let people into your life through self-disclosure.

> Develop relationships with people from a variety of backgrounds.

> Maintain close friendships through honesty and loyalty.

> Learn to manage conflict instead of ignoring or running from it.

KNOWLEDGE in BLOOM

Managing Conflict in Interpersonal Relationships

Each chapter-end assessment is based on *Bloom's Taxonomy of Learning.* See the inside front cover for a quick review.

UTILIZES LEVELS 1–6 ON THE TAXONOMY

EXPLANATION: Read the following brief case study. After you have familiarized yourself with the situation, work through each level of Bloom's Taxonomy to discuss, analyze, and solve the conflict.

CASE: My (choose one: *boyfriend, girlfriend, husband, wife, partner, best friend*) is a nice person. Most of the time, he or she is very affectionate and passionate toward me. He or she is supportive of my career and most of the time, we get along well. However, it seems that when something goes wrong or he or she gets angry or stressed, I am the person who receives the brunt of his or her aggression regardless of the cause. He or she can become very verbally abusive, sometimes yelling, screaming, cursing, and hurling insults. Sometimes, I just get the "silent treatment." On certain occasions, he or she has used personal and private information that I shared with him or her to hurt me or insult me. He or she has never physically abused me, but I sometimes worry that the verbal aggression may turn into physical aggression. I'm not sure what to do or what to make of this situation.

PROCEDURE: Answer the following questions from each level of Bloom's Taxonomy. Be specific and use the information from this chapter, your own experiences, and outside research to aid in your responses.

BLOOM LEVEL	QUESTION	RESPONSE
Level 1 Remembering	In your own words, define the conflict and its causes.	
Level 2 Understanding	Identify at least three major problems with this interpersonal relationship.	
Level 3 Applying	What solutions would you offer to both parties?	
Level 4 Analyzing	Compare and contrast this interpersonal relationship with a "healthier," more mature, productive relationship.	
Level 5 Evaluating	Develop a brief argument as to why you think this relationship is more the norm than unusual.	
Level 6 Creating	Develop/design a plan by which you would make this situation better. List at least five positive steps to bring about change.	

SQ3R *Mastery* STUDY SHEET

EXAMPLE QUESTION: *(from page 76)* What are the six elements of the communication process?		**ANSWER:**
EXAMPLE QUESTION: *(from page 82)* What is self-disclosure and why is it important for healthy relationships?		**ANSWER:**
AUTHOR QUESTION: *(from page 77)* Why is interpersonal communication important to your professional growth?		**ANSWER:**
AUTHOR QUESTION: *(from page 80)* What is Computer Mediated Communication (CMC)?		**ANSWER:**
AUTHOR QUESTION: *(from page 81)* In your own words, define "technological recluse."		**ANSWER:**
AUTHOR QUESTION: *(from page 85)* Discuss three issues that may cause tension in a relationship.		**ANSWER:**
AUTHOR QUESTION: *(from page 91)* Discuss at least two strategies for managing conflict.		**ANSWER:**
YOUR QUESTION: *(from page ____)*		**ANSWER:**
YOUR QUESTION: *(from page ____)*		**ANSWER:**
YOUR QUESTION: *(from page ____)*		**ANSWER:**
YOUR QUESTION: *(from page ____)*		**ANSWER:**
YOUR QUESTION: *(from page ____)*		**ANSWER:**

Finally, after answering these questions, recite this chapter's major points in your mind. Consider the following general questions to help you master this material.

▶ What was it about?
▶ What does it mean?
▶ What was the most important thing I learned? Why?
▶ What were the key points to remember?

CHAPTER 5
THINK

EXPANDING YOUR APTITUDE FOR CRITICAL THINKING, EMOTIONAL INTELLIGENCE, AND INFORMATION LITERACY SKILLS

PART ONE CHANGING YOUR THOUGHTS

WHY READ THIS CHAPTER?

What's in it for me?

WHY do I need to understand my emotions and know about emotional intelligence? WHY will a chapter on problem solving help me with my studies? WHY is information literacy important? WHY do I need to read a chapter on critical thinking when I'm thinking all the time?

Why? Because critical thinking affects your life positively or negatively every day. You use it when you go to the grocery store, you use it when you purchase gasoline, you use it when you choose what TV program to watch, you use it when you select classes for your degree, and you use it when you discuss important issues with your friends. Critical thinking is a major aspect of your daily life, affecting the very nature of the way you live and function in society. It helps you make decisions that will enhance your quality of life. Learning how to think more critically means that you are going to be able to look at situations differently, evaluate research sources more effectively, manage your emotions more closely, and solve problems more effectively than ever before. Your ability to think critically, solve problems, and become information literate is going to help you greatly in all of your classes and well into your career.

By carefully reading this chapter and taking the information provided seriously, you will be able to:

1. Define the eight steps in critical thinking, recognize their uses, and understand their importance.
2. Use emotional restraint, emotional intelligence, and emotional guidelines to aid in logical, rational thinking.
3. Manage information and become more information literate.
4. Learn to identify, narrow, and solve problems.
5. Learn to use creative thinking to become more resourceful.

CHAPTER 5 / THINK

"A person who does not think for himself does not think at all."

—Oscar Wilde

WHY READ THIS CHAPTER

. . . FROM MY PERSPECTIVE

NAME: Martin Cram
INSTITUTION: Butler Community College, El Dorado, KS
MAJOR: Music Education
AGE: 19

For years, I thought that my life was everyone's life. I was raised and educated in a rather rural part of Kansas where everybody was basically "the same." Little did I know that in a few short weeks of college, my life, my attitude, and my views would be tested and changed.

I soon learned that everyone had a different story, a different life, a different background, and a different perspective on world events. Learning how to be a more open-minded person through critical thinking helped me grow and change in ways I had never imagined. I was in class with people who are African American, Latino, Native American, and yes, Caucasians who were not from Kansas. I quickly learned that my life was not everyone's life and that my views were not everyone's views. This was a great gift that I received from learning more about critical thinking.

Critical thinking has also helped me become a much more effective manager of my time. I work on campus in the office of financial aid and with this job, my choral activities, classes, and other obligations, I quickly learned that I had to think about my schedule and learn how to plan and plot a course to success. Critical thinking taught me how to

look down the road, plan ahead, and get things done. It taught me how to ask for help, how to ask the right questions, and how to apply what I was learning to everyday life, my major, and my future.

Perhaps one of the most important areas where critical thinking helped me was my major. I sat down and made a list of all of the things I liked and what I was good at. I began to analyze my abilities and look for patterns. Critical thinking helped me decide that music was the one thing that I could not live without. It was then that I changed my major to music education.

I know that in the future, my critical thinking skills will help me become a better show choir director and educator. I also know that it will help me be more adept at thinking on my feet during job interviews and when things get rough in my profession. I learned that critical thinking affects my life every day. This chapter will help you learn how to look at the world with an open mind, embrace change, plan your activities, and plot a course to your future.

SCAN & QUESTION

In the preface of this book (page xix), you read about the **SQ3R Study Method**. Right now, take a few moments, **scan this chapter**, and on page 122, write **five questions** that you think will be important to your mastery of this material. In addition to the two questions below, you will find five questions from your authors. Use one of your "**Study for Quiz**" stickers to flag this page for easy reference.

EXAMPLES:

▶ **Why is emotional intelligence important to critical thinking?** (from page 99)

▶ **What is information literacy?** (from page 106)

THINKING ABOUT THINKING

Do You Know *Why* You Think *What* You Think?

Same-sex couples should be able to marry and adopt children. Think about that statement for a moment. You may be saying to yourself, *"I don't have to think about it—I know what my opinions on same-sex marriage and adoption are."* However, do you know WHY you have these opinions? Can you trace your decisions back to certain events or moments in your life? Do you think that your emotions cloud your thoughts on this issue? Is there a right or wrong side to this debate? Does your religion or culture come into play when thinking about this issue? Did someone else influence your thoughts or are they your very own, developed through research and conversations regarding this issue?

What are you thinking right now? More importantly, why are you thinking the way you are right now? What is causing you to believe, feel, or think one way or the other regarding this issue? What are the facts and/or opinions that have led you to your conclusion? At this moment, what are the origins on which you are basing your thoughts about this issue—emotions or facts, fallacies or truths, data or opinions, interviews or hearsay, reason or misjudgment, fear or empathy?

We purposefully chose a "hot topic" issue to open this chapter because understanding why and how we formulate thoughts and ideas is the main objective of this chapter and critical thinking in general. This chapter is about believing and disbelieving, seeking, uncovering, debunking myths, uncovering biases, identifying and solving problems, using information correctly, and proving the impossible possible. It is about proof, logic, evidence, and developing ideas and opinions based on hard-core facts and credible research. This chapter is about seeking truth and expanding your mind to unimaginable limits. This chapter is about the fundamental hallmarks of becoming an educated citizen; it is about human thought and reasoning.

THE IMPORTANCE OF CRITICAL THINKING

When Will I Ever Use it?

Have you ever made a decision that turned out to be a mistake? Have you ever said to yourself, *"If only I could go back and . . . "*? Have you ever regretted actions you took toward a person or situation? Have you ever planned a paper or speech that was flawless? Have you ever had to make a hard, painful decision that turned out to be "the best decision of your life"? If the answer to any of these questions is yes, you might be able to trace the consequences back to your *thought process* at the time of the decision. Let's face it, sometimes good and bad things just happen out of luck or circumstance. More often than not, however, many events in our lives are driven by the thought processes involved when we made the initial decision and chose to act on that decision.

Critical thinking can serve us in many areas as students and citizens in a free society. As a student, ***critical thinking can help you***:

- ▶ focus on relevant issues/problems and avoid wasting time on trivia.

- ▶ gather relevant, accurate information regarding finances, goals, decision making, relationships, civic responsibility, and environmental issues, to name a few.

- ▶ understand and remember facts and organize thoughts logically.

- ▶ look more deeply at problems, analyze their causes, and solve them more accurately.

- ▶ develop appropriate and meaningful study plans and manage your priorities.

- ▶ improve your problem-solving skills.

- ▶ control your emotions so that you can make rational judgments and become more open-minded.

- ▶ produce new knowledge through research and analysis.

- ▶ determine the accuracy of printed and spoken words.

- ▶ detect bias and determine the relevance of arguments and persuasion.

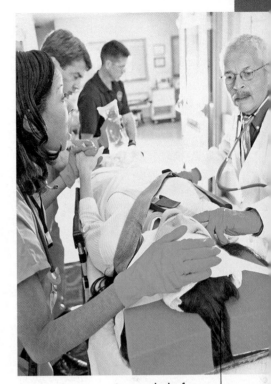

Can you think of a professional career where critical thinking will not be required?

AN EIGHT-POINT PLAN FOR CRITICAL THINKING

Can You Really Make Critical Thinking Work for You in Everyday Life?

Does critical thinking really matter? Seriously? Can it do anything to improve the quality of your life? The answer is yes. Critical thinking has daily, practical uses, from making sound financial decisions to improving personal relationships to helping you become a better student. You can improve your critical thinking skills by watching your emotional reactions, using solid research and facts to build your examples and thoughts, and practicing open-mindedness.

Conversely, can the lack of critical thinking skills cause real problems? The answer, once again, is yes. Poor critical thinking skills can impair your judgment, lead you to make rash decisions, and even cause you to let your emotions rule (and sometimes ruin) your life. Critical thinking can be hampered by a number of factors including closed-mindedness, unflappable opinions based on rumor instead of facts, cultural and/or religious bias, lack of accurate information, faulty arguments, and negativity.

As you begin to build and expand your critical thinking skills, consider the eight steps in Figure 5.1.

Step One: Understanding and Using Emotional Intelligence

Emotions play a vital role in our lives. They help us feel compassion, help us help others, help us reach out in times of need, and help us relate to others. On the other hand, emotions can also cause some problems in your critical thinking process. You do not—and should not have to—eliminate emotions from your thoughts, but it is crucial that you know when your emotions are clouding an issue and causing you to act and speak before thinking.

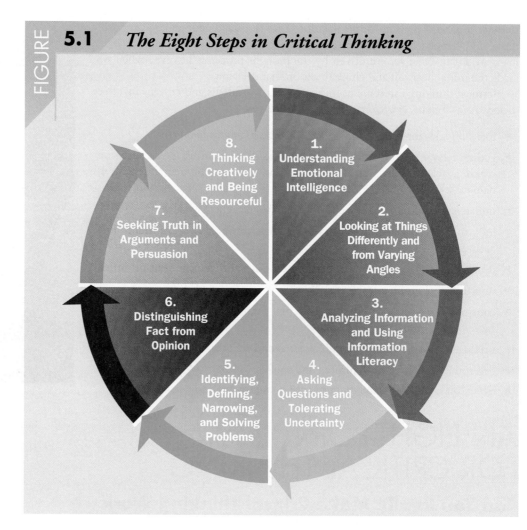

FIGURE

5.1　*The Eight Steps in Critical Thinking*

1. Understanding Emotional Intelligence
2. Looking at Things Differently and from Varying Angles
3. Analyzing Information and Using Information Literacy
4. Asking Questions and Tolerating Uncertainty
5. Identifying, Defining, Narrowing, and Solving Problems
6. Distinguishing Fact from Opinion
7. Seeking Truth in Arguments and Persuasion
8. Thinking Creatively and Being Resourceful

Consider the following topics:

▶ Should drugs and prostitution be totally legalized in the United States?

▶ Can the theories of evolution and creationism coexist?

▶ Can affirmative action reverse discrimination?

▶ Should illegal aliens be given amnesty and made U.S. citizens?

▶ Should the legal drinking age be lowered to 18?

▶ Should terminally ill patients have the right to assisted suicide?

▶ Should prayer be allowed in public schools?

As you read these topics, did you immediately form an opinion? Did old arguments surface? Did you feel your emotions coming into play as you thought about the questions? If you had an immediate answer, it is likely that you allowed some past judgments, opinions, and emotions to enter the decision-making process, unless you have just done a comprehensive, unbiased study of one of these issues. If you had to discuss these issues in class or with your friends and had to defend your position, how would you react? Do you think you would get angry? Would you find yourself groping for words? Would you find it hard to explain why you hold the opinion that you voiced? If so, these are warning signs that you are allowing your emotions to drive your decisions. If you allow your emotions to run rampant (not restrain them) and fail to use research, logic, and evidence, you may not be able to examine the issues critically or have a logical discussion regarding the statements.

"Simply stated, people who are emotionally intelligent harness emotions and work with them to improve problem solving and boost creativity."

—Snyder and Lopez

SHARPENING YOUR EMOTIONAL INTELLIGENCE (EI) SKILLS

How Does EI Affect Critical Thinking and Problem Solving?

If you have ever heard the old saying, "THINK before you act," you were actually being told to use *emotional intelligence EI*. Everyone knows that intelligence quotient is important to success in college, work, and life, but many experts believe that **EI** is just as important to being successful. EI helps people cope with the social and emotional demands in daily life. "Emotional intelligence is the single most influencing variable in personal achievement, career success, leadership, and life satisfaction" (Nelson and Low, 2003). "The data that exist suggest it can be *as powerful*, and at times *more powerful*, than IQ" (Goleman, 2006).

Exactly what is EI? EI includes all the skills and knowledge necessary for building strong, effective relationships through managing and understanding emotions. *It is knowing how you and others feel and managing those feelings in a rational manner that is good for both parties.* Consider Figure 5.2 (adapted from Snyder and Lopez, 2007).

We all have emotions and feelings that influence our thoughts and actions significantly. Emotions can manifest themselves in a wide range, from happiness to sadness, serenity to anger, and apathy to passion. You need to be able to recognize each of these emotions and employ appropriate skills for dealing with them. For example, let's say that you are discussing a political or religious issue with a friend of yours. You begin to sense that your friend is getting emotional and combative. You notice this in his or her voice and nonverbal behavior. An emotionally intelligent person would be able to sense what is going on, understand this situation and the consequences, and redirect the conversation to something more appropriate.

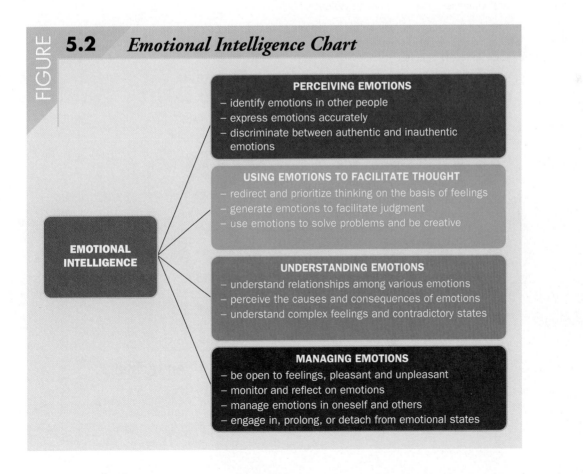

FIGURE 5.2   *Emotional Intelligence Chart*

EMOTIONAL INTELLIGENCE

PERCEIVING EMOTIONS
- identify emotions in other people
- express emotions accurately
- discriminate between authentic and inauthentic emotions

USING EMOTIONS TO FACILITATE THOUGHT
- redirect and prioritize thinking on the basis of feelings
- generate emotions to facilitate judgment
- use emotions to solve problems and be creative

UNDERSTANDING EMOTIONS
- understand relationships among various emotions
- perceive the causes and consequences of emotions
- understand complex feelings and contradictory states

MANAGING EMOTIONS
- be open to feelings, pleasant and unpleasant
- monitor and reflect on emotions
- manage emotions in oneself and others
- engage in, prolong, or detach from emotional states

Our emotions originate in the brain. If you have EI skills, your ***thinking mind*** and ***emotional mind*** should function together, making it more likely that you will craft sound, rational decisions. In other words, you will **think** before you **act**. When these two minds do not operate in harmony, you might make highly emotional decisions that can be viewed as irrational.

To become a successful, happy person, interpersonal relationships are important and learning to manage the entire spectrum of your personal emotions from the extreme **negative side** to the extreme **positive side** will be vitally important. This spectrum ranges from the darker side of your emotions (extreme negative pole) to the optimistic side (extreme positive pole).

FIGURE

5.3   *The Amygdala*

Don't let this word or concept frighten you. If you have never heard the word *"amygdala"* (pronounced ah-MIG-da-la), you're not alone. Most people have not. But this term and concept are important for you to be able to understand the overall aspects of EI. The amygdala, simply a part of the brain's emotional system, can cause us to go into default behavior based on what we remember from a similar experience. Do I use *fight* or *flight*? Basically, the amygdala is there to protect us when we become afraid or emotionally upset. When influenced by the amygdala, everything becomes *about us*. We become more judgmental. We don't stop to think about differences or the other person's feelings or the relationship. The amygdala can trigger an emotional response **before** the rest of the brain has had time to understand what is happening, and this situation causes us to have problems with others.

The amygdala remembers frustrations, fears, hurt feelings, and anger from our past. The tension from these past experiences causes the amygdala to go into default behavior—we *feel* before we *think*—and this can create a potentially explosive situation. If you had a bad experience several years ago and are placed in a similar situation, the amygdala will remember and trigger emotions that cause the body to respond. These feelings often cause people to bypass critical thinking (the logical brain) and to respond with angry words or actions (the emotional brain). For example:

- ▶ They get angry—you get angry.
- ▶ They curse you—you curse them.
- ▶ They use physical violence—you use physical violence.

However, if you remain calm and level-headed, you will begin to see that the other person usually begins to calm down, too. He or she will follow your emotional lead, positive or negative, and if you're calm and rational, anger and violence become out of place for most people.

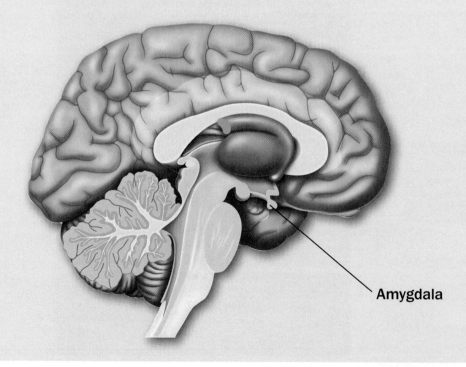

Amygdala

Study the spectrum of emotions illustrated in Figure 5.4. Think about which of these emotions you experience frequently and where you are located most of the time on this emotional continuum.

As you can see, the restraint and management of your personal emotional spectrum can impact you and your thinking skills greatly at home, at school, and at work. Today, this relatively new concept is being given a great deal of attention on college campuses and in the workplace. Not only will you find it helpful and necessary to manage your emotions at school, you will also need to be able to apply emotional management techniques at home and with family, friends, and work associates.

Think about one experience you've had in the past where your negative emotions "took over." Perhaps it was anger, fear, sorrow, hatred, or rage.

What was the situation and where were you when it happened? Be specific. _____

_____

_____

What triggered these emotions? _____

_____

_____

What were the negative consequences to you (or someone else) because of your emotions?

_____

_____

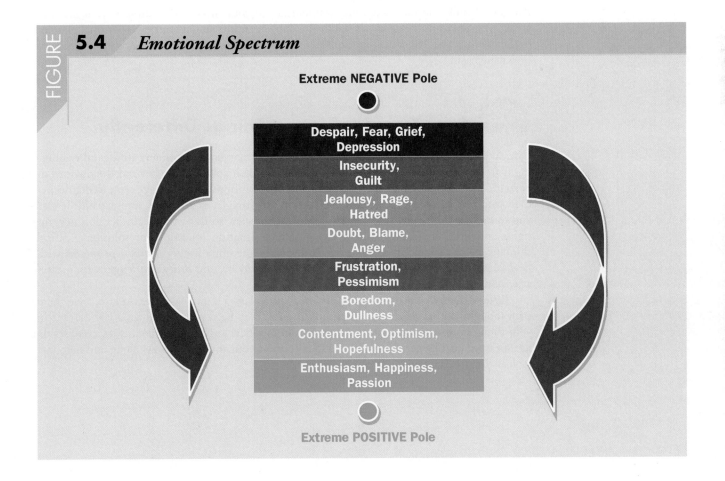

FIGURE 5.4 *Emotional Spectrum*

Extreme NEGATIVE Pole

Despair, Fear, Grief, Depression

Insecurity, Guilt

Jealousy, Rage, Hatred

Doubt, Blame, Anger

Frustration, Pessimism

Boredom, Dullness

Contentment, Optimism, Hopefulness

Enthusiasm, Happiness, Passion

Extreme POSITIVE Pole

FIGURE

5.5 *Guidelines for Emotional Management at School, Work, and Beyond*

▶ Face each day with an "I feel great, nothing is going to ruin my day" attitude.

▶ Hear all sides of an argument before you say anything, make a decision, or take an action.

▶ Practice a win-win philosophy at all times and work tirelessly to make it happen.

▶ Avoid letting your personal feelings about a person dictate your decisions.

▶ Never, never, never lose control!

▶ Avoid negative stereotyping and typecasting people into negative categories.

▶ Never look at or judge someone through someone else's eyes or experiences.

▶ Learn to keep a tight rein on any emotional "hotspots" such as anger, rage, and jealousy.

▶ Strive to treat people so well that you can always put your head on your pillow and sleep well, knowing that you have not been underhanded, rude, or unfair.

How did these emotions affect your ability to think clearly and critically? _____

_____

_____

_____

Because EI skills and knowledge are so important to your success in all areas of your life, you are encouraged to read extensively about this subject and to design your own personal plan for dealing with emotional concerns. Consider the tips in Figure 5.5 for managing your emotions on a daily basis.

Step Two: Looking at Things Differently

Critical thinking involves looking at something you may have seen many times and examining it from many different angles and perspectives. It involves going beyond the obvious or beyond "easy" to seek new understanding and rare solutions. It encourages you to dig deeper than you have before, to get below the surface, to struggle, experiment, and expand. It asks you to look at something from an entirely different view so that you might develop new insights and understand more about the problem, situation, question, or solution. Critical thinking involves looking at **common issues** with uncommon eyes, **known problems** with new skepticism, **everyday conflicts** with probing curiosity, and **daily challenges** with greater attention to detail.

Review the following "brain teasers" in Figures 5.6–5.8 and take the time to solve them even though you may not "get" them quickly. You may need to break down a few barriers in your thought process and look at the puzzles from a new angle. Remember, these exercises do not measure intelligence. They are included to prod your thought process along and help you look at things differently.

FIGURE

5.6   Brain Teaser #1:
Looking at Common Terms Backward

Consider the following clues. Two examples are given to help you get started. Answer the following 10 teasers based on the clues.

Examples

4 W on a C   Four Wheels on a Car

13 O C   Thirteen Original Colonies

1. SW and the 7D   _____

2. I H a D by MLK   _____

3. 2 Ps in a P   _____

4. HDD (TMRUTC)   _____

5. 3 S to a T   _____

6. 100 P in a D   _____

7. T no PLH   _____

8. 4 Q in a G   _____

9. I a SWAA   _____

10. 50 S in t U   _____

How did you do? Was it hard to look at the situation backward or have to look for clues within a series of letters and numbers? Most of us are not used to that. But part of critical thinking is trying to find *clues or patterns*. Perhaps the easiest teaser above was number two in Figure 5.6. Most people know MLK as Martin Luther King, Jr. When you figure that part out, the name of his most popular speech, *I Have a Dream*, becomes easy to figure out. Often, when trying to solve problems or dealing with unknowns, things become easier when you can find a clue or a pattern and build from WHAT you already know.

Examine the brain teaser in Figure 5.7. This teaser is included to help you look at an issue beyond what is actually given to you and considering what is not given.

Once again, you are given a basic clue, but you must go beyond what is given. You must look at the nine dots, but you must NOT let them confine you. You can't let the nine dots control your thoughts—you must move beyond what is given, beyond what you actually see. When you do this, the answer will come to you.

FIGURE

5.7   Brain Teaser #2:
Seeing What Is Not Given

Look at the design below. You will find nine dots. Your mission is to connect all nine dots with four straight lines without removing your pencil or pen from the paper. Do not retrace your lines.

FIGURE 5.8 *Brain Teaser #3: The Penny*

Pretend that all life on earth has ended and all traces of civilization are gone–there are no buildings, no people, no animals, no plants–nothing is left but dirt and one penny. Someone from another planet, who knows our language, comes to earth and finds the penny. List all of the things that could be inferred about our civilization based on this one small penny. You should find at least 10 for each side.

1. _____
2. _____
3. _____
4. _____
5. _____
6. _____
7. _____
8. _____
9. _____
10. _____

As you continue to look at common things differently and think beyond the obvious, examine the penny in Figure 5.8

Drawing inferences often takes the ability to look at things differently and take something very common and examine it like you have never examined it before. Just as you looked at the penny, you learned new things about it by studying it with different eyes. Think about how you might solve a common problem that you face every day simply by looking at that problem with different eyes, too.

While these activities may seem somewhat trivial, they are provided to help you begin to think about and consider information from different angles. This is a major step in becoming a critical thinker: looking beyond the obvious, thinking outside the box, examining details, and exploring possibilities—basically, looking BEYOND what is given to you.

Step Three: Managing Information and Becoming Information Literate

"The sheer abundance of information will not in itself create a more informed citizenry without a complementary cluster of abilities necessary to use information correctly."
—ACRL

Critical thinking involves knowing how to deal with all types of information, and ***information literacy*** refers to the skills a person needs to "recognize when information is needed and the ability to locate, evaluate, and effectively use the needed information" (American Library Association, 1989). *Information literacy* impacts all aspects of your college career and will later play a major role in your success in the workplace. You will use information literacy when you write a paper, read and evaluate an article, listen to presenters and determine if you believe what the speakers are saying, and prepare and make your own presentation.

Quite simply, if you are an information literate person, you have learned how to acquire and use information accurately and effectively. Figure 5.9 demonstrates a system for understanding and applying the concepts of information literacy.

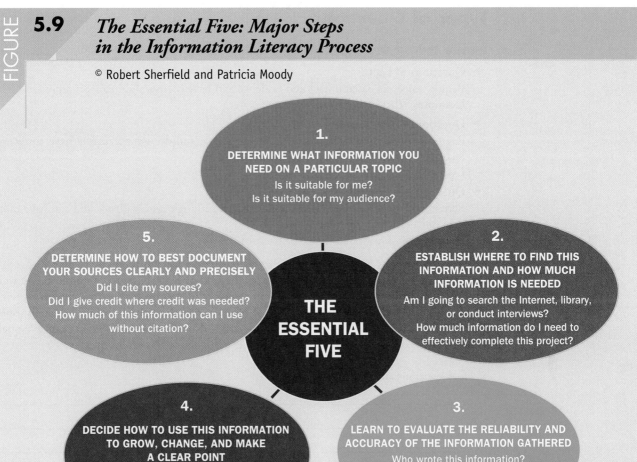

FIGURE 5.9 *The Essential Five: Major Steps in the Information Literacy Process*

© Robert Sherfield and Patricia Moody

THE ESSENTIAL FIVE

1. DETERMINE WHAT INFORMATION YOU NEED ON A PARTICULAR TOPIC
Is it suitable for me?
Is it suitable for my audience?

2. ESTABLISH WHERE TO FIND THIS INFORMATION AND HOW MUCH INFORMATION IS NEEDED
Am I going to search the Internet, library, or conduct interviews?
How much information do I need to effectively complete this project?

3. LEARN TO EVALUATE THE RELIABILITY AND ACCURACY OF THE INFORMATION GATHERED
Who wrote this information?
What are their associations?
Is it fair, balanced, and accurate?

4. DECIDE HOW TO USE THIS INFORMATION TO GROW, CHANGE, AND MAKE A CLEAR POINT
How can I use what I've learned to learn more?
How can I use what I've learned to make my point stronger?

5. DETERMINE HOW TO BEST DOCUMENT YOUR SOURCES CLEARLY AND PRECISELY
Did I cite my sources?
Did I give credit where credit was needed?
How much of this information can I use without citation?

Step Four: Asking Questions and Learning to Tolerate Uncertainty

You've asked questions all your life. As a child, you asked your parents, "What's that?" a million times. You probably asked them, "Why do I have to do this?" In later years, you've asked questions of your friends, teachers, strangers, store clerks, and significant others.

Questioning is not new to you, but it may be a new technique to you for exploring, developing, and honing your critical thinking skills. Curiosity may have killed the cat, but it was a smart cat when it died! Your curiosity is one of the most important traits you possess. It helps you grow and learn, and sometimes it may cause you to be uncomfortable. That's OK. This section is provided to assist you in learning how to ask questions to promote knowledge, solve problems, foster strong relationships, and critically analyze difficult situations. It is also included to help you understand the value of knowing how to tolerate uncertainty and avoid jumping to faulty conclusions because uncertainty "got the better of you." It is important to know that sometimes, *the question is more important than the answer*—especially a faulty answer.

> "It is not possible to become a good thinker and be a poor questioner. Thinking is not driven by answers, but, rather, by questions."
> —Paul and Elder

Types of Questions

Basically, there are three types of questions, according to Paul and Elder (2006):

▶ **Questions of Fact**
Requires answers based in fact and evidence and have correct and incorrect reponses
Example: What is the freezing point of water?

▶ **Questions of Preference**
Requires answers that state a subjective preference and do not necessarily have correct or incorrect responses
Example: What is your favorite color?

▶ **Questions of Judgment**
Requires answers based on your judgment based in logic and evidence and can have more than one defensible answer
Example: Should Roe vs. Wade be overturned?

Asking questions helps us gain insight where we may have limited knowledge. Answering properly posed questions can also help us expand our knowledge base. For example, if you were assigned to write a paper or give a speech on the topic of *creationism versus evolution*, what five questions would you definitely want that paper or speech to answer when you are finished writing/delivering it? Take some time to think about this issue. Write down at least five questions that you consider essential to the topic of creationism versus evolution.

My five questions are:

1. _____
2. _____
3. _____
4. _____
5. _____

Learning to ask probing questions can help you in everyday situations by challenging you to look beyond the obvious and critically examine everyday situations. **Examine the car advertisement in Figure 5.10.** The car dealership has provided some information, but it is not enough to make a smart, rational decision. What other questions would you ask the dealer to make sure that you are getting a good deal?

What additional questions would you need to ask the dealer to ensure that you are getting a "good" deal?

1. _____
2. _____
3. _____
4. _____
5. _____

I Am 100% Sure That I Am Not Sure

CAN YOU TOLERATE UNCERTAINTY?

Asking questions that can be answered is vitally important to critical thinking, but so is learning to tolerate uncertainty and learning to ask questions that may not have an **immediate answer**. Uncertainty causes you to keep going—to not get lazy or give up. If we thought we knew the

5.10   *Auto Ad*

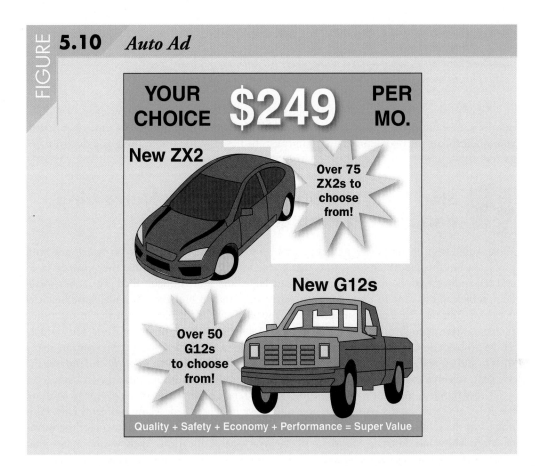

answers to everything, we would still be beating rocks together to make fire and we would still be walking everywhere instead of driving or flying. Uncertainty causes humanity to move forward and create new knowledge, to try new things, to consider the impossible. Uncertainty also breeds creative thinking.

Think about all of the uncertainty that can arise in your daily life:

"Can I be certain that my spouse/partner will not leave me?" No.
"Can I be certain that I will remain healthy?" No.
"Can I be certain that my children will turn out to be good, caring, loving adults?" No.
"Can I be certain what happens to me after I die?" No.
"Can I be certain that the plane won't crash or that someone won't crash into my car?" No.
"Can I be certain that this will not embarrass me or someone else?" No.
"Can I be certain that my investments will grow and I can retire comfortably?" No.

The inability to tolerate uncertainty can cause stress and anxiety. Sometimes, we just have to "let go" and accept that we do not know the answers. We can work hard to try to find the answers and/or direct our actions so that the answers will be favorable to us, but ultimately, many things in this universe require our tolerance of uncertainty. Sometimes, the best we can hope for is to keep asking questions and seeking the truth.

Think of the good things that initially unanswered questions and uncertainty brought to humanity in many fields of study.

"Can we send someone to the moon and have them return safely?"
"Can we transplant a human heart and have that person live and prosper afterward?"
"Can we establish a new country with a new constitution and have it work?"

*"Can we design and build a skyscraper that is over 140 stories high and have
  it remain safe?"*
"Can we create an automobile that will get over 50 miles per gallon of fuel?"
"Can we help reduce global warming and its effects on the polar ice caps?"

All of these uncertainties have contributed to the development of new knowledge, new skills, new jobs, new outlooks, and new ways of living. Therefore, it is important to remember that in your quest for answers, sometimes uncertainty can be the most important thing you discover.

Step Five: Identifying, Defining, Narrowing, and Solving Problems

What would your life be like if you had no problems? Most people do not like to face or deal with problems, but the critical thinker knows that problems exist every day and that they must be faced and hopefully solved. Some of our problems are larger and more difficult than others, but we all face problems from time to time. You may have transportation problems. You may have financial problems. You may have child care problems. You may have academic problems or interpersonal problems. Many people don't know how to solve problems at school, home, or work. They simply let the problem go unaddressed until it is too late to reach an amiable solution. But there are many ways to address and solve problems. In this section, we will discuss how to **identify and narrow** the problem, **research and develop** alternatives, **evaluate** the alternatives, and **solve** the problem.

Every problem may not have a solution. That can be a hard pill for many people to swallow, but it is a raw truth and a part of the uncertainty we just discussed. Many problems have solutions, but the solution may not be the one you wanted. It is imperative to remember the words of Mary Hatwood Futrell, President of the National Education Agency. She states that *"finding the right answer is important, of course. But more important is developing the ability to see that many problems have multiple solutions, that getting from X to Y demands basic skills and mental agility, imagination, persistence, patience."* Consider the problem-solving model in Figure 5.11.

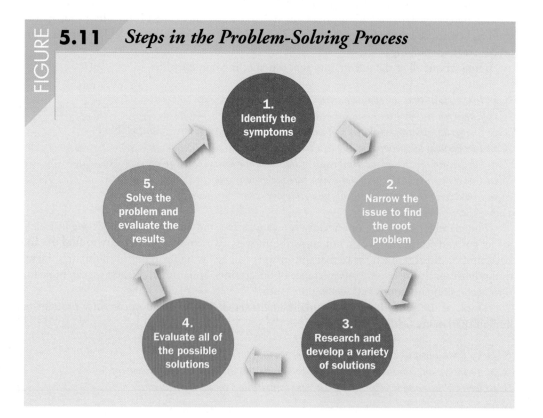

FIGURE **5.11**   *Steps in the Problem-Solving Process*

1. Identify the symptoms
2. Narrow the issue to find the root problem
3. Research and develop a variety of solutions
4. Evaluate all of the possible solutions
5. Solve the problem and evaluate the results

1. Identify the Symptoms

Symptoms and *problems* are not the same thing. Symptoms are PART of the problem, but may not be the problem itself. Think of a problem like you think of your health. For example, you may have aches in your joints, cold chills, and a severe headache. Those seem like problems; but in actuality, they are really symptoms of something larger—perhaps the flu or an infection. You can treat the headache with medicine, and soothe your joint pain with ointment, but until you get at the ROOT of the problem, these symptoms will come back. Problems are much the same way. If you don't move beyond the symptoms, the problem may seem to be solved, but shortly, it will reappear, usually worse than before. Therefore, it is imperative that you identify the symptoms of the *greater problem* before you begin solving anything.

> "When I'm getting ready to reason with a man, I spend one-third of my time thinking about myself and what I am going to say—and two-thirds thinking about him and what he is going to say."
> —Abraham Lincoln

2. Narrow the Symptoms to Find the Root Problem

Often, problems keep coming up because we did not deal with the *real problem*—the root problem—but, rather, we dealt with a symptom. Getting to the heart of a problem is hard work that requires a great deal of thought, research, and patience. Begin by putting your symptoms in writing, perhaps on note cards, so that you can lay them out and see them all at once. When doing this, be sure to jot down all of the major and minor symptoms such as:

▶ What are the daily challenges that keep coming up?

▶ Who is involved?

▶ How are the symptoms hindering your overall goals?

▶ Who or what is responsible for creating these symptoms?

▶ Are the symptoms internal (self-inflicted) or external (other-inflicted)?

▶ What obstacles are these symptoms creating?

▶ Are the symptoms part of ONE major problem or several problems?

3. Research and Develop a Variety of Solutions

It is a mistake to try to solve a problem when you don't have enough information to do so. It may be that you need to conduct interviews, research what others have done who face similar issues, read current data and reports, or even explore historical documents. Paul and Elder (2006) suggest that the type of information you need is determined by the type of problem you have and the question(s) you are trying to answer: "If you have a historical question, you need *historical information*. If you have a biological question, you need *biological information*. If you have an ethical question, you must identify at least one relevant *ethical principle*." Therefore, part of the problem-solving process is to gather your facts—the correct facts—before you try to reach a resolution.

4. Evaluate and Analyze All of the Possible Solutions

After you have gathered your research (through formal methods and/or brainstorming), you must now evaluate your solutions to determine which would work best and why. After careful study and deliberation, without emotional interference, analyze the solutions you came up with and determine if they are appropriate or inappropriate. To analyze them, create Columns A and B. Write the possible *solutions in Column A* and an evaluative *comment in Column B*.

ESSENTIAL CORNERSTONE

Creativity:
How can being more creative help you learn to be a better problem solver?

Social Networking Moment:
Share your response to this Essential Cornerstone with peers in your social network. Choose two responses from your peers and respond to their postings.

THINKING FOR CHANGE: An Activity for Critical Reflection

Carson's class was assigned an activity asking them to determine whom they would like to meet if they could meet anyone and which questions they would like to ask them. Some of the class members thought it was a stupid assignment—and Carson was not so sure that she wanted to spend any time on this "weird" activity, either. That evening, she began to think about the question seriously. "Who has been important to the world?" she thought. "Who has done something powerful and extraordinary?" "Who has been awful and caused needless pain?"

She decided that if she could ask anyone anything, she would choose Hitler. She decided that she would ask him these questions: (1) If you had to do it all over again, would you? (2) From where did your hatred come? (3) Why did you have everyone killed who could have revealed your own past? (4) You did not look like the master race you chose to promote. Why did you choose to promote it? (5) Why did you become such a coward in the end and kill yourself?

This interesting project led Carson to use WWII, Hitler, and the German occupation as the basis for her presentation in speech class. She did not just brush off what had seemed to be a "crazy" assignment.

In your own words, what three suggestions would you give to a classmate who thinks an assignment is crazy or useless? Be specific.

1. _____

2. _____

3. _____

Example (Using the problem "I don't have enough time to study due to my job"):
With your comments in Column B, you can now begin to eliminate some of the alternatives that are inappropriate at this time.

A (POSSIBLE SOLUTIONS)	B (COMMENTS)
Quit the job.	Very hard to do. I need the money for tuition and car.
Cut my hours at work.	Will ask my boss.
Find a new job.	Hard to do because of the job market—but will look into it.
Get a student loan.	Visit financial aid office tomorrow.
Quit school.	No—it is my only chance for a promotion.

5. Solve the Problem and Evaluate the Results

Now that you have a few strong possible solutions, you have some work to do. You will need to talk to your boss, go to the financial aid office, and possibly begin to search for a new job with flexible hours. Basically, you are creating a PLAN to bring this solution to life. After you have researched each possible solution further, you will be able to make a decision based on solid information and facts. You will be able to figure out which solution is the best option for you.

Using the diagram in Figure 5.12 on the next page, work through the following situation and determine the steps that could be taken to solve this problem.

YOUR TURN: Pretend that your best friend, Nathan, has just come to you with a problem. He tells you that his parents are really coming down hard on him for going to college. It is a strange problem. They believe that Nathan should be working full time and that he is just wasting his time and money, since he did

FIGURE **5.12** *Solutions in Bloom Diagram*

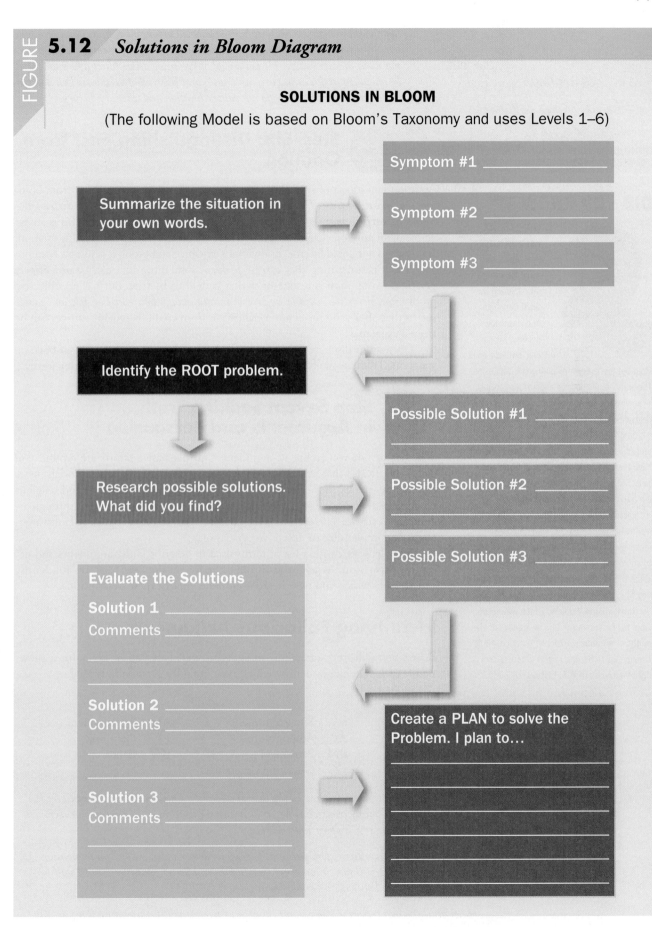

SOLUTIONS IN BLOOM
(The following Model is based on Bloom's Taxonomy and uses Levels 1–6)

Summarize the situation in your own words.

Symptom #1 _____

Symptom #2 _____

Symptom #3 _____

Identify the ROOT problem.

Possible Solution #1 _____
_____

Research possible solutions. What did you find?

Possible Solution #2 _____
_____

Possible Solution #3 _____
_____

Evaluate the Solutions

Solution 1 _____
Comments _____
_____
_____

Solution 2 _____
Comments _____
_____
_____

Solution 3 _____
Comments _____
_____
_____

Create a PLAN to solve the Problem. I plan to…
_____
_____
_____
_____
_____

DID YOU KNOW

CESAR CHAVEZ was born in 1927 near Yuma, Arizona. He was raised during the Great Depression in unspeakable poverty. His parents owned a small store but lost everything during the Depression. The entire family became migrant workers just to survive. He spent his youth working in the fields of Arizona and California. From the first to eighth grades (when he left school), he attended over 30 schools. Often his family did not have even the basic necessities of water and toilets to survive. They faced not only poverty, but also extreme prejudice and injustice.

Later, Chavez joined the Navy. Upon his return home, seeing the many problems faced by migrant families, he vowed to try to solve the problems and find a way to make life better for his family and the families living in such poverty. He thus founded the United Farm Workers, which was responsible for increasing public awareness of the plight of migrant workers in America. He is considered to be one of the greatest civil rights activists in U.S. history.

not do well in high school. They have threatened to take away his car and kick him out of the house if he does not find a full-time job. Nathan is doing well and does not want to leave college. He has a goal of becoming an architect and knows that he has talent in this area. He is making A's and B's in all of his classes. This does not matter to his parents. They do not value education and see it as a luxury.

Step Six: Distinguishing Fact from Opinion

An important aspect of critical thinking is the ability to distinguish fact from opinion. *In most media—TV, radio, newspapers, magazines, and the Internet—opinions surface more often than facts.* Reread the previous sentence. This is an example of an opinion cloaked as a fact. There is no research supporting this opinion. It sounds as if it could be true, but without evidence and proof, it is just an opinion.

A fact is something that can be **proven**, something that can be **objectively verified**. An opinion is a statement that is held to be true, but has no objective proof. *Statements that cannot be proven should always be treated as opinion.* Statements that offer valid proof and verification from credible, reliable sources can be treated as factual.

Learning to distinguish fact from opinion can be a paramount step in building your critical thinking skills at work, with family, and especially when analyzing media.

Step Seven: Seeking Truth in Arguments and Persuasion

Whether or not you realize it, arguments and persuasive efforts are around you daily—hourly, for that matter. They are in newspaper and TV ads, editorials, news commentaries, talk shows, TV magazine shows, political statements, and religious services. It seems at times that almost everyone is trying to persuade us through arguments or advice. This section is included to assist you in recognizing faulty arguments and implausible or deceptive persuasion.

First, let's start with a list of terms used to describe faulty arguments and deceptive persuasion. As you read through the list on the next page, try to identify situations in which you have heard arguments that fit these descriptions.

Identifying Fallacious Arguments

Below, you will find statements intended to persuade you or argue for a cause. Beside each statement, identify which type of faulty persuasion is used.

AB	Ad baculum	**SA**	Straw argument	**AH**	Ad hominem
AT	Appeal to tradition	**AP**	Ad populum	**PF**	Plain folks
AV	Ad verecundiam	**PM**	Patriotism	**BW**	Bandwagon
ST	Scare tactic	**GG**	Glittering generalities		

_____ 1. *This country has never faltered in the face of adversity. Our strong, united military has seen us through many troubled times, and it will see us through our current situation. This is your country; support your military.*

_____ 2. *If I am elected to office, I will personally lobby for lower taxes, a new comprehensive crime bill, a $2,500 tax cut on every new home, and better education, and I will personally work to lower the unemployment rate.*

_____ 3. *This is the best college in the region. All of your friends will be attending this fall. You don't want to be left out; you should join us, too.*

_____ 4. *If you really listen to Governor Wise's proposal on health care, you will see that there is no way that we can have a national system. You will not be able to select your doctor, you will not be able to go to the hospital of your choice, and you will not be able to get immediate attention. His proposal is not as comprehensive as our proposal.*

_____ 5. *My father went to Honors College, I went to Honors College, and you will go to Honors College. It is the way things have been for the people in this family. There is no need to break with tradition now.*

_____ 6. *The witness's testimony is useless. He is an alcoholic; he is dishonest and corrupt. To make matters worse, he was a member of the Leftist Party.*

_____ 7. *The gentleman on the witness stand is your neighbor, he is your friend, he is just like you. Sure, he may have more money and drive a Mercedes, but his heart never left the Elm Community.*

_____ 8. *John F. Kennedy once said, "Ask not what your country can do for you; ask what you can do for your country." This is the time to act, my fellow citizens. You can give $200 to our cause and you will be fulfilling the wish of President Kennedy.*

_____ 9. *Out of the 7,000 people polled, 72% believe that there is life beyond our planet. Therefore, there must be life beyond earth.*

_____10. *Without this new medication, you will die.*

_____11. *I don't care what anyone says. If you don't come around to our way of thinking, you'd better start watching your back.*

Why is it important to read and research possible solutions before you make decisions?

As you develop your critical thinking skills, you will begin to recognize the illogical nature of many thoughts, the falsehoods of many statements, the deception in some advertisements, and the irrational

Terminology for Fallacious Arguments

Ad baculum	Ad baculum is an argument that tries to persuade based on force. Threats of alienation, disapproval, or even violence may accompany this type of argument.
Ad hominem	Ad hominem is when someone initiates a personal attack on someone else rather than listening to and rationally debating the person's ideas. This is also referred to as "slander."
Ad populum	An ad populum argument is based on the opinions of the majority of people. It assumes that because the majority says X is right, then Y is not. It uses little logic.
Ad verecundiam	This argument uses quotes and phrases from people in authority or popular people to support one's own views.
Appeal to tradition	This argument looks only at the past and suggests that because we have always done it "this way," we should continue to do it "this way."
Bandwagon	The bandwagon approach tries to convince you to do something just because everyone else is doing it. It is also referred to as "peer pressure."
Glittering Generalities	This type of persuasion or argumentation is an appeal to generalities (Bosak, 1976). It suggests that a person, candidate, or professional is for all the "right" things: justice, low taxes, no inflation, rebates, full employment, low crime, free tuition, progress, privacy, and truth.
Patriotism	This form of persuasion asks you to ignore reason and logic and support what is right for state A or city B or nation C.
Plain folks	This type of persuasion is used to make you feel that the people making the argument are just like you. Usually, they are not; they are only using this appeal to connect with your sense of space and time.
Scare tactic	A scare tactic is used as a desperate measure to put fear in your life. If you don't do X, then Y is going to happen to you.
Straw argument	The straw argument attacks the opponent's argument to make one's own argument stronger. It does not necessarily make argument A stronger; it simply discounts argument B.

> *"There is nothing so powerful as truth, and often, nothing so strange."*
> —Daniel Webster

fears used to persuade. You will also begin to understand the depths to which you should delve to achieve objectivity, the thought and care that you should give to your own decisions and statements, and the methods by which you can build logical, truthful arguments.

Step Eight: Thinking Creatively and Being Resourceful

Creative thinking is a major and important aspect of critical thinking, in that you are producing something that is uniquely yours—introducing something to the world that is new, innovative, and useful. Creative thinking does not mean that you have to be an artist, a musician, or a writer. Creative thinking instead means that you have examined a situation and developed a new way of explaining information, delivering a product, or using an item. It can be as simple as discovering that you can use a small rolling suitcase to carry your books around campus instead of the traditional backpack. Creative thinking means that you have opened your mind to possibilities!

Creative thinking is really about being resourceful—and in today's times, resourcefulness is a powerful tool. Resourcefulness is an **internal** quality, not an **external** gift. If you have ever seen the TV series *Survivorman* or *Man vs. Wild*, you know that it takes a strong person to eat a slug just carved out of a tree trunk. It takes internal will to drink water with so many bacteria that flies die when they drink it. Yes, both shows are somewhat staged, but they show the basics of creativity, intelligence, imagination, and **resourcefulness**.

To truly understand resourcefulness, you need look no further than a child playing in the backyard. *"What does a worthless, old stick become?"* Because of a child's inability to see limitations, the stick becomes a medieval sword, Luke Skywalker's laser beam, an old man's cane, a crutch, a magic wand, a baseball bat, a witch's stirring stick, or a marshmallow roaster. An old stick now has limitless possibilities because the child refused to see it only as a stick. His refusal to be boxed into the confines of our adult reality created possibilities. Sometimes, we have to become that child and use every stick we have just to survive.

Think of internal resourcefulness as **renewable energy**. When you have to draw on your wits, creativity, and determination, these qualities multiply. The more you are required by circumstances to use these qualities, the stronger and more plentiful they become. Conversely, if you've always been able to buy anything you want or if all that you need is provided to you by an external force, your internal resourcefulness begins to wither and die like uneaten fruit on the winter vine. You are not forced to use the whole of yourself. Your energy fades. Your harvest dies.

Your inner resourcefulness and creativity also make you more secure and offer more protection from outside forces. When you know how to make ends meet, you can always do it. When you know how to pay the rent on limited income, you can always do it. When you know how to cut firewood to heat your home, you can always do it. When you know how to navigate the public transportation system in your town, you can always do it; even when the time comes that you don't have to "do it" anymore, you could if you had to. The more you know and the more inner strength and resourcefulness you have, the safer you are against the unknown. The more confidence you possess, the greater the likelihood that you can survive anything at any time. The more resourceful you are, the more you understand that this one quality will help you rebuild all that may have been lost. When the world *HAS* been handed to you on a silver platter, you cannot be ready for what the world *CAN* hand you.

To begin the creative process, consider the items in Figure 5.13. These are some of the characteristics creative thinkers have in common. Using your imaginative and innovative juices, think about how you would *creatively* solve the following problem. Write down at least five possibilities. Come on, make it count!

Jennifer is a first-year student who does not have enough money to pay her tuition, buy her books, and purchase a few new outfits and shoes to wear to class and her work-study job on campus.

If you had to use your creativity to "survive" in the wild, could you do it?

What should she do? Should she pay her tuition and purchase her books, or pay her tuition and buy new clothes and shoes to wear to class and work? What creative, resourceful ideas (solutions) can you give Jennifer?

MY CREATIVE SOLUTIONS:

1. _____

2. _____

3. _____

4. _____

5. _____

FIGURE **5.13** *Characteristics of Creative Thinking*

COMPASSION	Creative thinkers have a zest for life and genuinely care for the spirit of others.	**Example:** More than 40 years ago, community members who wanted to feed the elderly created Meals on Wheels, now a national organization feeding the elderly.
COURAGE	Creative thinkers are unafraid to try new things, to implement new thoughts and actions.	**Example:** An NBC executive moves the *Today Show* out of a closed studio onto the streets of New York, creating the number one morning news show in the United States.
TRUTH	Creative thinkers search for the true meaning of things.	**Example:** The astronomer and scientist Copernicus sought to prove that earth was *not* the center of the universe— an unpopular view at the time.
DREAMS	Creative thinkers allow themselves time to dream and ponder the unknown. They can see what is possible, not just what is actual.	**Example:** John F. Kennedy dreamed that space exploration was possible. His dream became reality.
RISK TAKING	Creative thinkers take positive risks every day. They are not afraid to go against popular opinion.	**Example:** Barack Obama took a risk and ran for President of the United States. He became one of only a few African Americans to ever run for the office and the only African American to be nominated by his party. In November of 2008, he became the first African-American President of the United States.
INNOVATION	Creative thinkers find new ways to do old things.	**Example:** Instead of continuing to fill the earth with waste such as aluminum, plastic, metal, and old cars, means were developed to recycle these materials for future productive use.
COMPETITION	Creative thinkers strive to be better, to think bolder thoughts, to do what is good and to be the best at any task.	**Example:** Tiger Woods had a several-season slump in golf. Most people thought he was a "has-been" especially after his knee surgery. He came back to win tournament after tournament because he knew that he could and he never gave up. He challenged himself.
INDIVIDUALITY	Creative thinkers are not carbon copies of other people. They strive to be true to themselves.	**Example:** A young man decides to take tap dancing instead of playing baseball. He excels and wins a fine arts dancing scholarship to college.
CURIOSITY	Creative thinkers are interested in all things; they want to know much about many things.	**Example:** A 65-year-old retired college professor goes back to college to learn more about music appreciation and computer programming to expand her possibilities.
PERSEVERANCE	Creative thinkers do not give up. They stick to a project to its logical and reasonable end.	**Example:** Dr. Martin Luther King, Jr., did not give up on his dream in the face of adversity, danger, and death threats.

From Ordinary to Extraordinary

REAL PEOPLE | REAL LIVES | REAL CHANGE

DR. WAYNE A. JONES
Assistant Professor and Thurgood Marshall Pathways Fellow
Department of Political Science and Public Administration
Virginia State University, Petersburg, VA

I come from a fine family. My mother is a retired social worker, college professor and community activist and my father, a retired Presbyterian minister and college professor. They provided a safe, structured environment and always have encouraged me to do well. Clearly, I had the foundation to do well in school. However I have not always followed my parents' advice. This was especially true for my senior year in high school. The outcome was that I did not graduate. So at 18, I was working, had my own apartment and things were OK. At least, so I thought.

I had always been interested in anything that had wheels on it. If it has wheels, I could drive it —or wanted to! I drove a bus for a few years and then I drove an ambulance. One day, however, I saw our local bookmobile and I wanted to drive it. I applied to do so, but found out that I had to have a high school diploma to be able to drive the bookmobile. At 19, this was my reason for going back to get my GED. Now, I could master driving yet another "thing" with wheels. It was not, however, as exciting as I thought it would be.

My parents begged me to begin my college studies. Reluctantly, at age 21, I enrolled at Virginia Commonwealth University. After only one year, I knew that college was not for me. I dropped out. In 1975, I began working for the Police Department in Chesterfield, VA. I was only the second African American police officer on the force. I held this position for five years.

My desire for wheels was still with me. I left the police department and began working for the Virginia Overland Transportation Company as a safety supervisor. I worked my way up to become supervisor of transportation. With this experience under my belt, I went to work for a transit company in Richmond, VA driving a city transit bus. I left the second bus company after a year to drive for a local construction company. This work, however, turned out to be very "seasonal" and I found myself frequently without income. I asked to be allowed to drive one of their trash trucks so that I could have a steady income and overtime, too. So, there I was in my late twenties, without a college degree, driving a trash truck. There was not a lot to look forward to.

My late grandmother called me one day and asked me why I didn't go back to college. "You are far from dumb," I remember her telling me. I tried to explain to her that I was making decent money and I could not quit my job. I told her that it would take me at least eight years to get my degree. "I'll be too old by then," I told her. She then said the words that woke me up and changed my life. "Son," she said, "unless you die, you're going to be eight years older in eight years anyway, why not be eight years older with a college degree?"

That was my wake-up call. I found another job with more flexible hours and enrolled at John Tyler Community College with no idea of what I wanted to become. Shortly after I re-enrolled in college, my grandmother died. Her final gift to me was her wonderful words of wisdom.

So, there I was, working full-time, going to college full-time, and barely having enough time to even visit my family who lived nearby. One night, I received another phone call that changed my life again. My parents called me and told me that they wanted to talk with me about money. I visited them and to my surprise, they asked me to quit work and concentrate on my studies. "Grandmother had a vision," my mother told me. "She knew that you were going to do great things." They told me that if I quit, they would pay my bills until I finished college. I agreed to take their help.

I transferred from John Tyler Community College and enrolled again at Virginia Commonwealth University. My GPA was not great upon graduation. I took the Graduate Record Exam (GRE) and scored very badly. I was turned down for the graduate program in Public Administration. I was now 35. I met with the director of admissions and said to him, "Just give me a chance, I know I can do this."

In just a few short years, I managed to go from driving a trash truck to being a university professor.

After some conversation, he agreed to give me a chance. I completed my Masters of Public Administration in only 18 months. I applied to the doctoral program in public administration at VCU. The chairman of the doctoral program reviewed my GRE scores and basically told me that based on them, I should not have been able to obtain a master's degree. Then, I applied to George Washington University for their PhD program.

Once again, the admissions office looked at my scores and basically told me that my master's degree was "just a fluke." I was accepted provisionally and only five years later, I graduated with a 3.85. My dissertation won the Outstanding Dissertation of the Year Award in 2000 from the George Washington University chapter of Phi Delta Kappa. I was not a fluke anymore.

I began working as Director of Adult Day Care for a United Way Agency and loved it. It was then that the thought of becoming a college professor came to mind. I saw an ad in the paper for a part-time teaching position working with advanced-placement students. I found the love of my life — teaching. I later applied to become a full-time faculty member at Virginia State University and today, I teach freshman studies and public administration.

EXTRAORDINARY REFLECTION

Read the following statement and respond in your online journal or class notebook.

Dr. Jones was brave enough to take an enormous risk, quit his full-time job, accept help, and reach his goals. Whom do you have in your life that you can depend upon for support (maybe not monetary support, but crucial support of your goals, dreams, and educational plans)? Why?

CHANGING IDEAS TO *Reality*

REFLECTIONS ON CRITICAL AND CREATIVE THINKING

Critical thinking, emotional intelligence, and information literacy require a great deal of commitment on your part. They may not be easy for everyone at first, but with practice, dedication, and an understanding of the immense need of all three, everyone can think more critically and logically, evaluate information sources, and use emotional intelligence to best advantage.

Critical thinking and emotional intelligence can affect the way you live your life, from strengthening relationships to purchasing a new car, from solving family problems to investing money, from taking the appropriate classes for graduation to getting a promotion at work. Both are vitally important to your growth and education.

As you continue on in the semester and work toward personal and professional motivation and change, consider the following ideas:

> "The significant problems we face cannot be solved at the same level of thinking we were at when we created them."
> —Albert Einstein

▶ Use only *credible* and *reliable* sources.
▶ Learn to distinguish *fact* from *opinion*.
▶ Be *flexible* in your thinking and *avoid* generalizations.
▶ Use emotional intelligence and *restraint*.
▶ Avoid *stereotyping* and prejudging and strive for *objectivity* in your thinking.
▶ *Reserve* judgment until you have looked at every side.
▶ Do *not* assume—do the research and *ask* questions.
▶ Work hard to distinguish *symptoms from problems*.

Critical thinking is truly the hallmark of an educated person. It is a hallmark of character and integrity, and a hallmark of successful students. Let it be yours.

KNOWLEDGE *in* BLOOM

Developing a Rational, Logical Argument

Each chapter-end assessment is based on *Bloom's Taxonomy of Learning*. See the inside front cover for a quick review.

UTILIZES LEVEL 3 OF THE TAXONOMY

EXPLANATION: Thousands of articles are written every day for magazines, newspapers, online journals, and other print media. Depending on the article or where it is published, it can have a slant. You may have heard this called bias (as in "liberal" or "conservative" bias). One of journalism's objectives should be to present the FACTS of what has happened in an incident or the facts of what is being discussed. Bias should not enter the argument unless it is an editorial.

PROCESS: For this activity, you are to find an article (not an editorial) in a mainstream newspaper or magazine (*USA Today, Newsweek, Time, The New York Times, The Washington Post, The National Review*, etc.), read the article, and determine if the article has bias, unsubstantiated opinions, or research that is weak.

The list of questions below will help you evaluate and assess your article.

Name of the article:

_____

Author of the article: _____

His or her affiliation: _____

Publication in which the article was found: _____

Date of publication: _____

Before you read this article, based on the title and subject matter, what five questions do you want to be able to answer once you have read the article?

1. _____
2. _____
3. _____
4. _____
5. _____

After reading the article, what is the author's main reason for writing it?

What is/are the most important fact(s) or information in the article? _____
_____

By writing this article, what is the author implying? _____
_____
_____

By writing this article, what is the author proving? _____
_____
_____

In writing this article, what assumptions were made? _____
_____
_____

What sources does the writer cite to prove his or her point? _____
_____
_____

Is the article fairly presented? In other words, does the author examine both sides of the issue or just one side? Justify your answer. _____
_____
_____

Do you believe and trust the article? Why or why not? Justify your answer. _____
_____
_____

If this article is accurate (or inaccurate, depending on your judgment), what are the implications for society? _____
_____
_____

Answer the five questions you wrote previously in this exercise. _____

1. _____
2. _____
3. _____
4. _____
5. _____

List one way that you can use the information in this article to enhance your creativity and/or resourcefulness. _____
_____
_____

(This project is adapted, in part, from the work of Richard Paul and Linda Elder, 2006.)

SQ3R *Mastery* STUDY SHEET

EXAMPLE QUESTION: *(from page 99)* Why is emotional intelligence important to critical thinking?		ANSWER:
EXAMPLE QUESTION: *(from page 106)* What is information literacy?		ANSWER:
AUTHOR QUESTION: *(from page 101)* Why is emotional intelligence important?		ANSWER:
AUTHOR QUESTION: *(from page 107)* Why is asking questions so important in critical thinking?		ANSWER:
AUTHOR QUESTION: *(from page 107)* Discuss the steps in information literacy.		ANSWER:
AUTHOR QUESTION: *(from page 114)* Define fact and opinion and give an example of each.		ANSWER:
AUTHOR QUESTION: *(from page 115)* Define ad hominem and find an example of this in a recent newspaper or magazine article.		ANSWER:
YOUR QUESTION: *(from page ____)*		ANSWER:
YOUR QUESTION: *(from page ____)*		ANSWER:
YOUR QUESTION: *(from page ____)*		ANSWER:
YOUR QUESTION: *(from page ____)*		ANSWER:
YOUR QUESTION: *(from page ____)*		ANSWER:

Finally, after answering these questions, recite this chapter's major points in your mind. Consider the following general questions to help you master this material.

- ▶ What was it about?
- ▶ What does it mean?
- ▶ What was the most important thing I learned? Why?
- ▶ What were the key points to remember?

ANSWERS TO TEASERS pp. 105–106

Brain Teaser #1, Looking at Common Terms Backwards

1. Snow White and the Seven Dwarfs

2. I Have a Dream by Martin Luther King, Jr.

3. Two peas in a pod

4. Hickory dickory dock, the mouse ran up the clock

5. Three sides to a triangle

6. One hundred pennies in a dollar

7. There's no place like home

8. Four quarts in a gallon

9. *It's A Small World After All*

10. Fifty states in the Union

Brain Teaser #2, Seeing What Is Not Given

(Hint: You have to think "outside the box." Look beyond what is given to you.)

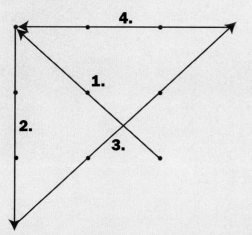

Brain Teaser #3, The Penny

Your answers might include things such as:

► We had more than one language.

► We knew geometry.

► We had a calendar system.

► We honored people.

► We knew metallurgy.

► We knew math.

► We knew architecture.

► We were united.

► We valued liberty.

CHAPTER 6
PRIORITIZE

PLANNING YOUR TIME AND REDUCING STRESS

PART TWO CHANGING YOUR PERFORMANCE

WHY READ THIS CHAPTER?

What's in it for me?

WHY does time management play a role in my value system and self-discipline? WHY is time management so important to the quality of my life? WHY do I need to know about stress and what causes it? WHY is learning to reduce anxiety and managing stress important to my overall success?

WHY? Because poor time management and stress are partners in crime. Poor time management leads to more stress and more stress leads to poor time management skills. It is a vicious circle. Time, of course, is not the only thing in your life that can cause stress. Stress can be brought on by relationships, work, family issues, and money problems, to name a few. However, by learning to effectively manage your time, you can reduce a major factor that contributes to the stress levels in your life. Have you ever looked at your peers who have children, a full-time job (or two jobs), and outside activities, and yet they still get it all done? *"How do they do that?"* The answer is they have figured out what they value and how to apply their values to their time management plans.

By carefully reading this chapter and taking the information provided seriously, you will be able to:

1. Discuss the relationship among time management, your value system, and self-discipline.
2. Beat procrastination and get more done.
3. Evaluate how you spend your time and develop a "to do" list based on your findings.
4. Understand the relationship between poor time management and stress.
5. Identify the major stressors in your life.

CHAPTER 6 / PRIORITIZE

"Nothing is a waste of time if you use the experience wisely."

—Rodin

NAME: Eric Despinis
INSTITUTION: ITT Technical Institute, Bensalem, PA
MAJOR: Computer Network Systems
AGE: 31

I am a full-time single parent, work a full-time job, and go to school full time. Having a lot of "free time" has not been a part of my life for years. But that is OK because I have learned how to manage my time so that I can devote enough energy, passion, and enthusiasm to all of the things I value in my life. We tend to spend our time and money on the things that we love and value. Managing my time at work and school is essential so that I can have as much time as possible with my son, who is my number-one priority. However, school is also a major priority because I want to have a career so I can provide a stable future for my son.

There are times when things get rough and everything seems to be crashing down around me. When that happens, I think about my son, my values, and my goals and this pulls me through. I think that the key to time management is having a clear vision of what you want from your future and then dedicating yourself to that vision. When you have a strong set of goals and you value those goals, you find that you do not allow common, everyday things to get in your way. You simply can't!

On the days when things seem overwhelming and out of balance, I step back, remember my overall plan, and play with my son. Creating balance in my life is very important.

I cannot devote every moment of every day to my job or to school because my son's life would suffer. Conversely, after he is settled and happy, my remaining time is devoted to reaching my goals of being a computer system administrator.

I also think it is important to find a strong support network of positive people in your life. My family has always been there for me and so has my advisor at ITT, Al Dornbach. He has helped me understand so much about life and work and family. His wisdom and guidance are paramount in helping me reach my goals. I suggest that you find people who support you and are behind you and this will help you develop a clear vision and a plan to help you succeed. The information in this chapter will be of great assistance to you as you begin to build your own time management plan for the future. Good luck.

SCAN & QUESTION

In the preface of this book (page xix), you read about the **SQ3R Study Method**. Right now, take a few moments, **scan this chapter,** and on page 155, write **five questions** that you think will be important to your mastery of this material. In addition to the two questions below, you will find five questions from your authors. Use one of your "**Study for Quiz**" stickers to flag this page for easy reference.

EXAMPLES:

▶ **How can I simplify my life and get more done?** (from page 138)

▶ **What are the components of self-discipline?** (from page 134)

TIME—YOU HAVE ALL THERE IS

Can You Take Control of Your Life and Make the *Most* of Your Time?

You can definitely say four things about time: ***It is fair. It does not discriminate. It treats everyone the same. Everyone has all there is.*** No person has any more or fewer hours in a day than the next person. It may seem that Gary or Tamisha has more time that you do, but they do not. In a 24-hour

span we all have 1,440 minutes. No more. No less. There is one more thing you can definitely say about time, too: ***It can be cruel and unrelenting.*** It is one of the few things in our lives that we cannot stop. There are no time-out periods, no breaks, and try as we might, we can't turn it back, shut it down, or stop it. The good news, however, is that by learning how to manage our time more effectively, we don't need to slow it down or stop it. We can learn how to get things done and have more time for joy and fun.

So, how do you spend your time? Some people are very productive, while others scramble to find a few moments to enjoy life and have quality relationships. According to time management and personal productivity expert Donald Wetmore (2008), "The average working person spends less than two minutes per day in ***meaningful*** communication with their spouse or significant other and less than 30 seconds per day in ***meaningful*** communication with their children." Think about that for a moment. THIRTY seconds. If you think that is amazing, consider the following list. As strange as it may seem, these figures are taken from the Bureau of Labor Statistics of the U.S. Department of the Census (2006). During your ***working years*** (age 20 to 65, a 45-year span), you spend an average of:

Do the figures regarding how we spend our time surprise you?
Where do you think most of your "free" time goes?

▶ 16 years sleeping.

▶ 2.3 years eating.

▶ 3.1 years doing housework.

▶ 6 years watching TV.

▶ 1.3 years on the telephone.

This totals ***28.7 years of your working life*** doing things that you may not even consider in your time management plan. What happens to the remaining 16.3 years? Well, you will spend ***14 of those years working***, which leaves you with 2.3 years, or only 20,000 hours, during your working life to embrace joy, spend time with your family, educate yourself, travel, and experience a host of other life-fulfilling activities. Dismal? Scary? It does not have to be. By learning how to manage your time, harness your energy and passion, and take control of your day-to-day activities, 2.3 years can be a long, exciting, productive time.

Why is it that some people seem to get so much more done than other people? They appear to always be calm and collected and have it together. Many people from this group work long hours in addition to going to school. They never appear to be stressed out, and they seem to be able to do it all with grace and charm. Uggh!

You are probably aware of others who are always late with assignments, never finish their projects on time, rarely seem to have time to study, and appear to have no concrete goals for their lives. Sometimes, we get the idea that the first group accomplishes more because they have more time or because they don't have to work or they don't have children or they are smarter or have more help. Actually, some of these reasons may be true, but in reality, many of the people in the first group have learned how to overcome and beat procrastination, tie their value systems to their time management plans, and use their personal energy and passion to accomplish more.

"I can't do any more than I am doing right now," you may say to yourself. But is that really true? One of the keys to managing your time is to consider your values. We discussed your value system in Chapter 2. What you value, enjoy, and love, you tend to put more passion, energy, and time toward. Do you value your family? If so, you make time for them. Do you value your friends? If so, you make time for them. Now you have to ask yourself, **how much do I value my education**? How important is it that I succeed in college and get my degree? If you make succeeding in college a high value for your life and your future, you will find that you make more time for your studies, your classes, and your projects. **We spend time on what we value!**

TIME MANAGEMENT AND SELF-DISCIPLINE

Do You Have What It Takes to Get It Done?

Time management is actually about managing you! It is about taking control and assuming responsibility for the time you are given on this earth. The sooner you understand this and take control of how you use your time, the quicker you will be on your way to becoming successful in college and many other activities. Learning to manage your time is a lesson that you will use throughout your studies and beyond. No, **you can't control time**, but you can control yourself. Time management is basically self-discipline—and self-discipline involves self-motivation. Time management is paying attention to how you are spending your most valuable resource—time—and then devising a plan to use it more effectively. This is one of the goals of this chapter.

The word "discipline" comes from a Latin word meaning "to teach." Therefore, **self-discipline** is really about "teaching ourselves" (Waitley, 1997). Self-discipline implies that you have the ability to teach yourself how to get more done when things are going well and when they are not going so well. If you have self-discipline, you have learned how to hold it all together when things get tough, when you feel beaten, and when defeat seems just around the corner. It also means that when you have important tasks to complete, you can temporarily pull yourself away from enjoyable situations and fun times until those tasks are completed. Consider the chart in Figure 6.1 regarding self-discipline. **Self-discipline is really about four things.**

> *"Self-discipline is teaching ourselves to do the things necessary to reach our goals without becoming sidetracked by bad habits."*
> —Denis Waitley

Once you have made the **choice** to engage in your education, stop procrastinating, and manage your time more effectively, you have to make the **changes** in your thoughts and behaviors to bring those choices to fruition. Then, you have to **accept responsibility** for your actions and take control of your life. You have to call upon your **inner strength** or **willpower**—and you DO have willpower; it may just be hidden or forgotten, but you do have it. You have the ability to empower yourself to get things done. No one can do this for you. You are responsible for your life, your actions, and your willpower. Self-discipline and willpower help you move in the direction of your dreams. Even in the face of fear, anxiety, stress, defeat, and darkness, self-discipline will help you find your way.

Willpower and self-discipline are all about **retraining your mind** to do what YOU want it to do and not what IT wants to do. It is about eliminating the negative self-talk that so often derails us and causes us to procrastinate and get stressed out. By retraining your mind and resisting the urge to simply "obey" your subconscious, you are basically retraining your life. Consider the following situations:

▶ You come home after three classes and are tired and weary. Your subconscious mind tells you to sit down, put your feet up, and watch TV for a while. But you have to tell your mind, *"NO! I am going to take a short walk around the block to get my adrenaline flowing and then I'm going to read my chapter for homework."*

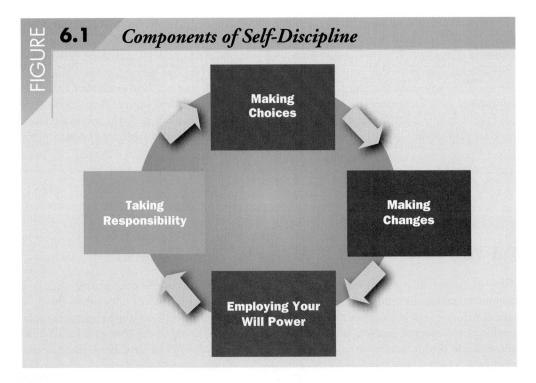

FIGURE

6.1   *Components of Self-Discipline*

Making Choices

Making Changes

Employing Your Will Power

Taking Responsibility

How can becoming a more organized person help you manage your time more effectively?

► You look at your desk or study space, and you see all of the books and papers you have gathered for your research paper and your subconscious mind tells you to just ignore it for a while; there's still time to get it done! You have to tell your mind, *"ABSOLUTELY NOT! I'm going to get those articles organized and make an outline of my paper before I do anything else today. Period."*

► You come home tired and hungry, and your mind tells you to eat that candy bar or donut. You have to tell your mind, *"NO WAY! I am going to have an apple instead. It is better for me and my memory to avoid sugar right now."*

By retraining your mind and ignoring your subconscious, you can retrain yourself to develop the self-discipline and willpower you need to get things done and avoid the stress caused by procrastination. Willpower gives you strength to stay on track and avoid the guilt associated with putting things off or not doing them at all. Guilt turns into frustration and frustration turns into anger, and before you know it, your negative self-talk and subconscious mind have "won" and nothing gets done. You DO have the power to change this.

I'LL DO IT WHEN I HAVE A LITTLE FREE TIME

Is Time Really "Free"?

What is *"free time"* and when does it occur? We've all used that expression at one time or another: *"I'll do that when I get a little more free time,"* or *"I'm going to wait until I find a little more time."* Can time be found? Is time free? Do we ever have a moment to call our own? The answer is "maybe," but you have to create free time, and you can create it only by getting the things done that must be completed for your success.

Free time is NOT time that you simply create by putting off work that needs to be done. Free time is NOT time that is spent procrastinating. Free time is NOT time that you take away from your duties, chores, studies, family, and obligations. That is **borrowed time** and if you know the rules of good behavior, you know that anything you borrow, you must repay. When are you going to find the time to "repay" these blocks of time to yourself? Usually, you don't and that is when and where you get into trouble and your stress levels start to rise.

Free time IS time that you reward yourself when you have completed your studies, tasks, chores, and obligations. Free time IS time that you have created by planning ahead and avoiding procrastination. Free time IS time that you enjoy when your work is done and you can sit and enjoy your life, family, and friends because the pressures and guilt of poor time management are not haunting you. One of your goals in managing your time more effectively should be to create more free time in your life for joy. Joy will not come to you, however, if you have projects looming over your head.

> "Begin doing what you want to do now. We are not living in eternity. We have only this moment, sparkling like a star in our hand and melting like a snowflake."
> —Marie B. Ray

PLANNING, DOODLING, OR BEGGING

What Type of Person Are You, Anyway?

We all have different personality types, but did you know that we also have different time management personalities? Consider the list in Figure 6.2 explaining the different negative time management personalities. Respond YES or NO to the types you think most resemble you and your management style. Then, in the next column explain why you think this type represents you and your daily thoughts on time. Finally, in the last column, list at least one strategy that you can begin to implement to overcome this type of negative time management style.

ABSOLUTELY NO . . . WELL, MAYBE

Do You Know How to Say No?

"NO, I'm sorry, I can't do that," is perhaps one of the most difficult phrases you must learn to say when it comes to effective time management. **"Jeez, I should have never agreed to do this in the first place"** is perhaps one of the most common phrases used when you don't know how to say "no." If you continually say yes to everyone and every project, then you'll quickly have no time left for yourself, your family, your friends, and your other projects. Many of us are taught from an early age that "no" is a bad word and that we should always try to avoid saying it to others. However, we are not taught that never saying "no" can cause us undue stress and feelings of guilt and frustration, and throw our time management plans into disarray. Now that you have so much going on from so many different projects, saying "no" needs to become a part of your everyday vocabulary. By learning to say "NO" to a few things, you can begin to say "YES" to many other things—things that you want to do, need to do, and that will actually help others in the long run. "No" is not rude; it is simply a way of managing your time so that you have more time to say "Yes" to what is important and useful.

> "Time is the most valuable and most perishable of our possessions."
> —John Randolph

FIGURE

6.2 *Time Management Types*

TYPE	EXPLANATION	Do YOU have any of these tendencies?	WHAT actions make you like this type of person?	What can YOU DO to begin eliminating this type of behavior?
THE CIRCLER	Doing the same things over and over again and again and hoping for a different result; basically, going around in circles.	YES / NO		
THE DOODLER	Not paying attention to details, doing things that do not really matter to the completion of your project.	YES / NO		
THE SQUANDERER	Wasting too much time trying to "get ready" to study or work and never really getting anything done; then it is too late to do a good job.	YES / NO		
THE BEGGAR	Expecting time to "stop" for you after you've wasted time doing nothing or going in circles. Then, becoming frustrated when you don't have enough time.	YES / NO		
THE PLANNER	Planning out your project so carefully and meticulously that by the time you have everything you think you need, there is no time to really do the project.	YES / NO		
THE HUN	Waiting too late to plan or get things done and then stomping on anyone or anything to get the project done with no regard for others' feelings, time, or relationships.	YES / NO		
THE PASSIVIST	Convincing yourself that you'll never get it all done and that there is no use to try anyway.	YES / NO		

Steps to Learning to Say No—It's as Simple as NOT Saying Yes:

► Think before you answer out loud with an insincere or untrue "Yes."

► Make sure you understand exactly what is being asked of you and what the project involves before you give a "Yes" or "No" answer.

► Review your schedule to see if you really have the time to do a quality job. ("If you have to have an answer immediately, it is 'No.' If you can wait a few days for me to finish project X, and review my schedule, the answer may be 'Yes.'")

► Learn the difference between assertiveness (politely declining) and rudeness (responding, "Have you lost your mind?").

► Say "No" at the right times (i.e., to the wrong things) so that you can say "Yes" at the appropriate times (i.e., to the right things).

▶ Learn how to put yourself and your future first (for a change). By doing this, you can say "Yes" more often later on.

▶ Inform others of your time management schedule so that they will have a better understanding of why you say "No."

▶ If you must say "Yes" to an unwanted project (something at work, for example), try to negotiate a deadline that works for everyone—you first!

▶ Keep your "No" short. If you have to offer an explanation, be brief so that you don't talk yourself into doing something you can't do and so that you avoid giving false hope to the other person. If the answer is "No" right now and it will be "No" in the future, say "No" now.

▶ Offer suggestions to the other person as to who may be able to help him or her or when you might be available (if it is in your best interest to accept this request at any time).

▶ If you feel you simply have to say yes, try to trade off with the other person and ask him or her to do something on your list.

▶ Put a time limit on your "Yes." For example, you might agree to help someone, but you could say, "I can give you 30 minutes and then I have to leave."

Your Turn

You are taking four classes and the reading and homework are mounting day by day. Your family needs you, your friends think you've abandoned them, and you want to continue to do a good job at work. Your schedule is tight and you have things planned down to the hour in order to be able to get it all done and done well. Suddenly, you are asked to help with a project for disadvantaged children that seems very worthy and timely. You know that your schedule is full but your conscience begins to gnaw at you and you really do want to help.

Applying the tips from the list above, predict how you might be able to address this situation.

_____

_____

_____

_____

Do you think saying "no" is rude or necessary?

BLOOM LEVEL 3
QUESTION

BEGINNING YOUR DAY WITH PEACE

Can You Start Your Day as a Blank Page and Simplify Your Life?

Imagine a day with nothing to do! That may be difficult, if not impossible, for you to conceive right now. But as an exercise in building your own day from scratch and simplifying your life, think about having a day where YOU build your schedule and where you do not have to be constrained by activities and projects that others have thrust upon you. Think about a day where you are in charge. Crazy? Impossible? Outrageous? Maybe not as much as you think.

Yes, you will need to plot activities such as work, class, and family duties into your daily calendar, but you also need to learn how to schedule time for fun activities, time for silence and peace,

THINKING ~ for CHANGE: An Activity for Critical Reflection

Darius is a single father of two young daughters. He and his wife divorced several years ago and he was granted custody of Alice and Marianne. Shortly after the divorce, Darius was laid off from his job as a construction foreman. He had been making a very good living, but now it was hard to make ends meet. He could not find another job that paid well enough to support the three of them.

Therefore, he decided to go back to school to pursue his dream of becoming a draftsman. His classes, along with his new part-time job, demand much of his time. He has found that he is spending much less time with his daughters than he had in the past—and he does not like this at all.

His daughters were cast in the school play and the performance is scheduled for Friday night—the same night as one of his drafting classes. He knows that he has a conflict on his hands. He knows that class is very important, but so is supporting his daughters. In your own words, what would you suggest that Darius do at this point? List at least three things that he could do handle this situation, manage his time to meet all of his obligations, and maintain his sanity.

1. _____

2. _____

3. _____

and time to be alone with your thoughts. By learning how to build your schedule each evening from scratch, you will have the opportunity to plan a day where you simplify your life. There is an old quote that states, "If you want to know what you value in your life, look at your checkbook and your calendar." Basically, this suggests that we spend our money and time on things we value.

12 Ways to Simplify Your Life:

> Know what you value, and work hard to eliminate activities that are not in conjunction with your core value system. This can be whittled down to one statement: ***"Identify what is important to you. Eliminate everything else."***

> Get away from technology for a few hours a day. Turn off your computer, cell phone, iPod, and other devices that can take time away from doing what you value.

> Learn to delegate to others. You may say to yourself, "My family does not know how to use the washing machine." Guess what? When all of their underwear is dirty, they'll learn how to use it. Don't enable others to avoid activities that complicate your life.

> Make a list of everything you are doing. Prioritize this list into what you enjoy doing and what fits into your value system. If you can feasibly do only three or four of these activities per day, draw a line after number four and eliminate the rest of the list.

> Do what is essential for the well-being of you and your family and eliminate everything else.

> Don't waste time saving money. Spend money to save time. In other words, don't drive across town to save 3 cents per gallon on fuel or 10 cents for a gallon of milk. Pay the extra money and have more time to do what you like.

> Clean your home of clutter and mess. Work from cleanliness. Declutter and organize. Make sure everything has a place.

Do you find it difficult or easy to simplify and declutter your life? Why?

FIGURE

6.3	*Ways to Simplify Your Life*	
Two things I can do to simplify my life at home		
Two things I can do to simplify my life at work		
Two things I can do to simplify my life at school		
Two things I can do to simplify my life with my children		
Two things I can do to simplify my life with my spouse/partner/loved one		
Two things I can do to simplify my economics (financial matters)		

▶ Donate everything you don't need or use to charity. Simplifying your life may also mean simplifying your closets, drawers, cabinets, and garage.

▶ Go through your home or apartment and eliminate everything that does not bring you joy or have sentimental value. If you don't love it, ditch it.

▶ Clean up the files on your computer. Erase everything that you don't need or want so that you can find material more easily. If you have not used the file in a month, put it on a flash drive for later use.

▶ Live in the moment. Yes, it is important to plan for the future, but if you ignore "the moment," your future will not be as bright.

▶ Spend a few moments each morning and afternoon reflecting on all of the abundance in your life. Learn to give thanks and learn to do nothing.

(Adapted from *Zen Habits,* 2008, and *Get More Done,* 2008)

In the space in Figure 6.3, compile a list that can help you simplify your life in each category. Add ONLY those things to the list that you can actually DO on a daily basis.

BLOOM LEVEL 6
QUESTION

THE DREADED "P" WORD

Why Is Procrastination So Easy to Do and How Can You Beat It Once and for All?

It's not just you! Almost everyone procrastinates, and then we worry and tell ourselves, "I'll never do it again if I can just get through this one project." We say things to ourselves like, "If I can just live through this paper, I will never wait until the last minute again." But then someone comes along with a great idea for fun, and off we go. Or there is a great movie on TV, the kids want to play a game of catch, you go to the refrigerator for a snack, and before you know it, you are rewarding yourself *with FREE time* before you have done your work.

The truth is simple: We tend to avoid the hard jobs in favor of the easy ones. Even many of the list makers fool themselves. They mark off a long list of easy tasks while the big ones still loom in front of them. Many of us put off unpleasant tasks until our backs are against the wall. So why do we procrastinate when we all know how unpleasant the results can be? Why aren't we disciplined and organized and controlled so that we can reap the rewards that come from being prepared? Why do we put ourselves through so much stress by putting things off?

"If you have to eat two frogs, eat the ugliest one first."
—Brian Tracy

The biggest problem with procrastination, even beyond not getting the job, task, or paper completed on time, *is doing it poorly* and then suffering the stress caused by having put it off or turning in a subpar project. By putting the project off, you have cheated yourself out of the time needed to bring your best to the table and, most likely, you are going to hand over a project, with your name on it, that is not even close to your potential. And to top it off, more stress is created by this vicious cycle of "I'll do it tomorrow—or this weekend."

What has procrastination cost you? This is perhaps one of the most important questions that you can ask and answer with regard to managing your time more effectively. Did it cost you a good grade? Did it cost you money? Did it cost you your reputation? Did it cost you your dignity? Did it cost you your ability to do your best? ***Procrastination is not free.*** Every time you do it, it costs you something. You need to determine what it is worth.

In order to beat procrastination, you will also need to consider ***what type*** of procrastinator you are (Figure 6.4). Each type requires a different strategy and different energy to overcome, but make no doubt about it, success requires overcoming all degrees and types of procrastination. Before you complete the Time Management Assessment, examine Figure 6.4 to determine if any of these procrastination types fit you.

Take a moment to complete the ***Time Management Assessment*** on the next page. Be honest and truthful in your responses. The results of your score are located after the assessment.

Procrastination is quite simply a bad habit formed after many years of practice. There are reasons, however, that cause us to keep doing this to ourselves. Often, we let our negative self-talk cause us to procrastinate. We allow our negative attitude to override what we know is best for us. An attitude adjustment may be just the thing you need to overcome and beat the trap of procrastination.

FIGURE

6.4 *Procrastinator Types*

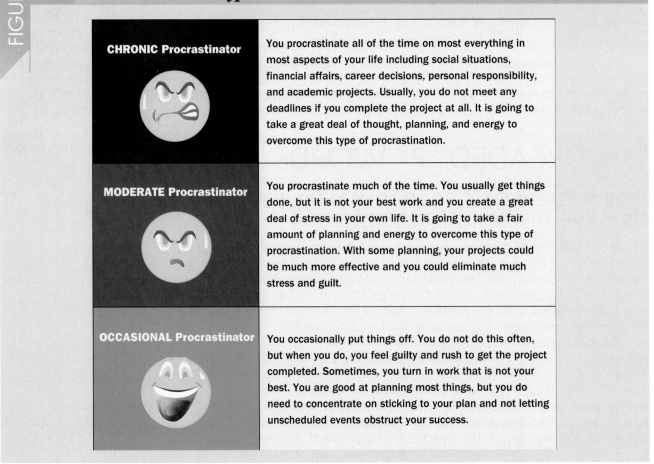

CHRONIC Procrastinator

You procrastinate all of the time on most everything in most aspects of your life including social situations, financial affairs, career decisions, personal responsibility, and academic projects. Usually, you do not meet any deadlines if you complete the project at all. It is going to take a great deal of thought, planning, and energy to overcome this type of procrastination.

MODERATE Procrastinator

You procrastinate much of the time. You usually get things done, but it is not your best work and you create a great deal of stress in your own life. It is going to take a fair amount of planning and energy to overcome this type of procrastination. With some planning, your projects could be much more effective and you could eliminate much stress and guilt.

OCCASIONAL Procrastinator

You occasionally put things off. You do not do this often, but when you do, you feel guilty and rush to get the project completed. Sometimes, you turn in work that is not your best. You are good at planning most things, but you do need to concentrate on sticking to your plan and not letting unscheduled events obstruct your success.

FIGURE **6.5**   *Time Management Assessment*

Answer the following questions with the following scale:

1 = Not at all   2 = Rarely   3 = Sometimes   4 = Often   5 = Very often

1. I prioritize my tasks every day and work from my priority list.	1 2 3 4 5
2. I work hard to complete tasks on time and not put them off until the last minute.	1 2 3 4 5
3. I take time to plan and schedule the next day's activities the night before.	1 2 3 4 5
4. I have made time during my daily schedule to study and get my projects completed so that I can have more quality time at home.	1 2 3 4 5
5. I study and get my work done before I take fun breaks.	1 2 3 4 5
6. I analyze my assignments to determine which ones are going to take the most time and then work on them first and most often.	1 2 3 4 5
7. I have analyzed my daily activities and determined where I actually spend my time.	1 2 3 4 5
8. I know how to say no and do so frequently.	1 2 3 4 5
9. I know how to avoid distractions and how to work through unexpected interruptions.	1 2 3 4 5
10. I do not let "fear of the unknown" keep me from working on a project.	1 2 3 4 5
11. I know how to overcome apathy toward a project.	1 2 3 4 5
12. I know how to fight and overcome my own laziness.	1 2 3 4 5
13. I know how to reframe a project that may not interest me so that I can see the benefits from it and learn from it.	1 2 3 4 5
14. I know how to break down a major, complex, or overwhelming task to get it done in pieces and then put it all together.	1 2 3 4 5
15. I build time into my schedule on a daily or weekly basis to deal with "unexpected" interruptions or distractions.	1 2 3 4 5

YOUR TOTAL SCORE: _____

RESULTS:

60–75   You manage your time well and you know how to build a schedule to get things done. Your productivity is high. You don't let procrastination rule your life.

45–59   You are good at doing some things on time, but you tend to procrastinate too much. Learning how to build and work from a priority list may help you manage your time more effectively.

30–44   You need to work hard to change your time management skills and learn how to set realistic goals. Procrastination is probably a major issue for you, causing you much stress and worry. Working from a priority list can help you greatly.

29–below   Your time management skills are very weak and without change and improvement, your success plan could be in jeopardy. You could benefit from learning to set realistic goals, working from a priority list, and reframing your thought process toward tasks.

Consider the following negative statements. On the right-hand side, rewrite each statement to make it a positive, procrastination-beating statement.

NEGATIVE STATEMENT	POSITIVE STATEMENT
I'll do it at 9:30 when this TV show is off.	_____ _____
I'm tired.	_____ _____
I can't concentrate.	_____ _____
This is too hard.	_____ _____

This is boring.

_____

_____

I don't know why anyone would ask me to do this crazy stuff.

_____

_____

Learning to apply this type of positive thinking can help you beat the Procrastination Trap and manage your time and life more effectively.

GETTING THE MOST OUT OF THIS MOMENT

Do You Know the Causes of and Cures for Procrastination?

Below, you will find a list of the 10 most COMMON CAUSES of procrastination and some simple, doable, everyday strategies that you can employ to overcome each cause. We have provided three strategies for each cause. Add at least two of your own strategies to overcome this type of procrastination.

ESSENTIAL CORNERSTONE

Accountability:
How can being a more responsible and accountable person help you overcome procrastination and "make the most of now"?

Social Networking Moment:
Share your response to this Essential Cornerstone with peers in your social network. Choose two responses from your peers and respond to their postings.

▶ **Superhuman expectations and trying to be a perfectionist**
  ▶ Allow yourself **more time than you think you need** to complete a project.
  ▶ Realize that no one, including you, is (or ever will be) perfect. Perfection does not exist.
  ▶ **Allow enough time to do your very best** and let that be that. If you plan and allow time for excellence, you can't do more.
  ▶ _____
  ▶ _____

▶ **Fear of not knowing how to do the task**
  ▶ **Ask for clarification** from whoever asked you to do the project.
  ▶ **Read** as much as you can about the task at hand and **ask for help**.
  ▶ Break up big tasks into **small ones**.
  ▶ _____
  ▶ _____

▶ **Lack of motivation and the inability to find internal motivation**
  ▶ **Reframe your attitude** to find the good and beneficial in any task.
  ▶ Consider how this task will help you **reach your overall goals and dreams**.
  ▶ Take time to do the **things you love**, which will create a healthy balance in your life.
  ▶ _____
  ▶ _____

▶ **Fear of failing or fear of the task being too hard**
  ▶ Start the project with **positive, optimistic thoughts**.
  ▶ **Face your fears**; look them right in the face and make a decision to defeat them.
  ▶ **Visualize your successful completion** of the project.
  ▶ _____
  ▶ _____

▶ **No real plan or goal for getting the task done**

    ▶ Set reasonable, concrete goals that you can reach in about **20–25 minutes**.

    ▶ **Draw up an action plan** the night before you begin the project.

    ▶ Look at completing the project in terms of your **long-range goals** and your overall life plan.

    ▶ _____

    ▶ _____

▶ **Considering the task too unpleasant or uninteresting**

    ▶ **Realize** that most tasks are not as unpleasant as we've made them out to be.

    ▶ **Do the hardest tasks first** and save the easiest for last.

    ▶ Schedule tasks that you consider unpleasant to be done **during your peak hours**.

    ▶ _____

    ▶ _____

▶ **Utter laziness and/or apathy**

    ▶ **Concentrate on the rewards** of managing yourself and your time more effectively.

    ▶ Give yourself a **time limit** to accomplish a task.

    ▶ Set a regular, realistic time for study, and **stick to it**.

    ▶ _____

    ▶ _____

Is there a difference among laziness, procrastination, and resting?

▶ **Distractions and/or lack of focus**

    ▶ **Ask for help** from your professors, advisor, counselor, or other professionals.

    ▶ Start on the difficult, **most boring tasks first**.

    ▶ Weed out your personal belongings and living space. Organization helps you manage your time and **get to work**.

    ▶ _____

    ▶ _____

▶ **Choosing "fun" before responsibility**

    ▶ Actually **reward yourself** when you have accomplished an important body of work.

    ▶ **Don't get involved** in too many organizations, accept too many commitments, or overextend yourself so that you can concentrate on what needs to be done.

    ▶ **Consider the consequences** of not doing what you're responsible for doing.

    ▶ _____

    ▶ _____

▶ **Waiting for the "right" mood**

    ▶ **Avoid whining and complaining** and realize that you can create the right mood at any time.

    ▶ **Just do it!** Force yourself to jump into the task.

    ▶ Work during your **peak hours of the day**.

    ▶ _____

    ▶ _____

From Ordinary to Extraordinary

REAL PEOPLE | REAL LIVES | REAL CHANGE

MAUREEN RIOPELLE
President & Founder
Mary's Circle of Hope—The Mary Maguire Foundation
Milford, OH

Things could not have been going better! I was a star basketball player recruited by hundreds of colleges and was a top pick by the University of Iowa. My dream of going to college, becoming an Olympic athlete, and later a sportscaster was so close I could see it all happening. But, life has a funny way of turning on a dime.

I had suffered knee problems for many years and most doctors attributed it to "growing pains." I continued to play sports in high school despite the pain. By the time I got to the University of Iowa, at the urging of my coaches I finally saw a few specialists but the diagnosis was inconclusive. They knew my knee was in serious disrepair and that I had lost over 35% of the range of motion. They just couldn't figure out why.

After surgery, my knees actually began to worsen. The doctors feared a massive infection and after more tests, another surgery was scheduled. It was then determined that the plica in my knees had hardened and formed so much scar tissue that it seemed to almost form another "bone" in my leg. I was told that I would probably have to have surgery every two years to repair the damage and that I only had a 50/50 chance of ever walking again.

In a relatively brief period of time, I went from a college basketball stand-out and Olympic hopeful to losing my scholarship, dropping out of college, and potentially facing the rest of my life on crutches or in a wheelchair. I had five surgeries in seven months and I spent that summer in a wheelchair and on crutches, but within a year, I was walking on my own again. Within a year and half I walked my first 5K.

I attribute my recovery to my drive and determination. When necessary, I am the most stubborn person you'll ever meet. When I was told that I would not walk, run, or play basketball again, I took it as a *personal challenge* to prove everyone wrong—*"I'll show you."* I eventually went back to college, graduating with a 4.0 GPA. After graduation, I began working, and life was moving along. Little did I know that within a few short years, I would have to call upon that teenager who years earlier had told herself, *"I'll show you."*

One morning I found a lump in my breast and immediately met with my doctor, who scheduled a mammo-

> *In a relatively brief period of time, I went from a college basketball standout and Olympic hopeful to losing my scholarship, dropping out of college, and potentially facing the rest of my life on crutches or in a wheelchair.*

140

From Ordinary to Extraordinary

REAL PEOPLE | REAL LIVES | REAL CHANGE

gram. After the test, I was told that everything was fine. But there was a little voice in my head that said, "You need to ask someone else. Get a second opinion." This little voice saved my life. I did, indeed, have breast cancer and it had even spread to my lymph nodes. My determination and strong will to live and beat the odds became my salvation once again. After surgery and treatment, there are no signs of cancer.

Both of these experiences, while trying and frightening, led me to my real calling in life—founding Mary's Circle of Hope—The Mary Maguire Foundation, a nonprofit organization dedicated to the support of women cancer survivors. We help provide financial assistance; health, fitness, and nutritional assistance; empowerment retreats and workshops; and additional services that help the women go from surviving to thriving. Being able to help others thrive in the face of adversity has become my passion and focus in life. Visit us at www.marymaguirefoundation.org.

EXTRAORDINARY REFLECTION

Read the following statement and respond in your online journal or class notebook.

Ms. Riopelle suffered a major setback with her health, causing her to lose her scholarship and drop out of college for a time. What advice regarding persistence, internal motivation, positive thinking, and determination would you give to someone who is facing a life-threatening health problem?

EVALUATING HOW YOU SPEND YOUR TIME

Do You Know Where Your Time Goes?

So, how do you find out where your time goes? The same way that you find out where your money goes—you track it. Every 15 minutes for one week, record exactly how you spent that time. This exercise may seem a little tedious at first, but if you complete the process over a period of a week, you will have a much better concept of where your time is being used. Yes, that's right—for a week, you need to keep a written record of how much time you spend sleeping, studying, eating, working, getting to class and back, cooking, caring for children, watching television, doing yard work, going to movies, attending athletic events, hanging out, doing laundry, whatever.

Take your plan with you and keep track of your activities during the day. To make things simple, round off tasks to 15-minute intervals. For example, if you start walking to the cafeteria at 7:08, you might want to mark off the time block that begins with 7:00. If you finish eating and return to your dorm at 7:49, you can mark off the next two blocks. You will also want to note the activity so that you can later evaluate how you spent your time. Study the example that is provided for you in Figure 6.6.

In Figure 6.7 on pages 143–144, you will find a daily time log that you can use for this exercise. Remember to take these pages with you and record how you are spending your time during the day. As you progress through the week, try to improve the use of your time. When you finish this exercise, review how you spent your time.

FIGURE **6.6** ***How You Really Spend Your Time***

7:00	get up & shower	7:00			12:15
		7:15			12:30
	X	7:30		Walked to Union	12:45
	Breakfast	7:45	1:00	Ate lunch	1:00
8:00		8:00			1:15
		8:15			1:30
	Read paper	8:30		Talked w/ Joe	1:45
	Walked to class	8:45	2:00		2:00
9:00	English 101	9:00		Went to book	2:15
		9:15		store	2:30
		9:30		Walked to	2:45
		9:45	3:00	my room	3:00
10:00		10:00		Called Ron	3:15
		10:15			3:30
		10:30			3:45
	Walked to class	10:45	4:00	Watched	4:00
11:00	History 210	11:00		Friends	4:15
		11:15			4:30
		11:30		Walked to	4:45
		11:45	5:00	library	5:00
12:00		12:00			5:15

FIGURE **6.7**   *Daily Time Sheet*

Monday		Tuesday		Wednesday	
6:00	6:00	6:00	6:00	6:00	6:00
	6:15		6:15		6:15
	6:30		6:30		6:30
	6:45		6:45		6:45
7:00	7:00	7:00	7:00	7:00	7:00
	7:15		7:15		7:15
	7:30		7:30		7:30
	7:45		7:45		7:45
8:00	8:00	8:00	8:00	8:00	8:00
	8:15		8:15		8:15
	8:30		8:30		8:30
	8:45		8:45		8:45
9:00	9:00	9:00	9:00	9:00	9:00
	9:15		9:15		9:15
	9:30		9:30		9:30
	9:45		9:45		9:45
10:00	10:00	10:00	10:00	10:00	10:00
	10:15		10:15		10:15
	10:30		10:30		10:30
	10:45		10:45		10:45
11:00	11:00	11:00	11:00	11:00	11:00
	11:15		11:15		11:15
	11:30		11:30		11:30
	11:45		11:45		11:45
12:00	12:00	12:00	12:00	12:00	12:00
	12:15		12:15		12:15
	12:30		12:30		12:30
	12:45		12:45		12:45
1:00	1:00	1:00	1:00	1:00	1:00
	1:15		1:15		1:15
	1:30		1:30		1:30
	1:45		1:45		1:45
2:00	2:00	2:00	2:00	2:00	2:00
	2:15		2:15		2:15
	2:30		2:30		2:30
	2:45		2:45		2:45
3:00	3:00	3:00	3:00	3:00	3:00
	3:15		3:15		3:15
	3:30		3:30		3:30
	3:45		3:45		3:45
4:00	4:00	4:00	4:00	4:00	4:00
	4:15		4:15		4:15
	4:30		4:30		4:30
	4:45		4:45		4:45
5:00	5:00	5:00	5:00	5:00	5:00
	5:15		5:15		5:15
	5:30		5:30		5:30
	5:45		5:45		5:45
6:00	6:00	6:00	6:00	6:00	6:00
	6:15		6:15		6:15
	6:30		6:30		6:30
	6:45		6:45		6:45
7:00	7:00	7:00	7:00	7:00	7:00
	7:15		7:15		7:15
	7:30		7:30		7:30
	7:45		7:45		7:45
8:00	8:00	8:00	8:00	8:00	8:00
	8:15		8:15		8:15
	8:30		8:30		8:30
	8:45		8:45		8:45
9:00	9:00	9:00	9:00	9:00	9:00
	9:15		9:15		9:15
	9:30		9:30		9:30
	9:45		9:45		9:45
10:00	10:00	10:00	10:00	10:00	10:00
	10:15		10:15		10:15
	10:30		10:30		10:30
	10:45		10:45		10:45
11:00	11:00	11:00	11:00	11:00	11:00
	11:15		11:15		11:15
	11:30		11:30		11:30
	11:45		11:45		11:45
12:00	12:00	12:00	12:00	12:00	12:00

FIGURE

6.7 *Daily Time Sheet (continued)*

Thursday		Friday		Saturday		Sunday	
6:00	6:00	6:00	6:00	6:00	6:00	6:00	6:00
	6:15		6:15		6:15		6:15
	6:30		6:30		6:30		6:30
	6:45		6:45		6:45		6:45
7:00	7:00	7:00	7:00	7:00	7:00	7:00	7:00
	7:15		7:15		7:15		7:15
	7:30		7:30		7:30		7:30
	7:45		7:45		7:45		7:45
8:00	8:00	8:00	8:00	8:00	8:00	8:00	8:00
	8:15		8:15		8:15		8:15
	8:30		8:30		8:30		8:30
	8:45		8:45		8:45		8:45
9:00	9:00	9:00	9:00	9:00	9:00	9:00	9:00
	9:15		9:15		9:15		9:15
	9:30		9:30		9:30		9:30
	9:45		9:45		9:45		9:45
10:00	10:00	10:00	10:00	10:00	10:00	10:00	10:00
	10:15		10:15		10:15		10:15
	10:30		10:30		10:30		10:30
	10:45		10:45		10:45		10:45
11:00	11:00	11:00	11:00	11:00	11:00	11:00	11:00
	11:15		11:15		11:15		11:15
	11:30		11:30		11:30		11:30
	11:45		11:45		11:45		11:45
12:00	12:00	12:00	12:00	12:00	12:00	12:00	12:00
	12:15		12:15		12:15		12:15
	12:30		12:30		12:30		12:30
	12:45		12:45		12:45		12:45
1:00	1:00	1:00	1:00	1:00	1:00	1:00	1:00
	1:15		1:15		1:15		1:15
	1:30		1:30		1:30		1:30
	1:45		1:45		1:45		1:45
2:00	2:00	2:00	2:00	2:00	2:00	2:00	2:00
	2:15		2:15		2:15		2:15
	2:30		2:30		2:30		2:30
	2:45		2:45		2:45		2:45
3:00	3:00	3:00	3:00	3:00	3:00	3:00	3:00
	3:15		3:15		3:15		3:15
	3:30		3:30		3:30		3:30
	3:45		3:45		3:45		3:45
4:00	4:00	4:00	4:00	4:00	4:00	4:00	4:00
	4:15		4:15		4:15		4:15
	4:30		4:30		4:30		4:30
	4:45		4:45		4:45		4:45
5:00	5:00	5:00	5:00	5:00	5:00	5:00	5:00
	5:15		5:15		5:15		5:15
	5:30		5:30		5:30		5:30
	5:45		5:45		5:45		5:45
6:00	6:00	6:00	6:00	6:00	6:00	6:00	6:00
	6:15		6:15		6:15		6:15
	6:30		6:30		6:30		6:30
	6:45		6:45		6:45		6:45
7:00	7:00	7:00	7:00	7:00	7:00	7:00	7:00
	7:15		7:15		7:15		7:15
	7:30		7:30		7:30		7:30
	7:45		7:45		7:45		7:45
8:00	8:00	8:00	8:00	8:00	8:00	8:00	8:00
	8:15		8:15		8:15		8:15
	8:30		8:30		8:30		8:30
	8:45		8:45		8:45		8:45
9:00	9:00	9:00	9:00	9:00	9:00	9:00	9:00
	9:15		9:15		9:15		9:15
	9:30		9:30		9:30		9:30
	9:45		9:45		9:45		9:45
10:00	10:00	10:00	10:00	10:00	10:00	10:00	10:00
	10:15		10:15		10:15		10:15
	10:30		10:30		10:30		10:30
	10:45		10:45		10:45		10:45
11:00	11:00	11:00	11:00	11:00	11:00	11:00	11:00
	11:15		11:15		11:15		11:15
	11:30		11:30		11:30		11:30
	11:45		11:45		11:45		11:45
12:00	12:00	12:00	12:00	12:00	12:00	12:00	12:00

FOCUSING ON AND ELIMINATING DISTRACTIONS AND INTERRUPTIONS

When Is Enough Really Enough?

If you were diligent and kept an accurate account of all of your time, your evaluation probably reveals that much of your time is spent dealing with distractions, getting side-tracked, and handling interruptions. These three things account for much of the time wasted within a 24-hour period. Below, in Figure 6.8 you will find a list of some of the most common distractions faced by college students. Consider how you might deal with these distractions in an effective, assertive manner.

PLANNING AND PREPARING

Is There a Secret to Time Management?

In the past, you may have said to yourself, *"I don't have time to plan." "I don't like to be fenced in and tied to a rigid schedule." "I have so many duties that planning never works."* Scheduling does not have to be a tedious chore or something you dread. Scheduling can be your lifeline to more free time. After all, if YOU build your own schedule, it is yours! As much as you are able, build your schedule the way you want and need it.

FIGURE

6.8 *Common Distractions*

COMMON DISTRACTIONS	MY PLAN TO OVERCOME THESE DISTRACTIONS
Friends / family dropping by unexpectedly	
Technology (playing on YouTube, FaceBook, iTunes, Google, etc. . . .)	
Constant phone calls that do not pertain to anything in particular or of importance	
Not setting aside any time during the day to deal with "the unexpected"	
Friends / family demanding things of you because they do not understand your schedule or commitments	
Not blocking private time in your daily schedule	
Being unorganized and spending hours upon hours dawdling and calling it "work"	
Playing with your children or pets before your tasks are complete (and not scheduling time to be with them in the first place)	
Saying "Yes" when you need to say "NO"	
Other distractions faced by you . . .	

To manage your time successfully, you need to spend some time planning. To plan successfully, you need a calendar that has at least a week-at-a-glance or a month-at-a-glance section as well as sections for daily notes and appointments. If you have not bought a calendar, you can download one from the Internet or create one using Word or another computer program.

Planning and Organizing for School

Each evening, you should take a few minutes (and literally, that is all it will take) and sit in a quiet place and make a list of all that needs to be done tomorrow. Successful time management comes from **planning the NIGHT BEFORE!** Let's say your list includes

Research speech project	Exercise
Study, finance test on Friday	Buy birthday card for Mom
Read Chapter 13 for chemistry	Wash the car
Meet with chemistry study group	Take shirts to dry cleaner
Attend English class at 8:00 a.m.	Buy groceries
Attend mgt. class at 10:00 a.m.	Call Janice about weekend
Work from 2:00 to 6:00 p.m.	

Now you have created a list of tasks that you will face tomorrow. Next, separate this list into three categories:

MUST DO	NEED TO DO	WOULD LIKE TO DO
Read Ch. 13 for chem.	Research speech project	Wash the car
Study for finance test on Fri.	Buy birthday card for Mom	Call Janice @ w/end
Exercise	Shirts to cleaner	
English class @ 8:00	Buy groceries	
Mgt. class @ 10:00		
Meet w/chem study gp.		
Work 2:00–6:00 p.m.		

Don't get too excited yet! Your time management plan is ***NOT finished***. The most important part is still ahead of you. Now you will need to rank the items in order of their importance. You will put a 1 by the most important tasks, a 2 by the next most important tasks, etc., in each category.

MUST DO	NEED TO DO	WOULD LIKE TO DO
1 Read Ch. 13 for chem.	1 Research speech project	2 Wash the car
2 Study for finance test on Fri.	2 Buy birthday card for Mom	1 Janice @ w/end
3 Exercise	3 Shirts to cleaner	
1 English class @ 8:00	2 Buy groceries	
1 Mgt. class @ 10:00		
2 Meet w/ chem study gp.		
1 Work 2:00–6:00 p.m.		

Now you have created a PLAN to actually get these tasks done! Not only have you created your list, but you have also divided them into important categories, ranked them, and made a written commitment to these tasks.

FIGURE **6.9** *Daily Calendar*

DAY Monday		Priority	Complete?
Time	**Task**		
6:00			__ Yes __ No
6:30			__ Yes __ No
7:00	Study for finance		__ Yes __ No
7:30	↓		__ Yes __ No
8:00	English 101		__ Yes __ No
8:30			__ Yes __ No
9:00	↓		__ Yes __ No
9:30	Read Pg. 1–10 of Chem. Chapter		__ Yes __ No
10:00	Management 210		__ Yes __ No
10:30			__ Yes __ No
11:00	↓		__ Yes __ No
11:30	Finish Reading Chem. Chapter		__ Yes __ No
12:00			__ Yes __ No
12:30	↓		__ Yes __ No
1:00	Meet w/Chemistry group (take lunch)		__ Yes __ No
1:30	↓		__ Yes __ No
2:00	Work		__ Yes __ No
2:30			__ Yes __ No
3:00			__ Yes __ No
3:30			__ Yes __ No
4:00			__ Yes __ No
4:30			__ Yes __ No
5:00			__ Yes __ No
5:30			__ Yes __ No
6:00			__ Yes __ No
6:30	Dinner/run by grocery store		__ Yes __ No
7:00	↓		__ Yes __ No
7:30	Internet Research for speech		__ Yes __ No
8:00	↓		__ Yes __ No
8:30	↓		__ Yes __ No
9:00	call Janice @ w/end		__ Yes __ No
9:30			__ Yes __ No

Now, take these tasks and write them into your daily calendar (see Figure 6.9). You would schedule category 1 (MUST DO) first, category 2 (NEED TO DO) next, and category 3 (WOULD LIKE TO DO) next. Remember, NEVER keep more than one calendar. Always carry it with you and always schedule your tasks immediately so that you won't forget them.

STRESS? I DON'T HAVE ENOUGH TIME FOR STRESS!

Do You Feel Like You're Going to Explode?

The word *stress* is derived from the Latin word *strictus,* meaning "to draw tight." Stress is your body's response to people and events in your life; it is the mental and physical wear and tear on your body as a result of everyday life and all that you have to accomplish. Stress is inevitable,

ESSENTIAL CORNERSTONE

Creativity:
How can managing your time more effectively, thus reducing stress, help you become a more creative person?

Social Networking Moment:
Share your response to this Essential Cornerstone with peers in your social network. Choose two responses from your peers and respond to their postings.

but it is not in itself bad. It is your response to stress that determines whether it is good stress (*eustress*) or bad stress (*distress*). The same event can provoke eustress or distress, depending on the person experiencing the event; just as "one person's trash is another's treasure," so one person's eustress may be another person's distress.

The primary difference between eustress and distress is your body's response. It is impossible to exist in a totally stress-free environment; in fact, some stress is important to your health and well-being. Good stress can help you become more motivated and even more productive. It helps your energy level, too. It is only when stress gets out of hand that your body becomes distressed.

FIGURE 6.10   *Test Your Stress*

Take the following **Stress Assessment** to determine the level of distress you are currently experiencing in your life. Check the items that reflect your behavior at home, work, or school, or in a social setting.

☐ 1. Your stomach tightens when you think about your schoolwork and all that you have to do.
☐ 2. You are not able to sleep at night.
☐ 3. You race from place to place trying to get everything done that is required of you.
☐ 4. Small things make you angry.
☐ 5. At the end of the day, you are frustrated that you did not accomplish all that you needed to do.
☐ 6. You get tired throughout the day.
☐ 7. You need some type of drug, alcohol, or tobacco to get through the day.
☐ 8. You often find it hard to be around people.
☐ 9. You don't take care of yourself physically or mentally.
☐ 10. You tend to keep everything inside.
☐ 11. You overreact.
☐ 12. You fail to find the humor in many situations others see as funny.
☐ 13. You do not eat properly.
☐ 14. Everything upsets you.
☐ 15. You are impatient and get angry when you have to wait for things.
☐ 16. You don't trust others.
☐ 17. You feel that most people move too slowly for you.
☐ 18. You feel guilty when you take time for yourself or your friends.
☐ 19. You interrupt people so that you can tell them your side of the story.
☐ 20. You experience memory loss.

Total Number of Check Marks

0–5 = Low, manageable stress

6–10 = Moderate stress

11+ = High stress, could cause medical or emotional problems

Some physical signs of distress are:

Headaches	Muscular tension and pain	Fatigue
Coughs	Abdominal pain and diarrhea	Mental disorders
Dry mouth	Hypertension and chest pain	Insomnia
Impotence	Heartburn and indigestion	Suicidal tendencies
Twitching/Trembling	Abdominal pain	Apprehension
Jitters	Diminished performance	Decreased coping ability

If you begin to experience any of these reactions for an extended period of time, you know that your body and mind are probably suffering from undue stress, anxiety, and pressure. This can lead to a very unhealthy situation. You may even require medical attention for hypertension.

I DON'T THINK I FEEL SO WELL

What Is the Relationship Among Poor Time Management, Monumental Stress, and Your Health?

There are probably as many stressors in this world as there are people alive. For some people, loud music causes stress. For others, a hectic day at the office, with people demanding things and equipment breaking down, causes stress. For others, that loud music and busy day at the office are just what the doctor ordered—they love it and thrive off of the energy and demands. For some people, being idle and sitting around reading a book cause stress, while others long for a moment of peace walking on the beach or just sitting out in the backyard with a good book. One thing is for sure: Poor planning and "running out of time" are on most people's lists of major stressors.

Most stress does not "just happen" to us. We allow it to happen by not planning our day or week. We allow our "to do" list to get out of hand (or we do not create a to-do list), and before we know it, our lives are out of control because of all the activities we are required to accomplish or because of all the things we agreed to by saying "Yes." Because of poor planning and procrastination, we become anxious and nervous about not getting it all done. By planning, prioritizing, and developing an action strategy, we can actually lower our stress level and improve our general, overall health and our memory.

Medical research has shown that exposure to stress over a long period of time can be damaging to one's body. Many of the physical and mental symptoms of stress are previously mentioned, but consider these effects as well: Stress can also have an effect on *memory*. When you are stressed, your brain releases *cortisol*, which has effects on the neurons in your brain. Over time, cortisol can be toxic and damage parts of the hippocampus—the part of the brain that deals with memory and learning. Therefore, learning to control stress through managing your time more effectively can be a key to better memory. In Chapter 5, "Think," we discussed the amygdala (the part of the brain that causes "fight or flight"). The amygdala is also affected negatively by prolonged stress, causing you to say and do things you regret later.

Other physical symptoms include *exhaustion,* where one part of the body weakens and shifts its responsibility to another part and causes complete failure of key organ functions.

Have you ever allowed procrastination to stress you out? What was the result?

Tips for Personal Success

Consider the following tips for dealing with and reducing stress in your life:

▶ Use relaxation techniques such as visualization, listening to music, and practicing yoga.

▶ Let minor hassles and annoyances go. Ask yourself, *"Is this situation worth a heart attack, stroke, or high blood pressure?"*

▶ Don't be afraid to take a break. Managing your time can help you take more relaxation breaks.

Now, it is your turn. Create a list of at least two more tips that you would offer a fellow classmate to assist him or her with reducing unhealthy stress in his or her life.

1. _____

2. _____

Chronic muscle pain and malfunction are also caused by unchecked stress. "Chronically tense muscles also result in numerous stress-related disorders including headaches, backaches, spasms of the esophagus and colon (causing diarrhea and constipation), posture problems, asthma, tightness in the throat and chest cavity, some eye problems, lockjaw, muscle tears and pulls, and perhaps rheumatoid arthritis" (Girdano et al., 2009).

As you can see from this medical research, stress is not something that you can just ignore and hope it will go away. It is not something that is overblown and insignificant. It is a real, bona fide condition that can cause many physical and mental problems from simple exhaustion to death. By learning how to recognize the signs of stress, what causes you to be "stressed out," and effectively dealing with your stress, you can actually control many of the negative physical and emotional side effects caused by prolonged stress. Examine Figure 6.11.

FIGURE

6.11 *Three Types of Major Stressors in Life*

TYPE	CAUSE	WHAT YOU CAN DO TO REDUCE STRESS
SITUATIONAL		
	Change in physical environment	▶ If at all possible, change your residence or physical environment to better suit your needs. If you can't change it, talk to the people involved and explain your feelings.
	Change in social environment	▶ Work hard to meet new friends who support you and upon whom you can rely in times of need. ▶ Get involved in some type of school activity. ▶ Enroll in classes with friends and find a campus support group.
	Daily hassles	▶ Try to keep things in perspective and work to reduce the things that you allow to stress you out. ▶ Allow time in your schedule for unexpected events. ▶ Find a quiet place to relax and study.
	Poor time management	▶ Work out a time management plan that allows time to get your projects complete while allowing time for rest and joy, too. ▶ Create "to do" lists.

FIGURE

6.11 *Three Types of Major Stressors in Life (continued)*

TYPE	CAUSE	WHAT YOU CAN DO TO REDUCE STRESS
SITUATIONAL		
	Conflicts at work, home, and school	▶ Read about conflict management (Chapter 4 in this text) and realize that conflict can be managed. ▶ Avoid "hot" topics such as religion or politics if you feel this causes you to engage in conflicts. ▶ Be assertive, not aggressive or rude.
	People	▶ Try to avoid people who stress you out. ▶ Put people into perspective and realize that we're all different with different needs, wants, and desires. ▶ Realize that everyone is not going to be like you.
	Relationships	▶ Work hard to develop healthy, positive relationships. ▶ Move away from toxic, unhealthy relationships and people who bring you down. ▶ Understand that you can NEVER change the way another person feels, acts, or thinks.
	Death of a loved one	▶ Try to focus on the good times you shared and what they meant to your life. ▶ Remember that death is as much a part of life as living. ▶ Talk about the person with your friends and family—share your memories. ▶ Consider what the deceased person would have wanted you to do.
	Financial problems	▶ Cut back on your spending. Seek the help of a financial planner. ▶ Determine why your financial planning or spending patterns are causing you problems. ▶ Apply for financial assistance.
PSYCHOLOGICAL		
	Unrealistic expectations	▶ Surround yourself with positive people and work hard to set realistic goals with doable timelines and results. ▶ Expect and anticipate less.
	Homesickness	▶ Surround yourself with people who support you. ▶ Call or visit home as often as you can until you get more comfortable. ▶ Meet new friends on campus through organizations and clubs.

(continued)

FIGURE

6.11 *Three Types of Major Stressors in Life (continued)*

TYPE	CAUSE	WHAT YOU CAN DO TO REDUCE STRESS
PSYCHOLOGICAL		
	Fear	▶ Talk to professors, counselors, family, and friends about your fears. Put them into perspective. ▶ Visualize success and not failure. ▶ Do one thing every day that scares you to expand your comfort zone.
	Anxiety over your future and what is going to happen	▶ Put things into perspective and work hard to plan and prepare, but accept that life is about constant change. ▶ Talk to a counselor or advisor about your future plans and develop a strategy to meet your goals. ▶ Don't try to control the uncontrollable.
	Anxiety over your past	▶ Try to see the big picture and how "the puzzle" is going to come together. ▶ Work hard to overcome past challenges and remember that your past does not have to dictate your future. ▶ Learn to forgive. ▶ Focus on your future and what you really want to accomplish.
BIOLOGICAL		
	Insomnia	▶ Watch your caffeine intake. ▶ Avoid naps. ▶ Do not exercise two hours prior to your normal bedtime. ▶ Complete all of your activities before going to bed (studying, watching TV, e-mailing, texting, etc.) Your bed is for sleeping.
	Anxiety	▶ Laugh more. Share a joke. ▶ Enjoy your friends and family. ▶ Practice breathing exercises. ▶ Talk it out with friends. ▶ Learn to say "No" and then do it. ▶ Turn off the TV if the news makes you anxious or nervous.
	Weight loss/gain	▶ Develop an exercise and healthy eating plan. ▶ Meet with a nutrition specialist on campus or in the community. ▶ Join a health-related club or group.

FIGURE **6.11** *Three Types of Major Stressors in Life (continued)*

TYPE	CAUSE	WHAT YOU CAN DO TO REDUCE STRESS
BIOLOGICAL		
	Reduced physical activities	▶ Increase your daily activity. ▶ If possible, walk to class instead of drive. ▶ Take the stairs instead of the elevator.
	Sexual difficulties/ dysfunction	▶ Seek medical help in case something is physically wrong. ▶ Determine if your actions are in contradiction with you value system.

CHANGING IDEAS TO *Reality*

REFLECTIONS ON TIME AND STRESS MANAGEMENT

Managing your time and reducing your levels of stress are two skills that you will need for the rest of your life. By learning to avoid procrastinating and taking the time to enhance the quality of your life, you are actually increasing your staying power as a college student. Further, as you enter the world of work, both of these skills will be necessary for your success. Technological advances, fewer people doing more work, and pressure to perform at unprecedented levels can put your life in a tailspin, but with the ability to plan your time and reduce your own stress level, you are making a contribution to your own success.

As you continue this term in college and work toward managing your time and stress levels, consider the following ideas:

▶ Make a to-do list every evening to plan for the next day.

▶ Always include time for friends, joy, and adventure in your schedule.

▶ Avoid procrastination by practicing the "Just Do It" mentality.

▶ Work hard to lose the "Superhuman" and perfectionist attitudes.

▶ Delegate everything that you can.

▶ Plan your day and week to avoid becoming too stressed.

▶ To reduce stress, take a few moments to relax in private.

▶ When stress is overwhelming, take time to decompress.

Good luck to you as you develop your plan for managing your time and stress.

"I wanted a perfect ending. Now I've learned, the hard way, that some poems don't rhyme, and some stories don't have a clear beginning, middle and end. Life is about knowing, having to change, taking the moment and making the best of it without knowing what is going to happen next."
—Gilda Radner

KNOWLEDGE in BLOOM

Reducing Stress In Your Everyday Life

Each chapter-end assessment is based on *Bloom's Taxonomy of Learning*. See the inside front cover for a quick review.

UTILIZES LEVELS 4, 5, AND 6 OF THE TAXONOMY

Take a moment and examine your academic and personal life right now. You probably have many things going on and may feel as if you're torn in many directions.

If you had to list the one major stress in your life at this moment, what would it be?

_____

_____

Why is this a major cause of stress in your life? _____

_____

_____

Are there other people or things contributing to this stress? In other words, is someone or something making the matter worse? If so, who or what?

_____

_____

In Chapter 1, you learned to write a narrative statement. This is the statement that "paints a verbal picture" of how your life is going to look once a goal is reached. Reflect for a moment and then write a paragraph predicting how your life would change if this major source of stress was gone from your life. Be realistic and optimistic.

_____

_____

_____

_____

_____

_____

_____

_____

_____

As you know, accomplishing anything requires action. Now that you have a picture of how your life would look if this stress was gone, develop a plan from beginning to end to eliminate this stressor from your life.

Step 1 _____

_____

Step 2 _____

_____

Step 3 _____

_____

Step 4 _____

_____

Step 5 _____

_____

SQ3R *Mastery* STUDY SHEET

EXAMPLE QUESTION *(from page 133)* How can I simplify my life and get more done?	**ANSWER:**
EXAMPLE QUESTION *(from page 129)* What are the components of self-discipline?	**ANSWER:**
AUTHOR QUESTION *(from page 129)* What is self-discipline and how is it related to time management?	**ANSWER:**
AUTHOR QUESTION *(from page 131)* What are the benefits of learning how to say no?	**ANSWER:**
AUTHOR QUESTION *(from page 133)* What are three strategies to effective time management and planning?	**ANSWER:**
AUTHOR QUESTION *(from page 147)* How does good stress differ from bad stress?	**ANSWER:**
AUTHOR QUESTION *(from page 149)* What are some of the physical and mental symptoms of stress?	**ANSWER:**
YOUR QUESTION *(from page ____)*	**ANSWER:**
YOUR QUESTION *(from page ____)*	**ANSWER:**
YOUR QUESTION *(from page ____)*	**ANSWER:**
YOUR QUESTION *(from page ____)*	**ANSWER:**
YOUR QUESTION *(from page ____)*	**ANSWER:**

Finally, after answering these questions, recite this chapter's major points in your mind. Consider the following general questions to help you master this material.

- ► What was it about?
- ► What does it mean?
- ► What was the most important thing I learned? Why?
- ► What were the key points to remember?

CHAPTER 7
LEARN

USING YOUR
DOMINANT
INTELLIGENCE,
PREFERRED
LEARNING
STYLE, AND
UNIQUE
PERSONALITY
TYPE TO
BECOME AN
ACTIVE
LEARNER

"We are led to truth by our weaknesses as well as our strengths."
—Parker Palmer

WHY READ THIS CHAPTER?

What's in it for me?

Why? Because discovering how "*TO* LEARN" and discovering how "*YOU* LEARN" are two of the most important things you will ever do for yourself as a college student. Learning **how TO learn** means that you know where to find information, how to store information in your brain so that it is easily retrievable, and how to make connections between one thing and another. Learning **how you learn** means that you know your own learning style, your primary intelligence, and your personality type and understand how to apply these characteristics to various learning situations. Knowing how you learn also affects the way you approach the task of mastering content. It is a dynamic discovery that will help you change your academic performance.

By carefully reading this chapter and taking the information provided seriously, you will be able to:

1. Define learning and discuss several historical learning theories.
2. Identify and discuss the steps in the learning process.
3. Identify and use your learning style to increase active and authentic learning.
4. Identify and use your primary intelligence to increase active and authentic learning.
5. Identify and use your personality type to increase active and authentic learning.

WHY is it important to understand what some old guy said about learning theory? *WHY* do I need to know my personality type? *WHY* will a chapter on discovering my learning style and dominant intelligence help me study better? *WHY* is it important to know the difference between my learning style and a learning strategy?

CHAPTER 7 / LEARN

"Learn everything you can, anytime you can, from anyone you can—there will always come a time when you will be grateful you did."

—Sarah Caldwell

NAME: Sakinah Pendergrass
INSTITUTION: The Art Institute of Philadelphia, Philadelphia, PA
MAJOR: Hospitality—Culinary Arts
AGE: 27

There were times when I thought I might not make it. I struggled with some of my classes and had a few problems that almost sidetracked me, but I was determined to be a success and after my first term, I was determined to do whatever was necessary to learn how to study, how to process information, and how to make that information "stick." I had not had much success with this in the past and I quickly learned that it was because I did not know how I learned best.

I quickly found that learning *how I learn* was very important to every aspect of my academic life. When you're going to college, working, studying, and trying to have a life, your time is limited and valuable. Learning how to learn and learning how to use your memory correctly are two very important aspects of success. I found that I am a tactile and visual learner and this has helped me greatly. I know that classes where I do not have the opportunity to have a "hands-on approach" will require me to work harder. I learned that it also takes me longer to process information when the lecture is all I have to go on. The student success class I took showed me how to make the best of this situation by creating charts and pictures in my notes. I also found that using color is important to my retention as well.

I have found that for me, my classes in culinary arts are easiest—certainly because this is my major and I enjoy them, but also because these classes are very tactile. We don't just listen to a lecture, we actually "do" things. The more I can do and see, the better I learn. Whatever your learning style, discover it, use it to your best advantage, and work hard to develop skills to get you through the classes that do not match your learning or memory style. By keeping this in mind, I am constantly working hard to overcome any barriers where my learning style and the professor's teaching style do not match.

This chapter will give you the opportunity to discover your learning style, dominant intelligence, and personality type. When you discover which style and type you are, things will begin to change for you and you will have the tools necessary to make some important decisions about learning.

SCAN & QUESTION

In the preface of this book (page xix), you read about the **SQ3R Study Method.** Right now, take a few moments, **scan this chapter**, and on page 183 write **five questions** that you think will be important to your mastery of this material. In addition to the two questions below, you will find five questions from your authors. Use one of your **"Study for Quiz"** stickers to flag this page for easy reference.

EXAMPLES:

▶ **What is the difference between a learning style and a learning strategy?** (from page 172)

▶ **What is the definition of tactile learning and how do you use it?** (from page 177)

Objective listening can be a difficult skill to learn. Have you encountered people with views radically different from your own? How do you respond?

WE HOPE YOU LEARNED YOUR LESSON!

What Is This Thing Called Learning, Anyway?

In its purest and simplest form, learning is a ***cognitive mental action*** in which new information is acquired or in which you learn to use old information in a new way. Learning can be ***conscious*** and/or ***unconscious***. Do you remember the very day you learned how to walk or talk? Probably not. This learning was more of an unconscious nature. However, you probably do remember learning about the 50 states or subtraction or reading an Edgar Allan Poe poem for the first time. This learning was more conscious in nature. Learning can also be ***formal*** (schooling) or ***informal*** ("street knowledge"). Learning can happen in many ways such as through play, trial and error, mistakes, successes, repetition, environmental conditioning, parental discipline, social interactions, media, observation, and, yes, through formal study methods.

Learning is what you do ***FOR*** yourself; it is not done ***TO*** you. Parents may discipline you time and time and time again, but try as they might, until YOU learn the lesson trying to be taught, it will NOT be learned. Teachers can preach and talk until they are blue in the face about the 13 original colonies, but until you learn them and commit them to memory, they will NOT be learned. That is what this chapter is all about—helping you discover how you learn, why you learn, and assisting you in finding the best way to learn so that you can DO the learning for yourself on a more effective level.

What Do the Experts Say?

The question still begs: ***HOW do we really learn?*** By studying a textbook? By reading a newspaper? By looking at pictures? By interviewing someone about a topic? By watching a movie? By trying something to see if it works? Yes, but the process is much more complex than this. Around 300 BC, the great Greek philosopher Socrates introduced his theory of learning. He believed that we learn by asking questions. This is called the Socratic Method. His student, Plato, expanded on this theory, believing that we learn best by dialogue, called the Dialectic Method, which involves "the searcher" beginning a conversation on a topic and having a dialogue with "an expert" on the other side. He believed that through this back-and-forth conversation, knowledge could be acquired.

In the 5th century BC, the Chinese philosopher Lao-Tse wrote, *"If you tell me, I will listen. If you show me, I will see. But if you let me experience, I will learn."* He was one of the first to proclaim that active, involved learning was a viable form of acquiring information. Kung Fu-tse (Confucius) first introduced the case study, which includes telling stories or parables and then having people discuss the issues or the case to learn and acquire knowledge. In 1690, the English philosopher John Locke introduced the theory of "the blank slate." He believed that all humans were born with empty minds and that we learn information about the world through what our senses bring to us (sensory learning). He felt that learning was like a pyramid—we learn the basics and then build on those simple principles until we can master complex ideas.

In the 1760s, the French philosopher Jean-Jacques Rousseau expanded on a theory that suggested that people learn best by experiencing rather

"The mind is not a vessel to be filled, but rather a fire to be kindled."
—Plutarch

than by authority. In other words, we learn best by doing something rather than being told how someone else did it. He was the first to thoroughly introduce the concept of individual learning styles, believing that learning should be natural to us and follow our basic instincts and feelings. In the early 1900s, the American psychologist J. B. Watson developed the theory of behaviorism, believing that we learn best by conditioning. His theory was based on that of Pavlov (and his dog) and held the tenant that we act and learn in certain ways because we have been conditioned to do so. If a dog (or a person) is fed when it rings a bell, the dog (or the person) quickly learns to ring the bell when it *wants* to be fed.

In the mid 1900s, Swiss psychologist Jean Piaget introduced the groundbreaking theory of holistic learning. This theory is widely held today as one of the most important breakthroughs in educational psychology. Piaget believed that we learn best by experiencing a wide variety of stimuli such as reading, listening, experimenting, exploring, and questioning. In 1956, Benjamin Bloom introduced his taxonomy (modeled and discussed in this text on page 25). Bloom believed in a mastery approach to learning. This theory suggests that we learn simple information and then transform that information into more complex ideas, solutions, and creations. His was an idea of learning how to process and actually use information in a meaningful way.

As you can see from these historical experts in the fields of learning, educational psychology, and philosophy, there are many theories on just HOW we learn best. Perhaps the most important thing to take from these examples is tied into Jean Piaget's theory of holistic learning—that as individuals with diverse and varied needs, backgrounds, and experiences, we require a variety of stimuli to help us learn and that we all learn differently at different stages in our lives.

> "Many things in life cannot be transmitted well by words, concepts, or books. Colors that we see cannot be described to a person born blind. Only a swimmer knows how swimming feels; the non-swimmer can get only the faintest idea of it with all the words and books in the world. And so it goes. Perhaps it is better to say that all of life must first be known experientially. There is no substitute for experience, none at all."
> —Abraham H. Maslow

GIVE YOUR BRAIN A WORKOUT

Can I Really Learn All This Stuff?

YES! YES! YES! YOU CAN LEARN! Think about all that you have already learned in your lifetime. You learned how to eat, walk, talk, play, make decisions, dress yourself, have a conversation, tie your shoes, make your bed, ride a bicycle, play a sport, drive a car, protect yourself, make associations based on observations, use a cell phone, play a video game, ask questions, and countless other simple and highly complex skills. The *proof* that you **CAN learn** is that you **HAVE learned** in the past. The old excuse of *"I can't learn this stuff"* is simply hogwash! You have the capacity to know more, do more, experience more, and acquire more knowledge. Your brain is a natural learning machine just as your heart is a natural pumping machine. It is in our nature to learn every single day. You just have to understand how this process works in order to make the most of your brain's natural learning power. And you have to **devote the time necessary to learn** the basics of something new and then build on that knowledge base. Time and effort are very important aspects of the learning process.

You also have to give your brain a "workout" to make sure it stays in shape. Just as your body needs exercise and activities to stay in shape, your brain does too. When you "work out" your brain and use it to learn new material, your brain releases a chemical called **cypin** (SIGH-pin). Cypin is found throughout the body, but in the brain, it helps build new branches, like a tree sprouting new growth. In a nutshell, when you exercise your brain, your brain rewards you with new learning patterns and new learning receptors. This is sometimes referred to as **neuroplasticity** (new-ro-plas-TIS-i-ty), or the brain's ability to change with new knowledge.

THE LEARNING PROCESS

What Are the Steps to Active, Authentic Learning?

"Human beings have an innate learning process, which includes a motivation to learn" (Smilkstein, 2003). You may be saying to yourself, *"If I have a natural, innate ability to learn, then why is chemistry so difficult for me to master?"* or *"Why is English such a crazy language with so many rules?"* The answer to both could rest in the notion that you are going AGAINST your natural, neurological learning pattern—that you are being taught, or are trying to learn by yourself, in a way that is unnatural to you, and your brain simply is having trouble adapting to this unnatural process.

If you learn best by doing and touching, ***you need to do and touch***. If you learn best by listening and questioning, you need to ***listen and question***. If you learn best by reading and studying in a quiet place, you need to ***find a quiet place to read and study***. Basically, you must figure out your natural inclination for learning and build on it. You will also need to understand that learning takes time and that people need different amounts of time to master material. Janet may learn Concept X in a few hours, but it may take William three days of constant practice to learn the same concept. One thing is true for everyone: The more INVOLVED you are with the information you are trying to learn, the more you will retain.

In Figure 7.1 and the exercise shown in Figure 7.2, we have tried to simplify thousands of years of educational study on the topic of learning. Basically, learning something new can happen in the six steps outlined in Figure 7.1.

If you are trying to learn new facts, concepts, procedures, principles, systems, solutions, or processes, you could achieve this goal by using these six steps. Take a moment and carefully review them now.

As a practice activity, research one of the following topics (all of which we purposefully chose because of their uniqueness . . . OK, weirdness) using the six steps in the Learning Process chart (Figure 7.1). You can do this in your notebook or online journal. Remember, however, that you will need to devote some time to this activity. Learning new information does not happen instantaneously. You will also need to use a variety of sources. Do not depend solely on Wikipedia! Yes, there are other sources out there!

BLOOM LEVEL 2 QUESTION

Possible topics:

▶ What was The Night of Long Knives?

▶ What is the mystery of the pyramid at Cheops?

▶ Why and how long can a cockroach live without a head?

▶ Who invented the electric chair and why?

▶ What is Sanskrit?

▶ How is paper made?

▶ Who invented the zero and what is its duel function?

▶ Who was Vlad the Impaler? What famous character did his life inspire?

UNDERSTANDING YOUR STRENGTHS

What Are the Advantages of Discovering and Polishing Your Talents?

On the next few pages, you will have the opportunity to complete three inventories: one to identify your **learning style**, one to identify your **personality type**, and one to identify your **dominant in-**

FIGURE

7.1   *The Learning Process*

1. Motivation to learn the material is the first step in the learning process. You have to possess the internal motivation and passion to WANT to learn what is being presented or what you are studying. You must also be motivated enough to devote the time to learning something new. Deep, purposeful learning does not happen in an instant; it takes work, patience and yes, motivation.

2. Understand the material through ambitious curiousity, keen observations, purposeful questioning, intense studying, eager determination, robust effort, and time devoted to task. You must answer questions such as: Who is involved? What happened? When did it happen? Where did it happen? How did it happen? How could it have happened? What does it all mean? Why is it important? What is the relationship between x and y? You should be able to describe it, discuss it, give examples, put the information into your own words, and tell others about it clearly.

3. Internalizie the material by asking: How can this information affect my life, my career, my studies, and my future? Why does this information matter? How can I control my emotions regarding the value of this information? If I think this information is useless, how can I change this perception?

4. Apply the material by asking: How can I use this information to improve? How can I use this information to work with others, to develop new ideas, or to build meaningful conclusions? Can I demonstrate it? Can I share this information with, or teach this information to, others intelligently? Is it possible to practice what I have learned?

5. Evaluate the material by determining the value of what I just learned. Do I trust my research and sources? Have I consulted others about their findings and knowledge? What did they learn? What can I learn from them? Have I asked for feedback? Can I debate this information with others?

6. Use the material to grow and change. How could I take this information (or the process of learning this information) and change my life, attitudes, or emotions? How could this information help me grow? What can I create out of this new information? How can I expand on this knowledge to learn more?

telligence. At the end of the chapter, you will have the opportunity to pull all of this information together to help you understand your learning patterns and to formulate a learning plan for the future.

These assessments are in no way intended to "label you." They are not a measure of how smart you are. They do not measure your worth or your capacities as a student or a citizen. The three assessments are included so that you might gain a better understanding of your dominant intelligence, identify your learning style, and discover your strongest personality type.

There are no right or wrong answers and there is no one best way to learn. We hope that by the end of this chapter, you will have experienced a "Wow" or "Ah-ha!" moment as you explore and discover new and exciting components of your education. We also hope that by the end of this chapter, you will have the skills you need to more effectively use your dominant traits and improve your less dominant characteristics.

7.2 *Take the MIS*

The Multiple Intelligences Survey
© *Robert M. Sherfield, Ph.D.*

Directions: Read each statement carefully and thoroughly. After reading the statement, rate your response using the scale below. There are no right or wrong answers. This is not a timed survey. The MIS is based, in part, on *Frames of Mind* by Howard Gardner, 1983.

3 = Often Applies

2 = Sometimes Applies

1 = Never or Almost Never Applies

____ 1. When someone gives me directions, I have to visualize them in my mind in order to understand them.

____ 2. I enjoy crossword puzzles and word games like Scrabble.

____ 3. I enjoy dancing and can keep up with the beat of music.

____ 4. I have little or no trouble conceptualizing information or facts.

____ 5. I like to repair things that are broken such as toasters, small engines, bicycles, and cars.

____ 6. I enjoy leadership activities on campus and in the community.

____ 7. I have the ability to get others to listen to me.

____ 8. I enjoy working with nature, animals, and plants.

____ 9. I know where everything is in my home such as supplies, gloves, flashlights, camera, and compact discs.

____10. I am a good speller.

____11. I often sing or hum to myself in the shower or car or while walking or just sitting.

____12. I am a very logical, orderly thinker.

____13. I use a lot of gestures when I talk to people.

____14. I can recognize and empathize with people's attitudes and emotions.

____15. I prefer to study alone.

____16. I can name many different things in the environment such as clouds, rocks, and plant types.

____17. I like to draw pictures, graphs, or charts to better understand information.

____18. I have a good memory for names and dates.

____19. When I hear music, I "get into it" by moving, humming, tapping, or even singing.

____20. I learn better by asking a lot of questions.

____21. I enjoy playing competitive sports.

____22. I communicate very well with other people.

____23. I know what I want and I set goals to accomplish it.

____24. I have some interest in herbal remedies and natural medicine.

____25. I enjoy working puzzles or mazes.

____26. I am a good storyteller.

____27. I can easily remember the words and melodies of songs.

____28. I enjoy solving problems in math and chemistry and working with computer programming problems.

____29. I usually touch people or pat them on the back when I talk to them.

____30. I understand my family and friends better than most other people do.

____31. I don't always talk about my accomplishments with others.

____32. I would rather work outside around nature than inside around people and equipment.

____33. I enjoy and learn more when seeing movies, slides, or videos in class.

____34. I am a very good listener and I enjoy listening to others' stories.

____35. I need to study with music.

____36. I enjoy games like Clue, Battleship, chess, and Rubik's Cube.

FIGURE

7.2   *Take the MIS (continued)*

____37. I enjoy physical activities such as bicycling, jogging, dancing, snowboarding, skateboarding, or swimming.

____38. I am good at solving people's problems and conflicts.

____39. I have to have time alone to think about new information in order to remember it.

____40. I enjoy sorting and organizing information, objects, and collectibles.

Refer to your score on each individual question. Place that score beside the appropriate question number below. Then, tally each line at the side.

Score					Total Across	Code
1____	9____	17____	25____	33____	_____	Visual/Spatial
2____	10____	18____	26____	34____	_____	Verbal/Linguistic
3____	11____	19____	27____	35____	_____	Musical/Rhythm
4____	12____	20____	28____	36____	_____	Logic/Math
5____	13____	21____	29____	37____	_____	Body/Kinesthetic
6____	14____	22____	30____	38____	_____	Interpersonal
7____	15____	23____	31____	39____	_____	Intrapersonal
8____	16____	24____	32____	40____	_____	Naturalistic

MIS Tally

Multiple Intelligences

Look at the scores on the MIS. What are your top three scores? Write them in the spaces below.

Top Score _____   Code _____

Second Score _____   Code _____

Third Score _____   Code _____

This tally can help you understand where some of your strengths may be. Again, this is not a measure of your worth or capacities, nor is it an indicator of your future successes. Read the following section to better understand multiple intelligences.

UNDERSTANDING MULTIPLE INTELLIGENCES

Why Is It Important to Discover New Ways of Looking at Yourself?

In 1983, Howard Gardner, a Harvard University professor, developed a theory called Multiple Intelligences. In his book *Frames of Mind,* he outlines seven intelligences that he feels are possessed by everyone: visual/spatial, verbal/linguistic, musical/rhythm, logic/math, body/kinesthetic, interpersonal, and intrapersonal. In 1996, he added an eighth intelligence: naturalistic. In short, if you have ever done things that came easily for you, you were probably drawing on one of your well-developed intelligences. On the other hand, if you have tried to do things that are very difficult to master or understand, you may be dealing with material that calls on one of your less developed intelligences. If playing the piano by ear comes easily to you, your musical/rhythm intelligence may be very strong. If you have trouble writing or understanding poetry, your verbal/linguistic intelligence may not be as well developed. This does not mean that you will never be able to write poetry; it simply means that this is not your dominant intelligence and you may need to spend more time on this activity.

DID YOU KNOW

PABLO PICASSO, the world-renowned, trend-setting artist, was born in Spain. He had a hard time in school and is said to have had a very difficult time with reading. He was diagnosed with a learning disability and his formal education never really benefited him. He left his college-level courses at the Academy of Arts in Madrid after less than a year of study. However, because of his immense artistic talent and his cubist interpretation of the universe, he changed the way the world looks at art. He is listed in the *Guinness Book of World Records* as THE most prolific painter in history, having completed nearly 14,000 paintings.

FIGURE **7.3** *The Eight Intelligences*

VISUAL/SPATIAL
- Picture Smart
- Thinks in pictures; knows where things are in the house; loves to create images and work with graphs, charts, pictures, and maps.

VERBAL/LINGUISTIC
- Word Smart
- Communicates well through language, likes to write, is good at spelling, great at telling stories, loves to read books.

MUSICAL/RHYTHM
- Music Smart
- Loves to sing, hum, and whistle; comprehends music; responds to music immediately; performs music.

LOGICAL/MATHEMATICAL
- Number Smart
- Can easily conceptualize and reason, uses logic, has good problem-solving skills, enjoys math and science.

BODY/KINESTHETIC
- Body Smart
- Learns through body sensation, moves around a lot, enjoys work involving the hands, is graced with some athletic ability.

INTERPERSONAL
- People Smart
- Loves to communicate with other people, possesses great leadership skills, has lots of friends, is involved in extracurricular activities.

INTRAPERSONAL
- Self Smart
- Has a deep awareness of own feelings, is very reflective, requires time to be alone, does not get involved with group activities.

NATURALISTIC
- Environment Smart
- Has interest in the environment and in nature; can easily recognize plants, animals, rocks, and cloud formations; may like hiking, camping, and fishing.

USING MULTIPLE INTELLIGENCES TO ENHANCE STUDYING AND LEARNING

Can You Make Them Work for You?

In Figure 7.4, you will find some helpful tips to assist you in creating a study environment and study habits using your multiple intelligences. Read each category because you may need to improve your less dominant intelligence in some of the classes you take. This list can help you build on your strengths and develop your less dominant areas.

FIGURE **7.4** *Using the Multiple Intelligences*

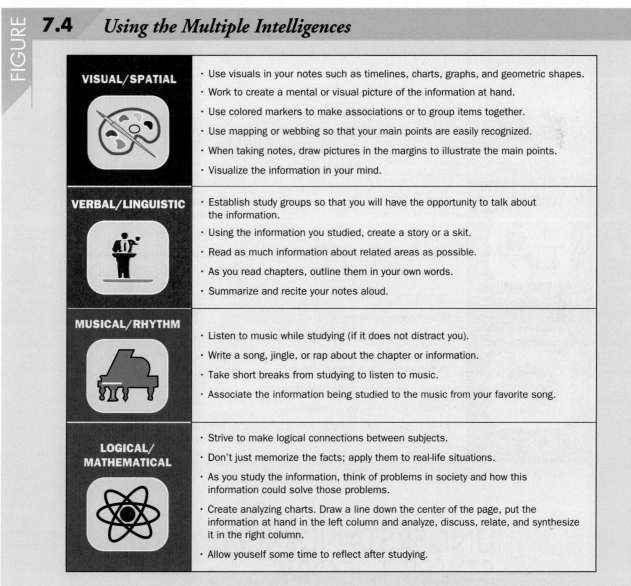

VISUAL/SPATIAL
- Use visuals in your notes such as timelines, charts, graphs, and geometric shapes.
- Work to create a mental or visual picture of the information at hand.
- Use colored markers to make associations or to group items together.
- Use mapping or webbing so that your main points are easily recognized.
- When taking notes, draw pictures in the margins to illustrate the main points.
- Visualize the information in your mind.

VERBAL/LINGUISTIC
- Establish study groups so that you will have the opportunity to talk about the information.
- Using the information you studied, create a story or a skit.
- Read as much information about related areas as possible.
- As you read chapters, outline them in your own words.
- Summarize and recite your notes aloud.

MUSICAL/RHYTHM
- Listen to music while studying (if it does not distract you).
- Write a song, jingle, or rap about the chapter or information.
- Take short breaks from studying to listen to music.
- Associate the information being studied to the music from your favorite song.

LOGICAL/ MATHEMATICAL
- Strive to make logical connections between subjects.
- Don't just memorize the facts; apply them to real-life situations.
- As you study the information, think of problems in society and how this information could solve those problems.
- Create analyzing charts. Draw a line down the center of the page, put the information at hand in the left column and analyze, discuss, relate, and synthesize it in the right column.
- Allow youself some time to reflect after studying.

(continued)

FIGURE 7.4 *Using the Multiple Intelligences (continued)*

BODY/KINESTHETIC	· Don't confine your study area to a desk or chair; move around, explore, go outside. · Act out the information. · Study in a group of people and change groups often. · Use charts, posters, flash cards, and chalkboards to study. · When appropriate or possible, build models using the information studied. · Verbalize the information to others. · Use games such as chess, Monopoly, Twister, or Clue when studying. · Trace words as you study them. · Use repetition to learn facts; write them many times. · Make study sheets.
INTERPERSONAL	· Study in groups. · Share the information with other people. · Teach the information to others. · Interview outside sources to learn more about the material at hand. · Have a debate with others about the information.
INTRAPERSONAL	· Study in a quiet area. · Study by youself. · Allow time for reflection and meditation about the subject matter. · Study in short time blocks and then spend some time absorbing the information. · Work at your own pace.
NATURALISTIC	· Study outside whenever possible. · Relate the information to the effect on the environment whenever possible. · When given the opportunity to choose your own topics or research projects, choose something related to nature. · Collect your own study data and resources. · Organize and label your information. · Keep separate notebooks on individual topics so that you can add new information to each topic as it becomes available to you.

UNDERSTANDING LEARNING STYLES THEORY

Why Is It Important to Know HOW I Learn?

A learning style is "the way in which each learner begins to concentrate on, process, and retain new and difficult information" (Dunn and Griggs, 2000). There is a difference between a *learning style* and a *learning strategy*. A learning *style* is innate and involves your five senses. It is how you best process information that comes to you. A learning *strategy* is how you might choose to learn or study, such as by using note cards, flip charts, color slides, or cooperative learning groups. Your learning strategy also involves where you study (such as at a desk, in bed, at the library, in a quiet place, with music, etc.), how long you study, and what techniques you use to help you study (such as mnemonics, cooperative learning teams, or SQ3R).

If you learn best by *seeing* **information**, you have a more dominant *visual learning style*. If you learn best by *hearing* **information**, you have a more dominant *auditory learning style*. If you learn best by *touching or doing*, you have a more dominant *tactile learning style*. You may also hear the tactile learning style referred to as kinesthetic or hands-on.

FIGURE

7.5   *Take the Lead*

The Learning Evaluation and Assessment Directory

© *Robert M. Sherfield, Ph.D.*

Directions: Read each statement carefully and thoroughly. After reading the statement, rate your response using the scale below. There are no right or wrong answers. This is not a timed survey. The LEAD is based, in part, on research conducted by Rita Dunn.

3 = Often Applies

2 = Sometimes Applies

1 = Never or Almost Never Applies

1. I remember information better if I write it down or draw a picture of it.
2. I remember things better when I hear them instead of just reading or seeing them.
3. When I get something that has to be assembled, I just start doing it. I don't read the directions.
4. If I am taking a test, I can "see" the page of the text or lecture notes where the answer is located.
5. I would rather the professor explain a graph, chart, or diagram than just show it to me.
6. When learning new things, I want to "do it" rather than hear about it.
7. I would rather the instructor write the information on the board or overhead instead of just lecturing.
8. I would rather listen to a book on tape than read it.
9. I enjoy making things, putting things together, and working with my hands.
10. I am able to quickly conceptualize and visualize information.
11. I learn best by hearing words.
12. I have been called hyperactive by my parents, spouse, partner, or professor.
13. I have no trouble reading maps, charts, or diagrams.
14. I can usually pick up on small sounds like bells, crickets, or frogs, or distant sounds like train whistles.
15. I use my hands and gesture a lot when I speak to others.

Refer to your score on each individual question. Place that score beside the appropriate question number below. Then, tally each line at the side.

Score					Total Across	Code
1	4	7	10	13		Visual
2	5	8	11	14		Auditory
3	6	9	12	15		Tactile

LEAD (Learning Styles) SCORE

Look at the scores on the LEAD. What is your top score?

Top Score _____

Code _____

CHEF ODETTE SMITH-RANSOME
Hospitality Instructor
The Art Institute of Pittsburgh, Pittsburgh, PA

At the age of 15, I found myself constantly in conflict with my mother, until one day I stood before her as she held a gun to my head. It was at that moment I knew I had to leave my parents' home, not just for my emotional well-being, but for my actual life and survival. My father was a good man, but he did not understand the entire situation with my mother's alcohol and diet pill addiction and he could do little to smooth out the situation between my mother and me. To complicate matters even more, my brother had just returned home from fighting in Viet-

> *So, I packed my clothes, dropped out of the 10th grade, and ran away over 1,000 miles to Charleston, South Carolina.*

nam and everyone was trying to adjust. It was a horrible time in the house where my ancestors had lived for over 100 years. So, I packed my clothes, dropped out of the 10th grade, and ran away over 1,000 miles to Charleston, South Carolina.

My first job was as a waitress. I worked in that job for over three years, realizing more every day that I was not using my talents and that without an education, I was doomed to work for minimum wage for the rest of my life. During this time, I met a friend in Charleston who was in the Navy. When he was re-

leased, he offered to take me back to Pittsburgh. I agreed and upon my return, I went to work in the kitchen of a family-owned restaurant. They began to take an interest in me and made me feel proud of my work. I then decided to get my GED and determine what road to take that would allow me to use my culinary talents and help others at the same time.

I began my associate's degree, which required that students complete an apprenticeship. We worked 40 hours per week, Monday through Thursday, under the direction of a master chef and we were in class 8 hours a day on Friday. My apprenticeship was at the Hyatt Regency in Pittsburgh. In order to obtain your degree, you had to pass the apprenticeship, all of the classes, and a bank of tests that proved your proficiency in a variety of areas. If you failed one part of the tests, you could not get your degree. Proudly, I passed every test, every class, and my apprenticeship.

My first professional job came to me upon the recommendation of a friend. I interviewed for and was hired to become the Private Chef for the Chancellor of the University of Pittsburgh. I loved the job and it afforded me the opportunity to get my bachelor's degree. So, I juggled a full-time job, a two-year-old child, and a full load of classes. As I neared the end of my degree, I was offered a fellowship at the University of Pittsburgh that trained people to teach students with special needs. I graduated Cum Laude and began teaching and working with people who had cerebral palsy at Con-

nelley Academy. I loved the work, and the position solidified my desire to work with adults.

From there I taught at the Good Will Training Center and later at the Pittsburgh Job Corps, where my culinary team won a major national competition. Today, I am an Instructor at The Art Institute® of Pittsburgh, helping others reach their dreams of working in the hospitality industry. In 2005, I was named *Culinary Educator of the Year* by the American Culinary Federation®. I try to let my life and my struggles serve as a light for students who have faced adversity and may have felt that their past was going to determine their future. My advice to my students—and to you—is this: NEVER let anyone tell you that you can't do it, that you're not able to do it,

that you don't have the means to do it, or that you'll never succeed. YOU set your own course in life and you determine the direction of your future.

EXTRAORDINARY REFLECTION

Read the following statement and respond in your online journal or class notebook.

Chef Smith-Ransome had to literally leave her family to protect her life. Think about your family situation at the moment. Are your family members supportive of your efforts? Do they offer you support? Are they working with you to help you achieve your goals? If so, how does this make you stronger? Do they offer you guidance?

THINKING *for* CHANGE: An Activity for Critical Reflection

Kristin knew that her most powerful learning style was visual. She knew that she had always learned best when she could "see" the information in pictures, charts, graphs, PowerPoint® slides, videos, or other powerful visuals. Kristin also knew that when she was able to get involved with the information, she seemed to retain it better. She did not at first know what this was called, but later learned that she was also a tactile or "hands-on" learner.

When she discovered that different people have different ways of learning and instructors have different ways of teaching, things began to make more sense to her. She had wondered why she had always done poorly in classes that were all lecture—like her history class. This semester, she was becoming increasingly worried about her performance in her literature class. It, too, was all lecture—information about poems, plays, and sonnets. She decided to go to the Tutoring Center to find out what she could do to retain the information

more effectively. Her tutor showed her how to make the terms and ideas more "visual" by drawing pictures beside each one, using colors in her notes, creating small story boards, and creating a visual image of what was being discussed.

In your own words, what would you suggest that a classmate do if he or she is having trouble understanding, interpreting, or remembering information from a class where there is very little discussion or lecture and he or she is a very strong auditory learner? List at least three things that your classmate could do to strengthen his or her less dominant intelligence or learning style. Think about what services are offered on your campus and what people might be of assistance to him or her.

1. _____

2. _____

3. _____

Some of the most successful students master information and techniques by using all three styles. If you were learning how to skateboard, you might learn best by *hearing someone* talk about the different styles or techniques. Others might learn best by *watching a video* in which someone demonstrates the techniques. Still others would learn best by actually getting on the board and *trying it out.* Those who engage all of their senses gain the most.

After taking the LEAD and reading more about learning styles (Figure 7.6) list at least three concrete strategies that you can employ to enhance your learning strategies for each of the three areas.

WANTED: A VISUAL LEARNER WITH TACTILE SKILLS

Do You Know the Differences Between Your Primary Learning Style and Your Dominant Intelligence?

As discussed previously, a **learning style** and a **learning strategy** are different. A learning style and a **dominant intelligence** are also quite different. When you read over the descriptions of multiple intelligences theory and learning styles theory, you probably noticed several common elements. Both theories deal with the visual, auditory, and tactile (or kinesthetic). There are also similarities between the two theories, but the differences are great and important.

FIGURE

7.6   *Learning Styles*

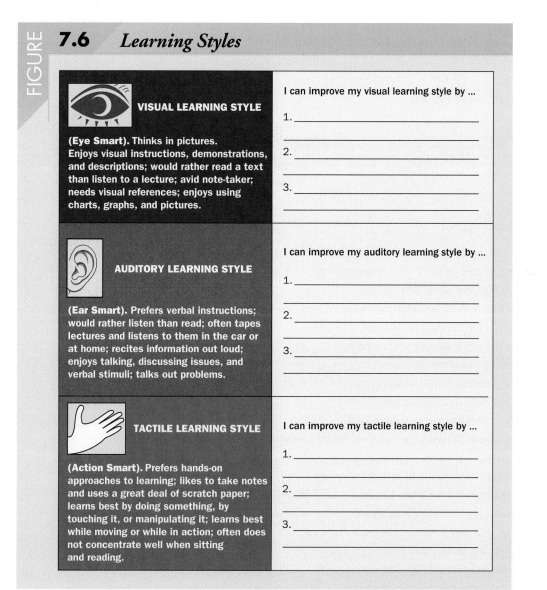

VISUAL LEARNING STYLE

(Eye Smart). Thinks in pictures. Enjoys visual instructions, demonstrations, and descriptions; would rather read a text than listen to a lecture; avid note-taker; needs visual references; enjoys using charts, graphs, and pictures.

I can improve my visual learning style by ...

1. _____
   _____
2. _____
   _____
3. _____
   _____

AUDITORY LEARNING STYLE

(Ear Smart). Prefers verbal instructions; would rather listen than read; often tapes lectures and listens to them in the car or at home; recites information out loud; enjoys talking, discussing issues, and verbal stimuli; talks out problems.

I can improve my auditory learning style by ...

1. _____
   _____
2. _____
   _____
3. _____
   _____

TACTILE LEARNING STYLE

(Action Smart). Prefers hands-on approaches to learning; likes to take notes and uses a great deal of scratch paper; learns best by doing something, by touching it, or manipulating it; learns best while moving or while in action; often does not concentrate well when sitting and reading.

I can improve my tactile learning style by ...

1. _____
   _____
2. _____
   _____
3. _____
   _____

Simply stated, you can have a visual learning style and yet ***not have*** visual/spatial as your dominant intelligence. *"How can this be possible?"* you may be asking. It may be that you **learn best** how to paint a picture by watching someone paint a picture—watching his or her brush-strokes, his or her method of mixing paints, and his or her spatial layout (this is your dominant visual learning style). However, you may not be as engaged or as talented at actually painting as the person you watched. Your painting may lack feeling, depth, and expression. You may find it hard to paint anything that is not copied from something else. You can't visualize a landscape in your mind because your visual/spatial intelligence is not very strong. In other words, you are not an innate artist at heart. This is an example of how your ***visual learning style*** can be a strong way for you to learn, but your visual/spatial intelligence may not be your dominant intelligence.

In your own words, compare and contrast YOUR primary learning style with your dominant intelligences. Give one example.

_____

_____

_____

_____

2

BLOOM LEVEL 2
QUESTION

FIGURE

7.7 *What Can You Learn about Personality?*

TAKE THE P.A.P.

The Personality Assessment Profile

© *Robert M. Sherfield, Ph.D.*

Directions: Read each statement carefully and thoroughly. After reading the statement, rate your response using the scale below. There are no right or wrong answers. This is not a timed survey. The PAP is based, in part, on the Myers-Briggs Type Indicator®(MBTI) by Katharine Briggs and Isabel Briggs-Myers.

3 = Often Applies

2 = Sometimes Applies

1 = Never or Almost Never Applies

_____ 1a. I am a very talkative person.

_____ 1b. I am a more reflective person than a verbal person.

_____ 2a. I am a very factual and literal person.

_____ 2b. I look to the future and I can see possibilities.

_____ 3a. I value truth and justice over tact and emotion.

_____ 3b. I find it easy to empathize with other people.

_____ 4a. I am very ordered and efficient.

_____ 4b. I enjoy having freedom from control.

_____ 5a. I am a very friendly and social person.

_____ 5b. I enjoy listening to others more than talking.

_____ 6a. I enjoy being around and working with people who have a great deal of common sense.

_____ 6b. I enjoy being around and working with people who are dreamers and have a great deal of imagination.

_____ 7a. One of my motivating forces is to do a job very well.

_____ 7b. I like to be recognized. I am motivated by my accomplishments and awards.

_____ 8a. I like to plan out my day before I go to bed.

_____ 8b. When I get up on a non-school or non-work day, I just like to let the day "plan itself."

_____ 9a. I like to express my feelings and thoughts.

_____ 9b. I enjoy a great deal of tranquility and quiet time to myself.

_____10a. I am a very pragmatic and realistic person.

_____10b. I like to create new ideas, methods, or ways of doing things.

_____11a. I make decisions with my brain.

_____11b. I make decisions with my heart.

_____12a. I am a very disciplined and orderly person.

_____12b. I don't make a lot of plans.

_____13a. I like to work with a group of people.

_____13b. I would rather work independently.

_____14a. I learn best if I can see it, touch it, smell it, taste it, or hear it.

_____14b. I learn best by relying on my gut feelings or intuition.

_____15a. I am quick to criticize others.

_____15b. I compliment others very easily and quickly.

_____16a. My life is systematic and organized.

_____16b. I don't really pay attention to deadlines.

_____17a. I can be myself when I am around others.

_____17b. I can be myself when I am alone.

_____18a. I live in the here and now, in the present.

(continued)

FIGURE **7.7**   *What Can You Learn about Personality? (continued)*

____18b. I live in the future, planning and dreaming.

____19a. I think that if someone breaks the rules, the person should be punished.

____19b. I think that if someone breaks the rules, we should look at the person who broke the rules, examine the rules, and look at the situation at hand before a decision is made.

____20a. I do my work, then I play.

____20b. I play, then do my work.

Refer to your score on each individual question. Place that score beside the appropriate question number below. Then, tally each line at the side.

Score					Total Across	Code
1a _____	5a _____	9a _____	13a _____	17a _____	_____	E Extrovert
1b _____	5b _____	9b _____	13b _____	17b _____	_____	I Introvert
2a _____	6a _____	10a _____	14a _____	18a _____	_____	S Sensing
2b _____	6b _____	10b _____	14b _____	18b _____	_____	N Intuition
3a _____	7a _____	11a _____	15a _____	19a _____	_____	T Thinking
3b _____	7b _____	11b _____	15b _____	19b _____	_____	F Feeling
4a _____	8a _____	12a _____	16a _____	20a _____	_____	J Judging
4b _____	8b _____	12b _____	16b _____	20b _____	_____	P Perceiving

PAP Scores

Personality Indicator

Look at the scores on your PAP. Is your score higher in the *E or the I* line? Is your score higher in the *S or the N* line? Is your score higher in the *T or the F* line? Is your score higher in the *J or the P* line? Write the code to the side of each section below.

Is your higher score   **E or I**   Code _____

Is your higher score   **S or N**   Code _____

Is your higher score   **T or F**   Code _____

Is your higher score   **J or P**   Code _____

UNDERSTANDING PERSONALITY TYPE

Are You ENFJ, ISTP, or ENTJ, and Why Does It Matter?

In 1921, Swiss psychologist **Carl Jung** (1875–1961) published his work *Psychological Types*. In this book, Jung suggested that human behavior is not random. He felt that behavior follows patterns and that these patterns are caused by differences in the way people use their minds. In 1942, Isabel Briggs-Myers and her mother, Katharine Briggs, began to put Jung's theory into practice. They developed the Myers-Briggs Type Indicator®, which after more than 50 years of research and refinement, has become the most widely used instrument for identifying and studying personality.

Personality typing can "help us discover what best motivates and energizes each of us as individuals" (Tieger and Barron-Tieger, 2007). The questions on the PAP helped you discover whether you are an **E** or an **I** (**E**xtroverted or **I**ntroverted), an **S** or an **N**

ESSENTIAL CORNERSTONE

Communication:
How can learning more about your personality, and the personalities of those around you, help you enhance your communication skills?

Social Networking Moment:
Share your response to this Essential Cornerstone with peers in your social network. Choose two responses from your peers and respond to their postings.

(**S**ensing or i**N**tuitive), a **T** or an **F** (**T**hinking or **F**eeling), and a **J** or a **P** (**J**udging or **P**erceiving). When all of the combinations of E/I, S/N, T/F, and J/P are combined, there are 16 personality types. Everyone will fit into **ONE** of the following categories:

ISTJ   ISFJ   INFJ   INTJ
ISTP   ISFP   INFP   INTP
ESTP   ESFP   ENFP   ENTP
ESTJ   ESFJ   ENFJ   ENTJ

Let's take a look at the four major categories of typing. Notice that the higher your score in one area, the stronger your personality type is for that area. For instance, if you scored 15 on the E (extroversion) questions, this means that you are a strong extrovert. If you scored 15 on the I (introversion) questions, this means that you are a strong introvert. However, if you scored 7 on the E questions and 8 on the I questions, your score indicates that you possess almost the same amount of extroverted and introverted qualities. The same is true for every other category of the PAP.

E versus I (Extroversion/Introversion)

This category deals with the way we *interact with others and the world around us; how we draw our energy*.

Extroverts prefer to live in the outside world, drawing their strength from other people. They are outgoing and love interaction. They usually make decisions with others in mind. They enjoy being the center of attention. There are usually few secrets about extroverts.

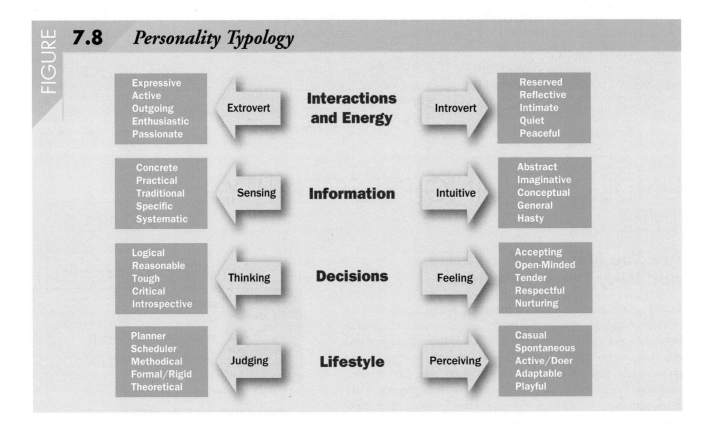

FIGURE 7.8 *Personality Typology*

Extrovert	Interactions and Energy	Introvert
Expressive, Active, Outgoing, Enthusiastic, Passionate		Reserved, Reflective, Intimate, Quiet, Peaceful
Sensing	**Information**	**Intuitive**
Concrete, Practical, Traditional, Specific, Systematic		Abstract, Imaginative, Conceptual, General, Hasty
Thinking	**Decisions**	**Feeling**
Logical, Reasonable, Tough, Critical, Introspective		Accepting, Open-Minded, Tender, Respectful, Nurturing
Judging	**Lifestyle**	**Perceiving**
Planner, Scheduler, Methodical, Formal/Rigid, Theoretical		Casual, Spontaneous, Active/Doer, Adaptable, Playful

Introverts draw their strength from the inner world. They need to spend time alone to think and ponder. They are usually quiet and reflective. They usually make decisions by themselves. They do not like being the center of attention. They are private

S versus N (Sensing/iNtuition)

This category deals with the way we *learn and deal with information*.

Sensing types gather information through their five senses. They have a hard time believing something if it cannot be seen, touched, smelled, tasted, or heard. They like concrete facts and details. They do not rely on intuition or gut feelings. They usually have a great deal of common sense.

Intuitive types are not very detail-oriented. They can see possibilities, and they rely on their gut feelings. Usually, they are very innovative people. They tend to live in the future and often get bored once they have mastered a task.

T versus F (Thinking/Feeling)

This category deals with the way we *make decisions*.

Thinkers are very logical people. They do not make decisions based on feelings or emotions. They are analytical and sometimes do not take others' values into consideration when making decisions. They can easily identify the flaws of others. They can sometimes be seen as insensitive and lacking compassion.

Feelers make decisions based on what they feel is right and just. They like to have harmony, and they value others' opinions and feelings. They are usually very tactful people who like to please others. They are very warm people.

J versus P (Judging/Perceiving)

This category deals with the way we *live and our overall lifestyle*.

Judgers are very orderly people. They must have a great deal of structure in their lives. They are good at setting goals and sticking to them. They are the type of people who would seldom, if ever, play before their work was completed.

Perceivers are just the opposite. They are less structured and more spontaneous. They do not like timelines. Unlike the judgers, they will play before their work is done. They will take every chance to delay a decision or judgment. Sometimes, they can become involved in too many things at one time.

After you have studied the the Personality Type Chart (Figure 7.9) and other information in the chapter regarding your personality type, you can make some decisions about your study habits and even your career choices. For instance, if you scored very high in the extroversion section, it may not serve you well to pursue a career where you would be forced to work alone. It would probably also be unwise to try to spend all of your time studying alone. If you are a strong extrovert, you would want to work and study around people.

bring the CHANGE

Tips for Personal Success

Consider the following tips for making the most of your learning style, personality type, and dominant intelligence.

▶ Improve your weaker learning styles by incorporating at least one aspect of those learning styles into your daily study plans.

▶ If your personality type clashes with your professor's personality type, try to make adjustments that enable you to get through the class successfully.

▶ Adjust your learning style to match your professor's teaching style if possible.

▶ Use your primary intelligence to help you decide on your life's vocation.

Now, it is your turn. Create a list of at least three more tips that you would offer a fellow classmate to assist him or her in making the most of his or her learning style, intelligence, and personality type. Develop one strategy for each category.

1. Learning Style Tip _____

2. Multiple Intelligence Tip _____

3. Personality Type Tip _____

FIGURE

7.9   *A Closer Look at Your Personality Type*

ISTJ–THE DUTIFUL

(7–10% of Americans)

Have great power of concentration; very serious; dependable; logical and realistic; take responsibility for their own actions; they are not easily distracted.

ISTP–THE MECHANIC

(4–7% of Americans)

Very reserved; good at making things clear to others; interested in how and why things work; like to work with their hands; can sometimes be misunderstood as idle.

ESTP–THE DOER

(6–8% of Americans)

They are usually very happy; they don't let trivial things upset them; they have very good memories; very good at working with things and taking them apart.

ESTJ–THE GUARDIAN

(12–15% of Americans)

They are "take charge" people; they like to get things done; focus on results; very good at organizing; good at seeing what will not work; responsible; realists.

ISFJ–THE NURTURER

(7–10% of Americans)

Hard workers; detail-oriented; considerate of others' feelings; friendly and warm to others; very conscientious; they are down-to-earth and like to be around the same.

ISFP–THE ARTIST

(5–7% of Americans)

Very sensitive and modest; adapt easily to change; they are respectful of others' feelings and values; take criticism personally; don't enjoy leadership roles.

ESFP–THE PERFORMER

(8–10% of Americans)

Very good at sports and active exercises; good common sense; easygoing; good at communication; can be impulsive; do not enjoy working alone; have fun and enjoy living and life.

ESFJ–THE CAREGIVER

(11–14% of Americans)

Enjoy many friendly relationships; popular; love to help others; do not take criticism very well; need praise; need to work with people; organized; talkative; active.

INFJ–THE PROTECTOR

(2–3% of Americans)

Enjoy an atmosphere where all get along; they do what is needed of them; they have strong beliefs and principles; enjoy helping others achieve their goals.

INFP–THE IDEALIST

(3–4% of Americans)

They work well alone; must know others well to interact; faithful to others and their jobs; excellent at communication; open-minded; dreamers; tend to do too much.

ENFP–THE INSPIRERS

(6–7% of Americans)

Creative and industrious; can easily find success in activities and projects that interest them; good at motivating others; organized; do not like routine.

ENFJ–THE GIVER

(3–5% of Americans)

Very concerned about others' feelings; respect others; good leaders; usually popular; good at public speaking; can make decisions too quickly; trust easily.

INTJ–THE SCIENTIST

(2–3% of Americans)

They are very independent; enjoy challenges; inventors; can be skeptical; they are perfectionists; they believe in their own work, sometimes to a fault.

INTP–THE THINKER

(3–4% of Americans)

Extremely logical; very analytical; good at planning; love to learn; excellent problem solvers; they don't enjoy needless conversation; hard to understand at times.

ENTP–THE VISIONARY

(4–6% of Americans)

Great problem solvers; love to argue either side; can do almost anything; good at speaking/motivating; love challenges; very creative; do not like routine; over-confident.

ENTJ–THE EXECUTIVE

(3–5% of Americans)

Excellent leaders; speak very well; hard-working; may be workaholics; may not give enough praise; like to learn; great planners; enjoy helping others reach their goals.

Adapted from Tieger and Barron-Tieger, Do What You Are, 2007, and The Personality Type Portraits at www.personalitypage.com.

REFLECTIONS ON LEARNING HOW TO LEARN

Unlike an IQ test, learning style, multiple intelligence, and personality type assessments do not pretend to determine if you are "smart" or not. These assessments simply allow you to look more closely at how you learn, what innate strengths you possess, and what your dominant intelligence may be.

Discovering your learning style can greatly enhance your classroom performance. For example, finally understanding that your learning style is visual and that your professor's teaching style is totally verbal (oral) can answer many questions about why you may have performed poorly in the past in a "strictly lecture" class. Now that you have discovered that you are a feeling extrovert, you can better understand why you love associating with others and learn a great deal by working in groups. And now that you have discovered that your primary intelligence is logical/mathematical, you know why math and science are easier for you than history or literature.

Possessing this knowledge and developing the tools to make your learning style, dominant intelligence, and personality type work for you, not against you, will be paramount to your success. As you continue to use your learning style, dominant intelligence, and personality type to enhance your learning, consider the following:

▶ Get involved in a *variety* of learning and social situations.
▶ Use your less dominant areas more often to *strengthen* them.
▶ *Read more* about personality typing and learning styles.
▶ *Surround yourself* with people who learn differently from the way you do.
▶ Try *different ways* of learning and studying.
▶ Remember that inventories *do not* measure your worth.

By understanding how you process information, learning can become an entirely new and exciting venture for you. Good luck to you on this new journey.

"Education is learning what you did not know you did not know."
—Daniel Boorstin

KNOWLEDGE *in* BLOOM

CREATING Your Personal Life Profile

Each chapter-end assessment is based on *Bloom's Taxonomy of Learning*. See the inside front cover for a quick review.

UTILIZES LEVELS 4 AND 5 OF THE TAXONOMY

Throughout the chapter, you have discovered three things about the way you learn best: your multiple intelligence, your learning style, and your personality type. Write them down in the spaces below:

My **dominant intelligence** is _____

My **primary learning style** is _____

My **strongest personality type** is _____

Now that you see them all together, think of them as a puzzle for which you need to "connect the dots." In other words, put them all together and what do they look like? What do they mean? How do they affect your studies, your relationships, your communication skills, and your career choices?

EXAMPLE: If Mike's dominant intelligence is **interpersonal**, his learning style is **verbal**, and his personality type is **ENFJ**, *connecting the dots* may suggest that he is the type of person who loves to be around other people and is an extrovert who learns best by listening to other people or explaining how something is done. He is a person who would probably speak up in class, be more of a leader than a follower, and start a study group if one did not exist because he is outgoing, organized, and very much a goal setter. Mike is the type of person who values relationships and listens to what others are saying. He is a person who shares and does not mind taking the time to explain things to others. He could easily become a good friend.

Some of the challenges that Mike could encounter might involve taking a class where discussions are rare, having to sit and never being able to share ideas or views, or having a professor who is not very organized and skips around. He would not deal very well with peers who are disrespectful and do not pull their own weight in the study group. He might also have a hard time with group members or classmates who are very quiet and prefer to observe rather than contribute. He would have trouble being around people who have no goals or direction in life. He might also run into some trouble because he is a very social person and loves to be around others in social settings. He may thus overcommit himself to groups and clubs and, on occasion, socialize more than study.

As you can see, by connecting the dots, Mike's **Personal Life Profile** tells us a great deal about his strengths and challenges. It also gives him an understanding of how to approach many different situations, capitalize on his strengths, and work to improve his weaker areas.

Now, it is your turn.

Take your time and refer to the chapter for any information you may need. Examine your assessments and create your own profile in the four areas listed below. Discuss your strengths and challenges for each area.

THE PERSONAL LIFE PROFILE OF _____

Academic Strengths: I found that I . . .

_____
_____
_____
_____
_____
_____
_____
_____
_____
_____
_____

Academic Challenges: I found that I . . .

_____
_____
_____
_____
_____
_____
_____
_____
_____
_____
_____
_____
_____
_____

Communication Strengths: I found that I . . .

_____
_____
_____
_____
_____
_____
_____
_____
_____
_____
_____
_____

Communication Challenges: I found that I . . .

_____
_____
_____
_____
_____
_____
_____
_____
_____
_____
_____
_____

Relationship Strengths: I found that I . . .

_____
_____
_____
_____
_____
_____
_____
_____
_____
_____
_____

Relationship Challenges: I found that I . . .

_____
_____
_____
_____
_____
_____
_____
_____

Career Strengths: I found that I . . .

_____
_____
_____
_____
_____
_____
_____
_____

Career Challenges: I found that I . . .

_____
_____
_____
_____
_____
_____
_____

Looking at all of this together, write an extensive paragraph about what all of this means about you. Include thoughts on your learning style, your personality, your study habits, your communication skills, and your overall success strategy.

_____
_____
_____
_____
_____
_____
_____

SQ3R *Mastery* Study Sheet

EXAMPLE QUESTION: *(from page 172)* What is the difference between a learning style and a learning strategy?		**ANSWER:**
EXAMPLE QUESTION: *(from page 173)* What is the definition of tactile and how do you use it?		**ANSWER:**
AUTHOR QUESTION: *(from page 160)* Discuss at least three theories of learning from the historical figures discussed.		**ANSWER:**
AUTHOR QUESTION: *(from page 165)* Who is Howard Gardner and why is his work important?		**ANSWER:**
AUTHOR QUESTION: *(from page 172)* Explain the difference between your learning style and your dominant intelligence.		**ANSWER:**
AUTHOR QUESTION: *(from page 173)* What is the difference between a visual learning style and visual intelligence?		**ANSWER:**
AUTHOR QUESTION: *(from page 175)* How can your personality type affect your study time?		**ANSWER:**
YOUR QUESTION: *(from page ____)*		**ANSWER:**
YOUR QUESTION: *(from page ____)*		**ANSWER:**
YOUR QUESTION: *(from page ____)*		**ANSWER:**
YOUR QUESTION: *(from page ____)*		**ANSWER:**
YOUR QUESTION: *(from page ____)*		**ANSWER:**

Finally, after answering these questions, recite this chapter's major points in your mind. Consider the following general questions to help you master this material.

- ▶ What was it about?
- ▶ What does it mean?
- ▶ What was the most important thing I learned? Why?
- ▶ What were the key points to remember?

BUILDING YOUR READING AND COMPREHENSION SKILLS

"The difference between the right word and the almost right word is the difference between lightning and the lightning bug."

—Mark Twain

WHY READ THIS CHAPTER?

What's in it for me?

WHY is it important to know my reading speed? *WHY* will a chapter on reading and comprehension help me study better? *WHY* do I need to know how to identify a main point? *WHY*, since I'm already in college, is learning how to read more effectively such a big deal?

WHY? Because there is a monumental difference between recognizing and pronouncing the words on a page and being able to comprehend, interpret, analyze, evaluate, and remember those written words. Your having hands does not make you a mechanic. Having a voice does not make you a singer, and being able to read words does not mean that you comprehend what the author intended. Reading makes you smarter and more knowledgeable about many subjects. You can sit in your easy chair and read all about the Renaissance, the painting of Mona Lisa, the statue of David, the Gold Coast of Australia, Alexander the Great, or the priceless antiquities of China. You might one day learn to do your job better by reading professional journals. Reading covers many terrains, from history to human-interest stories to cutting-edge ideas to scholars' research results. If you really want to learn, reading is the key. No other single skill comes close to offering you the benefits of knowing how to effectively read and comprehend information.

By carefully reading this chapter and taking the information provided seriously, you will be able to:

1. Understand the value of reading and identify whether you are an active or a passive reader.
2. Calculate and understand your reading speed and how it affects your study time.
3. Apply strategies to increase your reading comprehension.
4. Understand the skills associated with effective reading, including dictionary usage, fixation and locating main ideas.
5. Understand and use the SQ3R method of reading.

CHAPTER 8 / READ

"It is impossible for people to learn what they think they already know."

—Epictetus

NAME: Thomas Paddock
INSTITUTION: Louisville Technical Institute, Louisville, KY
MAJOR: Computer Networking Administration
AGE: 21

For me, reading was an elusive subject in high school. While students were strongly encouraged to read, most of us didn't have any free time to read, and those who did have free time were busy with other activities. While I was lucky enough to be in an AP English class for two years, I still didn't read as much as I should have. We were exposed to several great works of literature, but even more so, we were exposed to several chances for developing reading skills that I really wish I had honed before I arrived at college. It used to be, "Read Chapters 1–5 by Friday." Now it's, "Read Chapters 1–5 by tomorrow, and be prepared for a quiz."

Fortunately, I was able to recover from the shock of college rush, and I've adapted rather quickly. My career field requires me to read books that are on the level of technical manuals, and whether or not I can even get a job will depend on this knowledge. Every little detail mentioned counts, and oftentimes I've found that what may have seemed to be an obscure or unimportant detail has come back to haunt me later on certification exams, which is why it's important to be able to soak in as much information as possible. Even a small blurb or tip in a textbook may reveal a common network problem that can lead to a world of trouble if ignored.

Proper reading skills and techniques are some of the most important tools I've developed in college—and this will be true for you, too. There is so much information in our textbooks that it's impossible to cover all of it in class, so being able to actually understand that information without the aid of a teacher is a great benefit. Reading is something that I'm definitely not going to have a lack of, whether in the present or the future, and I can't see myself living or working without highly efficient reading skills. This chapter can help you become a more active reader and it can help you increase your comprehension, too.

SCAN & QUESTION

In the preface of this book (page xix), you read about the **SQ3R Study Method**. Right now, take a few moments, **scan this chapter**, and on page 209, write **five questions** that you think will be important to your mastery of this material. In addition to the two questions below, you will find five questions from your authors. Use one of your **"Study for Quiz"** stickers to flag this page for easy reference.

EXAMPLES:

▶ **Describe the process of fixation.** (from page 194)

▶ **Why is comprehension more important than speed?** (from page 191)

IS READING *FUNDAMENTAL* OR JUST PURE TORTURE?

The Answer Can Change Your Life

Quick question: "What are the top two academic problems among college students today?" According to faculty members, assessments, national tests, and yes, even your peers around the nation, the two greatest problems students face today are college math classes and reading comprehension—and some of the math problems can even be attributed to poor reading skills.

FIGURE 8.1 *A Six Pack that Can Help You with Effective Reading.*

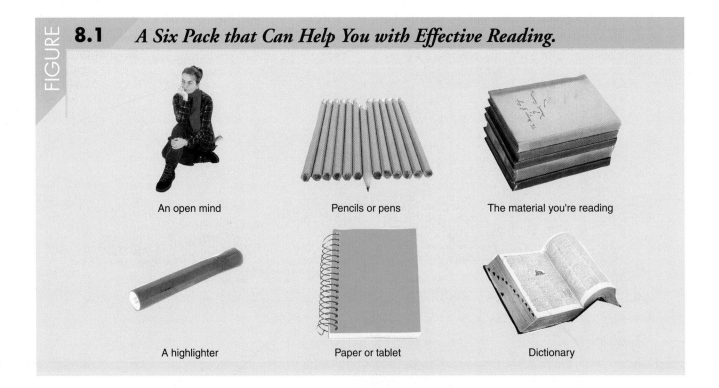

An open mind

Pencils or pens

The material you're reading

A highlighter

Paper or tablet

Dictionary

How many times have you read to the bottom of a page or completed a section in a text-book and said to yourself, ***"I don't remember a thing I just read."*** In actuality, all of us have experienced this at one time or another. The strategies outlined in this chapter will help you eliminate this common occurrence from your study time. By applying the strategies discussed herein, you will be able to read a page, a section, or an entire chapter so that when you reach the end, you will *comprehend and remember* what you just read.

It may seem elementary, but without the proper tools, you can't improve your reading comprehension, analysis, or speed. Enough said!

DISCOVERING YOUR READING STYLE

Are You Active or Passive?

Take a few moments and circle TRUE or FALSE for each of the statements in Figure 8.2 to determine whether you are more of an active or a passive reader.

Active reading is really nothing more than a mind-set. It is the attitude you have as you begin the reading process. For the next few days, try approaching your reading assignments with a positive, open-minded approach and notice the difference in your own satisfaction, understanding, and overall comprehension. Instead of saying things like, "I hate reading" or "This stuff is worthless," reframe your self-talk into statements such as "I'm going to learn from this" and "I think I can apply this to my life now."

FIGURE

8.2 *Discovering Your Reading Style*

Take a few moments and circle true or false for each of the following statements to determine if you are more of an active or passive reader.

DISCOVERING YOUR READING STYLE

1.	I enjoy reading for pleasure.	TRUE	FALSE
2.	College textbooks have little connection to my real life.	TRUE	FALSE
3.	I look for the deeper meaning in words and phrases.	TRUE	FALSE
4.	I seldom visualize what I am reading.	TRUE	FALSE
5.	I look up words that I do not understand.	TRUE	FALSE
6.	I read only what I have to read, and that is a stretch for me.	TRUE	FALSE
7.	I stop reading to ponder what something means.	TRUE	FALSE
8.	I never take notes when reading.	TRUE	FALSE
9.	Reading brings me great joy.	TRUE	FALSE
10.	My mind wanders constantly when I read.	TRUE	FALSE
11.	I make time for reading even when I am not required to read.	TRUE	FALSE
12.	Words are just words—they add no real meaning to my life or work.	TRUE	FALSE
13.	I get excited about reading something new because I know I will learn something new and useful.	TRUE	FALSE
14.	When reading, I just want to get it over with.	TRUE	FALSE
15.	I usually have no trouble concentrating when reading.	TRUE	FALSE
16.	I never look up words; I just read on.	TRUE	FALSE

Total of even-numbered TRUE responses _____

Total of odd-numbered TRUE responses _____

If you answered TRUE to more even numbers, you tend to be a more passive reader.
If you answered TRUE to more odd numbers, you tend to be a more active reader.

I FEEL THE NEED . . . THE NEED FOR SPEED!

Do You Know Your Personal Reading Rate?

You've heard the advertisements: "Breeze through a novel on your lunch hour," "Read an entire computer instruction book over dinner," or "Read *The New York Times* in 10 minutes." Sure, there are people who have an incredible gift for speed reading and a photographic memory, but those people are not the norm.

This section is included in your text to give you some idea about how long it will take to read a chapter so that you can *plan your reading time* more effectively. There is an average of 450 words on a college textbook page. If you read at 150 words per minute, each page may take you an average of three minutes to read.

> Have you ever timed yourself to determine how long it takes you to read a complete chapter?

FIGURE

8.3 *Calculating Your Reading Rate*

Start Time _____ _____   Minutes _____ Seconds _____

BINGE DRINKING

Binge drinking is classified as having more than five drinks at one time. Many people say, "I only drink once a week." However, if that one drinking spell includes drink after drink after drink, it can be extremely detrimental to your liver, your memory, your digestive system, and your overall health.

Most college students report that they do not mean to binge drink, but it is caused by the situation, such as a ballgame, a party, a campus event, or special occasions. Researchers at Michigan State University found that only 5 percent of students surveyed say they party to "get drunk" (Warner, 2002).

In their breakthrough work, *Dying to Drink*, Harvard researcher Henry Wechsler and science writer Bernice Wuethrich explore the problem of binge drinking. They suggest, "two out of every five college students regularly binge drink, resulting in approximately 1,400 student deaths, a distressing number of assaults and rapes, a shameful amount of vandalism, and countless cases of academic suicide" (Wechsler and Wuethrich, 2002).

It is a situation reminiscent of the old saying, "Letting the fox guard the henhouse." After a few drinks, it is hard to "self-police," meaning that you may not be able to control your actions once the drinking starts.

Perhaps the greatest tragedy of drug and alcohol abuse is the residual damage of pregnancy, sexually transmitted diseases, traffic fatalities, verbal/physical abuse, and accidental death. You know that drugs and alcohol lower your resistance and can cause you to do things that you would not normally do, such as drive drunk or have unprotected sex. Surveys and research results suggest that students who participate in heavy episodic (HE) or binge drinking are more likely to participate in unprotected sex with multiple sex partners. One survey found that 61 percent of men who do binge drink participated in unprotected sex as compared to 23 percent of men who do not binge drink. The survey also found that 48 percent of women who do binge drink participated in unprotected sex as compared to only 8 percent of women who do not binge drink (Cooper, 2002).

These staggering statistics suggest one thing: alcohol consumption can cause people to act in ways in which they may never have acted without alcohol—and those actions can result in personal damage from which recovery may be impossible.
(387 words)

Finishing Time _____   _____ Minutes _____ Seconds _____

Reading time in SECONDS = _____

Words per MINUTE (use the following chart) = _____

(continued)

FIGURE

8.3   *Calculating Your Reading Rate (continued)*

Example: If you read this passage in 2 minutes and 38 seconds, your reading time in seconds would be 158. Using the Rate Calculator Chart, your reading rate would be about 146 words per minute.

RATE CALCULATOR FOR RELATIVELY EASY PASSAGES

Time in Seconds and Minutes	Words Per Minute
40	581
50	464
60 (1 minute)	387
120 (2 minute)	194
130	179
140	165
150	155
160	145
170	137
180 (3 minute)	129
190	122
200	116
210	110
220	106
230	101

Source: B. Smith, *Breaking Through,* 8th ed. (2007).

Test Your Comprehension Skills

Answer the following questions with T (true) or F (false) without looking back over the material.

_____ 1. Binge drinking has resulted in the deaths of students.
_____ 2. Men who binge drink have unprotected sex more often than men who do not binge drink.
_____ 3. Women who binge drink have unprotected sex no more often than women who do not binge drink.
_____ 4. "Self-policing" means that you are able to look out for yourself.
_____ 5. Binge drinking is classified as having more than three drinks at one time.

Each question is worth 20%.   Comprehension = _____%

Example: If you answered two correctly, your comprehension rate would be 40% (2 × 20%). If you answered four correctly, your comprehension rate would be 80% (4 × 20%).

Test Your Comprehension Skills Answers: 1 = T, 2 = T, 3 = F, 4 = T, 5 = F.

This is a ***raw number*** for basic reading. It DOES NOT allow for marking, highlighting, taking notes, looking up words, reflecting, or comprehending. When these necessary skills are coupled with basic reading, they can sometimes triple the amount of reading time required. So, that page that you estimated would take you 3 minutes to read may actually take you 9 to 10 minutes to read.

In the reading activity (Figure 8.3), you will find a passage about binge drinking. Read the section at your normal pace. Use a stopwatch or a watch with a second hand to accurately record your time, and then calculate your rate and comprehension level using the directions provided.

ESSENTIAL CORNERSTONE

Passion:
    How can learning to read more effectively and frequently increase your passion for learning?

Social Networking Moment:
Share your response to this Essential Cornerstone with peers in your social network. Choose two responses from your peers and respond to their postings.

SPEED AND COMPREHENSION

Why Does It Matter So Much and How Does It Impact My Education?

According to Brenda D. Smith (2007), professor and reading expert, "rate calculators vary according to the difficulty of the material. Research indicates, however, that on relatively easy material, the average adult reading speed is approximately 250 words per minute at 70% comprehension. For college students, the rate is sometimes estimated at closer to 300 words per minute." The passage that you just read would be classified as relatively easy.

If you are reading below the average, 250-words-per-minute rate, several factors could be contributing to this situation. They include:

▶ Not concentrating on the passage.

▶ Vocabulary words with which you are not familiar.

▶ Stopping too long on any given single word (called fixations; discussed later).

▶ Not reading often enough to build your speed.

The remainder of this chapter is intended to assist you with improving your reading speed AND comprehension.

YOU DON'T HAVE TO BE A LOGODAEDALIAN TO ENJOY WORDS

Can a Powerful Vocabulary Really Be Developed?

Thankfully, it is not every day that you run across words like *logodaedalian*. (A logodaedalian is a person who has a great passion for unique, sly, and clever words and phrases.) Perhaps the best way to develop a dynamic vocabulary is by reading. While reading, you may come across words with which you are not familiar. You may be exposed to aspects of language that you have not experienced with your family, friends, or geographic location. These unfamiliar words will not become a part of your **vernacular** unless you STOP and look them up. This is the way to begin building a masterful vocabulary.

Let's start by looking up the word *vernacular*. Take a moment and jot down the definition.

BLOOM LEVEL 3 QUESTION

Vernacular means: _____

_____

_____

_____

See how simple that was? Now you have a new word in your vocabulary—actually, you have two new words from just a few paragraphs: *vernacular* and *logodaedalian*. You have taken a step toward becoming a logophile!

IT'S NOT JUST A DOORSTOP

How Can a Dictionary Aid in Reading Comprehension?

Your dictionary will become a good friend to you in college. There may be many words and phrases that you do not understand when reading your college textbooks. This is somewhat common, as many college texts are written on the 13th- and 14th-grade levels. You will need to stop and look up the words you don't understand. When you look up a word in the dictionary, you are given more than just a definition (see Figure 8.4). You are also given the phonetic pronunciation, the spelling, the meaning, the part of speech in which the word can be used, the origin of the word, and usually several definitions. You may have to choose the definition that best suits the context of the sentence. It can be beneficial to you to jot down definitions in the margins of your text.

Using the definition for *magnitude,* determine which definition would be best suited to this sentence: ***The magnitude of the power she had over him was truly amazing.***

FIGURE 8.4 *Annotated Dictionary Entry*

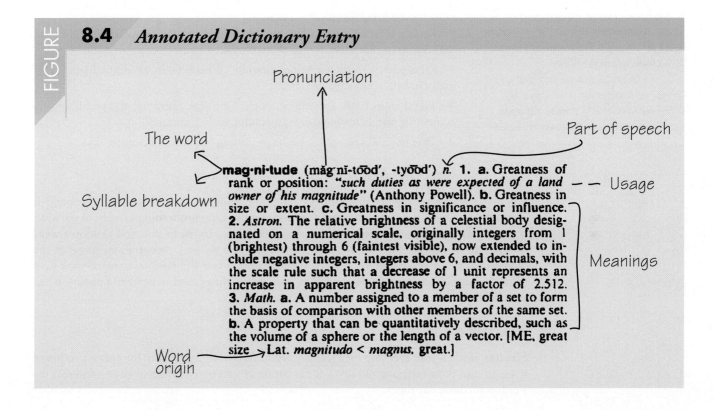

LEARNING TO READ FASTER AND SMARTER

Can Speed and Comprehension Be Improved?

As you begin to practice your reading comprehension, review the following tips for helping you read the material more quickly and understand it more clearly. Whenever you are faced with having to choose between comprehension and speed, choose comprehension every time.

Concentration

Speed and comprehension both require deep, mindful concentration. Neither can be achieved without it. Your body needs to be ready to concentrate. It will be nearly impossible to concentrate if you are tired and hungry. To increase your concentration for active reading, consider the following:

▶ Reduce outside distractions such as people talking, rooms that are too hot or cold, cell phones ringing, etc.

▶ Reduce internal distractions such as fatigue, self-talk, daydreaming, hunger, and emotions that cause you to think of other things.

▶ Set a goal of reading a certain amount of material in an allotted time. This goal can help you focus.

▶ Take a short break every 20 minutes. Don't get distracted and go off and do something else; come back to your reading in 3–5 minutes.

▶ Take notes as you read. This helps reading become an active process.

Vocabulary

Building a strong vocabulary may not be the easiest thing to do, and you will not build it overnight. However, it is important that you work on this aspect of reading as often as possible. If you do not know a word, you must stop and look it up. Having to stop and look up a word that you do not know may slow you down and cause you to lose concentration; however, the more words you have in your vocabulary, the fewer times you will need to stop and look up a word. It is difficult and nearly impossible to read, comprehend, and remember a passage when you do not know or understand one or more words.

Fixation

Fixation is when your eyes stop on a single word to read it. Your eyes stop for only a fraction of a second, but those fractions add up over the course of a section or chapter. Your mind sees the words something like this:

Nutrition   is   important   to   good   health.

As you read this, you probably had six fixations because the words are spaced out. However, even if they were not spaced out, many people would still have six fixations. To increase your speed, try to see two or three words with one fixation; this will cut your reading time nearly in half. Try to see the sentence like this:

Nutrition is important   to good health.

Smith (2007) states: "research has shown that the average reader can see approximately 2.5 words per fixation."

To reduce your fixation time for active reading, consider the following:

▶ Practice seeing two or more words with one fixation.

▶ As you practice, try to read in phrases like the example below:

Nutrition is important   to good health. Therefore,   you should   work hard to eat   proper meals   every day.   By doing this   you can maintain good health.

Read the following passage using the fixation procedure:

Motivation is an important asset to all students, and it must come from within. No one—not your professors, your parents, or your friends—can motivate you unless you want to be motivated. You will be motivated by one of two things—fear or desire. Fear will cause you to be afraid and not take risks, while desire will make you take a chance on yourself and move out of your comfort zone.

How did you do? Was this easy or difficult? Why?

_____

_____

_____

BLOOM LEVEL 5
QUESTION

FINDING THE TOPIC AND MAIN IDEAS IN PARAGRAPHS AND SECTIONS

Can You Get to the Main Point?

Typically, each paragraph has a main idea. You're no doubt familiar with this from your English classes. It is usually called a topic sentence. The topic statement is what the paragraph is about. Identifying the main idea of a paragraph can greatly aid your comprehension of that paragraph and eventually the entire section or chapter.

Read the following paragraph and determine the main idea—the point.

Without exception, the conclusion should be one of the most carefully crafted components of your paper or speech. Long after your reader has finished reading or your listener has finished listening, the last part of your work is more than likely going to be the part they remember the most. Some writers and speakers suggest that you write your conclusion first, so that your paper or speech is directed toward a specific end result. That decision, of course, is up to you. However, a great piece of advice from writing experts tells us that captivating writers always know how their stories will end long before they begin writing them.

From *Cornerstone: Building on Your Best,* 5th edition

Can you determine what the above paragraph is about? We know that the opening statement talks about writing the conclusion of a paper or speech. But it also talks about the importance

ESSENTIAL CORNERSTONE

Resourcefulness:
How can reading help you find creative ways to solve old and new problems?

Social Networking Moment:
Share your response to this Essential Cornerstone with peers in your social network. Choose two responses from your peers and respond to their postings.

From Ordinary to Extraordinary

REAL PEOPLE | REAL LIVES | REAL CHANGE

SYLVIA EBERHARDT
Fashion Model, Abercrombie and Fitch, *Hollister Magazine*, and Other Top Agencies
Honors Graduate, Fairfax High School, Fairfax, VA
Honors Student—Howard University, Washington, D.C.

If you read my resume and looked at my professional credits, you might think I had it made—that the world had been handed to me on a silver platter and that I never wanted for anything. Nothing could be further from the truth. Although I am an honors student at Howard University and a fashion model who has worked with some of the top stores and magazines in the nation, my beginnings were anything but easy and beautiful.

I was born into a crack-infested, gang-ridden, one-bedroom house in inner-city Washington, D.C. I was raised a few doors down from a major crack house, where I saw junkies, prostitutes, and pimps on a daily basis. It was simply a way of life. Poverty surrounded me and my two siblings at every turn. Unemployment was rampant and the streets were filled with trash and used needles. I slept in a bunk bed where nightly I could hear drug deals being made outside my window. The iron bars on the windows were the only things that separated me from the ugliness of the world outside my home.

My mother died just before I entered high school and I was raised from that point on by my father. I was constantly teased and tormented growing up because I was so thin. My peers nicknamed me Anna (for "Anorexic"). What they did not know was that I suffered (and continue to suffer) from Crohn's disease, a life-threatening disability. Crohn's is an autoimmune disease that affects the gastrointestinal system and causes rashes, severe abdominal pain, arthritis, vomiting, and weight loss.

How did I survive? How did I become an honors student at one of the top high schools in the nation? How did I become a fashion model at the age of 15? I am blessed to have an amazing, supportive father who taught me that you never have to let your past or present dictate your future. He believed and taught me that no matter how humble one's beginnings, no matter where you were born or the circumstances of your life, the test of a person's character is knowing that he or she holds his or her destiny in his or her own hands.

He taught me that I had to take responsibility for my own life. I had to be my own savior. Further, he taught my siblings and me that "you may live

> My father taught me that "you may live in the ghetto, but the ghetto does not have to live in you."

From Ordinary to Extraordinary

REAL PEOPLE | REAL LIVES | REAL CHANGE

in the ghetto, but the ghetto does not have to live in you." He always told us that you do not have to think and act poor simply because you live in a lower-class neighborhood. He also taught us that in order to enjoy the finer things in life, you first have to experience hard times. He would say to us, "You have to ride in an old, ragged car before you can appreciate a Mercedes." His attitude helped guide and change my life.

After we moved to Virginia, I began working hard and taking college-level classes at Northern Virginia Community College while still in high school. My dream is to become a heart surgeon. I knew from the very beginning that I would have to study hard and give up many things I enjoyed doing. It paid off, however. By the end of my senior year in high school, I had over 30 college credits in math, science, anatomy, microbiology, calculus, and physiology, with a 4.0 grade point average. I won a full scholarship to Howard University and finished my first semester with a 3.92 GPA.

I write all of this to you to say, "Your life is what you make of it. You can let your past and present dictate and ruin your future, or you can get over it, work hard, believe in yourself, push yourself, and work toward your dreams." I wish you so much good luck and good fortune in your future.

EXTRAORDINARY REFLECTION

Read the following statement and respond in your online journal or class notebook.

Sylvia mentions that her father would say to her, "in order to enjoy the finer things in life, you first have to experience hard times. You have to ride in an old, ragged car before you can appreciate a Mercedes." How do you plan to use your past experiences, positive or negative, to bring about positive change in your future?

of your conclusion and that some writers actually write their conclusions first. The main topic of this paragraph happens to be the first sentence. The remaining sentences simply add information and credibility to the topic sentence.

Read and study the following paragraph.

Do you remember where you were and what you were doing when you heard that Barack Obama had been elected the first African-American president of the United States? Chances are good that you remember some of the details surrounding what you were doing when you heard this historic news. Experts report that most people remember exactly where they were and what they were doing when a major event occurred. Depending on your age, you or your parents probably remember where you were when you heard about the World Trade Center attacks. Many people who were alive when John Kennedy was assassinated still remember vividly where they were when they heard the news, even though this event happened many years ago. Events of this magnitude seem to be seared into our memories.

Circle the one option below that best describes the topic sentence of this paragraph.

1. The election of Barack Obama

2. John Kennedy's assassination

3. The fact that we tend to remember what we were doing when events of great magnitude happened

Which did you choose? Statements one and two have very little to do with the paragraph's intended message. They are simply prompts or examples. Statement three is the correct topic for this paragraph.

According to Dorothy Seyler (2003), professor and reading expert, you can identify the topic of a paragraph in four easy steps:

► The topic is the subject of the paragraph.

► You can identify the topic by answering the question, "What or who is the paragraph about?"

► The topic statement should be general enough to cover all of the specifics of the paragraph.

► The topic statement should be specific enough to exclude other paragraphs on related topics.

Finding the topic sentence or main idea of a paragraph, section, or chapter is not hard, but it does take concentration and a degree of analytical skills. If you approach each paragraph as a detective searching for clues, you will soon find out how easy and effortless it is to determine main points.

Read the following paragraph and identify the topic in your own words. Justify your answer. Then, identify the main idea of the paragraph. See if you can determine what the author really wants you to know.

When reading, do you stop after each paragraph and think about the meaning?

Finally, develop one test question for the paragraph.

You *will not* have to do this for every paragraph you read in college. As you become a stronger reader, you will do this type of analysis after each heading or chapter section. But for now, as you work on building your skills as a reader, take the time to learn how to fully analyze a small portion of a chapter.

The origin of emotion is the brain. You might say that there are two minds—one that thinks (the thinking mind) and one that feels (the emotional mind). Think of thoughts and emotions as two different mechanisms for knowing and making sense of the world. The two minds are not adversarial or physically separate; rather, they operate interactively to construct your mental life. Passion (the heart) dominates reason (the mind) when feelings are intense.

—EMOTIONAL INTELLIGENCE, NELSON AND LOW

VOCABULARY BUILDER (DEFINE THE FOLLOWING)

mechanism _____

adversarial _____

dominate _____

The TOPIC *of this paragraph is* _____
_____
_____

Who or what is the paragraph about (the MAIN IDEA*)?* _____
_____
_____
_____

What do the authors of the paragraph really want you TO KNOW*?* _____
_____
_____
_____
_____

Develop one TEST QUESTION *from this paragraph using Bloom's Taxonomy test prompts.*
_____
_____
_____

BLOOM LEVEL 4 QUESTION

SQ3R TO THE RESCUE
How Can You Do it Right the First Time?

There are as many ways to approach a chapter in a textbook as there are students who read textbooks. One of the most effective and often-used reading and studying systems is the **SQ3R Method**, developed by Francis P. Robinson in 1941. This simple, yet highly valuable, system has proved to be a successful study tool for millions of students. SQ3R involves five steps: Scan, Question, Read, Recite, and Review. The most important thing to remember about SQ3R is that it should be used on a daily basis, not as a method for cramming. See Figure 8.5.

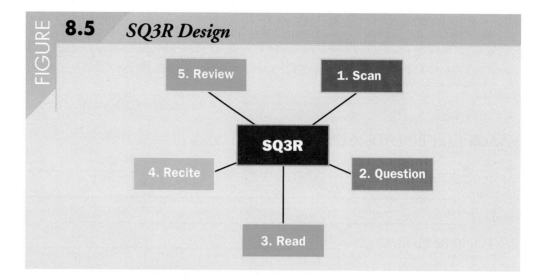

FIGURE **8.5** *SQ3R Design*

Scan

The first step of SQ3R is to *scan*, or preread, an assigned chapter. You've been doing this since you began reading Chapter 1 of this text. You begin by reading the title of the chapter, the headings, and each subheading. Look carefully at the vocabulary, timelines, graphs, charts, pictures, and drawings included in each chapter. If there is a chapter summary, read it. Scanning also includes reading the first and last sentences in each paragraph. Scanning is not a substitute for reading a chapter. Reading is discussed later. Before going any further, scan Chapter 9 of this text using the following seven questions.

Chapter Scan

*What is the title of the chapter?*_____

*What is the subtitle of the chapter?*_____

*List the chapter's major headings.*_____

_____

_____

_____

Who is introduced in the "Did You Know?" feature? List one thing you learned about him or her.

_____

_____

_____

If the chapter contains quotations, which one means the most to you? Why?

_____

_____

_____

What is the most important graph or chart in the chapter? Why?

_____

_____

_____

Without looking back, list five topics that this chapter will cover.

_____

_____

_____

Question

The second step is to *question*. There are five common questions you should ask yourself when you are reading a chapter: Who? When? What? Where? and Why? As you scan and read the chapter, turn the information into questions and see if you can answer them. If you do not know the answers to the questions, you should find them as you read along. You have been doing this for each chapter in this book thus far.

Another way to approach the chapter is to turn the major headings of each section into questions (see an example in Figure 8.6). When you get to the end of the section, having carefully read the material, looked up unfamiliar words, taken notes, and highlighted important information, answer the questions that you wrote at the beginning of the section.

FIGURE

8.6   *Forming Questions from Headings*

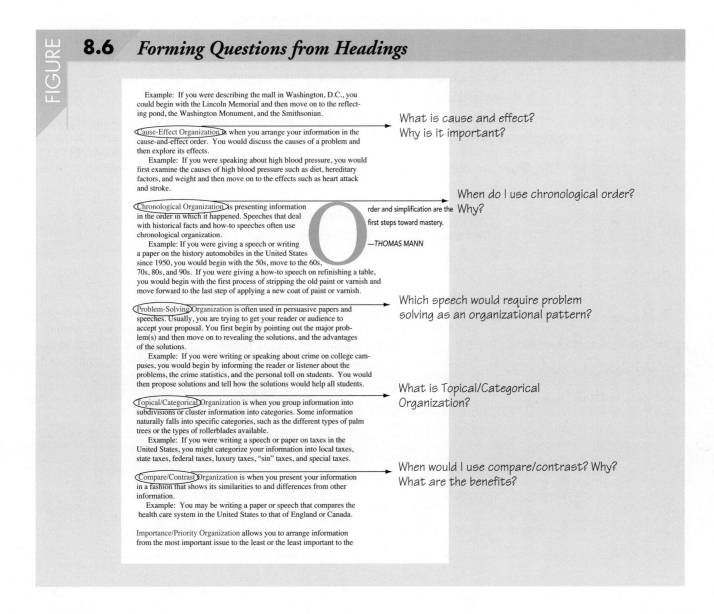

"There are worse crimes than burning books. One of them is not reading them."
—Joseph Brodsky

Read

After you scan the chapter and develop some questions to be answered from the chapter, the next step is to **read the chapter**. Remember, scanning is not reading. There is no substitute for reading in your success plan. Read slowly and carefully. The SQ3R method requires a substantial amount of time, but if you take each step slowly and completely, you will be amazed at how much you can learn and how much your grades will improve.

Read through each section. It is best not to jump around or move ahead if you did not understand the previous section. Paragraphs are usually built on each other, and so you need to understand the first before you can move on to the next. You may have to read a chapter or section more than once, especially if the information is new, technical, or difficult.

Take notes, highlight, and make marginal notes in your textbook as you read along. You own your textbook and should personalize it as you would your lecture notes. Highlight areas that you feel are important, underline words and phrases that you do not understand or that you feel are important, and jot down notes in the margins. Refer to page xxii in the preface to see how a text page should look after using SQ3R.

As you begin to read your chapter, mark the text, and take notes, keep the following in mind:

- ▶ Read the entire paragraph before you mark anything.
- ▶ Identify the topic or thesis statement of each paragraph and highlight it.
- ▶ Highlight key phrases.
- ▶ Don't highlight too much; the text will lose its significance.
- ▶ Stop and look up words that you do not know or understand.

While reading, you will want to take notes that are more elaborate than your highlighting or marginal notes. Taking notes while reading the text will assist you in studying the material and committing it to memory. **This is a major part of LEARNING ACTIVELY.** There are several effective methods of taking notes while reading (see Figure 8.7). They include:

Charts	Outlines	Flash cards
Mind maps	Timelines	Summaries
Key words		

"The man who does not read good books has no advantage over the man who can't read."
—Mark Twain

As you read through a chapter in your textbook, you may find that you have to use a variety of these techniques to capture information. Try them for one week. Although taking notes while reading a chapter thoroughly is time consuming, you will be amazed at how much you remember and how much you are able to contribute in class after using these techniques. They work!

FIGURE

8.7 *Sample Note-Taking Methods*

KEY WORDS

CHARTS

Fat Soluble Vitamins: A, D, E & K (p. 237)

VitaminA — 1st to have been recognized; there are 3 forms: retinol, retinal & retinoic acid

VitaminD — Different from all other nutrients Body can't synthesize it w/out help of sunlight

Aeschylus	Tragedy	* 7 Against Thebes * Agamemnon * The Persians
Sophocles	Tragedy	* Oedipus The King * Antigone * Electra
Euripides	Tragedy	* Medea * Hippolytus * The Cyclops
Aristophanes	Comedy	* The Clouds * The Birds
Menander	New Comedy	* The Grouch * The Arbitration * The Shorn Girl

Key words help define terminology, phrases, names, and people.

Steps to Successful Speaking   p. 114

I. Select the Topic
   1. What are your talents?
   2. Can you find sufficient materials?
   3. Is the topic appropriate for the audience?
II. Audience Analysis
   1. Conduct demographic study
   2. Use Maslow's Hierarchy of Basic Needs
III. Write a Purpose Statement
   1. What do you want your audience to understand?
   2. What is the main idea of your speech?
IV. Research Your Speech
   1. The Internet
   2. Personal interviews
   3. Electronic or print indexes
   4. Books
   5. Periodicals
V. Organize Your Speech
   1. Spatial organization
   2. Cause-effect
   3. Chronological
   4. Problem solving

Charts assist visual learners in seeing relationships and differences.

OUTLINES

Outlines organize information into clusters or under separate headings.

IT'S NOT OVER UNTIL IT'S OVER

What Is Reading Piece by Piece and How Can It Help?

If you are reading material that is completely **new to you—difficult to understand** yet important to remember—you may have to disregard entire paragraphs or read pieces of certain paragraphs. When you get to a point where you have "read enough," or your mind begins to wander, put a tick mark at that point (see Figure 8.8). The placement of the tick marks will be different for every person reading based on individual skills and experience. After your first tick mark, continue reading until you get to another stopping point, putting tick marks in the places where you feel you have read a complete thought. You will not want to read an entire chapter at one time this way—only sections.

When you get to the end of a major section, reread the material in your first "ticked section." Out to the side, paraphrase that section (indicated in matching colors in Figure 8.8). Then go on to the next section. Figure 8.8 gives you a visual of this technique. The paragraph on criminal justice is shown with its original paragraph breaks. However, you will also see **"tick marks"** indicated with a "/" showing where the reader felt this was enough to try to comprehend at one time. The "ticked section" and paraphrased remarks are shown in corresponding colors.

Few techniques will assist your comprehension and retention more than this one because it requires you to be actively involved in the reading process.

FIGURE 8.8 *Original Paragraph Breaks and New "Tick Mark Breaks" Indicated with a "/"*

A Brief History of Crime in America
(from *Criminal Justice: A Brief Introduction, 6th Edition.* F. Schmalleger, Prentice Hall, 2006.)

What we call criminal activity has undoubtedly been with us since the dawn of history, and crime control has long been a primary concern of politicians and government leaders world-wide./ Still, the American experience with crime during the last half century has been especially influential in shaping the criminal justice system of today./

Criminal activity has been around since the beginning of time and has been a concern to politicians and leaders.

Crime in Am. has greatly shaped our criminal justice system in the past 50 years.

In this country, crime waves have come and gone, including an 1850-1880 crime epidemic, which was apparently related to social upheaval caused by large-scale immigration, and the spurt of widespread organized criminal activity associated with the prohibition years of the early twentieth century./ Following World War II, however, American crime rates remained relatively stable until the 1960s./

Crime in Am. has come in waves including the 1850-1880 epidemic due to immigration and prohibition.

After WWII, crime in Am. remained stable until the '60's.

The 1960s and 1970s saw a burgeoning concern for the rights of ethnic and racial minorities, women, the physically and mentally challenged, and many other groups. The civil rights movement of the period emphasized the equality of opportunity and respect for individuals, regardless of race, color, creed, or personal attributes./ As new laws were passed and suits filed, court involvement in the movement grew. Soon, a plethora of hard-won individual rights and prerogatives, based on the U.S. Constitution, the Bill of Rights, and the new federal and state legislation, were recognized and guaranteed. By the 1980s, the civil rights movement had profoundly affected all areas of social life—from education throughout employment to the activities of the criminal justice system./

During the 60's and 70's, Am. saw the rise of individual rights regardless of race, creed, or attributes.

Due to laws based on the US Constitution the C.R. Movement profoundly impacted all aspects of life in Am. including the C.J. system.

Recite

Recitation is simple, but crucial. Skipping this step may result in less-than-full mastery of the chapter. Once you have read a section using one or more of the techniques already discussed, ask yourself this simple question: *"What was that all about?"* Find a classmate, sit down together, and ask questions of each other. Discuss with each other the main points of the chapter. Try to explain the information to each other without looking at your notes. If you are at home, sit back in your chair, recite the information, and determine what it means. If you have trouble explaining the information to your friend or reciting it to yourself, you probably did not understand the section and you should go back and reread it. If you can tell your classmate and yourself exactly what you just read and what it means, you are ready to move on to the next section of the chapter.

Review

After you have read the chapter, immediately go back and read it again. **"What?!! I just read it!"** Yes, you did. And the best way to determine whether you have mastered the information is once again to survey the chapter; review marginal notes, highlighted areas, and vocabulary words; and determine whether you can answer the questions you posed during the *"Question Step"* of SQ3R. This step will help you store and retain this information in long-term memory.

**REFLECTIONS ON
READING
AND COMPREHENSION**

SQ3R can be a lifesaver when it comes to understanding material that is overwhelming. It is an efficient, comprehensive, and DOABLE practice that can dramatically assist you in your reading efforts. It may take more time than your old method, but you will begin to see the results almost immediately. Seriously considering and practicing the strategies outlined in this chapter will help increase your comprehension level and also help your ability to recall the information when you need it later on.

As you continue to work to become an active, engaged learner, consider the following tips for reading comprehension and retention:

▶ Approach the text, chapter, or article with an *open mind.*

▶ *Free your mind* to focus on your reading.

▶ Always read with your *"six pack"* at your side.

▶ Underline and look up words you do not *understand.*

▶ Write down your *vocabulary words,* and review them often.

▶ Use *SQ3R* to increase and test your comprehension.

▶ If you're having trouble, *get a tutor* to help you.

▶ Understand that *the more you read,* the better you'll become at it.

"The knowledge of words is the gateway to learning."
—W. Wilson

KNOWLEDGE in BLOOM

Reading for Comprehension

Each chapter-end assessment is based on *Bloom's Taxonomy of Learning*. See the inside front cover for a quick review.

UTILIZES LEVELS 1–6 ON THE TAXONOMY

PROCESS: Read the following story carefully, looking up words that you do not understand, highlighting phrases that you think are important, and paraphrasing in the spaces provided. When reading the story, use the SQ3R method. We've done paragraph #1 for you as an example.

The Life and Death of Harvey Milk.

DIRECTIONS: READ THIS SECTION, IDENTIFY UNFAMILIAR WORDS WITH UNDERLINING, HIGHLIGHT IMPORTANT WORDS AND PHRASES	LOOK UP WORDS THAT NEED TO BE DEFINED	PARAPHRASE THE MAIN IDEA IN YOUR OWN WORDS
More perplexing things have happened, but a Twinkie caused the death of Harvey Milk. That's right. In 1978, defense lawyers using the "Twinkie Defense" explained an inexplicable murder away. This was the first mainstream trial to use the, "I am not responsible for my actions" defense.	*Unfamiliar words and definitions* *Perplexing = confusing or puzzling* *Inexplicable = not easily explained, unreasonable*	*The main idea of this paragraph is: In 1978, defense lawyers used a new strategy called "the Twinkie Defense" (I'm not responsible for my actions) to explain why someone murdered Harvey Milk.*
Harvey Milk was the first openly gay man elected to a significant office in America. In 1977, Milk was elected as a member of the San Francisco Board of Supervisors. This was quite arduous at this point in American history, when most people, including many psychologists and religious leaders, still classified homosexuality as deviant and a mental illness.	*Unfamiliar words and definitions*	*The main idea of this paragraph is:*
Harvey Milk is to the Gay Rights Movement what Martin Luther King, Jr. is to the Civil Rights Movement. Before King, little was happening with the CRM, and before Milk, little was happening with the GRM. He changed the face of California politics and paved the way for countless other gays and lesbians to enter the world of politics.	*Unfamiliar words and definitions*	*The main idea of this paragraph is:*

DIRECTIONS: READ THIS SECTION, IDENTIFY UNFAMILIAR WORDS WITH UNDERLINING, HIGHLIGHT IMPORTANT WORDS AND PHRASES	**LOOK UP WORDS THAT NEED TO BE DEFINED**	**PARAPHRASE THE MAIN IDEA IN YOUR OWN WORDS**
Dan White, a staunch antigay advocate, served on the board with Milk. They were constantly at odds with each other and often engaged in verbal confrontations.	*Unfamiliar words and definitions*	*The main idea of this paragraph is:*
White had been a policeman and a fireman in San Francisco before running for office. While running for office, he vowed to restore "family values" to the city government. He vowed to "rid San Francisco of radicals, social deviants, and incorrigibles."	*Unfamiliar words and definitions*	*The main idea of this paragraph is:*
Dan White was one of the most conservative members of the board, and many proposals brought to the board by Milk and the mayor of San Francisco, George Moscone, were defeated because of the heavily conservative vote led by White.	*Unfamiliar words and definitions*	*The main idea of this paragraph is:*
At that time, the Board of Supervisors was made up of 11 members; six of them, including Dan White, were conservative and had the power to defeat most, if not all, of the liberal measures brought before the board. This did not fare well with Harvey Milk and the other liberal members of the board.	*Unfamiliar words and definitions*	*The main idea of this paragraph is:*
Because the job offered diminutive wages, Dan White soon realized that he could not support his family on $9,800 per year, and he submitted his resignation to Mayor Moscone. This did not sit well with the people who'd elected him. They urged him to reconsider and when he tried to rescind his resignation, Mayor Moscone refused. This decision was made, in part, because Harvey Milk had convinced Moscone to deny White's reinstatement.	*Unfamiliar words and definitions*	*The main idea of this paragraph is:*
In a fit of wrath over the decision, Dan White entered the San Francisco City Hall on the morning of November 27, 1978, through a basement window. He went to Mayor Moscone's office and shot him in the chest, and as he lay dying, shot him again in the head.	*Unfamiliar words and definitions*	*The main idea of this paragraph is:*
He then walked calmly down the hall and asked to see Harvey Milk. Once inside the office, he slew Milk with two bullets to the brain. He then left City Hall, called his wife, spoke with her in person at St. Mary's Cathedral, and then turned himself in.	*Unfamiliar words and definitions*	*The main idea of this paragraph is:*
It is reported that policemen representing the city of San Francisco shouted, cheered, and applauded when news of the murders reached the police department.	*Unfamiliar words and definitions*	*The main idea of this paragraph is:*

Dan White's defense lawyers used a "diminished capacity" defense, suggesting that he was led to his actions by too much sugar from junk food. The lawyers convinced a jury that he was not himself and his senses were off-kilter. This became known as the "Twinkie Defense."	*Unfamiliar words and definitions*	*The main idea of this paragraph is:* _____ _____ _____ _____
Dan White was convicted of second-degree manslaughter and was sentenced to only seven years for two premeditated murders. After serving only five years, he was released. The "Twinkie Defense" had worked.	*Unfamiliar words and definitions*	*The main idea of this paragraph is:* _____ _____ _____ _____
In 1985, after being released from Soledad Prison, Dan White walked into his garage, took a rubber hose, connected it to his car's exhaust, and killed himself with carbon monoxide poisoning. He was 39 years old. His tombstone reads, *"Daniel J. White (1946–October 21, 1985), Sgt. U. S. Army, Vietnam. Cause of death: Suicide."*	*Unfamiliar words and definitions*	*The main idea of this paragraph is:* _____ _____ _____ _____

Sources: "He Got Away with Murder" at www.findagrave.com; "The Pioneer Harvey Milk" at www.time.com; "Remembering Harvey Milk" at www.lambda.net.

In 100 words or less, thoroughly summarize this entire article. Be certain to include dates, names, places, and circumstances. Pretend that you have to explain this entire story to a 10-year-old. This exercise will help you become more adept at the ESSENTIAL CORNERSTONE skill of KNOWLEDGE.

_____
_____
_____
_____
_____
_____
_____
_____
_____
_____
_____
_____
_____
_____
_____
_____
_____
_____

SQ3R *Mastery* Study Sheet

EXAMPLE QUESTION: *(from page 194)* Describe the process of fixation.		**ANSWER:**
EXAMPLE QUESTION: *(from page 191)* Why is comprehension more important than speed?		**ANSWER:**
AUTHOR QUESTION: *(from page 189)* Differentiate between passive and active reading.		**ANSWER:**
AUTHOR QUESTION: *(from page 192)* Why is having a dictionary on hand important to developing good reading comprehension?		**ANSWER:**
AUTHOR QUESTION: *(from page 194)* What are some of the effective methods to take notes while reading?		**ANSWER:**
AUTHOR QUESTION: *(from page 204)* How can you use tick marks to help you improve your reading ability?		**ANSWER:**
AUTHOR QUESTION: *(from page 204)* Why is recitation an important part of reading comprehension?		**ANSWER:**
YOUR QUESTION: *(from page ___)*		**ANSWER:**
YOUR QUESTION: *(from page ___)*		**ANSWER:**
YOUR QUESTION: *(from page ___)*		**ANSWER:**
YOUR QUESTION: *(from page ___)*		**ANSWER:**
YOUR QUESTION: *(from page ___)*		**ANSWER:**

Finally, after answering these questions, recite this chapter's major points in your mind. Consider the following general questions to help you master this material.

- ▶ What was it about?
- ▶ What does it mean?
- ▶ What was the most important thing I learned? Why?
- ▶ What were the key points to remember?

CHAPTER 9
RECORD

CULTIVATING
YOUR
LISTENING
SKILLS AND
DEVELOPING
A NOTE-TAKING
SYSTEM
THAT WORKS
FOR YOU

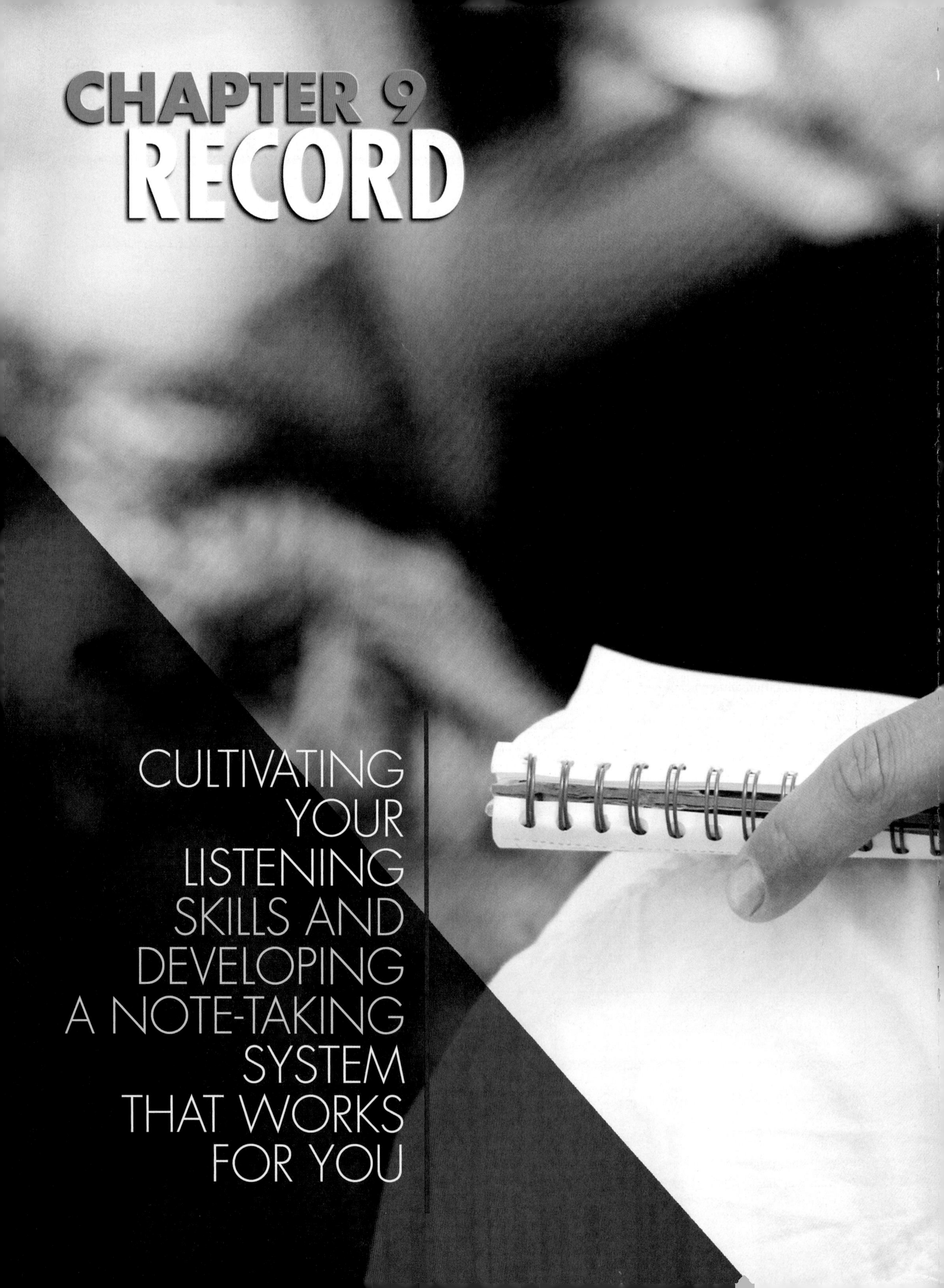

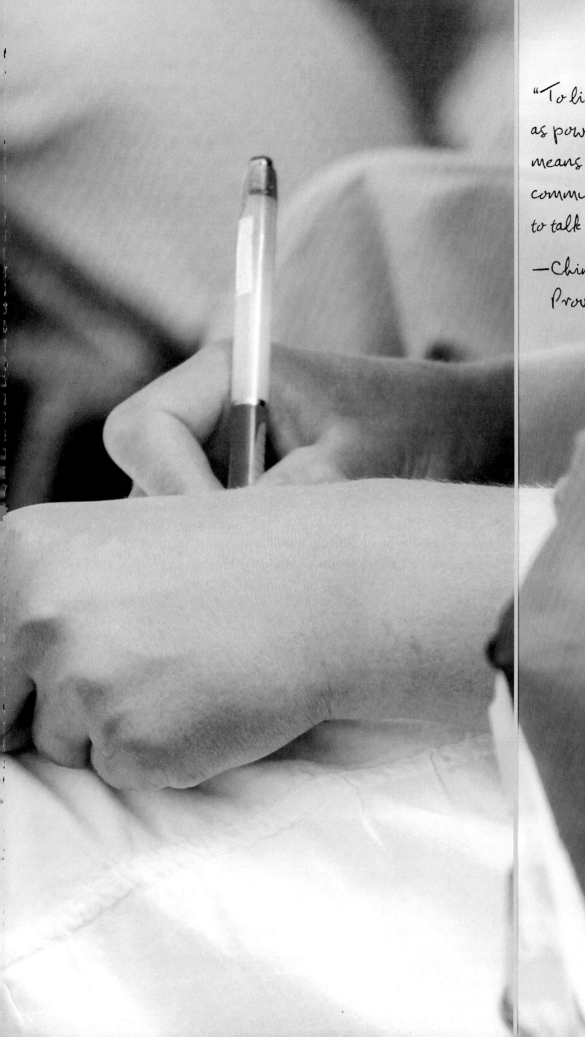

"To listen well is as powerful a means of communication as to talk well."

—Chinese Proverb

WHY READ THIS CHAPTER?

What's in it for me?

Why? Because listening is considered by many communication experts to be one of the, if not THE, most essential skills for building healthy relationships, solving problems, becoming open-minded, learning new information, and getting along in life. Listening will help you in terms of note taking, retaining information, and becoming actively involved in the learning process. The ability to listen in a variety of situations will also help you become a more efficient note-taker. Listening and note taking are important because well-designed notes create a history of your time in class, what you have read in your text and various articles, and what you might have studied with a group. You will find that there are different listening styles and note-taking styles and you will have to experiment to find which work best for you.

By carefully reading this chapter and taking the information provided seriously, you will be able to:

1. Understand the difference between listening and hearing.
2. Define the four listening styles.
3. Overcome the obstacles to listening and how to listen in different situations.
4. Discuss the importance of note taking and list specific tips to increase effectiveness.
5. Identify, discuss, and use the three types of note-taking systems: Cornell, outline, and mapping.

CHAPTER 9 / RECORD

"You cannot truly listen to anyone and do anything else at the same time."

—M. Scott Peck

WHY READ THIS CHAPTER?

. . . FROM MY PERSPECTIVE

NAME: Griffin Jones
INSTITUTION: Point Park University, Pittsburgh, PA
MAJOR: Cinema
AGE: 20

When you're making big decisions in your life, you will always have people who are older and more experienced than you bursting at the seams to give you "life lessons" and other advice. There is no point in your life where this will be more prevalent than when you first begin college. You will be bombarded with advice on sex, classes, drinking, relationships, and so on. A lot of it is just a rehash of all of the stuff you heard going into high school. However, many of the things we're asked to listen to can be helpful. Figuring out which ones are helpful is the hardest part. This is where listening comes in handy.

For most college students, listening to others is a ludicrous concept. We tend to want to try everything for ourselves. As someone who is quite stubborn, I completely understand, but over the past couple of years since enrolling in college, I've found that it's good to find a middle ground with these things. First, many people do actually know what they are talking about because they have "lived it," and we're just better off listening to their hard-earned advice and taking their word on it. On the other hand, trying something new for yourself isn't always a bad idea either. There are those people who don't know what they're talking about, either because they're completely oblivious to the real world or because they're trying to tell you stuff that doesn't necessarily apply to you. Again, this is where critical listening can come in very handy. Sometimes, you have to listen for what is not said. Also, trying something for yourself and failing is a great way of learning. Trial and error shouldn't be a forbidden activity.

What I have discovered is this: Find people who you know to be level-headed and in touch with the present and listen to them. Really listen to them. And even if you determine that they're not level-headed, take their advice and consider what they have to say anyway . . . store it away for another time; you never know when you will need their guidance. They may know what they're talking about but just don't know how to present it rationally. Just don't be afraid to step out of your boundaries and listen to others' viewpoints, listen to their lives, and use others' advice to live for yourself. This chapter on listening and note taking can help you become a much more active listener.

SCAN & QUESTION

In the preface of this book (page xix), you read about the **SQ3R Study Method**. Right now, take a few moments, **scan this chapter**, and on page 235, write **five questions** that you think will be important to your mastery of this material. In addition to the two questions below, you will find five questions from your authors. Use one of your **"Study for Quiz"** stickers to flag this page for easy reference.

EXAMPLES:

▶ **What are the four components of the Chinese verb "to listen"?** (from page 215)

▶ **Why is it important to identify key words during a lecture?** (from page 219)

THE IMPORTANCE OF LISTENING

Why Does Listening Really Matter in Classes and Relationships?

Listening is a survival skill. Period! It is that simple! *"I know listening is important,"* you might say, but few ever think of the paramount significance listening has in our everyday lives. It is necessary for:

How can becoming a critical listener help you in and out of the classroom?

▶ establishing and improving relationships,

▶ personal growth,

▶ showing respect to others,

▶ professional rapport,

▶ showing empathy and compassion,

▶ learning new information,

▶ understanding others' opinions and views,

▶ basic survival,

▶ entertainment, and

▶ health.

How much time do you think you spend listening every day? Research suggests that we spend almost 70% of our waking time communicating, and **53% of that time is spent in listening situations** (Adler et al., 2006). Effective listening skills can mean the difference between A's and F's, relationships and loneliness, and in some cases and careers, success and failure.

LISTENING DEFINED

Is There Really a Difference Between Listening and Hearing?

No doubt you've been in a communication situation in which a misunderstanding takes place. Either you hear something incorrectly or someone hears you incorrectly OR it could be that someone hears your message but misinterprets it. These communication blunders arise because we tend to view listening (and communicating in general) as an automatic response, when in fact it is not.

Listening is a learned, voluntary activity. You must choose to do it. It is a skill just like driving a car, painting a picture, or playing the piano. Becoming an active listener requires practice, time, mistakes, guidance, and active participation. **Hearing, however, is not learned; it is automatic and involuntary.** If you are within range of a sound, you will probably hear it even though you may not be listening to it. Hearing a sound does not guarantee that you know from where the sound comes. Listening actively, though, means making a conscious effort to focus on the sound you heard and to determine what it is.

According to Ronald Adler (Adler et al., 2006), the drawing of the Chinese verb "to listen" provides a comprehensive and practical definition of listening. (See Figure 9.1.)

In this figure, listening involves the ears, the eyes, undivided attention, and the heart. Do you make it a habit to listen with more than your ears? The Chinese view listening as a whole-body experience. At its core, listening is "the ability to hear, understand, analyze, respect, and appropriately respond to the meaning of another person's spoken and nonverbal messages" (Daly and Engleberg, 2006). Although this definition involves the word "hear," listening goes far beyond just the physical ability to catch sound waves.

FIGURE **9.1** *Chinese Verb "To Listen"*

Categories of Listening

The first step of listening *is* hearing, but true listening involves one's full attention and the ability to filter out distractions, emotional barriers, cultural differences, and religious biases. Listening means that you are making a conscious decision to understand and show reverence for the other person's communication efforts. Listening involves being open-minded as well. To understand listening as a whole-body experience, we can divide it into three different categories:

1. Listening with a **purpose**

2. Listening **objectively**

3. Listening **constructively**

Listening with a purpose suggests a need to recognize different types of listening situations— for example, class, worship, entertainment, and relationships. People do not listen the same way in every situation.

THINKING
FOR CHANGE: An Activity for Critical Reflection

Jennifer greatly disliked her biology instructor. She could not put her finger on exactly WHY she disliked her; she just knew that Dr. Lipmon rubbed her the wrong way. This had been the case since the first day of class. Other students seemed to like her and were able to carry on conversations with her—but Jennifer could not. "Why?" she thought. "Why do I dislike her so much? She's not a bad teacher," she reasoned, "but I just can't stand to listen to her."

Jennifer decided to sit in class for the next week and really try to figure out what the main problem was. As she sat in class and listened, she finally put her finger on the problem: She and Dr. Lipmon had completely different views on many things including evolution and women's reproductive rights. Every time Dr. Lipmon made a statement contrary to Jennifer's core beliefs, Jennifer cringed.

She "shut down" and refused to listen any further. She then transferred her dislike of Dr. Lipmon's lectures and opinions onto her as a person. She knew this was affecting her grade and her knowledge base in class, but did not know how to manage or change the situation.

In your own words, what would you suggest that Jennifer do at this point? Pretend that she is enrolled at your institution. List at least three things that she could do to ensure her success in her biology class. Think about what services are offered and what people might be of assistance to her.

1. _____

2. _____

3. _____

Listening objectively means listening with an open mind. You can give yourself few greater gifts than the gift of knowing how to listen without bias or prejudice. This is perhaps the most difficult aspect of listening. If you have ever been cut off in mid-conversation or mid-sentence by someone who disagreed with you, or if someone has left the room while you were giving your opinion of a situation, you have had the experience of talking to someone who does not know how to listen objectively.

Listening constructively means listening with the attitude: "How can this be helpful to my life, my education, my career, or my finances?" This type of listening involves evaluating the information you are hearing and determining whether it has meaning to your life. Sound easy? It is more difficult than it sounds because, again, we all tend to shut out information that we do not view as immediately helpful or useful. To listen constructively, you need to know how to listen and store information for later.

THE FOUR LISTENING STYLES
What Is Your Orientation?

According to Steven McCornack (2007), interpersonal communication expert, author, and educator, there are **four different listening styles**: action-oriented, time-oriented, people-oriented, and content-oriented. Study Figure 9.2 to determine which style best describes you as a listener.

Which style best describes you? _____

What are the "pros" of being this type of listener? _____

_____

_____

_____

FIGURE 9.2 *Four Listening Styles*

ACTION-ORIENTED LISTENERS

✓ want to get their messages quickly and to-the-point.
✓ do not like fluff and grow impatient when they perceive people to be "wasting their time."
✓ become frustrated when information is not orderly.
✓ are quick to dismiss people who "ramble" and falter when they speak.

TIME-ORIENTED LISTENERS

✓ want their information in brief, concise meetings
✓ are consumed with how much time is taken to convey a message
✓ set time limits for listening (and communicating in general)
✓ will ask people to "move the message along" if they feel it is taking too long

PEOPLE-ORIENTED LISTENERS

✓ are in contrast to time- and action-oriented listeners
✓ view listening as a chance to connect with other people
✓ enjoy listening to people so that relationships can be built
✓ become emotionally involved with the person communicating

CONTENT-ORIENTED LISTENERS

✓ enjoy an intellectual challenge
✓ like to listen to technical information, facts, and evidence
✓ enjoy complex information that must be deciphered and filtered
✓ carefully evaluate information and facts before forming an opinion
✓ enjoy asking questions

What are the "cons" of being this type of listener? _____
_____
_____
_____

LISTENING CAN BE SO HARD

Can You Really Overcome the Obstacles to Listening?

Several major obstacles stand in the way of becoming an effective listener. To begin building active listening skills, you first have to remove some barriers.

Obstacle One: Prejudging

Prejudging, the act of automatically shutting out what is being said, is one of the biggest obstacles to active listening. You may prejudge because you don't like or agree with the information or the person communicating it. You may also have prejudging problems because of your environment, culture, religion, social status, or attitude.

DO YOU PREJUDGE INFORMATION OR ITS SOURCE?

Answer yes or no to the following questions:

1. I tune out when something is boring.		YES	NO
2. I tune out when I do not agree with the information.		YES	NO
3. I argue mentally with the speaker about information.		YES	NO
4. I do not listen to people I do not like.		YES	NO
5. I make decisions about information before I understand all of its implications or consequences.		YES	NO

If you answered yes to two or more of these questions, you tend to prejudge in a listening situation.

TIPS FOR OVERCOMING PREJUDGING

▶ Listen for information that may be valuable to you as a student. Some material may not be pleasant to hear but may be useful to you later on.

▶ Listen to the message, not the messenger. If you do not like the speaker, try to go beyond personality and listen to what is being said, without regard to the person saying it. Conversely, you may like the speaker so much that you automatically accept the material or answers without listening objectively to what is being said.

▶ Try to remove cultural, racial, gender, social, and environmental barriers. Just because a person is different from you or holds a different point of view does not make that person wrong; and just because a person is like you or holds a similar point of view does not make that person right. Sometimes, you have to cross cultural and environmental barriers to learn new material and see with brighter eyes.

Obstacle Two: Talking

Not even the best listener in the world can listen while he or she is talking. The next time you are in a conversation with a friend, try speaking while your friend is speaking—then see if you know what your friend said. To become an effective listener, you need to learn the power of silence. Silence gives you the opportunity to think about what is being said before you respond. The first rule of listening is: Stop talking. The second rule of listening is: Stop talking. And, you guessed it, the third rule of listening is: Stop talking.

ARE YOU A TALKER RATHER THAN A LISTENER?

Answer yes or no to the following questions:

1. I often interrupt the speaker so that I can say what I want.		YES	NO
2. I am thinking of my next statement while others are talking.		YES	NO
3. My mind wanders when others talk.		YES	NO
4. I answer my own questions.		YES	NO
5. I answer questions that are asked of other people.		YES	NO

If you answered yes to two or more questions, you tend to talk too much in a listening situation.

TIPS FOR OVERCOMING THE URGE TO TALK TOO MUCH

▶ Avoid interrupting the speaker. Force yourself to be silent at parties, family gatherings, and friendly get-togethers. You should not be unsociable, but force yourself to be silent for 10 minutes. You'll be surprised at what you hear. You may also be surprised how hard it is to do this. Test yourself.

▶ Ask someone a question and then allow that person to answer the question.

▶ Too often we ask questions and answer them ourselves. Force yourself to wait until the person has formulated a response. If you ask questions and wait for answers, you will force yourself to listen.

▶ Concentrate on what is being said at the moment, not on what you want to say next.

Obstacle Three: Becoming Too Emotional

Emotions can form a strong barrier to active listening. Worries, problems, fears, and anger can keep you from listening to the greatest advantage. Have you ever sat in a lecture and before you knew what was happening, your mind was a million miles away because you were angry or worried about something? If you have, you know what it's like to bring your emotions to the table.

DO YOU BRING YOUR EMOTIONS TO THE LISTENING SITUATION?

Answer yes or no to the following questions:

1. I get angry before I hear the whole story.   YES   NO
2. I look for underlying or hidden messages in information.   YES   NO
3. Sometimes, I begin listening on a negative note.   YES   NO
4. I base my opinions of information on what others are saying or doing.   YES   NO
5. I readily accept information as correct from people whom I like or respect.   YES   NO

If you answered yes to two or more of these questions, you tend to bring your emotions to a listening situation.

TIPS FOR OVERCOMING EMOTIONS

▶ Know how you feel before you begin the listening experience. Take stock of your emotions and feelings ahead of time.

▶ Focus on the message; determine how to use the information.

▶ Create a positive image about the message you are hearing.

▶ Avoid overreacting and jumping to conclusions.

LISTENING FOR KEY WORDS, PHRASES, AND HINTS

Do Professors Really Offer Test Clues in Their Lectures?

Do you find it easy or hard to pick up on a professor's clues in class that may indicate important test information?

Learning how to listen for key words, phrases, and hints can help you become an active listener and an effective note-taker. For example, if your English instructor begins a lecture by saying, "There are 10 basic elements to writing poetry," jot down the number 10 under the heading "Poetry" or write the numbers 1 through 10 on your notebook page, leaving space for notes. If at the end of class you find that you listed only six elements to writing poetry, you know that you missed part of the lecture. At this point, you need to ask the instructor some questions.

ESSENTIAL CORNERSTONE

Knowledge:
How can learning to take more effective notes help you master knowledge and learn more?

Social Networking Moment:
Share your response to this Essential Cornerstone with peers in your social network. Choose two responses from your peers and respond to their postings.

Here are some key phrases and words to listen for:

in addition to	another way	above all
most important	such as	specifically
you'll see this again	therefore	finally
for example	to illustrate	as stated previously
in contrast	in comparison	nevertheless
the characteristics of	the main issue is	moreover
on the other hand	as a result of	because

Picking up on *transition words* such as these will help you filter out less important information and thus listen more carefully to what is most important.

LISTENING IN DIFFICULT SITUATIONS

What Do You Do When English Is Your Second Language?

For students whose first language is not English, the college classroom can present some uniquely challenging situations. One of the most pressing and important challenges is the ability to listen, translate, understand, and capture the message on paper in a quick and continuous manner. According to Lynn Forkos, professor and coordinator of the Conversation Center for International Students at the College of Southern Nevada, the following tips can be beneficial:

▶ Don't be afraid to stop the instructor to ask for clarification. Asking questions allows you to take an active part in the listening process. If the instructor doesn't answer your questions sufficiently, make an appointment to speak with him or her during office hours.

▶ If you are in a situation where the instructor can't stop or you're watching a movie or video in class, listen for words that you do understand and try to figure out unfamiliar words in the context of the sentence. Jot down questions to ask later.

▶ Enhance your vocabulary by watching and listening to TV programs such as *Dateline, 20/20, Primetime Live, 60 Minutes,* and the evening news. You might also try listening to radio stations such as National Public Radio as you walk or drive.

▶ Write down everything that the instructor puts on the board, overhead, or PowerPoint slide. You may not need every piece of this information, but this technique gives you (and hopefully your study group) the ability to sift through the information outside of class. It also gives you a visual history of what the instructor said.

▶ Join a study group with people who speak English well and have the patience to assist you.

▶ Finally, if there is a conversation group or club that meets on campus, take the opportunity to join. **By practicing language**, you become more attuned to common words and phrases. If a conversation group is not available, consider starting one of your own.

TAKING EFFECTIVE NOTES

Is It Just a Big, Crazy Chore?

Go to class, take notes. Listen, take notes. Read a text, take notes. Watch a film, take notes. Jeez! Is it really that important? Actually, knowing how to take useful, accurate notes can dramatically improve your academic life. If you are an effective listener and note-taker, you have two of the most valuable skills any student could ever use. There are several reasons why it is important to take notes:

▶ You become an active part of the listening process.

▶ You create a history of your course's content when you take notes.

▶ You have written criteria to follow when studying.

▶ You create a visual aid for your material.

▶ Studying becomes much easier.

▶ You retain information at a greater rate than non-note-takers.

▶ Effective note-takers average higher grades than non-note-takers (Kiewra and Fletcher, 1984).

TIPS FOR EFFECTIVE NOTE TAKING

How Can I Write It Right?

You have already learned several skills that you will need to take notes, such as cultivating your active listening skills, overcoming obstacles to effective listening, and familiarizing yourself with key phrases used by instructors. Next, prepare yourself mentally and physically to take notes that are going to be helpful to you. Consider the following ideas as you think about expanding your note-taking abilities.

▶ **Physically AND mentally attend class.** This may sound like stating the obvious, but it is surprising how many college students feel they do not need to go to class. Not only do you have to physically show up, you also have to be there mentally and emotionally—ready to listen, take notes, question, scrutinize, and interpret.

▶ **Come to class prepared.**   Scan, read, and use your textbook to establish a basic understanding of the material before coming to class It is always easier to take notes when you have a preliminary understanding of what is being said. Coming to class prepared also means bringing the proper materials for taking notes: lab manuals, pens, a notebook, and a highlighter.

▶ **Bring your textbook to class.**   Although many students think they do not need to bring their textbooks to class if they have read the homework assignment, you will find that many instructors repeatedly refer to the text while lecturing. The instructor may ask you to highlight, underline, or refer to the text in class, and following along in the text as the instructor lectures may also help you organize your notes.

▶ **Ask questions and participate in class.**   Two of the most critical actions you can perform in class are to ask questions and to participate in the class discussion. If you do not understand a concept or theory, ask questions. Don't leave class without understanding what has happened and assume you'll pick it up on your own.

Good note-taking skills help you do more than simply record what you learn in class or read in a book so that you can recall it. These skills can also help reinforce that information so that you actually know it.

YOU'LL BE SEEING STARS

What Is the L-STAR System and How Can I Use It?

One of the most effective ways to take notes begins with the **L-STAR system.**

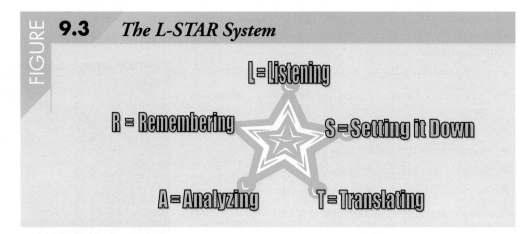

FIGURE 9.3   *The L-STAR System*

L = Listening

R = Remembering

S = Setting it Down

A = Analyzing

T = Translating

This five-step program will enable you to compile complete, accurate, and visual notes for future reference. Along with improving your note-taking skills, using this system will enhance your ability to participate in class, help other students, study more effectively, and perform well on exams and quizzes.

L—Listening

One of the best ways to become an effective note-taker is to become an active listener. A concrete step you can take toward becoming an active listener in class is to sit near the front of the room, where you can hear the instructor and see the board and overheads. Choose a spot that allows you to see the instructor's mouth and facial expressions. If you see that the instructor's face has become animated or expressive, you can bet that you are hearing important information. Write it down! If you sit in the back of the room, you may miss out on these important clues.

S—Setting It Down

The actual writing of notes can be a difficult task. Some instructors are organized in their delivery of information; others are not. Some stick to an easy-to-follow outline and others ramble around, making it more difficult to follow them and take notes. Your listening skills, once again, are going to play an important role in determining what needs to be written down. In most cases, you will not have time to take notes verbatim. Some instructors talk very fast. You will thus have to be selective about the information you choose to set down. One of the best ways to keep up with the information being presented is to develop a shorthand system of your own. Many of the symbols you use will be universal, but you may use some symbols, pictures, and markings that are uniquely your own. Some of the more common symbols are:

w/	with	w/o	without
=	equals	≠	does not equal
<	less than	>	greater than
%	percentage	#	number
&	and	^	increase
+	plus or addition	–	minus
*	important	etc.	and so on
e.g.	for example	vs.	against
esp	especially	"	quote
?	question	. . .	and so on

These symbols can save you valuable time when taking notes. Because you will use them frequently, it might be a good idea to memorize them.

T—Translating

Translating can save you hours of work as you begin to study for exams. Many students feel that this step is not important, or is too time consuming, and leave it out. Don't. Often, students take notes so quickly that they make mistakes or use abbreviations that they may not be able to decipher later.

After each class, go to the library or some other quiet place and review your notes. You don't have to do this immediately after class, but before the end of the day, you will need to rewrite and translate your classroom notes. This process gives you the opportunity to put the notes in your own words and to incorporate your text notes into your classroom notes. This practice also provides a first opportunity to commit this information to memory.

Translating your notes helps you make connections among previous material discussed, your own personal experiences, readings, and new material presented. Translating aids in recalling and applying new information. Few things are more difficult than trying to reconstruct your notes the night before a test, especially when they were made several weeks previously.

A—Analyzing

This step takes place while you translate your notes from class. When you analyze your notes, you are asking two basic questions: (1) What does this mean? and (2) Why is it important? If you can answer these two questions about your material, you have almost mastered the information. Though some instructors will want you to spit back the exact same information you were given, others will ask you for a more detailed understanding and a synthesis of the material. When you are translating your notes, begin to answer these two questions using your notes, textbook, supplemental materials, and information gathered from outside research. Once again, this process is not simple or quick, but testing your understanding of the material is important. Remember that many lectures are built on past lectures. If you do not understand what happened in class on September 17, you may not be able to understand what happens on September 19. Analyzing your notes while translating them will give you a more complete understanding of the material.

R—Remembering

Once you have listened to the lecture, set your notes on paper, and translated and analyzed the material, it is time to study, or remember, the information. Some effective ways to remember information include creating a visual picture, speaking the notes out loud, using mnemonic devices, and finding a study partner. Chapter 10 will help you with these techniques and other study aids.

Tips for Personal Success

Consider the following tips for improving your listening skills and taking notes more effectively:

▶ Sit near the front of the room and establish eye contact with the instructor.

▶ Read the text or handouts beforehand to familiarize yourself with the upcoming information.

▶ Come to class with an open mind and positive attitude about learning. Listen purposefully, objectively, and constructively.

Now, it is your turn. Create a list of at least three more tips that you would offer a fellow classmate to assist him or her with bringing about positive change in his or her listening and note-taking skills.

1. _____

2. _____

3. _____

THREE COMMON NOTE-TAKING SYSTEMS

Why Doesn't Everyone Take Notes the Same Way?

There are three common note-taking systems: (1) the **outline** technique; (2) the **Cornell**, or split-page, technique (also called the T system); and (3) the **mapping** technique. You may find each technique useful or you may find that one is more effective for you than the others.

IT'S AS SIMPLE AS A, B, C—1, 2, 3

The Outline Technique

The outline system uses a series of major headings and multiple subheadings formatted in hierarchical order (Figure 9.4). The outline technique is one of the most commonly used note-taking systems, yet it is also one of the most misused systems. It can be difficult to outline notes in class, especially if your instructor does not follow an outline format while lecturing.

When using the outline system, it is best to get all the information from the lecture and, afterward, combine your lecture notes and text notes to create an outline. Most instructors would advise against using the outline system of note taking during class, although you may be able to use a modified version. The most important thing to remember is not to get bogged down in a

FIGURE

9.4   *The Outline Technique*

October 20

Topic: Maslow's Hierarchy of Basic Needs

I. Abraham Maslow (1908–1970)
- American psychologist
- Born - Raised Brooklyn, N.Y.
- Parents = Uneducated Jewish immigrants
- Lonely - unhappy childhood
- 1st studied law @ city coll. of N.Y.
- Grad school - Univ of Wisconsin
- Studied human behavior & experience
- Leader of humanistic school of psy.

II. H of B. Needs (Theory)
- Written in <u>A Theory of Human Motivation</u> in 1943
- Needs of human arranged like a ladder
- Basic needs of food, air, water at bottom
- Higher needs "up" the ladder
- Lower needs must be met to experience the higher needs

III. H of B. Needs (Features)
- Physiological needs
  - Breathing
  - Food
  - Air & water
  - Sleep
- Safety needs
  - Security of body
  - Employment

system during class; what is critical is getting the ideas down on paper. You can always go back after class and rearrange your notes as needed.

If you are going to use a modified or informal outline while taking notes in class, you may want to consider grouping information together under a heading as a means of outlining. It is easier to remember information that is logically grouped than information that is scattered across several pages. If your study skills lecture is on listening, you might outline your notes using the headings "The Process of Listening" and "Definitions of Listening."

After you have rewritten your notes using class lecture information and material from your textbook, your notes may look like those in Figure 9.4.

IT'S A SPLIT DECISION

The Cornell (Modified Cornell, Split-Page, or T) System

The basic principle of the Cornell system, developed by Dr. Walter Pauk of Cornell University, is to split the page into two sections, each to be used for different information (see Figure 9.5). Section B (the larger section) is used for the actual notes from class or your text. Section A (the smaller section) should be used for headings OR questions. Review Figure 9.5 to see an example of Cornell note taking. An example of outline notes using the Cornell system appears in Figure 9.6.

FIGURE 9.5 *Cornell Note-Taking System Example*

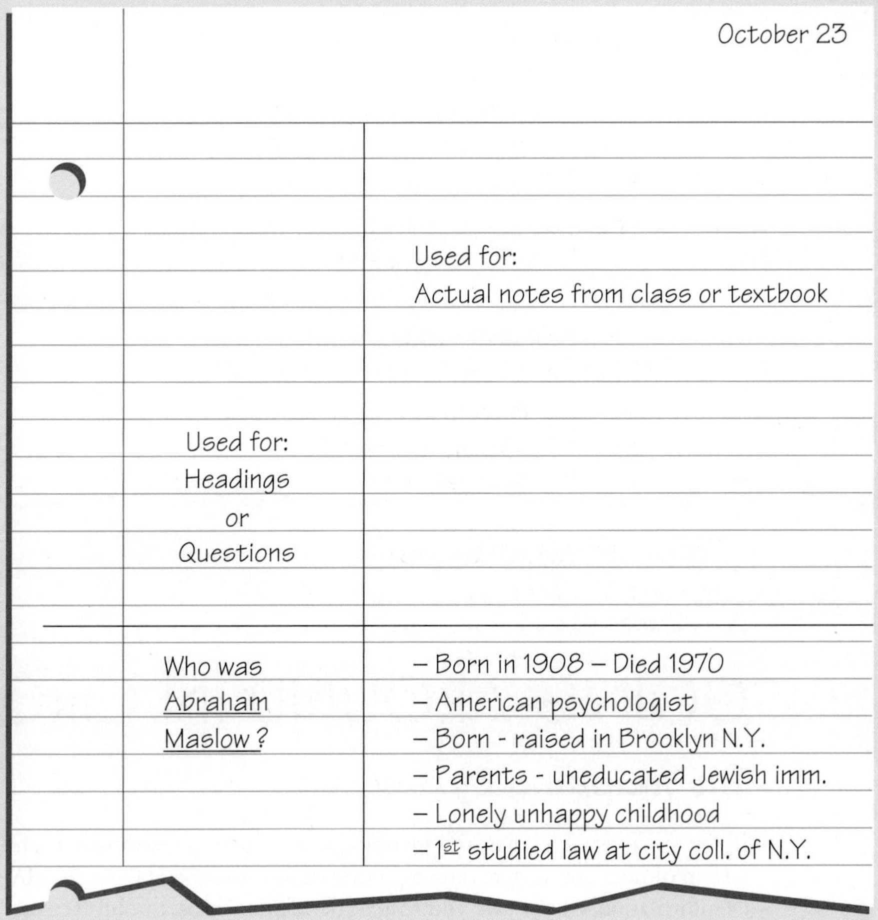

October 23

Used for:
Actual notes from class or textbook

Used for:
Headings
or
Questions

Who was Abraham Maslow ?	– Born in 1908 – Died 1970
	– American psychologist
	– Born - raised in Brooklyn N.Y.
	– Parents - uneducated Jewish imm.
	– Lonely unhappy childhood
	– 1st studied law at city coll. of N.Y.

FIGURE   **9.6**   *Outline Using a Cornell Frame*

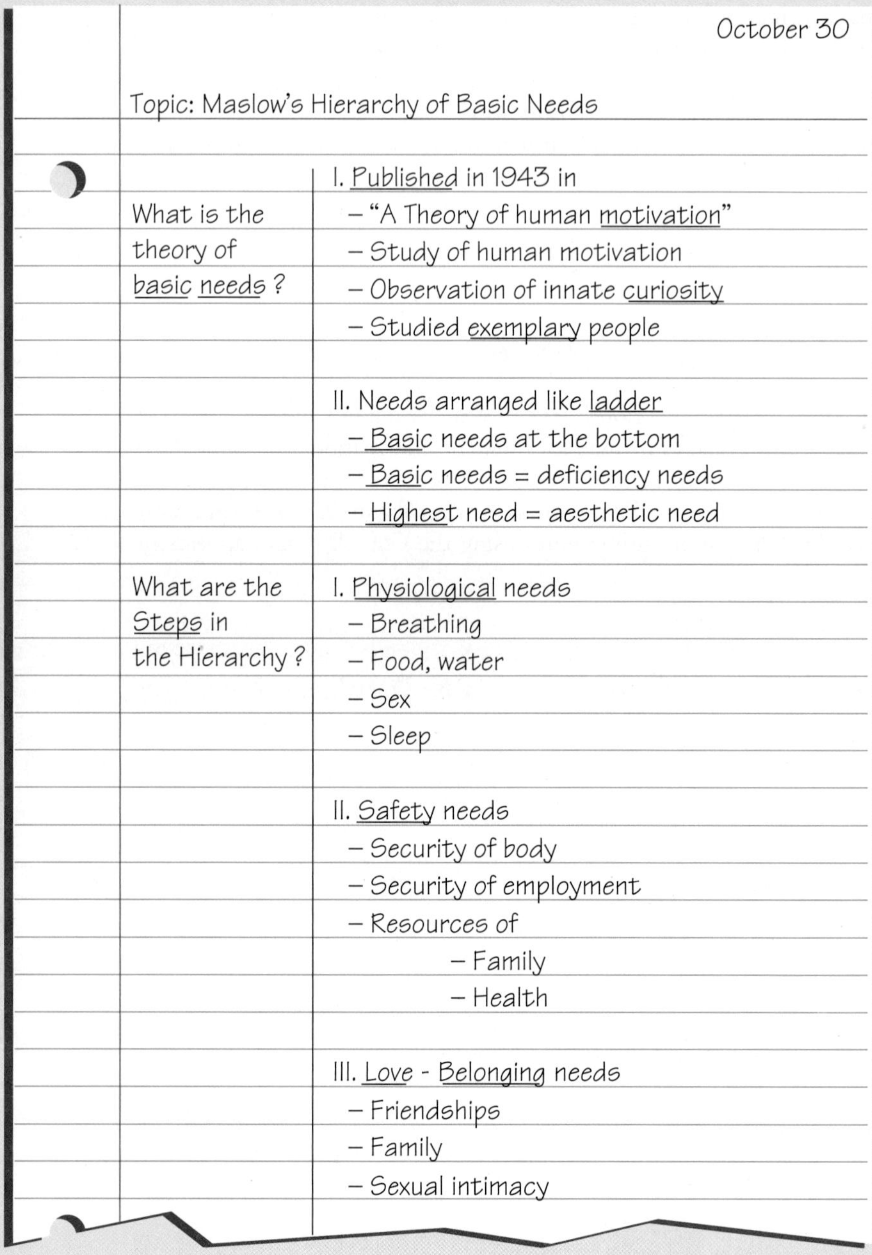

October 30

Topic: Maslow's Hierarchy of Basic Needs

What is the theory of <u>basic</u> <u>needs</u>?	I. <u>Published</u> in 1943 in
	  – "A Theory of human <u>motivation</u>"
	  – Study of human motivation
	  – Observation of innate <u>curiosity</u>
	  – Studied <u>exemplary</u> people
	
	II. Needs arranged like <u>ladder</u>
	  – <u>Basic</u> needs at the bottom
	  – <u>Basic</u> needs = deficiency needs
	  – <u>Highest</u> need = aesthetic need

What are the <u>Steps</u> in the Hierarchy?	I. <u>Physiological</u> needs
	  – Breathing
	  – Food, water
	  – Sex
	  – Sleep
	
	II. <u>Safety</u> needs
	  – Security of body
	  – Security of employment
	  – Resources of
	      – Family
	      – Health
	
	III. <u>Love</u> - <u>Belonging</u> needs
	  – Friendships
	  – Family
	  – Sexual intimacy

GOING AROUND IN CIRCLES

The Mapping System

If you are a visual learner, the mapping system may be especially useful for you. The mapping system of note taking generates a picture of information (Figure 9.7) by creating a map, or web, of information that allows you to see the relationships among facts or ideas. Figure 9.8 shows how to use the mapping system in a Cornell frame.

FIGURE

9.7 **The Mapping System**

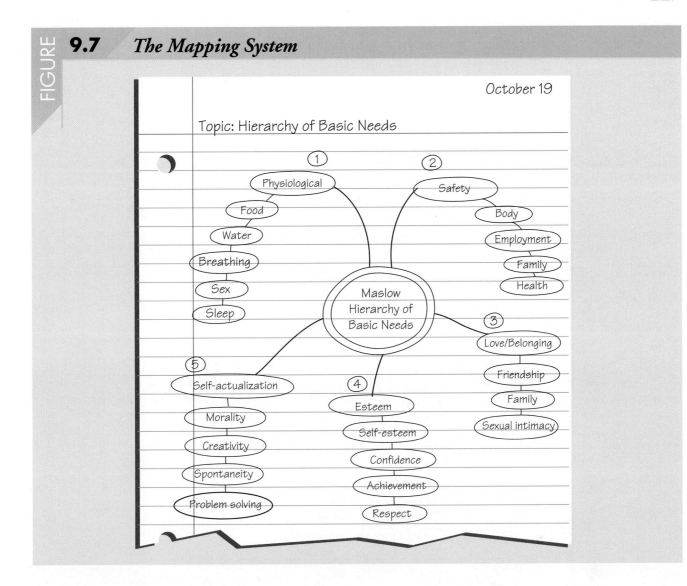

A note-taking system *must work for you*. Do not use a system because your friends use it or because you feel that you should use it. Experiment with each system or combination to determine which is best for you.

Always remember to keep your notes organized, dated, and neat. Notes that cannot be read are no good to you or to anyone else.

TMI! TMI! (TOO MUCH INFORMATION)

What Do I Do if I Get Lost While Taking Notes During the Lecture?

Have you ever been in a classroom trying to take notes, but the instructor is speaking so rapidly that you cannot possibly get all of the information? And just when you think you're caught up, you realize that he or she has made an important statement and you missed it. What do you do? How can you handle, or avoid, this difficult note-taking situation? Here are several hints:

ESSENTIAL CORNERSTONE

Adaptability:
How can the skill of adaptability help you if you get lost while taking notes during a lecture?

Social Networking Moment:
Share your response to this Essential Cornerstone with peers in your social network. Choose two responses from your peers and respond to their postings.

FIGURE

9.8   *The Mapping System in a Cornell Frame*

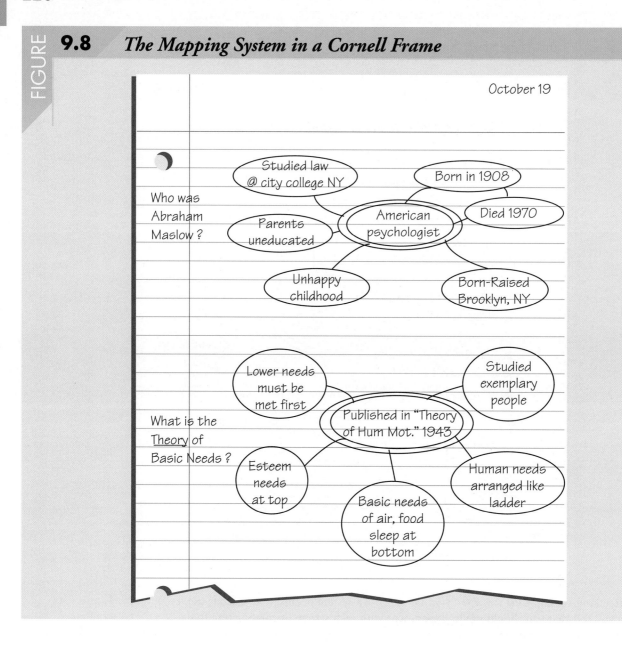

October 19

Who was Abraham Maslow?

- Studied law @ city college NY
- Born in 1908
- American psychologist
- Died 1970
- Parents uneducated
- Unhappy childhood
- Born-Raised Brooklyn, NY

What is the Theory of Basic Needs?

- Lower needs must be met first
- Studied exemplary people
- Published in "Theory of Hum Mot." 1943
- Esteem needs at top
- Human needs arranged like ladder
- Basic needs of air, food sleep at bottom

▶ Raise your hand and ask the instructor to repeat the information.

▶ Ask your instructor to slow down.

▶ If he or she will do neither, leave a blank space with a question mark in the side margin (Figure 9.9). You can get this information after class from your instructor, a classmate, or your study buddy. This can be a difficult task to master. The key is to focus on the information at hand. Focus on what is being said at the exact moment. Don't give up!

▶ Meet with your instructor immediately after class or at the earliest time convenient for both of you.

▶ Form a note-taking group that meets after each class. This serves two purposes: (1) you can discuss and review the lecture, and (2) you will be able to get the notes from one of your note-taking buddies.

FIGURE

9.9 *What To Do if You Get Lost*

October 20

Topic: Maslow's Hierachy of Basic Needs

I. Abraham Maslow (1908–1970)
- American psychologist
- Born - Raised Brooklyn, N.Y.
- Parents - Uneducated Jewish immigrants
- Lonely - unhappy childhood
- 1st studied law @ city coll. of N.Y.
- Grad school - Univ of Wisconsin
- Studied human behavior & experience
- Leader of humanistic school of psy.

II. H of B. Needs (Theory)
- written in 19 ?

?

Ask

} leave a blank space to fix in your notes later

III. H of B. Needs (Features)
- Physiological Needs
- Breathing
- Food
- Air & water
- Sleep
- Safety Needs
- Security of body
- Employment

▶ Never lean over and ask questions of another student during the lecture. This will cause that person to miss information as well. It will probably also annoy your peers and the instructor.

▶ Rehearse your note-taking skills at home by taking notes from TV news magazines or channels like the History Channel.

▶ Ask the instructor's permission to use a tape recorder during the lecture. Do not record a lecture without permission. We suggest that you try to use other avenues, such as the ones listed above, instead of taping your notes. It is a time-consuming task to listen to the lecture for a second time. However, if this system works for you, use it.

From Ordinary to *Extraordinary*

REAL PEOPLE | REAL LIVES | REAL CHANGE

CATHERINE SCHLEIGH
Customer Service Coordinator, Kinkos-FedEx, Inc.
Philadelphia, PA

I don't like to speculate, but I would say that few college students in America have to take a bus two and a half hours each way, five days a week, to attend classes. I did. I would also speculate that few college students became the primary caregiver for his or her mother at the age of seven. I did. I might also speculate that few people feel lucky, proud, and honored to simply be able to hold his or her head high and say, "I made it." I do. My name is Catherine Schleigh and despite my past family history and personal strug-

I was left to care for my mother, who is a diagnosed paranoid schizophrenic.

gles, I am a first-generation college graduate and hold a professional position with a major corporation in one of the most wonderful cities in America.

Growing up, I had no real family to speak of. My dad left my mom and me when I was young, and from the age of seven, I was left to care for my mother, who is a diagnosed paranoid schizophrenic. Growing up, I received no help, no support, and no encouragement from her or any other members of my family. Often, she would not take her

medications (or the medications had been improperly prescribed) and would thus be physically, emotionally, and verbally abusive to me. It was hard to watch her talk to herself or invisible people. We lived in a very poor, drug-infested, gang-populated area of Philly and many times, I could not see how I would ever survive.

I managed to complete high school and I began attending Job Corps, studying business. From there, I began my college studies and majored in business administration. I had to work very hard, and the adjustment from high school to college was massive. I had to learn how to motivate myself, but the most important thing I learned was that there are people in this world who will help you if you let them.

From Ordinary to Extraordinary

REAL PEOPLE | REAL LIVES | REAL CHANGE

Some of my instructors did not understand my situation at first. I cried a lot in class, did not have my projects completed from time to time, and basically lived the life of an introvert. Once everyone learned that I was caring for my mother, traveling five hours a day to class, and struggling just to eat, they became my family. They taught me that I had to put my education first. They taught me that without an education, I would most likely have to work in dead-end jobs for the rest of my life. I began to really look at all of the people in my neighborhood, and I made a committed decision that I was not going to fall prey to the temptations of alcohol, sex, unemployment, and drugs.

As I began to succeed in my classes, my self-esteem became healthier. I began to understand how to support myself, take pride in my successes, and help others in any way possible. I still struggle with my mother as she seeks therapy and better medical care, but I also know that I must take care of my own life and keep working toward my own goals. My life is my first priority.

Today, I am an honors graduate. I completed my Bachelor of Arts in business administration with a GPA of 3.50. At the graduation ceremony, I was presented an award by the faculty and staff for my dedication, hard work, and overcoming all odds to obtain my degree. I hope in some small way that my story can help you "hold on" and reach your dreams. Happiness and success are possible for you.

EXTRAORDINARY REFLECTION

Read the following statement and respond in your online journal or class notebook.

Ms. Schleigh had no family support in college. As a matter of fact, because her father was gone, she was the primary caregiver for her mother. How has your family support (or lack of support) affected your college studies? Do you think it is important to have your family's support to succeed?

CHANGING IDEAS TO *Reality*

Yes, listening is a learned skill, but it is more than that. It is a gift that you give to yourself. It is a gift that promotes knowledge, understanding, stronger relationships, and open-mindedness. Good listening skills can help you manage conflicts, avoid misunderstandings, and establish trusting relationships. Perhaps most importantly at this point in your life, listening can help you become a more successful student. Once you learn how to listen with your whole body and mind, you will begin to see how your notes, your grades, your attitude, your relationships, and your learning processes change. As you work toward improving your listening skills and developing your note-taking system, consider the following:

▶ When listening, evaluate the content before you judge the messenger.

▶ Keep your emotions and preconceived notions in check while listening.

▶ Sit where you can see and hear the instructor.

▶ Listen for "how" something is said.

▶ Listen to the "entire story" before making a judgment call.

▶ Listen for major ideas and key words.

▶ Use a separate notebook for every class.

▶ Use abbreviations whenever possible.

▶ Write down what the instructor puts on the board or PowerPoint slide.

Becoming adept at listening and developing your own note-taking system are two essential skills that can help you become a more active learner.

"Listening is an attitude of the heart, a genuine desire to be with another person."

—S. Isham

KNOWLEDGE *in* BLOOM

Listening with an Open Mind

Each chapter-end assessment is based on *Bloom's Taxonomy of Learning.* See the inside front cover for a quick review.

UTILIZES LEVELS 4 AND 5 ON THE TAXONOMY

EXPLANATION: Seldom (if ever) would you pop in a CD, click a song on your iPod, or tune your radio to a station that you strongly disliked. It just does not seem like a good use of time, and it is not something that you would probably enjoy doing on a daily basis. However, for this exercise, we are going to ask that you do precisely what we've described above and then apply what you've experienced and learned to several questions and four **ESSENTIAL CORNERSTONES** from Chapter 1.

PROCESS: Over the course of the next few days, find a song from your *least favorite* genre. If you are a huge fan of R&B, move away from that genre and choose something from a genre of which you are not particularly fond. You might choose an old country song or a song from rap or bluegrass. If you enjoy listening to "Easy Love Songs," try something different such as metal or swing. The only stipulation is that the **song must have lyrics**.

You will have to listen to the song several times to answer the questions. HOWEVER, it is important that you read the questions BEFORE you listen to the song—particularly question #2. The key to this exercise is to practice listening with an open mind, listening for content, and listening to words when barriers are in the way (the barrier in this case would be the music itself).

1. What is the song's title and artist? _____

_____

2. What emotional and mental responses did you have to the song the first time you listened to it? Why do you think you had this response? _____

_____

_____

_____

_____

3. While listening to the song, what happened to your appreciation level? Did it increase or decrease? Why?

_____

_____

_____

_____

4. In your opinion, what was the message (theme) of the song? _____

_____

_____

_____

_____

5. What about the song most surprised you? The lyrics? The actual music? Your like or dislike of the song? The artist's voice? Etc. . . . _____

_____

_____

_____

_____

6. If you HAD to say that you gained or learned one positive thing from this song, what would it be? _____

_____

_____

7. From memory, list at least two statements, comments, or quotes from the song. _____

_____

_____

_____

_____

Now, using the following **ESSENTIAL CORNERSTONES from page 8 of Chapter 1** consider how becoming a more effective listener can help you with each.

By enhancing my listening skills, I can become more **OPEN-MINDED** by

_____

_____

_____

_____

By enhancing my listening skills, I can become more **CREATIVE** by _____
_____
_____
_____
_____

By enhancing my listening skills, I can become more **KNOWLEDGEABLE** by _____
_____
_____
_____
_____

By enhancing my listening skills, I can increase my **RESOURCEFULNESS** level by
_____
_____
_____
_____

SQ3R *Mastery* STUDY SHEET

EXAMPLE QUESTION: *(from page 215)* What are the four components of the Chinese verb "to listen"?	ANSWER:
EXAMPLE QUESTION: *(from page 219)* Why is it important to identify key words during a lecture?	ANSWER:
AUTHOR QUESTION: *(from page 216)* What is objective listening?	ANSWER:
AUTHOR QUESTION: *(from page 217)* List and define the four listening styles.	ANSWER:
AUTHOR QUESTION: *(from page 222)* Discuss the five steps in the L-STAR note-taking system.	ANSWER:
AUTHOR QUESTION: *(from page 224)* Discuss the benefits and drawbacks of using outline technique to take notes during class.	ANSWER:
AUTHOR QUESTION: *(from page 226)* When would be the best time to use the mapping system of note taking? Justify your answer.	ANSWER:
YOUR QUESTION: *(from page ____)*	ANSWER:
YOUR QUESTION: *(from page ____)*	ANSWER:
YOUR QUESTION: *(from page ____)*	ANSWER:
YOUR QUESTION: *(from page ____)*	ANSWER:
YOUR QUESTION: *(from page ____)*	ANSWER:

Finally, after answering these questions, recite this chapter's major points in your mind. Consider the following general questions to help you master this material.

▶ What was it about?
▶ What does it mean?
▶ What was the most important thing I learned? Why?
▶ What were the key points to remember?

CHAPTER 10
UNDERSTAND

EMPOWERING
YOUR MEMORY,
STUDYING
EFFECTIVELY,
AND TAKING
TESTS WITH
CONFIDENCE

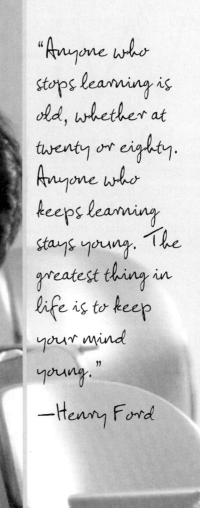

"Anyone who stops learning is old, whether at twenty or eighty. Anyone who keeps learning stays young. The greatest thing in life is to keep your mind young."

—Henry Ford

WHY READ THIS CHAPTER?

What's in it for me?

Why? Because when you read and study information, you learn amazing things. You may learn that Whoopi Goldberg has dyslexia, or that the Oedipus complex you read about in psychology class has its roots in a 2,500-year-old Greek tragedy, or that the first copying machine was invented in 1778. While you may not be tested on this material, you will certainly have many tests in college and beyond.

WHY do I need to keep remembering information and cramming my brain full? WHY will a chapter on studying and remembering help me pass my classes? WHY is it so important, since I'm not going to be in school forever, to learn how to take tests? WHY will learning how to use mnemonic devices help me in all my courses?

You will most likely be studying and taking tests for years to come. When you accept your first job, management may have you study their way of doing business and, in some cases, they will require you to pass an exam. If you go to graduate school, you will have to pass a test such as the G-MAT or the GRE or the MAT. Learning to study well and prepare for and take tests will be valuable lessons for you all your life. That is what this chapter is all about—learning how to study, how to increase your memory capacity, and how to take assessments more effectively.

By carefully reading this chapter and taking the information provided seriously, you will be able to:

1. Understand the importance of studying, how your memory works, and how to help it work better.

2. Identify the differences between short-term and long-term memory and how to commit information to long-term memory by using VCR3.

3. Use mnemonics to help you remember information.

4. Identify and use three different study strategies and apply these strategies to all your classes including math and science.

5. Identify the causes of your test anxiety and how to reduce anxiety by predicting test questions and formulating appropriate responses.

CHAPTER 10 / UNDERSTAND

"We can learn something new at any time we believe we can."

—Virginia Satir

NAME: Fernando Machado
INSTITUTION: El Paso Community College, El Paso, TX
MAJOR: Electrical Engineering
AGE: 19

I have had to learn to how to study and how to develop a note-taking system that works for me. I found that the freshman experience course and the *Cornerstone* textbook helped me become a much better student because they gave me a much better insight into how to better myself, how to organize, and how to study. I also learned about many differences between high school and college.

When I study, I first skim the chapter and make notes on major headings and bolded words. I then read the chapter carefully, highlighting important information. I always read with a dictionary close by to be sure I am grasping the correct meaning of words.

Being able to take good notes is imperative to succeed in college. Professors usually talk fast, and they don't spoon-feed students as much as teachers do in high school. You'll soon learn that you really are on your own, and you have to learn how to listen, write clear notes, and keep up with the professor. I try to get the main topics and important ideas down on paper during the professor's lecture. I use bulleted subheadings to emphasize certain ideas. It really helps me if I have read the chapter before the lecture and have taken notes as I read the chapter.

When I study for a test, I mainly review my notes rather than read the chapters again. I also like to study with a study group. Together we know much more than I know alone. I try to find a group that is serious about making good grades and learning and I am always sure that I am a contributor to the group. It is very important, however, to be self-reliant because you may not always be able to find a group or to make the meetings.

Finally, I would advise you to do your own work even if others are cheating. If you cheat now, you will most likely cheat the rest of your life. The way you are performing in school today is the way you will perform all your life.

SCAN & QUESTION

In the preface of this book (page xix), you read about the **SQ3R Study Method**. Right now, take a few moments, **scan this chapter**, and on page 263, write **five questions** that you think will be important to your mastery of this material. In addition to the two questions below, you will find five questions from your authors. Use one of your **"Study for Quiz"** stickers to flag this page for easy reference.

EXAMPLES:

▶ **Discuss three strategies for studying math.** (from page 251)

▶ **Why are mnemonics important?** (from page 245)

I FORGOT TO REMEMBER!

Do You Understand the FACTS and MYTHS about Memory Function?

"My brain is full." ***MYTH***
"Certain foods can help with memory development." ***FACT***
"Proper sleep and exercise can help you retain more information." ***FACT***
"I can't remember another thing." ***MYTH***
"Being closed-minded can hurt your memory development." ***FACT***
"Drugs and alcohol can help me remember more." ***MYTH***

> What study techniques have you used in the past to help you commit information to long-term memory?

Several studies suggest that it is impossible to fill our brains completely. One study in the 1970s concluded that if our brains were fed 10 new items of information every second for the rest of our lives, we would never fill even half of our memory's capacity (Texas A&M University).

At times, you may feel that if you study or read or learn any more, you'll forget everything. Some researchers suggest that we never forget anything—that the material is simply "covered up" by other material, but it is still in our brain. The reason we can't recall that information is that it was not important enough, not stored properly, or not used enough to keep it from being covered up. According to the German philosopher Friedrich Nietzsche (1844–1900), "The ***existence of forgetting has never been proved***; we only know that some things don't come to mind when we want them."

So, why is it so hard to remember the dates of the Civil War or who flew with Amelia Earhart or how to calculate the liquidation value of stocks or the six factors in the communication process? The primary problem is that we never properly filed or stored this information.

What would happen if you typed your English research paper into the computer and did not give it a file name? When you needed to retrieve that paper, you would not know how to find it. You would have to search through every file until you came across the paper you needed. Memory works in much the same way. We have to store it properly if we are to retrieve it easily at a later time.

This section will detail how memory works and why it is important to your studying efforts. Below, you will find some basic facts about memory.

- ▶ Everyone remembers some information and forgets other information.
- ▶ Your senses help you take in information.
- ▶ With very little effort, you can remember some information.
- ▶ With rehearsal (study), you can remember a great deal of information.
- ▶ Without rehearsal or use, information is forgotten.
- ▶ Incoming information needs to be filed in the brain if you are to retain it.
- ▶ Information stored, or filed, in the brain must have a retrieval method.
- ▶ Mnemonic devices, repetition, association, and rehearsal can help you store and retrieve information.

Psychologists have determined that there are three types of memory: **sensory** memory; **short-term,** or **working,** memory; and **long-term** memory.

Sensory memory stores information gathered from the five senses: taste, touch, smell, hearing, and sight. Sensory memory is usually temporary, lasting about one to three seconds, unless you decide that the information is of ultimate importance to you and make an effort to transfer it to long-term memory.

Short-term, or **working, memory** holds information for a short amount of time. Consider the following list of letters:

jmplngtoplntstsevng

Now, cover them with your hand and try to recite them.

It is almost impossible for the average person to do so. Why? Because your working memory bank can hold a limited amount of information, usually about five to nine separate new facts or pieces of information at once (Woolfolk, 2006). However, consider this exercise. If you break the letters down into smaller pieces and add MEANING to them, you are more likely to retain them. Example:

jum   lng   to   plnts   ts   evng

This may still not mean very much to you, but you can probably remember at least the first two sets of information, "jum" and "lng."

Now, if you were to say to yourself that this sentence means "Jump Long To Planets This Evening," you would be much more likely to begin to remember this information. Just as your memory can "play tricks" on you, you can "play tricks" on your memory.

Although it is sometimes frustrating when we "misplace" information, it is also useful and necessary to our brain's survival that every piece of information that we hear and see is not in the forefront of our minds. If you tried to remember everything, you would not be able to function. As a student, you would never be able to remember all that your instructor had said during a 50-minute lecture. You have to take steps to help you to remember important information. Taking notes, making associations, drawing pictures, and visualizing information are all techniques that can help you move information from your short-term memory to your long-term memory bank.

Long-term memory stores a lot of information. It is almost like a computer disk. You have to make an effort to put something into your long-term memory, but with effort and memory techniques such as rehearsal, practice, and mnemonic devices, you can store anything you want to remember there. Long-term memory consists of information that you have heard often, information that you use often, information that you might see often, and information that you have determined necessary and/or important to you. Just as you name a file on a computer disk, you name the files in your long-term memory. Sometimes, you have to wait a moment for the information to come to you. While you are waiting, your brain disk is spinning; if the information you seek is in long-term memory, your brain will eventually find it if you stored it properly. You may have to assist your brain in locating the information by using mnemonics and other memory devices.

THIS ISN'T YOUR DADDY'S VCR

How Can You Use VCR3 to Increase Memory Power?

Countless pieces of information are stored in your long-term memory. Some of them are triggered by necessity, some by the five senses, and some by experiences. The best way to commit information to long-term memory and retrieve it when needed can be expressed by:

V Visualizing
C Concentrating
R Relating
R Repeating
R Reviewing

Consider the following story:

As Katherine walked back to the dorm room after her evening class, she heard someone behind her. She turned to see two students holding hands walking about 20 feet behind her. She was relieved. This was the first night that she had walked back to the residence hall alone.

Katherine pulled her book bag closer to her as she increased her pace along the dimly lit sidewalk between the Salk Biology Building and the Horn Center for the Arts. "I can't believe that Shana didn't call me," she thought to herself. "She knows I hate to leave class alone."

As Katherine turned the corner onto Suddith Street, she heard someone else behind her. She turned but did not see anyone. As she continued to walk toward the residence hall, she heard the sound again. Turning to see if anyone was there, she saw a shadow disappear into the grove of hedges along the sidewalk.

Startled and frightened, Katherine crossed the street to walk beneath the streetlights and sped up to get closer to a group of students about 30 feet in front of her. She turned once more to see if anyone was behind her. Thankfully, she did not see anyone.

By this time, she was only one block from her residence hall. The lighting was better and other students were around. She felt better, but vowed never again to leave class alone at night.

To visualize information, try to create word pictures in your mind as you hear the information. If you are being told about a Revolutionary War battle in Camden, South Carolina, try to see the soldiers and the battlefield, or try to paint a mind picture that will help you to remember the information. You may also want to create visual aids as you read or study information.

As you read Katherine's story, were you able to visualize her journey? Could you see her walking along the sidewalk? Did you see the two buildings? What did they look like? Could you see the darkness of her path? Could you see the shadow disappearing into the bushes? Could you see her increasing her pace to catch up to the other students? What was she wearing?

If you could see all of this, then you were using your visual skills—your mind's eye. This is one of the most effective ways to commit information to long-term memory. See it, live it, feel it, and touch it as you read and study it, and it will become yours.

Concentrating on the information given will also help you commit it to long-term memory. Don't let your mind wander. Stay focused. If you find yourself having trouble concentrating, take a small break (two to five minutes) and then go back to work.

Relating the information to something that you already know or understand will assist you in filing or storing the information for easy retrieval. Relating the appearance of the African zebra to the American horse can help you remember what the zebra looks like. You may not know

Do you find that studying in the library, at home, or somewhere else is most effective for you? Why?

"If a man is given a fish, he eats for a day. If a man learns to fish, he eats forever."
—Chinese Proverb

BLOOM LEVEL 1 QUESTION

FIGURE

10.1   *Remembering Katherine*

Without looking back, answer the following questions about Katherine. Use the power of your visualization and concentration to recall the information.

1. What was the name of the biology building? _____

2. Did she see the shadow before or after she saw the two people behind her? _____

3. What were the two people behind her doing? _____

4. What was the name of the arts building? _____

5. Why did she cross the street? _____

6. How far ahead of her was the group of students? _____

7. When she saw the group of students in front of her, how far was she from her residence? _____

8. What was Katherine's friend's name? _____

BLOOM LEVEL 3 QUESTION

what the buildings in Katherine's story looked like, but try to see her in front of a building on *your campus*. Creating these types of relationships increases memory retention.

Repeating the information out loud to yourself or to a study partner facilitates its transfer to long-term memory. Some people have to hear information many times before they can commit it to long-term memory. Memory experts agree that repetition is one of the STRONGEST ways to increase the retention of material.

Reviewing the information is another means of repetition. The more you see and use the information, the easier it will be to remember it when the time comes. As you review, try to remember the main points of the information.

Walter Pauk (2007), educator and inventor of the Cornell note-taking method, concluded from a research study that people reading a textbook chapter forget 81% of what they had read after 28 days. With this in mind, it may behoove you to review Katherine's story (and other material in your texts) on a regular basis. Reviewing is a method of keeping information fresh.

THE CAPABILITY OF YOUR MEMORY

What Is the Difference Between Memorizing and Owning?

Why don't you forget your name? Why don't you forget your address? The answer is that you KNOW that information. *You OWN it.* It belongs to you. You've used it often enough and repeated it often enough that it is highly unlikely that you will ever forget it. Conversely, why might you have trouble remembering the details of Erickson's Stages of Development or Maslow's Hierarchy of Basic Needs? Most likely because you memorized it and never "owned" it.

Knowing something means that you have made a personal commitment to make this information a part of your life. For example, if you need to remember the name "Stephen" and his phone number of 925-6813, the likelihood of your remembering this information depends on *attitude*. Do you need to recall this information because he is in your study group and you might need to call him, or because he is the caregiver for your infant daughter while you are in class? How badly you need that name and number will determine the commitment level that you make to either *memorizing* it (and maybe forgetting it) or *knowing* it (and making it a part of your life).

Take a moment and refer to The Learning Process Chart in Chapter 7, "Learn" (Figure 7.1 on page 163). This will give you a good reminder of what it takes to learn new information and how to adjust your attitude about the value of that information.

FIGURE

10.2 *Seeing Clearly*

Consider the first picture. Study it carefully.
Look at everything from left to right, top to bottom.

Now, notice the picture and pay close attention to the areas marked.

Notice the number of people on the trampoline

Notice the storage building

Notice the color of the protective padding

Notice the green foliage

Notice the utility meter

FIGURE

10.2 *Seeing Clearly, continued*

Now, cover this picture and answer the following questions:

1. How many people are on the trampoline? _____

2. What color is the protective padding on the edge? _____

3. What is the season of the year based on the foliage color? _____

4. What colors are used on the storage building? _____

5. Is there one utility meter or two? _____

6. How many children are in the air? _____

7. Are the children all male, female, or mixed? _____

8. How many people are wearing striped shirts? _____

9. What type of fence surrounds the house? _____

10. What colors are used on the house? _____

11. Is the house made of one material or more? _____

12. What color are the flowers on the bush? _____

"NOT FAIR!" you may be saying right now. "We were not asked to look at the fence, the colors on the house, or what people are wearing." Regardless, could you answer all of the questions without looking? The purpose of this exercise is to help you understand the real difference between casually looking at something and REALLY looking at something. To truly know something, you have to go beyond what is on the surface—even going beyond reading and studying what was asked of you. You have to look and examine more than you are told or more than what is pointed out to you. In order to own information, you have to be totally committed to examining every detail, every inch, and every angle of it. You will need to practice and master the technique of "going beyond."

USING MNEMONIC DEVICES

What Does a Greek Goddess Have to Do with My Memory?

The word "mnemonic" is derived from the name of the Greek Goddess of Memory, **Mnemosyne** (pronounced Ne-MO-ze-knee). She was considered one of the most important goddesses of all time because it was believed that memory separates us from lower animal life forms. It was believed that memory is the very foundation of civilization (The Goddess Path, 2009). Memory was so very important because most of the transmission of human history depended on oral stories and parables committed only to memory, not on paper.

In modern times, a mnemonic (pronounced ni-MON-ik) device is a memory trick or technique that assists you in putting information into your long-term memory and pulling it out when you need it. According to research into mnemonics and their effectiveness, it was found that mnemonics can help create a phenomenon known as the *bizarreness effect*. This effect causes us to remember information that is "bizarre" or unusual more rapidly than "normal," everyday facts. "The bizarreness

The Greek goddess of memory, Mnemosyne.

effect occurs because unusual information and events trigger heightened levels of our attention and require us to work harder to make sense of them; thus we remember the information and its associated interaction better" (McCornack, 2007). The following types of mnemonics may help you with your long-term memory.

JINGLES/RHYMES. You can make up rhymes, songs, poems, or sayings to assist you in remembering information; for example, "Columbus sailed the ocean blue in fourteen hundred and ninety-two."

As a child, you learned many things through jingles and rhymes. You probably learned your ABC's, as well as your numbers, through a song pattern. If you think about it, you can probably still sing your ABC's, and maybe your numbers through the "Ten Little Indians" song. You can probably also sing every word to the opening of *The Brady Bunch, Scooby Doo,* or *Gilligan's Island* because of the continual reruns on TV. Some advertisements and commercials seem to stick with us even if we find them annoying. Jingles and rhymes have a strong and lasting impact on our memory—especially when repetition is involved.

SENTENCES. You can make up sentences such as "Some men can read backward fast" to help you remember information. Another example is "**P**lease **e**xcuse **m**y **d**ear **A**unt **S**ally," which corresponds to the mathematical operations **p**arentheses, **e**xponents, **m**ultiplication, **d**ivision, **a**ddition, and **s**ubtraction.

Other sentences in academic areas include:

1. **M**y **V**ery **E**lderly **M**other **J**ust **S**aved **U**s **N**icely. This is a sentence mnemonic for the eight planets **in order from the sun**: Mercury, Venus, Earth, Mars, Jupiter, Saturn, Uranus, Neptune.

2. **E**very **G**ood **B**ird **D**oes **F**ly is a sentence mnemonic for the line notes in the treble clef in music.

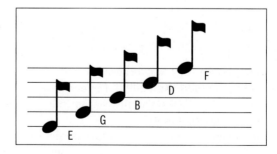

3. Some **M**en **H**elp **E**ach **O**ther is a sentence mnemonic for the Great Lakes from **west to east**: Superior, Michigan, Huron, Erie, Ontario.

WORDS. You can also create words. For example, **Roy G. Biv** may help you to remember the colors of the rainbow: **r**ed, **o**range, **y**ellow, **g**reen, **b**lue, **i**ndigo, and **v**iolet. Other word mnemonics include:

1. HOMES is a word mnemonic for the Great Lakes in no particular order: **H**uron, **O**ntario, **M**ichigan, **E**rie, **S**uperior.

2. FACE is a word mnemonic for the space notes in the treble clef.

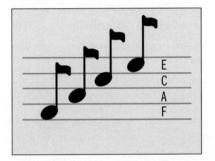

STORY LINES. If you find it easier to remember stories than raw information, you may want to translate the information into a story that you can easily tell. Weave the data and facts into a creative story that can be easily retrieved from your long-term memory. This technique can be especially beneficial if your instructor gives essay exams, because the "story" that you remember can be what was actually told in class.

ACRONYMS. An acronym is a word that is formed from the first letters of other words. You may see reruns for the famed TV show *M*A*S*H*. This is an acronym for "Mobile Army Surgical Hospital." If you scuba dive, you know that *SCUBA* is an acronym for "Self-Contained Underwater Breathing Apparatus." Other common acronyms include:

NASA (**N**ational **A**eronautics and **S**pace **A**dministration)
NASCAR (**N**ational **A**ssociation for **S**tock **C**ar **A**uto **R**acing)
NASDAQ (**N**ational **A**ssociation of **S**ecurities **D**ealers **A**utomated **Q**uotations)
NATO (**N**orth **A**tlantic **T**reaty **O**rganization)
BART (**B**ay **A**rea **R**apid **T**ransit)

PEGGING. The pegging system uses association, visualization, and attachment to aid in memory. With this system, you literally "attach" what you want to remember to something that is already familiar to you—the pegs that you create. This is a visual means of remembering lists, sequences, and even categories of information.

From Ordinary to Extraordinary

REAL PEOPLE | REAL LIVES | REAL CHANGE

H. P. RAMA
CEO, JHM Hotels
Greenville, SC

I have led a life filled with a great variety of experiences, trials, challenges, and triumphs. Born in Africa, I was sent to India to live with my grandparents and go to school when I was just five years old. I lived away from my parents, whom I missed greatly, in a little farming village in India, where I finished school and ultimately earned an undergraduate degree. I knew I wanted to go to America and pursue the American dream, so at age 21 I left India and arrived in this country with only $2 in my pocket.

I had to get a job quickly, so I took the first job offered to me, a dishwasher, which I quit after just four hours. My next job was as a waiter at a Howard Johnson's restaurant in Manhattan. While I worked as a waiter to support myself, I attended Xavier University to pursue my MBA. My life was primarily one of work and sacrifice as I worked hard to pay my expenses and to graduate with this degree I prized so much. While working at Howard Johnson's, I paid attention to everything that happened around me because I had no intention of remaining a waiter all my life. I was absorbing knowledge of the hotel and restaurant business, which I would put to use later. At the time, I had no intention of becoming a hotelier. My goal was to go into banking. I always say that I became an accidental hotelier, but this field has served me well and offered me many opportunities. I was pursuing the American dream, and that was all that mattered.

I considered myself fortunate to have this great opportunity to be in America, to be going to school, and to have a job that supported me.

After receiving my MBA from Xavier, I worked as a staff accountant for 14 months. In 1973 I had an opportunity to buy my first hotel in Pomona, California. My brother and I bought the hotel, and we had only two employees other than the two of us. We worked 24/7 and lived behind the office. There was no job that we did not do. But we were chasing the dream, and we were off and running with no idea of how many opportunities we would have.

> "At age 21 I left India and arrived in this country with only $2 in my pocket."

248

From Ordinary to Extraordinary

REAL PEOPLE | REAL LIVES | REAL CHANGE

Then I moved East, still focused on achieving the American dream, and bought a 36-room hotel in Buffalo, Tennessee. My wife and I did everything—front desk, night duty, all the maintenance. We both worked very hard, long hours. In 1977 we moved to Greenville, South Carolina, and bought a foreclosed property from a bank. In 1983 I bought four Howard Johnson's hotels—just 13 years after working for HJ as a waiter. Over the years my brothers and I have owned and developed 78 hotels and still own 38 today.

We developed a five-star hotel in India in 1990, and today we are expanding and adding other hotels. We are most proud of the fact that we are developing a mixed-use development in India that will include a Hospitality College campus, a retailing and enter-tainment campus, a hospital campus, and luxury accommodations. We are using our knowledge learned in this wonderful country to continue the dream in India.

In 1999, I was named chairman of the American Motel and Hotel Lodging Association, which was a significant honor for me. Because I wanted to give back to the field that has done so much for me, I donated $1 million for scholarships for hospitality students. In 1989 I was the founding member of the Asian American Hotel Owners Association. Today I serve on several boards of advisors for hospitality programs and was named an executive ambassador by Cornell University, a position in which I speak to graduate students about my experiences.

My advice to students today is this: Anything is possible if you have the vision, pay the price, work hard, and take risks. I have been very blessed, but I have also worked very hard. And I am living proof that the American dream is alive and well.

EXTRAORDINARY REFLECTION

Read the following statement and respond in your online journal or class notebook.

Mr. Rama worked his way up the ladder and became chairman of the American Motel and Hotel Lodging Association, a major organization. What top honors do you hope to achieve in your own career? Why? How would they change your life?

FIGURE **10.3** *The Pegging System*

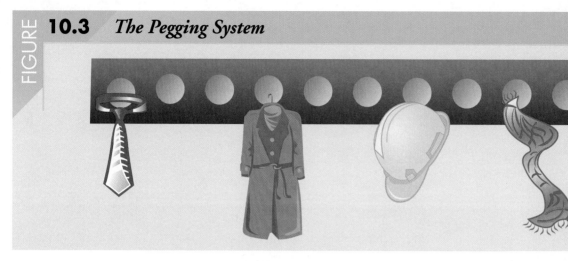

Pretend that you are looking at a coat rack mounted on the wall, with 10 pegs sticking out of it. Just as you would hang a hat or coat on the pegs of a rack, you can hang information there, too.

For the sake of explaining this technique more thoroughly, we have named the 10 pegs for you with corresponding rhyming words. You, however, can name your pegs anything that would be easy for you to remember. Once you memorize these peg names, you can attach anything to them with visualization and imagination. The key to using the pegging mnemonic system is to name your pegs ONCE and use those names each time you hook information to them. This way, they become second nature to you. For our example, our 10 pegs are named:

1	= sun	6	= sticks
2	= shoe	7	= heaven
3	= bee	8	= gate
4	= shore	9	= line
5	= alive	10	= pen

Repeat these until you have memorized them.

Let's use an example from your *Cornerstone* text. In Chapter 1 you were introduced to the **Ten Essential Cornerstones for Personal and Professional Success** (passion, motivation, knowledge, resourcefulness, creativity, adaptability, open-mindedness, communication, accountability, and vision). Using visualization, attach one of the cornerstones to each peg.

1 - sun	I look at the ***sun*** on a beautiful day with ***passion***.
2 - shoe	I walk in my ***shoes*** with ***motivation***.
3 - bee	I see a ***bee*** flying around that seems to be very ***knowledgeable***.
4 - shore	The ***shore*** washes many ***resources*** to the beach.
5 - alive	My brain is ***alive*** because I use ***creativity***.
6 - sticks	I see a ***stick*** bending into a half circle, making it very ***adaptable***.
7 - heaven	Believing in ***heaven*** takes ***open-mindedness***.
8 - gate	Many ***gates*** open for people who know how to ***communicate***.
9 - line	If you walk a straight ***line,*** you are ***accountable***.
10 - sin	Use a ***pen*** to write your ***vision***.

Read these over one more time, and then cover the list. You'll be amazed at how easy it is to repeat it. You will, of course, need to study each one to know what it means, but now, you have the list memorized, in order.

FIGURE

10.4 *A Quick Reference Guide to Studying Math and Science*

© **Robert M. Sherfield, Ph.D.**

Before Class

▶ **NEVER** take a math or science course (or any course for that matter) for which you are not prepared. If you think you need, or test into a basic, remedial, or transitional class *take it*!!! Look at it as a chance to start over with new hope and knowledge.

▶ **UNDERSTAND** that most math and science classes build on previous knowledge. If you begin the class with a weak background, you must work very hard to learn missed information.

▶ **AVOID** taking math or science classes during "short" terms if possible. The more time you spend with the material, the better, especially if math and/or science are not your strong suits.

▶ **KNOW** your own learning style. If you're visual, use colors, charts, and photos. If you're auditory, practice your listening skills. If you're tactile, work to create situations where you can "act out" or touch the material.

▶ **PREPARE** yourself *before class* by reading the chapter. EVEN if you don't understand all of it, read through the material and write down questions about material you did not understand.

▶ **SCAN** all of the introductory and summation materials provided in the text or study guides.

▶ **JOIN** a study group. If there is not one, start one. Cooperative learning teams can be life savers.

▶ **SEEK** tutorial assistance on campus from the first day. Go visit the center and get familiar with how it operates. Get to know the people who work there. Don't wait until you get behind to seek assistance.

During Class

▶ **COME to EVERY** class, study group, or lab.

▶ **CONTROL** your own anger and frustration. The past is the past and you can't change any part of it—but you can change YOUR future. Learn to make your negative self-talker "be quiet!"

▶ **ASK** questions. **ASK** questions. **ASK** questions. **ASK** questions. . . . and be specific in your questioning. Don't just say, "I don't understand that." Ask detailed and specific questions such as, *"I don't understand why f(x + h) doesn't equal f(x) + f(h)*. Or, *"I don't understand the difference between 'algia' and 'dynia.' Why are two different words used for pain?"*

▶ **SLOW DOWN** and read the material carefully.

▶ **FIND** the formulas and write them down on note cards.

▶ **WRITE** down the explanatory remarks made by the instructor such as:

    ▶ How do you get from one step to the next?

    ▶ How does this problem differ from other problems?

    ▶ Why do you need to use formula "x" instead of formula "y"?

    ▶ Were any steps combined—why or why not?

▶ **TRY** to learn from a *general to specific* end. That is, try to get a feeling of the overall goal of the material before you hone in on smaller problems.

▶ **WRITE** down any theorem, formula, or technique that the instructor puts on the board, overhead, or PowerPoint.

▶ **LEAVE** a space in your notes for any material you missed or did not understand. This will help you keep your notes organized when you go back after class and add the explanation.

▶ **BRING** Post-it ® Notes, strips of paper, or bookmarks to class with you so that you can "tag" pages with important information and concepts. Use the tabs included with your text to help you mark important information.

After Class

▶ **VISIT** your instructor's office (make an appointment to visit during office hours).

▶ **FILL** in the missing information in your notes by reviewing the text, going to your study group, or getting clarification from your instructor.

(continued)

FIGURE 10.4   *A Quick Reference Guide to Studying Math and Science (continued)*

▶ **PRACTICE** the problems in your text or study guide and then practice them again, and again, and again until they become second nature. Much of Math and Science is learned by DOING . . . so DO . . . and then DO again.

▶ **APPLY** what you learned in class or lab. Find a way to make it "speak" to your life in a practical way.

▶ **CONTINUALLY** review all of the theorems, formulas, concepts, and terms from each chapter so they become second nature to you.

▶ When doing practice tests, **PRETEND** that you are in an actual test and adhere to the timelines, rules, and policies of your instructor. This helps replicate the actual testing situation.

Before the Test

▶ **ASK** questions that will reduce your anxiety such as:

    ▶ What is the point value of each question?

    ▶ How many questions will be on the test?

    ▶ Will the questions be multiple choice, etc. . . . ?

    ▶ What materials do I need to bring to class?

    ▶ Will I be allowed to use a calculator or any other technology?

    ▶ Is there a time limit on the test?

    ▶ What is the overall grade value of the test?

▶ **MAKE** every effort to attend any study or review sessions offered by the instructor or peers.

During Tests

▶ **READ** the directions carefully.

▶ **QUICKLY** glance over the test to determine the number of questions and the degree of difficulty as related to the time you have to complete the test.

▶ **WORK** by the clock. If you have 60 minutes to take a test that has 120 questions, this means you have about 30 seconds per question.

▶ **BEGIN** by solving the problems that are easiest or most familiar to you.

▶ **READ** the questions on the test carefully and MORE than once and don't jump to conclusions.

▶ **DETERMINE** which formulas you will need to use.

▶ **DECIDE** how you want to solve the problem.

▶ **CHECK** your work by using multiple solving techniques. (If the problem is division, can it be rechecked with multiplication? This is called Opposite Operations).

▶ **DRAW** pictures if you encounter word problems. Visualization is very important.

▶ **SHOW** all of your work, even if it is not required. This will help the instructor (and you) see what you did correctly and/or incorrectly.

▶ **RECHECK** every answer if you have time.

▶ **WORK** backward if at all possible. This may help answer the question and catch mistakes.

▶ After you've completed the answer, **reread** the question to determine if you did everything the question asked you do to.

▶ **NEVER** erase your margin work or mistakes. This wastes time and you may erase something that you need (or worse, something that was correct).

After Tests

▶ **IMMEDIATELY** after the test, try to determine if the majority of test questions came from classroom notes, your textbook, your study guide, or from your homework. This will help you prepare for the next test.

▶ **THINK** about the way you studied for this test and how you could improve your techniques for the next time. Consider the amount of time spent studying for this test.

▶ Once the test is graded, **DETERMINE** what caused you to lose the most points: Simple errors? Applying incorrect formulas or theorems? Misunderstanding of the questions asked? Intensified test anxiety? Poor study habits in general?

HAKUNA MATATA

How in the World Can I Study with Small Children in the House?

For many college students, finding a place or time to study is the hardest part of studying. Some students live at home with younger siblings; some students have children of their own. If you have young children in the home, you may find the following hints helpful when it comes time to study.

STUDY AT SCHOOL. Your schedule may have you running from work to school directly to home. Try to squeeze in even as little as half an hour at school for studying, perhaps immediately before or after class. A half hour of pure study time can prove more valuable than five hours at home with constant interruptions.

CREATE CRAFTS AND HOBBIES. Your children need to be occupied while you study. Choose projects your children can do by themselves, without your help. Explain to your children that you are studying and that they can use this time to be creative; when everyone is finished, you'll share with each other what you've done. Give them little rewards for their work and for helping you have quiet time to study.

Do you think it is a good idea to involve your children (or younger siblings) in your education? Why or why not?

STUDY WITH YOUR CHILDREN. One of the best ways to instill the value of education in your children is to let them see you participating in your own education. Set aside one or two hours per night when you and your children study. You may be able to study in one place, or you may have separate study areas.

RENT MOVIES OR LET YOUR CHILDREN WATCH TV. Research has shown that viewing a limited amount of educational television, such as *Sesame Street, Reading Rainbow,* or *Barney and Friends,* can be beneficial for children. If you do not like what is on television, you might consider renting or purchasing age-appropriate educational videos for your children.

INVITE YOUR CHILDREN'S FRIENDS OVER. What?! That's right. A child who has a friend to play or study with may create less of a distraction for you. Chances are your children would rather be occupied with someone their own age, and you will gain valuable study time.

ESSENTIAL CORNERSTONE

Adaptability:
How can learning to be more adaptable help you study with your children or with distractions all around you?

Social Networking Moment:
Share your response to this Essential Cornerstone with peers in your social network. Choose two responses from your peers and respond to their postings.

HIRE A SITTER OR EXCHANGE SITTING SERVICES with another student. Arrange to have a sitter come to your house a couple of times a week if you can afford it. If you have a classmate who also has children at home, you might take turns watching the children for each other. You could each take the children for one day a week, or devise any other schedule that suits you both best.

FIND OUT IF YOUR COLLEGE HAS AN ON-SITE DAY-CARE center such as the Boys and Girls Club. Some colleges provide day-care facilities at a reduced cost, and some provide day care at no charge. It is certainly worth checking out.

TALK TO THE FINANCIAL AID OFFICE on your campus. In some instances, there will be grants or aid to assist you in finding affordable day care for your child.

STUDYING IN A CRUNCH
TOMORROW? What Do You Mean the Test Is Tomorrow?

Let's be straight up front. No study skills textbook will ever advise you to cram. It is simply a dangerous and often futile exercise in desperation. You will ***never read the words***, "Don't waste your time studying, just CRAM the night before so you can party harder and longer!" in a study skills textbook. Cramming is the complete opposite of what this whole chapter is about—knowing versus memorizing. Cramming will not help you own the material; it can only help you memorize a few things for storage in short-term memory. You may spend several hours cramming, and shortly after the test, the information is gone, evaporated, vanished! If you find yourself in this spot, consider the following tips and suggestions for cramming. These probably won't get you an A, but they may help you with a few questions.

DEPRESSURIZE. Just tell yourself up front what you are doing. Don't pretend that cramming is going to save you. Let yourself realize that you are memorizing material for short-term gain and that you won't be able to keep it all. With this admission, your stress will diminish.

KNOW THE SCORE. When cramming, it is important to know what you're cramming for. If you're cramming for a multiple-choice test, you'll need different types of information than for an essay test. Know what type of test it is for which you are studying.

READ IT QUICKLY. Think about **H2 FLIB.** This is a mnemonic for: read the **h**eadings, **h**ighlight the important words, read the **f**irst sentence of every paragraph, read the **l**ast sentence of every paragraph, read the **i**ndented and **b**oxed material. This can help you get through a chapter when pinched for time.

MAKE CONNECTIONS. As you are reading, quickly determine if any of the information has a connection with something else you know. Is there a relationship of any kind? Is there a cause and effect in motion? Can you pinpoint an example to clarify the information? Is there a mnemonic that can help you with this information? These questions can help you with retention and long-term memory commitment.

> "Don't just learn something from every experience, learn something positive."
> —Al Neuharth

USE YOUR SYLLABUS OR STUDY GUIDE. If your instructor lists questions in the syllabus that you should know the answers to (mastery questions), or if he or she gave you a study sheet (or you developed your own study sheet, like the one you have created at the end of each *Cornerstone* chapter), this is the place to start. Answer those questions. If you don't have either, look to see if the text gives study questions at the end of the chapter.

SEE IT. Visualizing the information through mapping, diagrams, photos, drawings, and outlines can help you commit this information to short-term memory.

CHECK YOUR NOTES. Did the professor indicate that certain things are important to know for the test?

CHOOSE WISELY. If you're cramming, you can't do it all. Make wise choices about which material you plan to study. This can be driven by your study sheet, your lecture notes, or questions in your syllabus (if they are listed).

Information you've crammed is going to leave you after the test. Don't rely on it for the next test or the final. You will need to go back and relearn (truly understand) the information you "crammed" in order to commit it to long-term memory.

THINKING ABOUT TESTING

Can Changing My Attitude and Reducing Stress Really Help?

Yes, both are necessary to help you get through tests. A positive or negative attitude can truly mean the difference between success and failure. With an attitude adjustment from negative to positive and some basic preparation, you can overcome a good deal of your anxiety about tests and do well. You can reduce anxiety when you are in control of the situation, and you can gain control by convincing yourself that you **can be** and **will be** successful. If you think positively and can honestly say that you have done everything possible to prepare for a test, then the results will most likely be positive.

Silencing *your negative self-talk* is one of the most powerful things you can do for yourself. Consider the following tips for reducing test anxiety during your next test. You will not be able to employ them all, but if you learn and use a few new ones each time, before you know it, you'll be a testing pro!

- ▶ Prepare yourself emotionally for the test, control your self-talk, and be positive.
- ▶ Study and learn the material—NO! You can't study too much.
- ▶ Ask peers who have had a certain professor what type of tests he or she gives.
- ▶ Arrive early for the test (at least 15 minutes early).
- ▶ Go to the test with everything you need: pencils, calculator, and other supplies.
- ▶ Listen to the instructor before the test begins, know his or her rules about testing, and READ the instructions.
- ▶ Keep an eye on the clock during the test so that you can finish on time. However, don't let time cause you undue stress or anxiety.
- ▶ Answer what you know first, the questions that are easiest for you.
- ▶ Check your answers, but remember, your first response is usually correct.
- ▶ Find out ahead of time exactly what the test will cover.
- ▶ Ask the instructor for a study sheet; you may not get one, but it does not hurt to ask!
- ▶ When you get the test, jot down on the back or at the top of a page any mnemonics you might have developed.

QUIZZING YOUR INSTRUCTOR AND KNOWING YOUR RESPONSE TYPE

What Are Some Techniques I Can Use to Help Me During Tests?

Several classes before the test is scheduled to be given, **quiz your instructor** about the logistics and specifics of the test. This information can help you

Tips for Personal Success

Consider the following tips for making time for studying and committing information to long-term memory:

- ▶ Study daily to avoid having to "cram" the night before your test.
- ▶ Form a study group with people who are motivated and keep you on track.
- ▶ Keep up with your daily readings and homework.

Now, it is your turn. Create a list of at three more tips that you would offer a fellow classmate to assist him or her in making time in his/her life to study.

1. _____

2. _____

3. _____

What techniques have you found help you reduce your anxiety and negative self-talk during quizzes and exams?

study more effectively and eliminate the anxiety that comes with uncertainty. If you don't know whether the test is going to be true-false or essay or both, it is much more difficult to study. Some questions you need to ask are:

1. What types of questions will be on the test?

2. How many questions will be on the test?

3. Is there a time limit on the test?

4. Will there be any special instructions, such as "use pen only" or "use a number 2 pencil"?

5. Is there a study sheet?

6. Will there be a review session?

7. What is the grade value of the test?

8. What chapters or sections will the test cover?

Asking these simple questions will help you know what type of test will be administered, how you should prepare for it, and what supplies you will need.

What Do I Do When I Can't Remember the Answer?

Almost every test question will elicit one of three types of responses from you as the test taker:

▶ Quick-time response

▶ Lag-time response

▶ No response

Your response is a *quick-time response* when you read a question and know the answer immediately. You may need to read only one key word in the test question to know the correct response. Even if you have a quick-time response, however, always read the entire question before answering it. The question may be worded in such a way that the correct response is not the one you originally thought of.

You have a *lag-time response* when you read a question and the answer does not come to you immediately. You may have to read the question several times or even move on to another question before you think of the correct response. Information in another question will sometimes trigger the response you need. Once you've begun to answer other questions, you usually begin to remember more, and the response may come to you.

No response is the least desirable situation when you are taking a test. You may read a question two or three times and still have no response. At this point, you should move on to another question to try to find some related information. When this happens, you have some options:

1. Leave this question until the very end of the test.

2. Make an intelligent guess.

3. Try to eliminate all unreasonable answers by association.

4. Watch for modifiers within the question.

It is very difficult to use intelligent guessing with essay or fill-in-the-blank questions. Remember these important tips about the three types of responses:

1. Don't be overly anxious if your *response is quick*; read the entire question and be careful not to make a mistake.

2. Don't get nervous if you have a *lag-time response*; the answer may come to you later, so just relax and move on.

3. Don't put down just anything if you have *no response*; take the remaining time and use intelligent guessing.

THINKING FOR CHANGE: An Activity for Critical Reflection

After the second week of classes, Jose was devastated by his first test score. The instructor put the range of grades on the board, and he was shocked to see that many people passed the test and that his score was in the bottom 10%.

He began asking classmates if they did well or not and found some who had made A's and others who had made D's. When he spoke with one classmate, Letty, she told him that he should just chill and take a "cheat sheet" to class. "The instructor never looks, man, and she left the classroom twice. She'll never know. That's how I got my A."

"Cheat," Jose thought, "I don't think I can do that." He knew that others had made better grades than he over the years, but he also knew that he had never once cheated on an exam. Never.

Jose went to the Tutoring Center and worked with a tutor on content and on how to take a test more effectively. On the next test, Jose scored a C. "It may not be the best grade in the class," he thought, "but it is all mine. I did it."

In your own words, what two suggestions would you give Jose to improve his grades without cheating?

1. _____

2. _____

TEST-TAKING STRATEGIES AND HINTS FOR SUCCESS

What Are Some Tips for Taking Tests?

Before you read about the strategies for answering these different types of questions, think about this: *There is no substitute for studying!* You can know all the tips, ways to reduce anxiety, mnemonics, and strategies on earth, but if you have not studied, they will be of little help to you.

Strategies for Matching Questions

Matching questions frequently involve knowledge of people, dates, places, or vocabulary. When answering matching questions, you should:

► Read the directions carefully.

► Read each column before you answer.

► Determine whether there is an equal number of items in each column.

► Match what you know first.

► Cross off information that is already used.

► Use the process of elimination for answers you might not know.

► Look for logical clues.

► Use the longer statement as a question; use the shorter statement as an answer.

Strategies for True-False Questions

True-false questions ask whether a statement is true or not. True-false questions can be some of the trickiest questions ever developed. Some students like them; some hate

Sample Test #1 MATCHING

DIRECTIONS: Match the information in column A with the correct information in column B. Use uppercase letters.

GOALS, MOTIVATION, & SELF-ESTEEM

A

_____ They can be long or short, social, academic, religious, or financial

_____ They bring out the worst in you

_____ I CAN'T Syndrome

_____ Your "true self"

_____ Listening with an open mind

B

A. Child within

B. Objectivity

C. Contaminated people

D. Negative thoughts

E. Goals

them. There is a 50/50 chance of answering correctly, but you can use the following strategies to increase your odds with true-false questions:

▶ Read each statement carefully and watch for key words in each statement.

▶ Read each statement for double negatives such as "not untruthful."

▶ Pay attention to words that may indicate that a statement is true, such as "some," "few," "many," and "often."

▶ Pay attention to words that may indicate that a statement is false, such as "never," "all," "every," and "only."

▶ Remember that if any part of a statement is false, the entire statement is false.

▶ Answer every question unless there is a penalty for guessing.

Sample Test #2 TRUE/FALSE

Place "T" for true or "F" for false beside each statement.

NOTE-TAKING SKILLS

1. _____ Note taking creates a history of your course content.
2. _____ "Most importantly" is not a key phrase.
3. _____ You should always write down everything the instructor says.
4. _____ You should never ask questions in class.
5. _____ The L-STAR system is a way of studying.

Strategies for Multiple-Choice Questions

Many college instructors give multiple-choice tests because they are easy to grade and provide quick, precise responses. A multiple-choice question asks you to choose from among, usually, two to five answers to complete a sentence. Some strategies for increasing your success when answering multiple-choice questions are the following:

▶ Read the question and try to answer it before you read the answers provided.

▶ Look for similar answers; one of them is usually the correct response.

▶ Recognize that answers containing extreme modifiers, such as *always, every,* and *never,* are usually wrong.

▶ Cross off answers that you know are incorrect.

▶ Read all the options before selecting your answer. Even if you believe that A is the correct response, read them all.

▶ Recognize that when the answers are all numbers, the highest and lowest numbers are usually incorrect.

▶ Understand that the most inclusive and longest answers are often correct.

▶ If you cannot answer a question, move on to the next one and continue through the test; another question may trigger the answer you couldn't come up with previously.

▶ Answer every question unless there is a penalty for guessing.

Sample Test #3 MULTIPLE CHOICE

DIRECTIONS: Read each statement and select the best response from the answers given below.

STUDY SKILLS

1. Which statement is true according to the 2007 Labor Statistics, Bureau of Census?
   A. Men earn more than women.
   B. Women earn more than men.
   C. People with a Master's degree earn the most money of any educational level.
   D. Unemployment is greatest among those with a doctorate degree.

2. To calculate a GPA, you would:
   A. Divide quality points by the number of semester hours.
   B. Multiply total points by quality points.
   C. Divide total points by the number of semester hours.
   D. Multiply the quality points by the total points.

3. To be an effective priority manager, you have to:
   A. Be very structured, organized, and self-disciplined.
   B. Be very unstructured and disorganized.
   C. Be mildly structured and organized.
   D. Know what type of person you are avoid working from that perspective.

Strategies for Short-Answer Questions

Short-answer questions, also called fill-in-the-blanks, ask you to supply the answer yourself, not select it from a list. Although "short answer" sounds easy, these questions are often very difficult. Short-answer questions require you to draw from your long-term memory. The following hints can help you answer this type of question successfully:

▶ Read each question and be sure that you know what is being asked.

▶ Be brief in your response.

▶ Give the same number of answers as there are blanks; for example, _____ and _____ would require two answers.

▶ Never assume that the length of the blank has anything to do with the length of the answer.

▶ Remember that your initial response is usually correct.

▶ Pay close attention to the word immediately preceding the blank; if the word is "an," give a response that begins with a vowel (a, e, i, o, u).

▶ Look for key words in the sentence that may trigger a response.

Sample Test #4 SHORT ANSWER

DIRECTIONS: Fill in the blanks with the correct response. Write clearly.

LISTENING SKILLS

1. Listening is a _____ act. We choose to do it.
2. The three elements of listening involve listening objectively, _____, and _____.
3. _____ is the same as listening with an open mind.
4. Prejudging is an _____ to listening.
5. Leaning forward, making eye contact, being patient, and leaving your emotions at home are characteristics of _____ listeners.

Strategies for Essay Questions

Most students look at essay questions with dismay because they take more time. Yet essay tests can be one of the easiest tests to take because they give you a chance to show what you really know. An essay question requires you to supply the information. If you have studied, you will find that once you begin to answer an essay question, your answer will flow more easily. Some tips for answering essay questions are the following:

▶ More is not always better; sometimes more is just more. Try to be as concise and informative as possible. An instructor would rather see one page of excellent material than five pages of fluff.

▶ Pay close attention to the action word used in the question and respond with the appropriate type of answer. Key words used in essay questions include the following:

discuss	illustrate	enumerate	describe
compare	define	relate	list
contrast	summarize	analyze	explain
trace	evaluate	critique	interpret
diagram	argue	justify	prove

▶ Write a thesis statement for each answer.

▶ Outline your thoughts before you begin to write.

▶ Watch your spelling, grammar, and punctuation.

▶ Use details, such as times, dates, places, and proper names, where appropriate.

▶ Be sure to answer all parts of the question; some essay questions have more than one part.

▶ Summarize your main ideas toward the end of your answer.

▶ Write neatly.

▶ Proofread your answer.

Learning how to take a test and learning how to reduce your anxiety are two of the most important gifts you can give yourself as a student. Although tips and hints may help you, don't forget that there is no substitute for studying and knowing the material.

Sample Test #5 ESSAY

DIRECTIONS: Answer each question completely. Use a separate paper if you wish.

STUDY SKILLS

1. Identify and discuss two examples of mnemonics.
2. Justify why it is important to use the SQ3R method when reading.
3. Compare an effective study environment with an ineffective study environment.

CHANGING IDEAS TO *Reality*

REFLECTIONS ON
NOTE TAKING AND TESTING

Just as reading is a learned skill, so are memory development, studying, and learning how to take assessments. You can improve your memory, but it will take practice, patience, and persistence. You can improve your study skills, but it will take time and work. And you can increase your ability to do well on tests, but it will take a commitment on your part to study smarter and put in the time and dedication required. By making the decision "I CAN DO THIS," you've won the battle, for when you make that decision, your studying and learning become easier.

Your challenge is to focus on developing excellent memory techniques, study patterns, and test-taking abilities while earning the best grades you can. When you have done this, you can look in the mirror and be proud of the person you see without having to be ashamed of your character or having to worry about being caught cheating or wondering if you really did your best. When studying for your next class or taking your next test, consider the following:

- ▶ Study the hardest material first.
- ▶ Review your classroom and textbook notes frequently.
- ▶ Use mnemonics to help you remember lists.
- ▶ Learn the material from many different angles.
- ▶ *Ask* questions of the instructor before the test.
- ▶ Glance at the entire test *before* beginning.
- ▶ *Ignore* the pace of your classmates.
- ▶ Watch *time* limits.
- ▶ Use academic integrity.

As you study and learn to enter your chosen profession, remember this: "You are building your character for the long haul—not just a few short years."

"Change occurs, progress is made, and difficulties are resolved if people merely do the right thing—and rarely do people NOT KNOW what the right thing is."
—Father Hessburg

KNOWLEDGE *in* BLOOM

Using and Evaluating your GUIDING STATEMENT

Each chapter-end assessment is based on *Bloom's Taxonomy of Learning.* See the inside front cover for a quick review.

UTILIZES LEVELS 3 AND 6 OF THE TAXONOMY

EXPLANATION: Now that you have read and studied this chapter and, no doubt, taken a few tests this semester, you have a better understanding of what happens to you physically and mentally during an exam.

Below, you will find listed six of the common physical or mental symptoms of anxiety reported by students while testing.

PROCESS: Beside each symptom, **create a list** of at least three concrete, doable, realistic strategies to overcome this physical or emotional anxiety symptom before or during a testing situation.

SYMPTOM	HOW TO REDUCE IT
Fatigue	1. 2. 3.
Frustration	1. 2. 3.
Fear	1. 2. 3.
Anger	1. 2. 3.
Nervousness/Nausea	1. 2. 3.
Uncertainty/Doubt	1. 2. 3.

SQ3R *Mastery* STUDY SHEET

EXAMPLE QUESTION: *(from page 251)* Discuss three strategies for studying math.	**ANSWER:**
EXAMPLE QUESTION: *(from page 245)* Why are mnemonics important?	**ANSWER:**
AUTHOR QUESTION: *(from page 241)* What is the difference between short-term and long-term memory?	**ANSWER:**
AUTHOR QUESTION: *(from page 242)* Discuss the five steps in VCR3.	**ANSWER:**
AUTHOR QUESTION: *(from page 254)* What is H2 FLIB and how can it help you?	**ANSWER:**
AUTHOR QUESTION: *(from page 255)* Discuss five ways to reduce test anxiety.	**ANSWER:**
AUTHOR QUESTION: *(from page 257)* Discuss one strategy for each type of testing situation.	**ANSWER:**
YOUR QUESTION: *(from page ____)*	**ANSWER:**
YOUR QUESTION: *(from page ____)*	**ANSWER:**
YOUR QUESTION: *(from page ____)*	**ANSWER:**
YOUR QUESTION: *(from page ____)*	**ANSWER:**
YOUR QUESTION: *(from page ____)*	**ANSWER:**

Finally, after answering these questions, recite this chapter's major points in your mind. Consider the following general questions to help you master this material.

- ▶ What was it about?
- ▶ What does it mean?
- ▶ What was the most important thing I learned? Why?
- ▶ What were the key points to remember?

CHAPTER 11
PROSPER

MANAGING YOUR MONEY AND DEBTS WISELY

"I've been rich and I've been poor—and rich is better."

—Sophie Tucker

WHY READ THIS CHAPTER?

What's in it for me?

WHY is learning to manage money so important at this stage of my life? WHY does it matter if I have big student loans and credit card debt when I graduate? WHY is it such a big deal to know how much my next semester will cost? WHY is it important to know and protect my FICO score?

Why? Because changing and strengthening your money management skills can impact your life forever and make you fiscally fit! You have probably heard the old saying, "Money won't buy happiness." Well, neither will poverty. As in many areas of your life, wealth accumulation needs to be balanced with a solid work experience, physical health, good relationships, hobbies, travel, and other things that you enjoy. Managing money—or the lack of managing money—will impact what kind of house you live in, what kind of car you drive, what kind of education your children will have, how much you can give to charities, and what kind of retirement you will have. Few skills will have more of a direct impact on your quality of life than managing your personal finances.

By carefully reading this chapter and taking the information provided seriously, you will be able to:

1. Understand the ramifications and the pitfalls of crushing, overwhelming debt.
2. Identify the types of financial aid available to you and identify how each type differs from the others.
3. Understand the importance of your credit history, how to keep it healthy, and how to protect your FICO score.
4. Construct and use a budget.
5. Protect your credit cards and other vital information from identity theft.

CHAPTER 11 / PROSPER

"Millions of Americans live paycheck to paycheck. More than half said they would need $500 more per paycheck to live comfortably."

—Careerbuilder.com, 2007

NAME: Melissa VonAschen
COLLEGE: Oklahoma State University, Stillwater, OK
MAJOR: Geography
AGE: 24

Learning to manage money, budget carefully, and pay your bills on time are some of the most important lessons students can learn, and the sooner you learn all this, the better. When I was much younger, I had some large medical bills, and I had no insurance. Since I am supporting myself, I was responsible for these bills. I couldn't pay the bills so I just ignored them and later had a collection agency calling me. The lesson I can pass on to you about not being able to pay your bills is to call the company to which you owe money and make an arrangement for a payment schedule that you can manage. If you don't do this, you may damage your credit score.

I think everyone needs to budget for large and small items, and be sure you can make payments on things like rent, cell phones, car payments, and groceries. One word of caution—I've found that the small miscellaneous items are the ones that cause me the most problems. Small expenditures add up in a hurry so I suggest that you keep track of what you are spending and try to stay within limits for each item. I have totally stayed away from credit cards because I have heard too many horror stories from my friends. Now that I am close to graduation, I am going to open up two credit card accounts and use them to establish credit. I'll charge small amounts and pay them off early for several months to help establish a good FICO score. You should really pay attention to your credit rating because it will be very important to you when you graduate and try to buy a car or rent an apartment.

My biggest concern about money is paying off student loans. Since I am self-supporting, I had no choice but to borrow money. When I was a first-year student, I was awarded several scholarships and really didn't need all the money that was given to me in student loans, but I took the money anyway. Now, I wish I had taken only the amount I needed to pay for my tuition and books because I am now looking at paying off a considerable amount in student loans. My advice to you is to borrow only what you must have to make it because a day of reckoning will be coming.

SCAN & QUESTION

In the preface of this book (page xix), you read about the **SQ3R Study Method**. Right now, take a few moments, **scan this chapter**, and on page 288, write **five questions** that you think will be important to your mastery of this material. In addition to the two questions below, you will also find five questions from your authors. Use one of your "**Study for Quiz**" stickers to flag this page for easy reference.

EXAMPLES:

▶ **What are four types of financial aid?** (from page 270)

▶ **How does a grant differ from a loan?** (from page 270)

THE OVERWHELMING BURDEN OF CRUSHING DEBT

Can You Take Control Before It's Too Late?

Most of this chapter will be devoted to teaching you vital points about your current and future finances. We'll discuss the many ways that you can get into financial trouble and incur the feeling of being literally crushed by debt, as well as ways you can avoid these problems. Reported below are several very serious facts quoted by Erica Williams (2008), in her testimony before the House Financial Services Sub-Committee on Financial Institutions and Consumer Credit, that should get your attention and make you determined not to become one of these statistics:

Have you ever had a class or workshop on money management?

▶ A 2006 poll of three million twentysomethings from *USA Today* and Experian, the credit-reporting agency, found that nearly half the twentysomethings had stopped paying a debt, forcing lenders to "charge off" the debt and sell it to a collection agency, or had cars repossessed or sought bankruptcy protection.

▶ Thirty percent of twentysomethings say they worry frequently about their debt.

▶ The Boomerang Effect, young adults returning to live with their parents, is quickly increasing. In 2006, Experience, Inc., which provides career serices to link college grads with jobs, found that 58% of the twentysomethings it surveyed had moved home after college for a year or longer.

▶ Debt forces some young people to change their career plans. Of those surveyed in the 2006 *USA Today* NEFE poll, 22% said they'd taken a job they otherwise wouldn't have because they needed the money to pay off student loan debt.

▶ Average credit card debt among indebted young adults increased by 55% between 1992 and 2001, to $4,088.

▶ The average credit card–indebted young adult household now spends nearly 24% of its income on debt payments.

▶ Among young adult households with incomes below $50,000 (two-thirds of young households), nearly one in five with credit card debt is in debt hardship—spending over 40% of their income servicing debt, including mortgages and student loans.

▶ Young Americans now have the second highest rate of bankruptcy, just after those aged 35 to 44.

PRACTICING DISCIPLINE AT THE RIGHT TIME

Can You Mind Your Own Business?

The time to learn to take care of your business and finances is right now so that you can hit the ground running when you graduate. You might already be working in a full-time position with an opportunity to participate in a 401-K program. Many people neglect to enroll because they don't understand the program and don't want to appear ignorant by asking someone to explain it. You may feel that you simply can't afford to enroll and allocate that money to a retirement fund. The truth? You really can't afford not to enroll! Your future depends on it. Even if you are a typical college student who is struggling to make ends meet and can't invest right now, this is the time to prepare for what comes ahead. We highly encourage you to make up your mind that you are going to be financially secure and that you are going to master the keys to wise investing.

Some important tips for preparing for the future RIGHT NOW include:

▶ Practice *delayed gratification.* This is the first key to personal wealth accumulation. Even though it will probably require changing your habits, learn to develop this habit now.

▶ Take a *personal finance course* as soon as possible. You will be able to put the information into practice much sooner if you take the course early in your college career.

▶ Learn to understand *financial lingo.* A beginning list is included in Figure 11.3. Add to the list as you learn more in-depth information.

▶ If you plan to operate any kind of business, *take accounting and tax law courses.* Even if you plan to run a dance studio or a physical fitness center, this tip applies to you.

▶ *Save your change every day.* You will be surprised how quickly it adds up. You can put it in savings or invest it. You may even need it to pay the rent one month.

▶ *Write down everything you spend.* Where can you cut costs? In what ways are you wasting money? At the end of this chapter, you will find a worksheet titled **Tracking Your Expenditures and Spending Habits Chart**. Use this sheet to track all of your spending for three days, and then analyze your habits and develop a change plan. You'll be amazed at where your money goes.

▶ *Apply for every type of financial aid* available to assist with your education. You may not be awarded every type, but every cent helps. The following section will help you with this.

How many credit cards do you currently have? Do you use them wisely?

PENNIES FROM HEAVEN

Is There a Secret World of Financial Aid?

Nearly two of every three undergraduate students are going into debt to go to college, owing an average of more than $19,000, most often to the government (Barrett, 2008). Chances are good that you have already borrowed money or might need to in the future. Therefore, understanding financial aid, scholarships, loans, and grants is very important as you make decisions that will impact you for a long time. If you have to borrow money to go to college, we think you should; on the other hand, we urge you to be very frugal—even stingy—when it comes to borrowing money. A day of reckoning will come, and for many people, that day is like getting hit by a freight train, when they realize what this debt means to them. Because they are relatively uninformed about personal finances, many young people make really bad financial decisions. Many college students don't have a clue as to the impact large student loans and other debts will have on their future well-being.

ESSENTIAL CORNERSTONE

Accountability: How can being accountable for your financial decisions help prepare you for the future?

Social Networking Moment: Share your response to this Essential Cornerstone with peers in your social network. Choose two responses from your peers and respond to their postings.

FIGURE 11.1 *Types of Aid*

TYPE	DESCRIPTION
Federal and state loans	Money that must be repaid with interest—usually beginning six months after your graduation date.
Federal and state grants	Monies you do not have to repay—often need-based awards given on a first-come, first-served basis.
Scholarships (local, regional, and national)	Money acquired from public and private sources that does not have to be repaid. Often, scholarships are merit based.
Work study programs	Money earned while working on campus for your institution. This money does not have to be repaid.

The most well-known sources of financial assistance are from federal and state governments. Federal and state financial aid programs have been in place for many years and are a staple of assistance for many college students. Figure 11.1 indicates the sources of aid.

Not every school participates in every federal or state assistance program. To determine which type of aid is available at your school, you need to contact the financial aid office.

One of the biggest mistakes students make when thinking about financial aid is forgetting about scholarships from private industry and social or civic organizations. Each year, millions of dollars are unclaimed because students do not know about these scholarships or where to find the necessary information about them. Speak with someone in your financial aid office regarding all types of scholarships.

Federal Financial Aid Eligibility And Types

PELL GRANT. This is a need-based grant awarded to qualified undergraduate students who have not been awarded a previous degree. Amounts vary based on need and costs.

FEDERAL SUPPLEMENTAL EDUCATIONAL OPPORTUNITY GRANT (FSEOG). This is a need-based grant awarded to institutions to allocate through their financial aid offices to students.

STAFFORD LOAN (FORMERLY KNOWN AS THE GUARANTEED STUDENT LOAN). The Stafford Direct Loan Program is a low-interest, subsidized loan. You must show need to qualify. The government pays the interest while you are in school, but you must be registered for at least half-time status. You begin repayments six months after you leave school.

How can learning about different loans, scholarships, and work study help you reach your goals?

UNSUBSIDIZED STAFFORD LOAN. This Stafford Loan is a low-interest, nonsubsidized loan. You DO NOT have to show need to qualify. You are responsible for the interest on the loan while you are enrolled. Even though the government does not pay the interest, you can defer the interest and the payment until six months after you have left school.

PLUS LOAN. This is a federally funded, but state-administered, low-interest loan to qualified parents of students in college. The student must be enrolled at least half-time. Parents must pass a credit check and payments begin 60 days after the last loan payment.

WORK STUDY. Work study is a federally funded, need-based program that pays students an hourly wage for working on (and sometimes off) campus. Students earn at least minimum wage.

HOPE SCHOLARSHIP TAX CREDIT. This tax credit is for students in their first two years of college who are enrolled at least half-time in a degree or certifi-

FIGURE

11.2 *Student Eligibility for Federal Financial Aid**

To receive aid from the major federal student aid programs, you must:

▶ Have financial need, except for some loan programs.

▶ Hold a high school diploma or GED, pass an independently administered test approved by the U.S. Department of Education, or meet the standards established by your state.

▶ Be enrolled as a regular student working toward a degree or certificate in an eligible program. You may not receive aid for correspondence or telecommunications courses unless they are a part of an associate, bachelor, or graduate degree program.

▶ Be a U.S. citizen.

▶ Have a valid Social Security number.

▶ Make satisfactory academic progress.

▶ Sign a statement of educational purpose.

▶ Sign a statement of updated information.

▶ Register with the Selective Service, if required.

▶ Some federal financial aid may be dependent on your not having a previous drug conviction.

*Source: Adapted from The Student Guide: Financial Aid from the U.S. Department of Education. U.S. Dept. of Education, Washington, DC, 2008–2009.

cate program. Each student taxpayer may receive a 100% tax credit for each year for the first $1,000 of qualified out-of-pocket expenses. They also may claim a 50% credit on the second $1,000 used for qualified expenses (U.S. Bank, 2002).

PERKINS LOAN. This is a need-based loan in which the amount of money you can borrow is determined by the government and the availability of funds. The interest rate is 5%, and repayment begins nine months after you leave school or drop below half-time status. You can take up to 10 years to repay the loan. (Note: The federal government may have eliminated this program by the time this book is published.)

Tips for Applying for Financial Aid

▶ You MUST complete a Free Application for Federal Student Aid (FAFSA) to be eligible to receive ANY federal or state assistance. ***You AND your parents*** must apply for and obtain a PIN number to complete the FAFSA ***if you are considered a dependent***. Because much federal and state money is awarded on a first-come, first-served basis, it is advisable to complete your application as soon after January 1 as possible—even if you have to use the previous year's tax returns and update your application later. Your college's financial aid office can assist you with this process. You can also log onto *www.fafsa.ed.gov* to learn more.

▶ *Do not miss a deadline.* There are *no* exceptions that allow you to make up for missing deadlines for federal financial aid!

▶ *Read all instructions* before beginning the process, always fill out the application completely, and have someone proof your work.

▶ If documentation is required, submit it according to the instructions. Do not fail to do all that the application asks you to do.

▶ Never lie about your financial status.

▶ Begin the application process as soon as possible. Do not wait until the last moment. Some aid is given on a first-come, first-served basis. Income tax preparation time is usually also financial aid application time.

▶ Talk to the financial aid officer at the institution you will attend. Person-to-person contact is always best. Never assume anything until you get it in writing.

FIGURE

11.3 *Financial Aid Glossary*

Borrower—The person who borrows the funds and agrees to repay them.

COA—Cost of attendance. This is the total amount it will cost you to go to college.

Cosigner—A person who signs a promissory note and agrees to repay the debt should the borrower default.

Default—The term used when you do not repay your student loan. This will prevent you from receiving any further funding. Your wages can be garnished until full restitution is made. Your tax refunds will also be held until full payment is made. This default will also be reported to credit agencies and your credit will be scarred for 7 to 10 years.

Deferment—A period of time when you do not have to make loan payments. This period usually applies to education loans and usually lasts only six to nine months.

EFC—Expected Family Contribution. The amount of money your family contributes to your educational costs.

FAFSA—Free Application for Federal Student Aid. The application that you (or your parents) fill out to determine your financial needs. This is the first step in any financial aid process.

FAT—Financial Aid Transcript. A record of your financial assistance from all institutions.

Gross income—Your income before taxes and deductions.

Interest—The fee (or amount of money) charged to you to borrow money.

Late fee—A fee charged to you if you do not make your payment on time.

Need analysis—A formula established by Congress to determine your financial need. This is based on your FAFSA form.

Net income—Your income after taxes and deductions.

Payoff—The total amount owed on a loan if you were to pay it off in one lump sum.

Principal—The exact dollar amount that you borrowed and the amount on which interest is charged.

Promissory note—A legal document that obligates the borrower to repay funds.

Selective Service Registration—If you are required by law to register with Selective Service, you must do so before you can qualify for federal student aid.

Have you allotted enough time in your schedule to fill out your financial aid application completely and accurately?

▶ Take copies of fliers and brochures that are available from the financial aid office. Private companies and civic groups will often notify the financial aid office if they have funds available.

▶ Always apply for admission as well as financial aid. Many awards are given by the college to students who have already been accepted.

▶ If you are running late with an application, find out if there are electronic means of filing.

▶ Always keep a copy of your tax returns for each year!

▶ To receive almost any money, including some scholarships, you must fill out the FAFSA form.

▶ Apply for everything possible. You will get nothing if you do not apply.

STUDENT LOANS

A Day of Reckoning Will Come. Will You Be Ready?

The high cost of college makes tuition out of reach for many families. In recent years, "college tuition has risen at twice the rate of consumer prices. Tuition has soared much faster than pay has for the kinds of low-wage jobs that students tend to hold" (Block, 2006), making it much more difficult for students to work in the summer and pay for the coming year of college. Today a student would have to work an entire year to pay for one year of public college education, and that assumes that he or she saved every penny of his or her earnings. For many students, the only way they can attend college is with student loans. If this is the only way you can go to college, borrow the money—but borrow no more than you absolutely must. Try not to borrow anything but tuition and perhaps room and board. Get a job, budget, cut out extras, work in the summers, attend college via a

FIGURE 11.4 *Total Interest Paid*

AMOUNT OF MONEY BORROWED BY YOU	YOUR INTEREST RATE (AVERAGE)	TOTAL YEARS TO REPAY (20 YEARS IS THE AVERAGE)	YOUR MONTHLY PAYMENT	TOTAL INETREST PAID BY YOU (YOUR COST TO BORROW THE MONEY)
$ 5,000	7%	10	$ 58.05	$ 1,966.00
		20	$ 38.76	$ 4,302.40
		30	$ 33.27	$ 6,977.20
$ 10,000	7%	10	$ 116.11	$ 3,933.20
		20	$ 77.53	$ 8,607.20
		30	$ 66.53	$ 13,950.80
$ 15,000	7%	10	$ 174.16	$ 5,899.20
		20	$ 116.29	$ 12,909.60
		30	$ 99.80	$ 20,928.00
$ 20,000	7%	10	$ 232.22	$ 7,866.40
		20	$ 155.06	$ 17,214.40
		30	$ 133.06	$ 27,901.60
$ 30,000	7%	10	$ 348.33	$ 11,799.60
		20	$ 232.59	$ 25,821.60
		30	$ 199.59	$ 41,852.40

cooperative program, enroll in online courses, take fewer credits even though it delays graduation, live at home—do everything possible not to borrow more money than you must.

Many students are finding it necessary to extend their student loans over a period of 30 years just to keep their heads above water; of course, if one does that, the interest paid is also higher. For example, a student who takes 30 years to pay off a $20,000 loan at 6.8% will pay about $27,000 in interest plus the principal, compared to $7,619 interest on a loan paid off in 10 years (Block, 2006). You will have to repay the money that you have borrowed. Period! ***Even bankruptcy will not relieve you of this debt*** because student loans are not subject to bankruptcy laws; so again, don't borrow any money that you don't absolutely need. Consider the examples in Figure 11.4.

KNOW THE SCORE

Why Is Understanding Your Credit History Important to Your Future?

Many college students don't even know they have a credit score, yet this score is the single most important factor that will determine if you get approved for a mortgage, car loan, credit card, insurance, etc. Furthermore, if you get approved, this credit score will determine what rate of interest you have to pay (Broderick, 2003). You can order one free credit score online by accessing the Web site *https://www.annualcreditreport.com*.

Range of Scores and What FICO Means for You

This information may seem trivial right now, and you might not want to be bothered with more information, but the truth is, you must pay attention to this because your FICO score has long-lasting implications for almost everything you want to do. The sooner you understand the importance of this score and take steps to keep it healthy, the better off you will be.

ESSENTIAL CORNERSTONE

Resourcefulness:
How can being resourceful help me reduce the amount I have to borrow in student loans?

Social Networking Moment:
Share your response to this Essential Cornerstone with peers in your social network. Choose two responses from your peers and respond to their postings.

11.5   *The Impact of FICO on Buying a Home*

FICO SCORE	INTEREST RATE	PAYMENT	30 YEARS OF INTEREST
500	9.3%	$1651	$394,362
560	8.5%	$1542	$355,200
620	7.3%	$1373	$294,247
675	6.1%	$1220	$239,250
700	5.6%	$1151	$214,518

> *"Just about every financial move you make for the rest of your life will be somehow linked to your FICO score."*
> —Suze Orman Financial Planning Expert

Your credit score is referred to as the FICO score. FICO is the acronym for **Fair Isaac Corporation**, the company that created the widely used credit score model. This score is calculated using information from your credit history and files. The FICO score is the reason it matters if you accumulate large debts, if you go over your credit card limits, if you are late with payments—these offenses stick with you and are not easily changed. Based on this score, you can be denied credit, pay a lower or higher interest rate, be required to provide extensive asset information in order to even get credit, or sail right through when you seek a loan.

FICO scores range from 300 to 850. A good score is considered 720 or above. The lower your FICO score, the higher the interest rate you will have to pay because you will be considered a poor risk. So what's the big deal about a few points? Study the chart (Figure 11.5), and you will see how important your FICO score is when you want to finance a house or seek credit for other reasons:

B IS FOR BUDGETING

Where Does My Money Go?

Most people have no idea where their money goes. Many just spend and spend and then borrow on credit cards to pay for additional expenses for which they had not budgeted. Knowing how much money you have and exactly how you spend it is a very important step toward financial security. Many college students pay more attention to buying than they do to budgeting, watching their credit scores, or controlling their credit card debt. If you fit that mold, this is one area where change is needed.

One of the main reasons to budget is to determine the exact amount of money you need to borrow to finance your college education. Poor planning while in college can easily result in a lower standard of life after you graduate and begin paying back enormous loans. Deciding how much to borrow will impact your life long after you have completed your degree. You should also remember that you will be required to repay your student loans even if you do not graduate. As previously mentioned, even bankruptcy won't eliminate student loans.

When budgeting, you must first determine how much income you earn monthly. Complete the following chart:

SOURCE OF INCOME	ESTIMATED AMOUNT
Work	$_____
Spouse/Partner/Parental Income	$_____
Scholarships/Loans	$_____
Savings/Investments	$_____
Alimony/Child Support	$_____
Other	$_____
TOTAL INCOME	$_____

Next, you must determine how much money you spend in a month. Complete the following chart:

SOURCE OF EXPENDITURE	ESTIMATED AMOUNT
Housing	$_____
Utilities (water, gas, power, etc.)	$_____
Phone (home and cell)	$_____
Internet Access	$_____
Car Payment	$_____
Car Insurance	$_____
Fuel	$_____
Clothing	$_____
Food	$_____
Household Items	$_____
Personal Hygiene Items	$_____
Health Care and/or Health Insurance	$_____
Entertainment/Fun	$_____
Savings	$_____
Other	$_____
TOTAL EXPENDITURES	$_____

Total Income _____ **minus Total Expenses** _____ = **$_____**

If the amount of your total expenditures is smaller than your monthly income, you are on your way to controlling your finances. If your total expenditures figure is larger than your monthly income, you are heading for a financial crisis. Furthermore, you are establishing bad habits for money management that may carry over into your life after college.

Now, consider your education and the costs associated with everything from books to supplies. Using the **Economic Readiness Assessment** (Figure 11.6), *do the research* to determine how much your education (tuition, books, room, board, etc.) will cost you next semester. You will have to go to the bookstore (or online) to research the cost of your texts, and you may need to refer to your college catalog for rules regarding some of the other questions. You can also use the Internet to answer a few of the questions, but it is important that you answer them all.

BLOOM LEVELS 4 & 6 QUESTIONS

LIVING ON BORROWED MONEY

Credit Cards! Are They Really the WORST Kind of Debt?

Credit card debt—one of the worst kinds of debt—is rising rapidly among college students as they struggle to pay tuition, buy books, and cover day-to-day living expenses. According to a Nellie Mae study (2005), 76% of all undergraduate college students have at least one credit card and carry an average balance of $2,169. One of the results of high credit card debt is lower GPAs and a higher dropout rate (Cooper-Arnold, 2006). As a result of over-the-top credit card marketing on campuses, terrible credit card terms and conditions, and an economy that no longer provides as many well-paying jobs with good benefits as it once did, graduates are facing overwhelming odds to achieve financial health, in large part as a result of the credit card debt from their undergraduate years (Williams, 2008).

Studies show that credit card shoppers, in general, are less price sensitive and more extravagant. When you pay with plastic, you lose track of how much

> *"If you can eat it, wear it, or drink it, it is not an emergency."*
> —Kim Rebel, Credit Counselor

FIGURE

11.6 *Economic Readiness Assessment*

In the spaces below, please read each question carefully, respond with Yes or No, and then answer the question based on your financial research for **next semester.** Be specific. You may have to visit the financial aid office, bookstore, or other campus resource center to answer the questions.

QUESTION	ANSWER	RESPONSE
I know exactly how much my tuition will cost next semester.	YES NO	Answer: $_____
I know the cost of lab fees, technology fees, and other fees associated with my courses.	YES NO	Answer: $_____
I know how much my textbooks will cost next semester.	YES NO	Answer: $_____
I know how much my transportation will cost next semester (car payment, gas, insurance, bus passes, etc.).	YES NO	Answer: $_____
I know how much I need to spend on supplies for next semester.	YES NO	Answer: $_____
I know how much child care will cost next semester.	YES NO	Answer: $_____
I know where my GPA must remain to keep my financial aid.	YES NO	Answer: _____
I know how much money I can borrow through the Guaranteed Student Loan Program in one academic year.	YES NO	Answer: $_____
I know how much money I need to manage my personal budget in a single semester.	YES NO	Answer: $_____
I have estimated miscellaneous and unexpected costs that might occur during the semester.	YES NO	Answer: $_____
I know what a FAFSA is and how and WHEN to apply.	YES NO	Answer: _____
I know how a drug arrest could affect my financial aid.	YES NO	Answer: _____
I know the scholarships available to me, how, when, and where to apply for them.	YES NO	Answer: _____
I know how and where to apply for work study.	YES NO	Answer: _____
I know how a felony charge affects my ability to get a job after graduation.	YES NO	Answer: _____
		TOTAL $_____

Can you imagine paying for a piece of pizza for 12 years?

you are spending. According to the article "Live Without Plastic" (Rosato, 2008), after McDonald's started accepting credit and debit cards in 2004, diners who paid with plastic spent $7 a visit on average compared to $4.50 when they paid in cash. The article also suggests that you are less aware of what you spend if you use plastic. For example, 68% of cash-paying students exiting a college bookstore knew how much they'd spent. Conversely, only 35% of students using plastic knew what they'd spent. Rosato also reports that you are willing to pay more for the same stuff if you are using plastic instead of real money.

"Imagine being 30 years old and still paying off a slice of pizza you bought when you were 18 and in college. Sounds crazy, but for plenty of people problems with credit card debt can lead to that very situation" (Collegeboard, 2008). If you borrow excessively and pay only the minimum each month, it will be very easy to find yourself over your head with credit card problems. Take the case of Joe. "Joe's average unpaid credit card bill over a year is $500, and his finance charge is 20 percent. He pays a $20 annual fee plus a $25 late fee (he was up late studying and forgot to mail in his check). Joe ends up owing $145 to his credit card company, and he still hasn't paid for any of his purchases" (Collegeboard, 2008).

11.7 *Important Facts You Need To Know About Credit Cards*

What you don't know can wreck your credit rating and can ruin your life. Listed below are some of the most important things you can learn about managing credit card debt.

✔ Understand that credit cards are nothing more than high interest loans—in some cases, very high! The system is designed to keep you in debt.

✔ Be aware that companies often add on new fees and change policies after customers already have signed up.

✔ If you fall behind on payments to one creditor or if your credit score drops for any reason, your rates can be raised on all your credit cards.

✔ Banks can and will abruptly switch your due date so pay attention. Always check your bill to see if any fees or charges have been added.

✔ Avoid cards that charge an annual fee just for the privilege of carrying their card. This fee can be as high as $100–$400 per year. If you charge this fee, it will be automatically added to your card and then you begin paying interest on the fee.

✔ Be sure your card allows for a grace period before interest is charged.

✔ Carry only one or two credit cards so you can manage your debt and not get in over your head. Do not accept or sign up for cards that you don't need.

✔ When you accept a card, sign it right away and keep records of your credit card numbers (in a secure location) and the phone number to contact in case they are lost or stolen. If you lose your card, report it immediately to avoid charges.

✔ Avoid the temptation to charge. You should use credit cards only when you absolutely must and only when you can pay the full amount before interest is added. "Buy now, pay later" is a dangerous game.

✔ When you pay off a card, celebrate and don't use that as a reason to charge again. Lock that card in a safe place and leave it there.

✔ Each month, always try to pay more than the "minimum payment due."

✔ Send the payment at least five days in advance. Late fees now represent the third-largest revenue stream for banks.

✔ Call the credit card company and negotiate a better rate. If they won't give you a better rate, tell them you are going to transfer the debt.

✔ If you have several credit card debts, consolidate all the amounts on the card where you have the lowest balance. Don't cancel your cards because it helps your credit score if you have cards on which you have no debt. Just don't use them again!

✔ Do not leave any personal information (credit cards, Social Security numbers, checking accounts) in places where roommates or other students have access to them. Purchase a metal file box with a lock and keep it in a secure place.

✔ Consider using a debit card. Money is deducted directly from your bank account and you cannot spend more than you actually have.

✔ If you have already gotten into credit card trouble, get **reputable** counseling. One of the best agencies is the National Foundation for Credit Counseling (NFCC).

✔ Be aware that using a credit card carelessly is similar to a drug addiction. Credit card use is habit forming and addictive!

✔ Ask yourself these questions: "If I can't pay this credit card in full this month, what is going to change next month? Will I have extra income or will I reduce my spending enough to pay for this purchase?" If the answers are "No," you don't need to make the purchase.

✔ Realize that you are building your future credit rating even though you are a student.

> *Once you get a credit card, immediately write, "CHECK ID" across the back in RED, permanent ink.*

Most credit card companies charge a very high rate of interest—18 to 21% or higher. If you are late with a payment, the interest rate can go even higher. For every $1,000 you charge, you will pay from $180 to $210 in interest each year, states Konowalow (2003). Don't be fooled by the ploy of "1.5% interest." This means 1.5% each month, which equates to 18% per year. The best practice is to charge no more than you can pay off each month while avoiding high interest rates. Consider the tips in Figure 11.7.

THE PITFALLS OF PAYDAY LOANS, CAR TITLE LOANS, AND RENT-TO-OWN CONTRACTS

Did You Know There's Someone Lurking on Every Corner to Take Your Money?

Many unsuspecting consumers have been duped into signing car title loans, payday loans, or rent-to-own contracts that resulted in very high monthly payments and penalties. Some were told by their title loan broker before they signed the contract that they could make a partial payment if they needed to and this would be OK. Unfortunately, the unsuspecting victims find out too late that their car is going to be repossessed due to one late or partial payment. Others realize too late that on a loan of

THINKING for CHANGE: An Activity for Critical Reflection

Jonathon is having a great time at college. He has joined a fraternity, is loving going to football games, and is managing to keep his grades up. But he's already got a major problem—keeping up with his expenses. He is spending much more money than he has coming in. His parents told him he could join a fraternity, but that he would have to pay these expenses from the allowance they provide him every month. He and his parents made the decision for him not to work his first year, so he is in a bind.

To compound his problems, he has met a great girl, and he has tried hard to impress her by taking her to expensive clubs and out to dinner. He took her to his frat dance and that cost a bundle. He didn't have the funds so he charged everything on his new credit card. Jonathon is getting very stressed about his money situation. He's having trouble sleeping well. Fraternity dues are coming up again soon. There is a big interfraternity/

sorority dance at the end of the semester that is high on his new girlfriend's list. Now she is talking about going on a cruise for spring break. He is very worried because he has already maxed out one credit card and has heavy charges on the other one. Jonathon has calculated that if he charges $1,000 on his card and makes only the minimum payment, it will take $15\frac{1}{2}$ years for him to pay for the cruise. He doesn't want to disappoint his girlfriend and fears losing her if he doesn't go on the cruise. But clearly, he has to make some changes.

What are two things you would advise Jonathon to do right away?

1. _____

2. _____

List two other suggestions that you would make to Jonathon to help him get control of his expenses.

1. _____

2. _____

$400, they must pay back over $500 that month. According to recent reports from consumer affairs groups, some institutions have been charging as much as 250% interest on an annualized basis (Cojonet, 2003). In some instances, interest rates as high as 900% have been charged due to poor government regulatory policies. Some states have recently enacted laws to prevent this.

Payday loans are extremely expensive compared to other cash loans. For example, a $300 cash advance on the average credit card, repaid in one month, would cost $13.99 in finance charges and an annual interest rate of almost 57%, which is very high. By comparison, however, a payday loan costing $17.50 per $100 for the same $300 would cost $105 if renewed one time or 426% annual interest (Pay Day Loan Consumer Information, 2008). As bad as credit card debt is, it pales in comparison to the pitfalls of payday loans.

SMALL COSTS ADD UP!
How Much Money Will You Throw Down the Drain in 10 Years?

Many people pay more money for convenience. If you are on a tight budget, you might want to give up some of the conveniences so that you can hold onto more of your money. Although we want you to really live and enjoy life, we also want you to take a hard look at where your money goes. Those dimes, quarters, and dollars add up quickly. In fact, small-amount money drains for the typical person can add up to $175,000 over a 10-year period. What if you could hold onto some of that money and invest it? What would that money be worth to you when you are 65 and want to retire? Is having sausage biscuits and orange juice from a fast-food restaurant really worth $3.50 a day or $1,274 if you have that *every day for one year*? Did you ever stop to think that if you spend $3.50 every day on fast food or coffee or whatever for 10 *years*, you would be spending $12,740?

The 10-Year Plan

According to the Web site The Digerati Life (2008), some other prime causes of money drain are:

- **Gum**—a pack a day will cost you $5,488 in 10 years.
- **Bottled water**—One bottle a day will cost you almost $5,500 in 10 years. (Most bottled water comes from no special source and is no better than tap water.)
- **Eating lunch out daily**—Even if you spend only $9, this will cost you over $35,000 in 10 years. If you can eat lunch at home, you will save so much money.
- **Junk food, vending machine snacks**—This will cost you at least $4,000 in 10 years if you are a light snacker, and they are empty calories.
- **Unused memberships**—Those gym memberships that look so enticing and, for many people, go unused will total over $7,500 in 10 years.
- **Expensive salon visits**—Fake nails along with the salon visit can cost over $30,000 in 10 years. Is that really how you want to spend your money?
- **Cigarettes**—Not only will this terrible habit kill you and make people want to avoid you, it will cost you over $25,000 in 10 years if you smoke a pack a day.

These are just a few of the drains that take our money and keep us from being wealthy when we are older. Maybe you want to splurge at times and go for the convenience, but day in and day out, you can really save a lot of money if you budget your time and do some of these things for yourself.

Examine the following information about *The Latte Factor*™ (Figure 11.8), and apply it to your own spending habits.

FIGURE 11.8 *The Latte Factor™*

In his book *The Finish Rich Notebook* (2003), Bach states, "How much you earn has no bearing on whether or not you will build wealth." As a rule, the more we make, the more we spend. Many people spend far more than they make and subject themselves to stress, exorbitant debt, fear, and an ultimate future of poverty.

Bach uses the Latte Factor™ to call people's attention to how much money we carelessly throw away when we should be saving and investing for the future. He uses the story of a young woman who said she could not invest because she had no money. Yet, almost every day she bought a large latte for $3.50 and a muffin for $1.50. If you add a candy bar here, a drink there, a shake at the gym, you could easily be spending $10 a day that could be invested.

If you take that $10 per day and invest it faithfully until retirement, you would have enough money to pay cash for a home and a new car, and have money left over. This is the power of compound interest! If you are a relatively young person, you will probably work that many years and more, so you could retire with an extra $1 million in addition to any other savings you might have accumulated.

The point is that most of us have the ability to become rich, but we either lack the knowledge or the discipline to do so. Remember the Latte Factor™ as you begin your college career and practice it, along with other sound financial strategies, if you want to become a millionaire.

Calculate your own Latte Factor™. For example, if you buy one diet soda each morning for $1.81, then your Latte Factor™ is $685.84 per year ($1.81 × 7 days/week × 52 weeks/year).

My daily "have to have it" is _____

It costs $ _____ per day

My Latte Factor™ is $ _____

Small expenditures add up. What you do today may inhibit your ability to buy a car, purchase a house, and even get certain jobs!

PROTECT YOURSELF FROM IDENTITY THEFT

Why Are College Campuses Ground Zero?

"Amid all the back-to-school activities and tasks that college students face, one of the most important is to protect their identities. You have such busy schedules that you may unknowingly expose yourself to identity theft and fraud, particularly when you're making online purchases or engaging in social-networking web sites. We're all living in an extremely open environment where free flow of information is the norm, as opposed to the exception," said Adam Levin, cofounder of Identity Theft 911 (Yip, 2008). Because college students tend to move often, their mail service may be interrupted if they don't follow through with change-of-address cards. By the time their information catches up to them, they may have already suffered from identity theft. "All these things make this group vulnerable," said Thomas Harkins, chief strategy officer of Secure Identity Systems (Yip, 2008).

People who may steal your identity are roommates, relatives, friends, estranged spouses, restaurant servers, and others who have ready access to your papers. They may steal your wallet, go through your trash, or take your mail. They can even legally photocopy your vital information at the courthouse if, for example, you have been divorced. The Internet provides thieves many other opportunities to use official-looking e-mail messages designed to obtain your personal information. Do not provide personal information over the Internet no matter how official the Web site might look. Reputable businesses will not inquire about your personal information in this manner.

It is very difficult, if not impossible, to catch identity thieves. While you may not be liable, you still have to spend your time filing expensive legal affidavits, writing letters, and making telephone calls to clear your good name.

How to Minimize Identity Theft Risk

Criminals are very clever, and many are adept at using electronic means to steal your personal information. According to a variety of financial sources, there are a number of ways to avoid having your identity stolen:

▶ Carry only the ID and cards you need at any given time.

▶ Do not make Internet purchases from sites that are unsecured (check for a padlock icon to ensure safety).

▶ Do not write your PIN number, Social Security number, or passcode on any information that can be stolen or that you are discarding. Do not keep this information in your wallet or exposed in your living space.

▶ Try to memorize your passwords instead of recording them on paper or in the computer.

▶ Buy a shredder and use it.

▶ Avoid providing your Social Security number to any organization until you have verified its legitimacy.

▶ Check your credit file periodically by requesting a copy of your report.

▶ Do not complete credit card applications at displays set up on campus. This exposes your personal information to people you don't know.

▶ Use your home address as your permanent mailing address rather than a temporary address while in school.

▶ Do not provide personal information on a social network that can be accessed by an identity thief. You don't know these people!

▶ Carry your wallet in your front pocket instead of your back pocket.

▶ Place security freezes on your credit scores. This prevents anyone from looking at your credit report except the companies that already have a financial relationship with you. Lenders who can't pull your credit report are unlikely to grant new credit to someone else in your name.

▶ Opt out of preapproved credit offers, which are easy ways for identity thieves to steal your personal identity. This stops credit bureaus from selling your name to lenders. Go to the opt-out Web site at *www.optoutprescreen.com* or call 888-567-8688.

▶ Don't use obvious passwords like your birthday, your mother's maiden name, or the last four digits of your Social Security number.

(Adapted from Consumer Response Center brochure, *Identity Theft and Fraud,* 2003; *ConsumerReport, Money Advisor,* 2008; *The State* Newspaper, August 31, 2008)

He later became a major shareholder in the firm Berkshire Hathaway, which purchased major shares in The *Washington Post* Company, ABC, Geico, Dairy Queen, and Coca-Cola. The most he has ever taken as an actual salary from all of his ventures and investments is $100 per year. It was reported in 2006 that Mr. Buffett does NOT carry a cell phone, does NOT have a computer at his desk, and drives his own car.

Upon his death, his children will NOT inherit much of his wealth. He has been quoted as saying, *"I want to give my kids just enough so that they would feel that they could do anything, but not so much that they would feel like doing nothing."*

(Adapted from Forbes, Wikipedia, and About.com)

Tips for Personal Success

Consider the following suggestions for improving your financial status during the semester:

▶ Practice delayed gratification.

▶ Reduce your Latte Factor™.

▶ Talk to an advisor about taking a personal finance course next semester as an elective.

Now, it is your turn. What three things could you implement to change your financial management practices?

1. _____
2. _____
3. _____

From Ordinary to Extraordinary

REAL PEOPLE | REAL LIVES | REAL CHANGE

LEO G. BORGES
Founder and Former CEO
Borges and Mahoney, San Francisco, CA

Tulare, California, is still a farming community today, but in 1928 when I was born, it was totally agricultural and an exceptionally rural, detached part of the world. My parents had immigrated to California from the Azore Islands years earlier in search of a better life—the American dream. My father died when I was 3 years old and when I was 11, my mother passed away. Even though I lived with and was raised by my sisters, the feelings of aloneness and isolation were the two primary feelings I had growing up. We were orphans. We were poor. We were farm kids. We were Portuguese—not Americans. Every day, someone reminded us of these realities. One positive thing remained, however. My mother always told us that we could be anything or

> *We were orphans. We were poor. We were farm kids. We were Portuguese—not Americans.*

have anything if we believed in it and worked hard for it.

I left home at 17 to attend a program in advertising in San Francisco. Later that year, I moved to Los Angeles and began working for a major advertising firm. From there I enlisted in the Coast Guard, and when my duty was over, I worked for an oil company and then a major leasing firm. In each position, I worked my way up the ladder, strove to do my very best, and proved that I was capable of doing anything regardless of my background.

When I was in my early forties, my best friend, Cliff, and I decided to start our own business. We were tired of working in "middle management" and knew that we could be successful if we worked hard. After much research and consulting with companies across the

country, we determined that we would start a company in the water treatment business.

You may be asking yourself, "What experience did an advertising agency, an oil company, and a leasing firm give him to start a business in water treatment?" The answer is none. However, Cliff was an excellent accountant and I was an excellent salesman. We found a third partner who was one of the leading water treatment experts in the world and we were off. It was not easy and we had to eat beans for many meals, but Borges and Mahoney, Inc. was born.

Our first office was a small storefront in San Francisco. Through the development of our superior products, expert advice to clients, and outstanding customer service, we grew and grew, finally moving to our largest location in San Rafael, California. By the time we sold our business some 20 years later, we had 15 full-time employees and annual revenues in the millions of dollars.

From Ordinary to Extraordinary

REAL PEOPLE | REAL LIVES | REAL CHANGE

To this day, I attribute my success to the fact that I was determined to show everyone—my sisters, cousins, aunts and uncles, former co-workers, friends and foes—that I would never let my past, my heritage, my economic background, or my history hold me back. I knew that I could be a success. Through hard work, determination, and surrounding myself with supportive, brilliant people, I proved that the American dream my parents sought years earlier is truly possible for anyone who works hard, believes in himself or herself, and doesn't give up. It is possible for you, too.

EXTRAORDINARY REFLECTION

Read the following statement and respond in your online journal or class notebook.

Mr. Borges states that through "hard work, determination, and surrounding himself with supportive, brilliant people," he and his partner, Cliff, were able to become very successful in business and beyond. Who can you call upon in your life to offer you support, advice, and provide you with solid, smart advice? What questions do you need to ask them?

How careful are you when it comes to protecting your financial and medical records?

BATTLING THE BIG "IF'S"

Do You Know What to Do When You Need Something?

Below, you will find some helpful tips for managing some important financial decisions in your life and protecting yourself when things get tough.

IF YOU NEED TO PURCHASE A CAR

▶ Do not purchase a new car. We know it is tempting, but the value will plummet 20 to 40% the moment you drive off the lot. It is just not worth it! Purchase a two- to three-year old car from a reputable dealer.

▶ DON'T fall in love with a car before you know everything about it. Love is blind when it comes to people . . . and cars, too!

▶ Purchase an extended warranty, BUT read the terms carefully.

▶ Always ask for a "Car-fax" and a title search and make the dealer pay for them.

▶ Check to see if your state has a "Lemon Law" and if so, read it carefully.

▶ Don't be pressured into a sale by lines such as: "This is our last one like this," or "I've got several people interested in this car." Let them have it!

▶ Make sure the car has passed the smog test if one is required in your state.

IF YOU NEED TO SAVE ON FUEL

▶ Consider carpooling.

▶ Make sure your car is in good running condition and that your tires are inflated properly. Get your car tuned up often.

▶ Drive slower and at a constant speed when possible. Driving 74 mph instead of 55 mph increases fuel consumption by as much as 20%.

▶ Check your car's air filter and fuel filter and replace them if they are dirty.

▶ Do not use "Jack Rabbit" starts. Accelerate easily after red lights and stop signs. "Flooring it" costs money.

▶ When stuck in traffic, try to drive at a steady pace and not stop and start. Watch how the large trucks do this—they seldom come to a complete stop.

▶ Plan your trips so that you can make the most number of right turns, thus saving time at lights. Also, combine your errands so that you can make fewer trips.

▶ Clean out your car. Carrying around just a few extra pounds in the trunk or backseat costs fuel.

▶ Stick with the wheels and tires that came with your car. Using larger wheels and tires than recommended creates more drag and weight on your car and costs you more fuel.

▶ Use the telephone. Often, many things can be accomplished without personal visits.

IF YOU FEEL THE URGE TO MAKE AN IMPULSE PURCHASE

▶ Use the 72-hour rule. Wait 72 hours to make any purchase over $50.

▶ If you still feel the need to purchase the item after 72 hours, consider your budget and how you are going to pay for the item.

▶ Consider waiting until you can pay cash for the item, or consider putting the item on lay-away. Do not charge it!

▶ Purchase the item later as a reward to yourself for getting all A's in your classes.

▶ Think about how purchasing this item will affect your family's budget.

▶ Make as few trips out shopping as possible to lower your temptation to purchase things you can't afford.

Do you work hard to control everyday and impulse spending?

IF YOUR GROCERY BILL IS OUT OF CONTROL

▶ Shop with a calculator and enter each item as you place it into your cart. This will give you a great idea of what you're spending.

▶ Create a menu for each day of the week and shop only for the items on your list. Do not shop when you are in a hurry, tired, or after working all day.

▶ Consider purchasing generic brands—often they are the same product as brand-name items, just with a different label.

▶ Clip coupons. They actually work. Go online to your favorite product's Web site and print out their online coupons. Try to shop when stores double or triple coupons' value.

▶ Consider cooking in bulk and then freezing leftovers for later in the week.

▶ Look for placement of the product in the store. Items at chest level are the most expensive. Look up and down on the shelves to find less expensive items.

▶ Do not shop for convenience items such as premade meals, bakery items, or boneless chicken breasts. Purchase an entire chicken and cut it up. You'll save a lot of money this way.

▶ Buy in bulk at one of the major warehouse stores. Often this can save a lot of money if you are buying for a large family.

Although many young people fail in the management of their personal finances, there is no reason that you cannot manage your financial business well. You should think about personal finance and the management of money and investments as basic survival skills that are very important to you now, as well as for the rest of your life.

Since only 10% of high school students graduate from high school with any kind of instruction in personal finance, learning to budget your money, make wise investments, and avoid credit card debt are priority needs of all college students. As you move toward establishing yourself in a career, it is important to remember that to get what you want out of life, a significant part of your success will depend on your ability to make sound money decisions. We hope you will learn to make money work for you instead of your having to work hard for money because of poor decisions made early in life. En route to becoming a good money manager, the following tips will assist you:

► Don't get caught in the credit card trap.

► Know exactly how you are spending your money.

► Protect your credit rating by using wise money management strategies.

► Learn all you can about scholarships and grants.

► Understand the regulations about repaying student loans.

► Don't borrow any more money than you absolutely have to.

► Ask for your credit score at least once a year and be sure you have a good one.

► Use only one or two credit cards.

► Try to pay off your credit card each month before any interest is charged.

► Write down your credit card numbers and keep them in a safe place in case your cards are lost or stolen.

► If you get into credit card trouble, get counseling.

► Learn everything you can about investments and retirement plans.

Learning to manage your money and protecting your credit rating will be as important to you as getting your degree. It is never too early to learn about money management. If you can do it when you have just a little money, it will be easier when you have more money.

"Never work just for money or for power. They won't save your soul or help you sleep at night."
—Marian Wright Edelman

KNOWLEDGE in BLOOM

Improving Your Money Management Skills

Each chapter-end assessment is based on *Bloom's Taxonomy of Learning*. See the inside front cover for a quick review.

UTILIZES LEVELS 1–6 ON THE TAXONOMY

PROCESS: As a beginning college student, it is not too early for you to map out your financial future. In this exercise, you will be asked to list some of your pressing financial concerns and discuss how you might spend more wisely. You will be asked to apply principles of financial management as you analyze your overall current financial management profile, design a plan for improvement, and critique your plan after practicing it for a week.

Level 1 Question: List three of your most pressing financial concerns:

1. _____

2. _____

3. _____

Level 2 Question: Give examples of how you might improve your money management techniques relative to these three concerns and spend more wisely.

_____

_____

_____

Level 3 Question: Prepare a plan for improving how you spend your money in these three areas only.

_____

_____

_____

Level 4 Question: Analyze your current financial management practices using the information you have studied in this chapter. Discuss your income, your expenses, student loans, credit card debt, impulse-buying habits, and overall financial situation at the moment. Be sure to list financial concerns.

_____

_____

_____

Level 5 Question: Now that you have been honest with yourself and have identified current financial practices and concerns, **design** a plan for improvement by listing steps that you will employ to practice better financial management.

_____

_____

_____

_____

Level 6 Question: Follow your plan for a week. Write down everything you spend, the things you resist that you might have typically bought, and strategies you have employed to improve. After a week, **evaluate your plan and your ability to stick with this plan at this point.**

_____

_____

_____

_____

SQ3R *Mastery* STUDY SHEET

EXAMPLE QUESTION: *(from page 270)* What are four types of financial aid?		**ANSWER:**
EXAMPLE QUESTION: *(from page 270)* How does a Pell grant differ from a loan?		**ANSWER:**
AUTHOR QUESTION: *(from page 271)* Discuss three steps for applying for financial aid.		**ANSWER:**
AUTHOR QUESTION: *(from page 272)* What have you learned about student loans that might help you make better decisions?		**ANSWER:**
AUTHOR QUESTION: *(from page 274)* Why is budgeting so important?		**ANSWER:**
AUTHOR QUESTION: *(from page 275)* What are some of the dangers of credit card debt?		**ANSWER:**
AUTHOR QUESTION: *(from page 281)* What practices will you employ to avoid becoming a victim of identity theft?		**ANSWER:**
YOUR QUESTION: *(from page ____)*		**ANSWER:**
YOUR QUESTION: *(from page ____)*		**ANSWER:**
YOUR QUESTION: *(from page ____)*		**ANSWER:**
YOUR QUESTION: *(from page ____)*		**ANSWER:**
YOUR QUESTION: *(from page ____)*		**ANSWER:**

Finally, after answering these questions, recite this chapter's major points in your mind.
Consider the following general questions to help you master this material.

- ▶ What was it about?
- ▶ What does it mean?
- ▶ What was the most important thing you learned? Why?
- ▶ What were the key points to remember?

11.9 *Tracking Your Expenditures and Spending Habits Chart*

Over the course of the **next three days**, **write down EVERY CENT you spend** including items such as fuel, food, bottled water, child care, newspapers, etc. EVERY CENT. After three days, analyze your spending habits and determine at least five ways that you can cut expenses.

DAY #1	DAY #2	DAY #3

TOTAL FOR DAY #1
$ _____

TOTAL FOR DAY #2
$ _____

TOTAL FOR DAY #3
$ _____

What is the biggest lesson you have learned from tracking your money? What was the most shocking? Why?

_____

_____

_____

List five ways that you can cut your expenses.

1. _____
2. _____
3. _____
4. _____
5. _____

CHAPTER 12
INFORM

IMPROVING YOUR RESEARCH, WRITING, AND SPEAKING SKILLS

"The limits of my language mean the limits of my world."

—Ludwig Wittgenstein

WHY READ THIS CHAPTER?

what's in it for me?

Why? Learning to speak and write properly will be two of the most valuable skills you will ever develop. Learning the proper techniques of speaking and writing will help you improve your relationships at school, work, and home and will help you present yourself professionally in many situations. This chapter will give you an opportunity to integrate and apply the skills you learned about *information literacy* in Chapter 5, "Think." You will learn to apply these skills while researching a written paper or spoken presentation. Learning to research and prepare a paper or presentation is a necessary skill that will help you be successful in so many endeavors in your life.

By carefully reading this chapter and taking the information provided seriously, you will be able to:

1. Understand the power and value of the written and the spoken word.
2. Understand the value of and how to use the campus library to aid your research.
3. Identify and discuss the similarities and differences between writing a college-level paper and delivering an oral presentation.
4. Identify the steps and processes of writing a college-level paper.
5. Identify the steps and processes of writing and delivering a college-level oral presentation.

CHAPTER 12 / INFORM

"Words are, of course, the most powerful drug used by mankind."

—Rudyard Kipling

NAME: Acacia Jamison
COLLEGE: University of South Carolina, Columbia, S.C.
MAJOR: Criminal Justice
AGE: 21

I took a course called University 101 that helped me adjust to college quickly. It also gave me an opportunity to make new friends early in the semester, and this helped me learn to feel at home more quickly. In this course, we also addressed topics like drinking responsibly and what to do about alcohol poisoning. I learned how to write a good speech in this class. First, I learned to do research and then I put my main points in bulleted items on note cards. Even though I wrote out the speech, I referred just to bullets when I delivered the speech because if you read a speech, it is very boring to your audience.

One of the most valuable skills I gained in this class was learning to speak in front of a group. My goal is to become an attorney, so this is a skill I will use the rest of my life. After you have researched the speech and decided on your bullet points, I recommend that you rehearse the speech out loud several times before you actually deliver it. Stand in front of a mirror and observe your body language. Time yourself to be sure you are meeting the guidelines. Record it and critique yourself, and try to avoid using filler words like "um" and "uh."

As you speak, establish eye contact, and put expression in your voice. A sing-song voice is boring to your audience.

Try to create a catchy beginning that gets your audience's attention. Summarize the main points and then end powerfully so they remember your presentation.

When you have to write research papers, first, read over the instructions from the professor to see what he or she is looking for. Research online at different Web sites, being careful to evaluate the information. Go to the library and get books to add to your paper's validity and interest. Get help from a librarian if you can't find information. Avoid copying information from Wikipedia. The best tip? Start early!

What advice do I have for you in general? Remember, the first impression is usually the most memorable. You want to be sure you are strong and confident so you leave a good impression on people you meet or to whom you are speaking.

SCAN & QUESTION

In the preface of this book (page xix), you read about the **SQ3R Study Method**. Right now, take a few moments, **scan this chapter**, and on page 313, write **five questions** that you think will be important to your mastery of this material. In addition to the two questions below, you will also find five questions from your authors. Use one of your **"Study for Quiz"** stickers to flag this page for easy reference.

EXAMPLES:

► **List three ways that speech preparation differs from preparation for writing a paper.** (from page 295)

► **How is writing a research paper like climbing a ladder?** (from page 296)

THE ENORMOUS AND VAST POWER OF WORDS

Why Is It Important to Know How to Harness the Power of Words?

Words are among the most powerful forces in existence when used by a skilled orator or writer. When people are able to get others to do what they want them to do, they usually employ words, not physical power. Words can inspire, comfort, teach, encourage, persuade, and sell. They can also be used to manipulate, misinform, and spread propaganda. Words can lift us up and bring us together. They can also tear us apart and create divisiveness. They can twist our thinking, cause us not to use common sense, and even control our behavior. Words can change our opinions, make us act foolishly, lead us to join a cause, and touch our emotions.

Do you find that it is easier to express yourself through writing or speaking?

Words have started wars, led people into battle, stirred entire nations to do the right thing—or the wrong thing. "Words influence how we think, and our thoughts determine our actions. There is a powerful connection between the words we use and the results we get. . . . Poorly chosen words can kill enthusiasm, impact self esteem, lower expectations and hold people back while well chosen ones can motivate, offer hope, create vision, impact thinking and alter results" (Russell, 2004). The written word can be more powerful than the spoken word because many people just accept what is written and in print as truth even though it may be a blatant lie. To underestimate the power of words is to do so at your own peril.

Words are powerful and can literally change the course of your life if you learn to use them effectively. If you have not taken the use of the spoken and written word seriously enough, this is one area where you need to change.

HOW TO WRITE A COLLEGE-LEVEL RESEARCH PAPER

Will I Ever Get This Thing Done?

Writing a research paper is not at the top of every college student's list of favorite things to do! In fact, it stands right up there with a major test in organic chemistry or a root canal. But

"I write to understand as much as I do to be understood.".
—Elie Wiesel, Holocaust Survivor and Nobel Prize Winner

it is something that millions of college students have to face daily, so it is important to start now and learn how to do it right. How important is writing? According to college seniors, the most important courses they took were those that required them to write. "Think of all the courses you have taken at college. Which course, or courses, had the most profound impact on you, on the way you think, about learning, about life, about the world?" When seniors answered this question, they tended to cite courses in which they had done a significant amount of writing (Light, 2001). So people just like you decided along the way

FIGURE **12.1** *Ten Steps to Communication Success: Overview of Similarities and Differences Between Writing and Speaking*

STEPS	WRITER	SPEAKER
TOPIC	Most likely assigned by the professor	May be assigned by the professor; most likely chosen by the student
	Can be very broad to appeal to a mass audience	Usually narrowed for a specific audience or class
	Can be narrative, informative, biographical, technical, analytical, etc.	Will usually be informative, demonstrative, or persuasive for classroom purposes
AUDIENCE ANALYSIS	Usually written for the professor	Usually written and delivered for the entire class
PURPOSE STATEMENT	Referred to as a thesis statement, it is usually at the beginning of the paragraph and introduces the topic	Referred to as a purpose or transition statement, it is usually at the end of the introduction and serves as a bridge to the body of the speech
RESEARCH PROCESS	Research based on your topic and thesis statement	Research based on your topic and thesis statement
ORGANIZATIONAL PROCESS	May be assigned by the professor	Usually determined by the type of speech
	May use a formal outline	Will probably use a less formal outline
WRITING PROCESS	Writer can create a draft and revise until polished	Speaker can create a draft and rehearse until polished
	May be allowed a rewrite after a grade is assigned	Seldom allowed a second chance for another grade
DOCUMENTATION	Presented at the end of the paper as a bibliography, endnotes, or reference page, depending on documentation style	Research and sources usually documented orally during speech and may be written at the end of the speech as required by the professor
OUTLINING DELIVERY NOTES	Not required for a written paper	Speaker can use a variety of notes such as key word outlines, note cards, or overheads if allowed by the professor
AUDIOVISUAL	Not required for a written paper although graphs, pictures and diagrams can support contents	Adds strength to the presentation Increases audience attention and retention Speaker must rehearse with the aids used
REHEARSAL AND DELIVERY	Not required for a written paper unless you have to talk to your class about your paper	Speaker must spend a great deal of time in rehearsal to deliver a polished presentation

that writing papers is pretty important. Let's see if we can shed some light on the process and make it more enjoyable for you. To begin, review Figure 12.2, The Writing Ladder.

Where Do I Start the Research Process?

First, take this assignment one step at a time. Think of the process as going up a ladder. You start at the bottom rung and work your way to the top. When you reach the top of the ladder, if you have worked hard, avoided cutting corners, and sought help from qualified people along the way, your paper is going to be a good one. As a writer, you will need to divide your paper into small, manageable tasks with two goals in mind—the quality of your paper and the due date. Writing a solid research paper (or presentation) of which you can be proud is not a task for a weekend or an overnighter.

Why do you think it might be important to use the library for research instead of the Internet?

Is the Library Still Important in the Digital Age?

Yes! The answer is yes! Many people still think of libraries as places that are as quiet as a tomb, with a crabby old woman presiding over it who is prepared to pounce on you if you ask a question or touch one of her precious books. Fortunately, that stereotype has started to go the way of the horse and buggy, and today, libraries are literally the hub of a college or university campus. Your library is the key that you can use to unlock the secrets to your education. Your authors think it is safe to say, "You can't get an education if you try to bypass the library." Certainly, you can't write a solid research paper without using the library and its resources. Although the Internet is an amazing tool, serious research requires you to use the library and its tools such as print books, maps, charts, government data, periodicals, and your librarian. It may be fun and easy to use Google, Dogpile, or Wikipedia, but you will also need to hone your library research skills. So, let's look at the steps and get started in using the library, research, and writing.

Step One: Clarify the Purpose

Why are you writing this paper? Exactly what does the assignment require that you accomplish? Since this is college-level work, you most likely will not be asked simply to report information; most likely you will be required to react to or defend a position or persuade someone to take

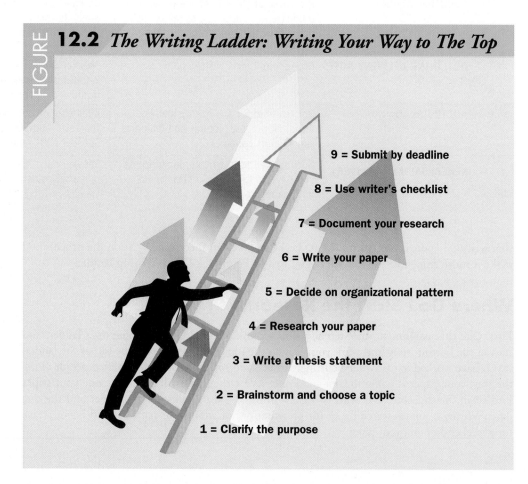

FIGURE **12.2** *The Writing Ladder: Writing Your Way to The Top*

9 = Submit by deadline

8 = Use writer's checklist

7 = Document your research

6 = Write your paper

5 = Decide on organizational pattern

4 = Research your paper

3 = Write a thesis statement

2 = Brainstorm and choose a topic

1 = Clarify the purpose

FIGURE

12.3   *Tips for Topic Selection*

▶ Study the assignment and understand exactly what the professor wants you to do.

▶ Know what type of paper you will be writing.

▶ Identify your talents, interests, and experiences.

▶ Determine if you find sufficient material and information for your paper.

▶ Decide if you can adequately discuss the topic within the given time frame or page length.

▶ When researching your topic, narrow your search. If your subject is *depression*, for example, it may be too broad. You may have to narrow that search to *depression among college students*.

action. Writing a research paper usually requires that you use higher-order thinking skills such as demonstrating, forecasting, inferring, justifying, validating, interpreting, and prioritizing.

Step Two: Brainstorm Ideas and Choose a Topic

Often students say, "I can't think of anything to write or speak about." Basically, that's bull. We all care deeply about something. Consider this exercise: When was the last time you got angry? What aroused that anger? This could be your topic. When was the last time you felt passion—real dynamic passion? That is a topic for you. When was the last time you felt really frustrated and agitated? There is a topic. When was the last time you were scared—really frightened about something? There is a topic. Your best topics will come from your heart and experiences and will be based on your desire to explain your anger, passion, fears, or other feelings. Some tips for topic selection are listed in Figure 12.3.

After you have brainstormed topics for your assignment, write the topic of your paper in the space below.

My TOPIC is: _____

Step Three: Write Your Thesis Statement—It's the Big Idea

A thesis statement is the big idea—the PURPOSE of your paper. Simply stated, what do you want to accomplish? Are you writing to entertain, to persuade, to defend, or to inform? What do you want your readers to do or feel at the end of your paper? Do you want them to change their minds, sign a petition, join a cause, give blood, or practice safer sex? If you can answer this question, you are on your way to writing an effective and engaging paper.

Your thesis statement is a single sentence that tells your readers *exactly* what you hope to accomplish in your paper. An example of a thesis statement for a paper on domestic abuse follows:

> *This paper will present the effects of domestic abuse, inform readers how to look for warning signs, provide information where they can find assistance, and attempt to persuade them that stronger laws need to be enacted.*

Using the topic you selected previously, write your thesis statement below.

In the past, have you found it easy or difficult to write an effective thesis statement? Why?

_____

_____

_____

Step Four: Research, Organize, and Verify Data for Your Paper

Now that you have selected and narrowed your topic and developed your thesis statement, you are ready to begin accumulating information to support your paper or speech. As you begin to consider resources, you will want to investigate and explore a variety of sources, including the following:

▶ Personal interviews with experts on your topic

▶ Electronic and print indexes

▶ Books, journals, and other periodicals on the subject

▶ Newspapers such as *The New York Times, Chicago Sun-Times,* and *Atlanta Constitution*

▶ Reference materials such as encyclopedias, dictionaries, directories, atlases, almanacs and yearbooks, books of quotations, and bibliographical directories

▶ Government documents

▶ The Internet (start with Yahoo!, Infoseek, Dogpile, or Google, for example)

Don't forget to use the information literacy skills you learned in Chapter 5, "Think." Consider using a card like the example in Figure 12.4 to record your research data and help you stay organized.

Verify the Validity of Sources and Authors

As a researcher, you should know the validity of the sources and research that you plan to use to write your papers and speeches. The credibility of your sources can mean the difference between having a valid argument or thesis and having unsubstantiated opinions. Does your research come from a reliable, respected source? Is your research related to the argument or point you are making? Is the person you are quoting highly respected and reputable in the field? Is the data skewed or biased by an organization or special interest?

You should always feel free to ask the reference librarian for assistance and advice regarding resources. Also, to critically analyze any information sources, whether Internet or print, use the following guidelines by Ormondroyd, Engle, and Cosgrave (2001) from Cornell University Libraries:

▶ Who is the author and what are his or her credentials, educational background, past writings, or experience?

▶ When was the source published? If it is a Web page, the date is usually found on the last page or the home page. Is the source current or out of date for your topic?

▶ What edition is the source? Books in second or third editions suggest that the source has been updated to reflect changes and new knowledge.

FIGURE **12.4** *Data Card*

SOURCE: (AUTHOR, TITLE, DATE, URL, MEDIA)	
SUBJECT:	
KEY SEARCH WORDS:	
QUOTE:	

▶ Who is the publisher? If the source is published by a university press, it is likely to be a scholarly publication.

▶ What is the title of the source? This will help you determine if the source is popular, sensational, or scholarly, which thus indicates the level of complexity. Popular journals are resources such as *Time, Newsweek, Vogue, Ebony,* and *Reader's Digest.* They seldom cite their sources. Sensational resources are often inflammatory and written on an elementary level. They usually have flashy headlines, and they cater to popular superstitions. Examples are *The Globe, The National Enquirer,* and *The Star.*

▶ Who is the intended audience of your source? Is the information too simple, too advanced, or too technical for your paper's audience?

▶ Is the source factually objective, opinionated, or propagandistic? Objective sources look at all angles and report on each one honestly.

▶ Does the information appear to be valid and well researched or does it just gloss over the material? Is it supported by evidence?

▶ When searching the Internet for resources, use extreme caution. Anyone can create a Web page or present information on the Internet.

To evaluate Web pages (UC-Berkeley, 2002), you should train your mind to think critically, even suspiciously, by asking a series of questions that will help you decide how much a Web page can be trusted:

▶ Is it someone's personal page? Personal pages are not necessarily "bad," but they may need to be investigated very carefully.

▶ What kind of domain does it come from? Look for appropriateness. What do you think is the most reliable source for your topic?

▶ Look for the date that the article was last updated.

▶ Who wrote the paper? Look for the name of the author or organization, agency, or institution who is responsible for the page.

▶ Is the page dated? Is it current enough for your research or is it "stale" and outdated?

▶ What are the author's credentials? Anyone can put anything on the Web. Your task is to distinguish between the reliable and questionable, and the knowledgeable and amateur.

▶ Are sources documented with footnotes or links? In scholarly works, the credibility of most writings is proven through the amount of footnote or endnote documentation.

▶ Ask yourself, "Why was this page put on the Web?"

▶ Could the article be parody, humor, or satire?

▶ Is this as good a resource as you could find if you used the library?

Using the topic you chose previously, access one popular source, one scholarly source, and one sensational source. What are the major differences among the data collected in each area? Which site offers you the most credible research? Why?

BLOOM LEVEL 4
QUESTION

_____

_____

_____

_____

_____

Step Five: Decide on an Organizational Pattern

Now that you have gathered enough information from a variety of resources, what are the most effective ways to present your findings and ideas? As you probably know, every good paper will have an introduction, a body, and a conclusion. These subjects will be discussed later in the chapter.

Organizing the body of your paper or speech can be done using one of several proven methods:

SPATIAL ORGANIZATION arranges information or items according to their location.

> **Example:** If you were describing the Mall in Washington, D.C., you could begin with the Lincoln Memorial and then move on to the reflecting pond, the Washington Monument, and the Smithsonian.

CAUSE-EFFECT ORGANIZATION arranges your information in the cause-and-effect order. You would discuss the causes of a problem and then explore its effects.

> **Example:** If you were speaking about high blood pressure, you would first examine the causes of high blood pressure such as diet, hereditary factors, and weight and then move on to the effects such as heart attack and stroke.

CHRONOLOGICAL ORGANIZATION presents information in the order in which it happened. Speeches that deal with historical facts and how-to speeches often use chronological organization.

> **Example:** If you were writing a paper on the history of automobiles in the United States since 1950, you would begin with the '50s and then move to the '60s, '70s, '80s, and '90s.

PROBLEM-SOLVING ORGANIZATION is often used in persuasive papers. Usually, you are trying to get your reader to accept your proposal. You first begin by pointing out the major problem(s) and then move on to revealing the solutions, and the advantages of the solutions.

> **Example:** If you were writing about crime on college campuses, you would begin by informing the reader or listener about the problems, the crime statistics, and the personal toll on students. You would then propose solutions and tell how the solutions would help all students.

TOPICAL/CATEGORICAL ORGANIZATION groups information into subdivisions or clusters information into categories. Some information naturally falls into specific categories, such as the different types of palm trees or the types of rollerblades available.

> **Example:** If you were writing a paper on taxes in the United States, you might categorize your information into local taxes, state taxes, federal taxes, luxury taxes, "sin" taxes, and special taxes.

COMPARE/CONTRAST ORGANIZATION presents your information in a fashion that shows its similarities to and differences from other information.

> **Example:** You may be writing a paper that compares the health care system in the United States to that of England or Canada.

IMPORTANCE/PRIORITY ORGANIZATION arranges information from the most important issue to the least or from the least important to the most important. You can also arrange your information from the top priority to the lowest priority or vice versa.

> **Example:** If you were writing a paper to inform readers and listeners about buying diamonds, you might arrange your information so that you speak first about the most important aspects of diamond buying—clarity, color, and cut—and later about less important factors.

Using the topic that you selected earlier, and referring to the up-to-date, valid research that you have gathered, which organizational pattern do you plan to use to write your paper? Why is this the best way?

_____

_____

_____

_____

Step Six: Write Your Paper

You have already done a lot of the hard work. Now it is time to get on with the task of writing a solid research paper. By now, you have decided on a topic and thesis statement, gathered data, validated and documented your sources, organized the data, and drafted an outline. You are ready to write!

ETHICAL CONSIDERATIONS

As a writer you have a personal responsibility to consider the ethics and consequences of your statements. Gamble and Gamble, in their book *Public Speaking in the Age of Diversity* (1998), suggest that you follow these guidelines when considering the ethical dimensions of writing and speaking:

▶ Share only what you know to be true.
▶ Be fully prepared and informed.
▶ Consider the best interests of your receivers.
▶ Make it easy for your receivers to understand your message.
▶ Refrain from using words as weapons.
▶ Don't wrap information in a positive spin just to succeed.
▶ Respect the cultural diversity of your receivers.
▶ Remember: You are accountable for what you say.

   Using these points as a checklist, evaluate your topic to ensure that it is ethically sound.

> "I am returning this otherwise good typing paper to you because someone has printed gibberish all over it and put your name at the top."
> —English Professor at Ohio State University

ORGANIZING THE BODY

One of the most effective ways to begin composing your paper or speech is to create a rough outline of the points you would like to cover. As you begin to outline, remember that your organizational pattern should guide you through this phase.
   Assume you are writing a paper on date rape. Your outline might look similar to this:

I. Introduction
   A. Thesis statement
   B. Overview of the paper
II. The problem of date rape
   A. What is date rape?
   B. Facts and statistics supporting its prevalence
   C. Laws relative to date rape
III. Where does date rape happen and why?
   A. What are the settings where date rape typically happens?
   B. What are the usual circumstances that cause date rape?
   C. Who does it typically happen to?
IV. How to prevent date rape
   A. Avoid excessive drinking and drugs
   B. Be responsible for watching your drink
   C. Get to know people before you are with them alone
   D. Go out in groups
   E. Check on each other
   F. Pay your own way

When writing your papers or speeches, do you ask yourself the "4W+1H" questions? Who? What? When? Where? How?

FIGURE
12.5 *Creating Effective Introductions*

- ▶ Telling a story or creating a vivid, visual illustration
- ▶ Using startling facts or statistics
- ▶ Referring to an accident with which the reader is familiar
- ▶ Asking rhetorical, yet pertinent questions
- ▶ Using novel ideas or striking statements
- ▶ Using quotations
- ▶ Using humor or humorous stories

V. What to do if it happens
    A. Report it to campus security or the police
    B. Do not destroy evidence
    C. Report it to the proper college authorities
    D. Press charges if advised
VI. Conclusion

Once you have developed your outline, you can begin to write your paper. Using the topic you selected previously, organize the body of your paper or speech by completing an outline of your resources. Use a separate sheet of paper for this exercise.

In Figure 12.5 you will find a variety of techniques that can help you start your paper by creating an effective introduction.

Using the topic you selected previously, choose one technique, or a combination of the techniques we've discussed, to construct an introduction to your topic and write a draft of your introduction.

_____

_____

_____

_____

_____

_____

WRITING CONCLUSIONS

Conclusions are very important to the overall quality of your paper. They are designed to leave the reader wanting more and remembering your words. Figure 12.6 features several techniques for helping you build an effective conclusion.

FIGURE
12.6 *Techniques for Concluding a Paper*

- ▶ Summarize and reemphasize the main points.
- ▶ Make a final appeal for action or challenge.
- ▶ Refer to the introduction (story, quote, or joke); this is parallelism.
- ▶ Complete the opening story.
- ▶ Reemphasize the impact of your topic.
- ▶ Use a vivid analogy or simile.
- ▶ End powerfully! You want your reader to remember your topic and your compelling points.

Using your topic, write a memorable, creative conclusion.

_____

_____

_____

_____

_____

_____

Step Seven: Documenting Your Paper

When writing your paper, and certainly once it has been written, you should take careful precautions to document all research and information that is not your own. If you have written a paper, you will need to document and cite all statistics, quotes, and excerpts from works that you referenced. The most common means of doing this is by quoting within the paper and then compiling a reference or bibliography sheet or page of endnotes at the end. We recommend that you review the section on plagiarism in Chapter 3 on page 60.

If you have questions about what to document, consider the following by Kirszner and Mandell (1995):

▶ Direct quotations

▶ Opinions, judgments, and insights of others that you summarize or paraphrase

▶ Information that is not widely known

▶ Information that is open to dispute

▶ Information that is not commonly accepted

▶ Tables, charts, graphs, and statistics taken from a source

Step Eight: Is Your Paper Ready to Turn In? Use the Writer's Checklist to Be Sure

Writing a really good paper that you can be proud of requires making several drafts, proofreading very carefully to eliminate grammatical and spelling errors, correcting mistakes, determining if you have really said what you wanted to say, being sure you have adequately covered the topic, checking to see if you have followed the correct style guidelines, and being sure you have correctly cited all sources. Good writers always write and rewrite before they are satisfied with the final document.

You can use the following checklist (Figure 12.7) to determine if you are finally ready to give your paper to the professor and feel proud and confident of your work.

Step Nine: Submit Your Paper by the Deadline

You've worked hard and created a paper on which you can be proud to place your name. Now, just make sure that you turn it in on time. Many professors DO NOT accept late work, or they severely penalize you for turning in late work. A paper that may have received an A may get a C because it was late. Always work hard to submit your best work—and submit it on time.

FIGURE

12.7 *Writer's Final Checklist*

Is My Paper Ready to Give to the Professor?

☐ My paper is the right length, not too long or too short.

☐ I have given my paper the best topic for the subject.

☐ My thesis statement is concise and clear.

☐ I have presented my topic in a comprehensive, convincing manner.

☐ My major points are presented in a logical sequence.

☐ I have revised my paper several times and improved it each time.

☐ I have been very careful not to use someone else's intellectual property as my own.

☐ I have used the style manual recommended by my professor and followed it carefully.

☐ I have checked carefully to be sure I followed all instructions assigned by the professor.

☐ I have double-checked my references and citations to be sure I reported them accurately.

☐ I have used several types of sources—books, articles, newspapers, Internet pamphlets, journals, and interviews.

☐ I have checked the validity of my sources.

☐ I have cited a variety of sources and not limited my research to only one or two sources.

☐ I have proofed my paper several times and made corrections, not relying solely on a spell checker to proof my paper.

☐ I have checked my paper to be sure that I have no run-on sentences.

☐ I have varied the length and type of sentences used to provide interest.

☐ I have avoided using "I" in a formal paper.

☐ If possible, I have had someone proof my paper and make suggestions.

How can learning to speak effectively help you reach your career goals?

PUBLIC SPEAKING

Do You Want a Chance to Shine?

"If I wanted to speak in front of people, I would have taken a public speaking course," you might be saying at this moment. Relax. You are not alone in your anxiety about speaking publicly. In fact, according to *The Book of Lists,* 3,000 of the Americans surveyed listed public speaking as their number-one fear. Public speaking ranked ahead of sickness, insects, financial troubles, deep water, and even death! Most people would rather die than speak in front of a group!

So, why do we include information on public speaking in a first-year-orientation text? You probably won't like the answer, but the simple truth is that you are going to be asked to speak in many of your classes; from history to chemistry, from engineering to computer programming, public speaking is going to be required of you. The more you know about researching, writing, and delivering presentations, the more confident you are going to feel in every class. We can't overemphasize the importance of mastering the written and spoken word now and in the future!

Is Writing a Speech Like Writing a Paper?

In some respects, writing a speech is similar to writing a paper, but by no means are they exactly alike. One of the worst things you can do is stand up in class and read a boring paper and call it a speech, especially if it is a paper that was written for another class or assignment. However, many of the points made previously about writing can be helpful to you in writing a speech. Because there are many similarities, your authors recommend that you review these previous sections as you prepare to write a speech. While these sections can help you develop your speech, you need to focus on the fact that speeches are different from papers in many regards. Speaking is sinking yourself into other people's hearts and souls; it is finding the right human-interest stories, the right humor, the right voice inflection, the right points to deliver your message, and using them at the right time—speaking is all this and more.

"If all my talents and powers were to be taken from me, and I had the choice of keeping but one, I would unhesitatingly ask to be allowed to keep the power of speaking, for through it, I would quickly recover the rest."

—Daniel Webster

Choosing a Topic for Your Speech

Sooner or later in one of your classes, you are going to have to make a presentation, which means you will have to choose a topic. Almost every writing and speaking expert will tell you to select a topic on which you are an expert, or a topic on which you have a keen interest and enough preparation time to become knowledgeable. This does not mean that you cannot speak on topics that are new or unfamiliar to you, but if you choose such a topic, your preparation time will need to be extended.

If you have a choice for your paper or speech, keep the tips shown in Figure 12.8 in mind.

FIGURE **12.8** *Topic Selection for Presentations*

▶ Know what type of speech you will be writing and/or delivering.

▶ Think about your talents, interests, and experiences and what appeals to you most.

▶ Determine if your topic is appropriate to you and your audience.

▶ Decide if you can adequately cover a speech on this topic in the allowed length of time.

▶ Build your speech around an interesting theme.

▶ Analyze your audience and their interests. Why will they want to hear your remarks?

▶ Be sure you can deliver a speech on this topic in a reasonable length of time.

Choosing a Theme or Thesis Statement

Writing a good speech is much more than just stringing together a few funny stories, telling a joke or two, using a few inspirational quotes, and inserting a few facts. President John Kennedy's famous inaugural address was built around the theme of freedom. He made many points, but he always went back to his basic theme of freedom. Martin Luther King, Jr.'s famous "I Have a Dream Speech" focused over and over on his dreams for the United States and his people. As you develop your speech, try to find a theme that is common to your points, one that your audience will relate to and remember. Refer to Step Three on page 297 and read the information about writing a thesis statement.

Have you ever looked around your class and really studied the diversity of your peers?

Analyzing Your Audience

Have you ever listened to someone speak about a topic that was so technical that you understood very little about it? It could be because the speech was poorly written, but it may be that the boring technical speech was unappealing to you because it was written for a different audience. If you don't understand your audience, it is unlikely that you will be able to maintain their attention, inform or persuade them, or expect them to act on your advice. Although your immediate speech will be written for your professor or class, there will be instances in the future when it will be advantageous for you to complete an analysis of your audience. This analysis will assist you in learning more about the diversity or homogeneity of your audience. Figure 12.9 will guide you in developing a comprehensive audience analysis.

Using your classroom setting as your audience, write a brief analysis of this audience. You may have to make some educated guesses based on observation and keen listening skills, but you may also have to interview your classmates or issue a questionnaire.

FIGURE **12.9** *Audience Demographic Wheel*

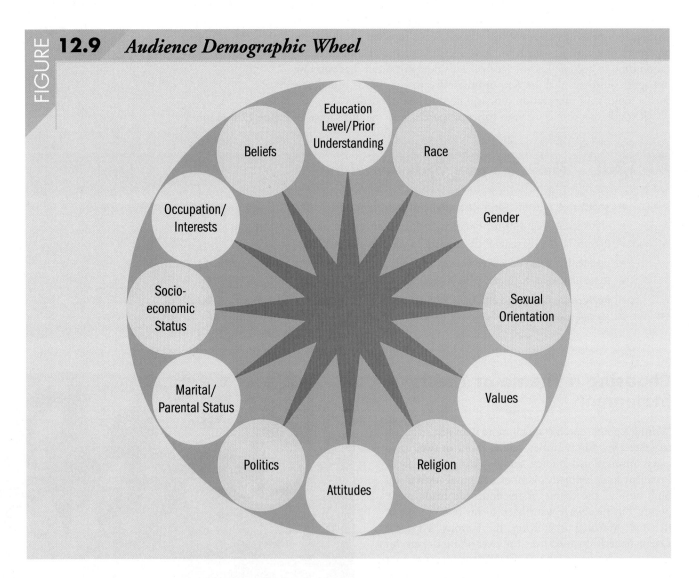

Organizing and Writing Your Speech

Speeches are typically written in three parts—introduction, body, and conclusion. Before you begin writing you need to review the purpose of the speech, the thesis, how much time you have to deliver it, and what your audience is like. There are many kinds of speeches. Some inform, some demonstrate, some persuade, and still others entertain. Decide what your purpose is before you begin writing. Narrow your topic so that you can present it well in the time allowed.

Effective speakers engage an audience; they reach out and grab people with their delivery style, their voices, and their stories. Good speakers use a variety of techniques, but they all use this one—a powerful introduction. You will either hold or lose your audience at the beginning, so your introduction needs to be powerful. If you are speaking to a class, your fellow classmates will have to sit and listen to several speeches in one class period. Before you speak, they could have already listened to five or six speeches and could have developed an "endurance" mentality.

Outlining Your Notes for Delivery

If you have ever watched and heard a disorganized speaker, or had to endure a speaker *read* an entire presentation, then you know the value of well-designed speaking notes.

After your speech has been formally written, it is time to outline your speaking notes. It is the mark of an unprofessional, unprepared—and usually, boring—speaker to read verbatim from pages and pages of typed notes. Instead, with rehearsal and a comprehensive key word outline, you can use surprisingly few notes as you gain experience.

An outline should be used to keep you organized and to assist you if you get lost or blank out during your presentation. It should not be used for reading your speech to the audience. Some speakers prefer to use note cards (3 × 5 or 5 × 7), while others prefer to use several sheets of paper in outline form. The choice is yours unless specified otherwise by your professor.

ESSENTIAL CORNERSTONE

Communication:
How will being able to speak and write well help you be more creative in all your classes and at work?

Social Networking Moment:
Share your response to this Essential Cornerstone with peers in your social network. Choose two responses from your peers and respond to their postings.

Using Audiovisual Aids Effectively

You have heard it said, "A picture is worth a thousand words." Nowhere is that more true than in public speaking. Visual aids can assist your audience in retaining the information longer. If you simply tell an audience some facts, three days later, they will remember only 10% of what you said. If you tell them and show them, three days later, they will remember 65% of what you said (Gamble & Gamble, 1998).

Several important factors should be considered when developing your visual aids. First, an audiovisual (AV) aid is a supplement to, **not a substitute** for, a presentation. Simply stated, even the most wonderfully creative visual aid will not support a poorly written and delivered speech. There are many types of aids available to you:

- Physical objects
- Models
- Drawings
- Maps
- Videotapes
- Audio recordings
- Real people
- PowerPoint presentations
- Graphs, tables, and charts
- Photographs and slides
- Slick boards and chalkboards
- Yourself (probably the most important)
- Posters and flip charts
- Computer-generated presentations (such as on CD-ROMs)

For a smooth, clean, polished presentation, consider the following guidelines when using your visual aids:

- ▶ *Always* rehearse with your AV aids.
- ▶ Make sure your AV is visible to all audience members.
- ▶ Make sure all equipment works before you begin your speech.
- ▶ Bring any item that you might need to make your AV work (such as extension cords, tape, push pins, and markers).

How can using a visual aid such as PowerPoint help you get your point across more effectively?

- ▶ Reveal and explain each AV when you are ready to use it, not all at once. Remove the AV when you have finished using it.
- ▶ Do not pass any AV around the room.
- ▶ Don't speak to the AV; speak to your audience.
- ▶ Use handouts with extreme caution. They should be issued only at the very end of your speech to prevent people from reading ahead and becoming bored with what you are saying.

PREPARING A POWERFUL POWERPOINT PRESENTATION

PowerPoint has become the "speaker's choice" for presenting information. While this is a valuable and creative tool, learning to use PowerPoint correctly can help you build a more dynamic presentation. Consider the following tips:

- ▶ Dynamic, visually appealing presentation slides take lots of time—begin early!
- ▶ Present your points in a logical order and place your most important points upfront.
- ▶ Don't put too much information on your slides.
- ▶ Do not use too many slides—using a few powerful slides is much better than many boring ones. Keep the size of the file manageable.
- ▶ Use a few key words—using too much text makes the slide unreadable and boring.
- ▶ Proofread carefully to be sure everything is spelled correctly and that grammar is correct.
- ▶ Use a font size of 44 for titles and a font size of 28 to 34 for subtitles with a bold font. Choose a font that is easy to read. Use no more than six to eight words per line.
- ▶ Do not use a wide variety of fonts or too many pictures or graphics because they will become distracting.
- ▶ Limit the number of colors on one screen.
- ▶ Avoid using all capital letters.
- ▶ Cite sources on the same slide where you present the information
- ▶ Using too much animation is distracting and may be confusing. Use with caution.
- ▶ Practice, practice, practice until your delivery becomes natural. DO NOT read from your slides—this is deadly! Allow time for audience questions and participation.

I'D RATHER DIE THAN MAKE THIS SPEECH

Can Anxiety Really Be Handled?

The time has come! All of your hard work, creativity, and energy will culminate in this one moment in the sun. You have taken all of the necessary steps for a successful presentation. Now, you need to consider only a few more details before you take the lectern.

Public speaking is an unfair beast. If you study for an exam and do well or fail to study and do poorly, the results are known only to you and the professor. However, the results of your public speaking performance are known to all present. You are evaluated immediately. That is just an accepted fact in the art of speaking. In order to do your very best, consider the following anxiety-reducing and delivery tips.

Reducing Anxiety

Your fears and anxiety are real, but they are also manageable. When faced with anxiety over public speaking, keep the following tips in mind:

- ▶ Choose a topic about which you know a great deal and about which you care deeply.
- ▶ Prepare for your speech thoroughly!
- ▶ When rehearsing, try to recreate the speaking environment, or if possible, rehearse in the room where the speech will be delivered.
- ▶ Approach the speech with an "I can" attitude. The more confident you act, the more confident you will eventually become.
- ▶ Realize that your small mistakes will not be seen and will rarely be heard by the audience; they are magnified in your own mind.
- ▶ Remember that listeners want you to succeed; most audiences are supportive.
- ▶ Instead of looking at the entire audience as a "room full of people," choose one person and look at him or her for a brief moment. Then, move on to the next person, and so on. This creates the feeling of speaking to only one person at a time.
- ▶ Don't try to be something that you are not. Just be yourself; use your own voice, your own style.
- ▶ Don't concentrate on the evaluation. If you have prepared and do your best, you will be evaluated fairly.

Tips for Personal Success

Consider the following strategies for improving your presentations:

- ▶ Select topics that interest you and your audience.
- ▶ Analyze your audience and how you might relate to them.
- ▶ Carefully research your papers and presentations.
- ▶ Document your sources carefully.
- ▶ Pay extra attention to Internet sources.
- ▶ Polish your presentation by practicing it aloud many times.
- ▶ Face your fears about speaking by presenting in public as often as you can.
- ▶ Keep in mind the slogan, "This is your moment in the sun." Use it wisely.

Now it is your turn. Create a list of at least three tips that you would offer fellow classmates to assist them when preparing to make a speech.

1. _____

2. _____

3. _____

WALKING TALL

How Do You Stand and Deliver with Confidence?

The day has finally come for you to deliver your speech—actually, it may have arrived way too early to suit you. However, if you have prepared using the steps outlined in this chapter, you have every reason to believe you are going to do well. Try to look at this presentation as an opportunity to practice a skill that will serve you well all your life. You may feel nervous, but you need to remember that no one else knows that but you. Some final tips are listed to help you perform well on "game day."

ESSENTIAL CORNERSTONE

Knowledge:
How will mastering your material and possessing good presentation skills help you reduce speech anxiety?

Social Networking Moment:
Share your response to this Essential Cornerstone with peers in your social network. Choose two responses from your peers and respond to their postings.

THINKING *for* CHANGE: An Activity for Critical Reflection

Mike is taking a first-year experience course that requires him to make an oral presentation. Although his class is small and he has gotten to know many of his classmates, he is terrified at the thought of making this speech. The date for his speech is two weeks away, and he needs to get moving, but he seems to be immobilized by his fears of speaking in front of a group.

Mike's fear of making oral presentations goes back to the eighth grade, when one of his teachers required him and his peers to make a speech. Mike didn't prepare very well. When it was his time to present, he panicked and forgot his speech. His classmates laughed at him, and his teacher rebuked him in front of his peers. He was humiliated! Mike has hated making presentations since that day and has avoided speaking in front of a group at all costs. He has built this bad event up in his mind until he cannot face the thought that this could happen again.

The time has come for him to get over this fear and move on. He knows that he has to overcome this fear because he will be making presentations all through college and later when he goes to work.

What suggestions would you make to Mike to help him focus on getting this task done and be able to get up and make this presentation? What advice would you give him for getting over his fears?

1. _____

2. _____

3. _____

What steps can you take to reduce your own anxiety over speaking publicly?

▶ Walk to the front of the room, taking a few deep breaths on the way, and turn and face your audience before you start speaking.

▶ Never, ever, under any circumstance begin by apologizing for your presentation. Remember, your introduction must grab your audience!

▶ Don't talk too fast or too slow. Use your normal conversation style.

▶ Use pauses for effect when appropriate.

▶ If you are using a lectern, don't lean on it.

▶ Watch your nonverbal communication (body language, facial expressions, and gestures).

▶ Remove temptations to fidget with things such as keys, change in your pocket, pens, and clips.

▶ Always establish and maintain eye contact with your audience. Focus on friendly, engaged faces.

▶ The occasion should dictate your dress, so dress for the occasion. Wear something that makes you feel confident and comfortable.

▶ Don't stand in front of your audience and read off your speech; know your topic and simply talk to them.

▶ Watch your timing! Don't ramble around after you have made your points.

▶ End powerfully! Never end by saying something like: "And that's about it." Or "That's all I've got."

▶ Try to enjoy yourself. The more you act like you are enjoying doing this, the quicker you will actually begin to have fun speaking. Fake it 'til you make it!

The steps outlined in this chapter will assist you in writing and delivering a public speech. However, without a positive "I can" attitude, much of your preparation will be fruitless. Writing and public speaking are exciting, rewarding experiences that will assist you in almost every endeavor of your collegiate and professional life. The more you practice, the better you'll become! This is a promise!

"The trouble with talking too fast is that you might say something you haven't thought about yet."
—Ann Landers

CHANGING IDEAS TO *Reality*

REFLECTIONS ON RESEARCH, WRITING, AND SPEAKING

As you learn to speak and write well, you will be following a tradition that has been practiced by scholars for thousands of years. Effective speech-making principles can be traced to Plato, Socrates, Cicero, and Quintilian. By learning to construct and deliver your own presentations and to write your own papers, you are becoming accomplished in skills that will serve you well all your life.

Learning to write well and to make effective presentations will help you succeed in every class you take. More than likely, the skills learned in this chapter will assist you in improving your relationships with friends and family. While you further hone your communications abilities, you will want to practice the following points:

▶ Use a comprehensive thesis statement.
▶ Use credible, documented research and carefully evaluate sources found on the Internet.
▶ Document sources carefully and completely.
▶ Use a logical organization pattern.
▶ Submit your work on time.
▶ Speak on subjects that you know.
▶ Always rehearse aloud and often.
▶ Take every opportunity to speak in public.
▶ Use a key word outline.
▶ Analyze the audience and relate to them.
▶ Learn to use technology to complement your presentations.

"As long as there are human rights to be defended; as long as there are great interests to be guarded; as long as the welfare of nations is a matter for discussion, so long will public speaking have its place."
—William Jennings Bryan

KNOWLEDGE *in* BLOOM

Improving your research skills and applications

Each chapter-end assessment is based on *Bloom's Taxonomy of Learning*. See the inside front cover for a quick review.

UTILIZES LEVELS 1, 2, 3, 4, 5, 6 ON THE TAXONOMY

EXPLANATION: This activity will require you to use each of the six steps in Bloom's Taxonomy: Remembering, Understanding, Applying, Analyzing, Evaluating, and Creating. Excellent research, writing, and speaking draw on all components of this taxonomy.

PROCESS: The exercises will ask you to use your critical thinking and research skills to build an effective paper or speech. You can use the Internet or any valid print media to answer the questions.

REMEMBER	**LIST** the steps in researching and verifying a paper or speech.
UNDERSTAND	**Explain** each step and give one **example** of each step.
APPLY	What **approach** would you take to begin researching your paper or speech? Why?
ANALYZE	Based on the guidelines laid out in this chapter regarding validity, how do you plan to ensure that your sources are accurate and up to date? **List and scrutinize** each of your steps to achieve this goal.
EVALUATE	Using the topic you selected previously in this chapter and based on your research, **prepare** an annotated bibliography of two of your research sources.
CREATE	**Generate a list** of questions that you want your paper to answer.

SQ3R *Mastery* STUDY SHEET

EXAMPLE QUESTION: *(from page 295)* List three ways that speech preparation differs from preparation for writing a paper.	**ANSWER:**
EXAMPLE QUESTION: *(from page 296)* How is writing a research paper like climbing a ladder?	**ANSWER:**
AUTHOR QUESTION: *(from page 298)* What are the steps to take in making sure your sources are valid?	**ANSWER:**
AUTHOR QUESTION: *(from page 302)* Discuss two means by which you could write an effective introduction.	**ANSWER:**
AUTHOR QUESTION: *(from page 302)* Discuss two means by which you could write an effective conclusion.	**ANSWER:**
AUTHOR QUESTION: *(from page 307)* List three ways to effectively use audiovisual aids.	**ANSWER:**
AUTHOR QUESTION: *(from page 309)* How can you reduce speaking anxiety?	**ANSWER:**
YOUR QUESTION: *(from page _____)*	**ANSWER:**
YOUR QUESTION: *(from page _____)*	**ANSWER:**
YOUR QUESTION: *(from page _____)*	**ANSWER:**
YOUR QUESTION: *(from page _____)*	**ANSWER:**
YOUR QUESTION: *(from page _____)*	**ANSWER:**

Finally, after answering these questions, recite this chapter's major points in your mind. Consider the following general questions to help you master this material.

▶ What was it about?
▶ What does it mean?
▶ What was the most important thing I learned? Why?
▶ What were the key points to remember?

CHAPTER 13
RELATE

CELEBRATING PEOPLE, CULTURES, AND DIVERSITY

"We must learn to live together as brothers or perish together as fools."

—Martin Luther King, Jr.

WHY READ THIS CHAPTER?

what's in it for me?

Why? Because when we think of change, there are few places where many people need more work than in the area of diversity awareness and appreciation. A truly educated person knows how to listen to others, learn from others, and grow from others' experiences and cultures. This chapter will provide a chance for you to rethink and evaluate some of your long-held beliefs and challenges you to open yourself and your thinking up to new possibilities regarding diversity—indeed, to learn to celebrate differences and to relate to all kinds of people. Few things will do more to make you an educated, sophisticated, and competitive person than expanding your thinking about diversity and being able to build lasting and rewarding relationships with people from many walks of life.

WHY is it important to study diversity? *WHY* does it matter whether I get along with people from cultures and backgrounds that are different from mine? *WHY* will learning to celebrate diversity help me be able to get along with other people? *WHY* does my personal community need to include people who are not just like me?

By carefully reading this chapter and taking the information provided seriously, you will be able to:

1. Understand the concept of globalization and its impact on personal and work relationships.
2. Define and discuss ethnocentrism and xenocentrism.
3. Identify and understand the dimensionsof diversity.
4. Understand the power of having an open mind.
5. Understand how the dimensions of diversity can bring people together.

CHAPTER 13 / RELATE

"I feel my heart break to see a nation ripped apart by its own greatest strength ... its diversity."

—Melissa Etheridge

. . . FROM MY PERSPECTIVE

NAME: Priscilla Renew
INSTITUTION: Houston Community College, Houston, TX
MAJOR: Business Technology
AGE: 49

As an older African-American student with four grown children, I am not the typical college student. I am, however, representative of a very diverse personal culture. I grew up in the South Carolina low country and am a descendant of the Gullah people. I am actually a Gullah Priestess with responsibilities for teaching young women about caring for families. As a high school student, I was privileged to attend an all-black Catholic high school where I graduated as Salutatorian. This environment was the beginning of my learning to embrace diversity and to grow from it.

I moved to Houston, where all my children live; this move opened up a new world of different kinds of diversity that I had not previously experienced. I encourage all college students to embrace diversity of all kinds because it is a big part of your college education. Everyone in my high school was basically very much alike, but in college I have met people from many different nationalities, religions, and races. On one team, we had students from five different nationalities. I learned as much from them about their cultures, their dress, their religions, and their dating and marital customs as I did from the project itself.

I recommend that you build solid relationships with fellow students, professors, and even college administrators. If you have a problem paying your tuition, for example, a college administrator will know how to advise you and walk you through requesting an extension or applying for financial aid.

The college environment is very different from high school. In college you will meet people who are there from all over the world. I have friends who are from Pakistan, Nigeria, Taiwan, Guatemala, and India. They have been a great part of my education, and I feel fortunate to have known them.

I also embrace diversity at work and have learned to be open to being friends with older and younger workers. They all have something to teach me that makes me a better person and a better employee.

As a person with a very diverse background myself, I know I have a lot I can teach, and I know I can learn so much from others. I highly recommend that college students open up their hearts and minds to all kinds of people because you will be blessed by the experiences and the knowledge.

In the preface of this book (page xix), you read about the **SQ3R Study Method**. Right now, take a few moments, **scan this chapter**, and on page 331, write **five questions** that you think will be important to your mastery of this material. In addition to the two questions below, you will find five questions from your authors. Use one of your **"Study for Quiz"** stickers to flag this page for easy reference.

EXAMPLES:

▶ **Define personal community and how it relates to diversity.** (from page 324)

▶ **Define the difference between age and generational diversity.** (from pages 324–325)

LEARNING TO THINK GLOBALLY WHILE MAKING LOCAL APPLICATIONS

Is It Really a Small World After All?

> "I am not a citizen of Athens or Greece but of the world."
> —Socrates

"Think Globally, Act Locally" was a phrase that emerged from an international conference on environmental issues in the early '70s. In the world where we live and work today, that phrase encompasses so much more than just the environment. Today we are connected by technology and economics, as well as social networks. Because we are so mobile and interconnected, what happens in another part of the world can have immediate implications for our part of the world. For example, war in a Middle Eastern country can interrupt oil supplies and thus impact our economy. As we have seen, a melt-down in U.S. financial markets can severely impact world markets because other countries' citizens own a significant portion of U.S. stocks and bonds.

Because of technology, primarily the Internet, we are now connected with people all over the world. "Internet users are roughly 35 percent English and 65 percent Non-English with Chinese at 14 percent. Google's Index now stands at over 8 billion pages. Today we have over a billion internet users and that number is growing rapidly" (21 Facts About the Internet, 2008). Consider the following statistics in Figure 13.1.

Technology has opened the doors to the world and brought with it amazing opportunities. But it has also brought a new set of problems and concerns as it exposes our differences to a

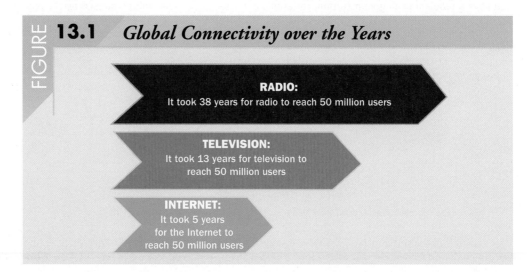

FIGURE 13.1 *Global Connectivity over the Years*

RADIO: It took 38 years for radio to reach 50 million users

TELEVISION: It took 13 years for television to reach 50 million users

INTERNET: It took 5 years for the Internet to reach 50 million users greater degree than in the past and pits us against each other as competitors for jobs, business ventures, and tourists. So we all have work to do to become good global citizens in this brave new world where we live and work. As a citizen and an employee, you will need new skills and knowledge to function at your best capacity. Some of the ideas to consider as you begin to *think globally and act locally* are:

▶ To act with compassion and understanding for people who are different from you.

▶ To develop a good understanding of the different cultures, beliefs, and issues embraced by people from locations all over the world that may be vastly different from yours.

▶ To travel internationally and experience firsthand people from other parts of the world.

▶ To examine multiple viewpoints and philosophies and make decisions that are respectful of many types of differences.

▶ To listen carefully, think differently, and solve problems that emerge in the workplace and in communities because of cultural differences.

▶ To study and grasp historical perspectives in order to understand reasons for the tensions between and among different cultures.

How has living in a global world affected your career path? Has it affected your current job?

Take a Virtual Global Field Trip

You may be thinking to yourself at the moment, "*Have these people gone crazy? Travel internationally? Associate with different cultures?* I don't have the time or money to leave my own backyard." That's OK. As a matter of fact, because we are all so connected through technology, you can travel to many places with the tips of your fingers. You can sit at your computer and learn a great deal about a country and its people without ever leaving your home. Sure, it would be nice to actually travel to China or Australia—and you will one day, if you so desire—but until that time, you can use the Internet to travel virtually.

In the spaces in Figure 13.2, take a virtual trip somewhere in the world. Think about a place you've always wanted to travel. Africa? India? Finland? Scotland? Saudi Arabia? You decide! Consider each question on the left and respond on the right. You might even consider asking your children, spouse, or friends to help you with this exercise. There is nothing that says you have to travel alone. If you have a child, this could be an excellent opportunity to introduce him or her to different parts of the world, the study of geography, and the opportunity to learn about other cultures. This is also an excellent opportunity to learn HOW to learn about other cultures, places, and peoples. Begin this assignment with an open mind and see where it takes you and what you learn. You may surprise yourself.

ESSENTIAL CORNERSTONE

Resourcefulness:
How can researching and learning more about a culture, subculture, or religion help you in the workplace?

Social Networking Moment:
Share your response to this Essential Cornerstone with peers in your social network. Choose two responses from your peers and respond to their postings.

ANYTHING YOU CAN DO, I CAN DO BETTER!

What Are Ethnocentrism and Xenocentrism?

Many people truly believe that they are not prejudiced against any group and that they have no stereotypes in their thought processes about certain groups of people. If we dig deep enough, how-

FIGURE

13.2 *My Virtual Global Fieldtrip*

QUESTION	RESPONSE
The place I've chosen to "travel" is . . .	
Why do you want to travel here?	
What is the population?	
What is the primary language spoken?	
What is the literacy rate of its people?	
What is their primary form of energy?	
What is the primary religion practiced?	
Who are their neighbors (other countries)?	
What is one cultural trait you learned about this country that surprised you?	
What is the normal temperature of this country during the summer and winter?	
What is this country's primary industry?	
What is this country's most treasured site?	
What is the country's health system like?	
How many of this country's citizens are college graduates?	

"We don't see things as THEY are, we see things as WE are."
—Anaïs Nin

Have you ever made a snap judgment about something unfamiliar to you?

ever, we would find that most of us have some kind of prejudice and that we all discriminate in some ways. Because most of us have lived in rather homogeneous neighborhoods and have primarily hung out with people like us, we may tend to be *ethnocentric*, believing that our particular ethnic background is superior and tending to stay with our own kind. If you remember, the idea of striving to be *"nonethnocentric"* was discussed in Chapter 5, "Think," as an important aspect of becoming a critical thinker.

Ethnocentrism suggests that we tend to fear people from other ethnic backgrounds or we lump them together and view them *as a group* rather than *as individuals*. We don't think that their culture, religion, or race could possibly be as important or worthwhile as our own. Think about the ramifications to your *own* life if you were judged by "your group" of people instead of as an individual—if everyone judged you *as a woman* and not as Suzanne; if everyone judged you *as a Northerner* and not as Joe; if everyone judged you *as a Pentecostal* and not as Raymond; if everyone judged you *as a lesbian* and not as Sandra.

Think about the negative terms many people use to describe a few practices from other cultures:

"People in England drive on the WRONG side of the road."
"The Islamic language is written and read BACKWARD."
"Europeans use the WRONG KIND of money."
"Africans dress FUNNY."
"Asians eat WEIRD things."

Ask yourself this: "Is it really wrong?" "Is it really backward?" "Is it really weird?" Or are these customs simply *different* from your own?

Xenocentrism is the opposite of ethnocentrism in that one believes that other cultures are superior to

FIGURE

13.3 *Getting a Grasp on Ethnocentrism*

Read each statement *very carefully* and then, based on YOUR personal feelings, experiences, and upbringing, circle the number on the scale that best reflects your opinion as to whether this behavior or action is *"good or bad."*

STATEMENT	BAD		NEUTRAL		GOOD
1. Looking at someone when you talk to them.	1	2	3	4	5
2. Eating any type of food with your bare hand.	1	2	3	4	5
3. Having a pierced eyebrow.	1	2	3	4	5
4. Smelling someone as a greeting.	1	2	3	4	5
5. Eating someone's cremated ashes as a tribute to him or her.	1	2	3	4	5
6. Being late for an appointment.	1	2	3	4	5
7. Participating in an arranged marriage.	1	2	3	4	5
8. Believing in more than one god.	1	2	3	4	5
9. Eating cows.	1	2	3	4	5
10. Eating pigs.	1	2	3	4	5
11. Eating dogs.	1	2	3	4	5
12. Eating horses.	1	2	3	4	5
13. Having sex before marriage.	1	2	3	4	5
14. Chewing food with your mouth open (smacking your food).	1	2	3	4	5
15. Believing that money is a good thing.	1	2	3	4	5
16. Requiring that women cover all body parts except their eyes.	1	2	3	4	5
17. Staring at someone.	1	2	3	4	5
18. Moving away or out of your parent's home.	1	2	3	4	5
19. Shaking hands with your right hand.	1	2	3	4	5
20. Taking a bath every day.	1	2	3	4	5
21. Duty and country should always come first.	1	2	3	4	5
22. Calling a person by their first name.	1	2	3	4	5
23. Everyone should have a chance to be educated.	1	2	3	4	5
24. Nose rings are ok.	1	2	3	4	5
25. Tattoos are ok on any part of the body.	1	2	3	4	5
26. Using profanity to express one's self.	1	2	3	4	5
27. Having more than one wife at a time.	1	2	3	4	5
28. Having "barn yard" animals live in your home.	1	2	3	4	5
29. Believing that all citizens have a right to know "the truth" about what its government does.	1	2	3	4	5
30. Showing no emotions to others.	1	2	3	4	5
31. Having healthy self-esteem.	1	2	3	4	5
32. Believing in fate.	1	2	3	4	5
33. Believing that the arrangement of furniture in your home can help determine your health and happiness.	1	2	3	4	5
34. Always finish what you start regardless of the cost or consequences.	1	2	3	4	5
35. Hard work is more important than fun.	1	2	3	4	5
36. Honesty is always the best policy.	1	2	3	4	5
37. Participating in a nomadic lifestyle.	1	2	3	4	5
38. Mercy or honor killing.	1	2	3	4	5
39. Marrying children under the age of 16.	1	2	3	4	5
40. Lying to protect someone's feelings.	1	2	3	4	5

one's own culture and that one's own culture has very little of value to offer. Some people use xenocentrism as an "overcorrection" for their ethnocentrism. This can be just as dangerous as ethnocentrism because once again, we cut ourselves off from learning from everyone and everything we encounter. All people, places, cultures, religions, races, genders, and orientations have something to offer. This does not mean that we have to accept and embrace every notion, but being an educated citizen does mean learning to listen, evaluate, analyze, and then make our decisions.

Take a few moments to complete Figure 13.3 on the previous page. As you consider each statement, respond as honestly as possible.

Analysis:

Now that you have circled a response for each statement, work with a group of students in your class or online to determine how your answers are different from or similar to theirs. This can be of significance when your responses vary by at least two numbers on the scale. (Example: If you responded with a 5 on #30 and your partner(s) responded with a 1, this is a major difference.) After you have discussed your responses with each other, write a brief statement about what conclusions can be drawn from this experience.

BLOOM LEVEL 4
QUESTION

_____

_____

_____

_____

LIVING AND LEARNING IN THE BRAVE NEW WORLD

What Are the Dimensions of Diversity?

Among the kinds of diversity you might encounter are race, religion, gender, age, ethnic group, nationality, cultural, sexual orientation, social class, geographic region, and physical challenges. It is important for you to become open and accepting of individuals in all categories of diversity. The most significant thing you can do is to think of people who are different from you as individuals, not as groups. Some people need to make bigger changes in their overall belief systems than others; it all depends on what kind of background they come from and what experiences they have had. An explanation of some major types of diversity follows.

Racial Diversity

What have you learned about a culture other than your own since beginning your studies?

Racism is a prejudicial feeling that exists when an individual has a negative attitude about any race or ethnic group. Racism can be institutionalized in actions such as racial profiling or refusing to hire certain races except for menial manual labor. It can also mean that certain races are charged higher interest rates when borrowing money or have to pay more for an automobile than another race. Racist language usually implies that one group of people or an individual is inferior in some way to others. In many cases, races that are discriminated against have been relegated to inferior positions in society due to economic and political oppression.

FIGURE **13.4**   *Dimension of Diversity Wheel*

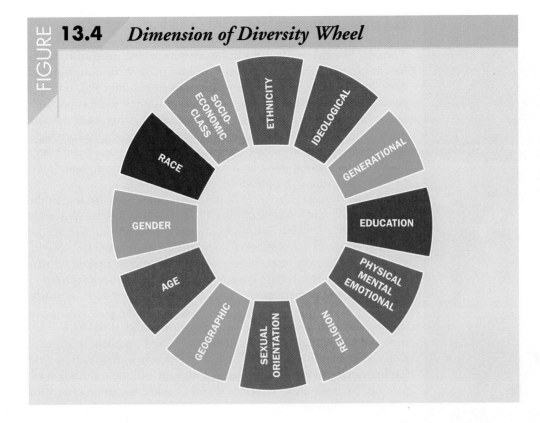

Religious Diversity

Many types of religions are practiced in this country and around the world. Ranging from orthodox practices that have been in place for hundreds of years to newly formed "cults," people who practice each of these forms of worship are sensitive to unkind remarks about their beliefs. There are actually three major beliefs people have about other religions: *exclusivism*, *inclusivism*, and *pluralism*. Those who believe in exclusivism think that other faiths are in grave error and often view them as opponents. Those who practice inclusivism believe that other faiths have some truth in them, but are only partly developed. Finally, those who believe in pluralism think that all faiths are legitimate and valid—when viewed from within their particular cultures.

The biggest problem, quite simply, is that people tend to believe their religion is the only right one and is superior to all others. Such a position can also be dangerous, as wars frequently break out over religious differences. The terrible events that took place in the United States on September 11, 2001, when the World Trade Center and Pentagon were attacked, were perpetrated by individuals who no doubt believed they were martyring themselves in the name of their religion. You live in a country where you are free to worship as you choose. We must all expand our worldviews to the point that we can allow others the same choice without judging them in a negative manner and without engaging in hate crimes against others because of their beliefs.

Tips for Personal Success

Consider the following tips for dealing with cultural diversity as you meet new and different kinds of people:

▶ Keep an open mind and don't make assumptions about people.

▶ Don't let your prejudices from the past interfere with your being an open-minded person.

▶ Make a point every day of talking to people who have different backgrounds from you.

Now it is your turn. Name three more tips that you would give a fellow classmate who is trying to enlarge his or her personal community of friends.

1. _____

2. _____

3. _____

What are your personal feelings about diverse groups of people succeeding in areas where there were previous limitations?

Gender Diversity

Since the '60s and the Women's Rights Movement, women in this country have made steady gains toward being treated as equals to men, although there are still biases to be found among some institutions and, certainly, among some individuals. The fact that Hillary Clinton was a strong contender for the 2008 Democratic Party presidential nomination and that Sarah Palin was named the Republican vice presidential candidate highlights the fact that women have made significant gains. There is still a large number of *men and women*, however, who will make the statement, "I just can't vote for a woman for president."

"Cross-cultural research indicates that gender roles are among the first that individuals learn and that all societies treat males differently from females. . . . What is considered natural behavior for each gender is based more on cultural belief than on biological necessity" (Slavin, 2009). Just a few years ago, boys were expected to grow up and be masculine and to pursue certain types of careers while girls were expected to be *feminine* and perhaps pursue roles as homemakers, nurses, or teachers. Many of the women who ventured out and did become involved in the business or academic world ran up against the "glass ceiling." Today men and women are attending college in record numbers, with more women actually in attendance than men. Although dramatic progress has been made to improve gender bias, there is still some confusion regarding "women's roles" as well as stigma attached to certain careers for men such as nursing.

Age Diversity

In your college classes, you are likely to find people ranging in age from 16 to 90. In fact, a large percentage of college students today are nontraditional students (24 and older), as many adults continue their educations and return to college to study in entirely new fields. Large numbers of older people return to college to take classes simply for enjoyment after they retire. You might very well find an older person on one of your teams. Certainly, when you enter the workforce, you will immediately be thrust into a community with people of all ages.

Older people are very much like you underneath their skin, which naturally looks older than that of typical 18-year-olds. They want to be treated with respect; they want to laugh and have fun; they want to see the latest movies; they are likely to enjoy sporting events; and they want to be included in discussions. The college years provide you a great opportunity to start learning to relate well to older people. You might find that some of the most helpful and valuable people in your classes are much older than you; certainly, there will be people of all ages when you enter the workplace. The fastest-growing group of people in this country consists of those age 85 and older.

Ethnic Diversity

The word *ethnic* is derived from the Greek word *ethnos,* meaning "nation," and some people refer to ethnic groups simply by the country from which they originated. Scholars don't always agree on exactly what constitutes an ethnic group. Some consider an ethnic group to be a social group that is typically distinguished by race, religion, or national origin. These groups may be identified by distinguishing features and physical characteristics. But in some cases, they can be identified by their religion or language when physical differences do not exist. Ethnicity might simply mean national origin to others. According to Feagin and Feagin (2008), an ethnic group is "a group socially distinguished or set apart, by others or by itself, primarily on the basis of cultural or national-origin characteristics."

Sexual Orientation

According to the American Psychological Association, sexual orientation "refers to an enduring pattern of emotional, romantic, and/or sexual attractions to men, women, or both sexes. Sexual orientation also refers to a person's sense of identity based on those attractions, related behaviors, and a membership in a community of others who share those attractions. . . . There is no consensus among scientists about the exact reasons that an individual develops a heterosexual, bisexual, gay, or lesbian orientation. Some think that both nature and nurture play complex roles" (2008). The conclusion, however, is that most people experience little or no sense of choice about their sexual orientation. "Most scientific thinking holds that one's sexuality is genetically determined rather than being a matter of choice" (DeVito, 2008).

Regardless of one's sexual orientation, a person needs to have a positive self-image and good mental health regarding his or her sexuality. It is a great misconception to assume that people of different sexual orientations have different goals and values than any other group. "Research shows that the factors that influence relationship satisfaction, commitment, and stability are remarkably similar for both same-sex cohabiting couples and heterosexual married couples" (American Psychological Association, 2008). So the truth is that there are very intelligent, engaging, attractive people of all sexual orientations—people who can become good friends and colleagues if you are open to expanding your views.

Social Class Diversity

Socioeconomic status or social class can be defined using the parameters of a person's income, education level, type of work he or she does, and family heritage. Someone may have social status because his grandfather was a U.S. senator, but he may still not have great wealth. In this country when class is discussed, this terminology is generally used: upper class (wealthy), middle class (people who have jobs requiring considerable education or who own businesses that afford them a certain level of income), and lower class (people who are unemployed or hold very low-level jobs that do not provide them with a good standard of living).

If you follow our advice and consider people as individuals rather than as part of a class, you will probably meet some really great people from all classes. Wealth and status certainly provide opportunities and advantages not enjoyed by everyone, but you can find outstanding people in all classes to include in your personal community.

ESSENTIAL CORNERSTONE

Adaptability:
How can learning about different types of diversity help you become more adaptable in a changing workplace?

Social Networking Moment:
Share your response to this Essential Cornerstone with peers in your social network. Choose two responses from your peers and respond to their postings.

What do you think a person who is older than you can teach you about "the world?"

Generational Diversity

While you may have heard of many different types of diversity, you are less likely to have been informed about generational diversity. More than likely, you know that different generations have been labeled with names such as the "Traditionals," the "Boomers," "Generation X," and the current generation, which is referred to as the "Millennials." For the first time, four distinctly different generations, each with its own loyalties, priorities, and expectations, are working side by side in the workplace (Glenn, 2007). Naturally, with such a wide range of ages, there are conflicts over how work should be completed, what constitutes company loyalty, how many hours one should work after closing time, and how best to communicate.

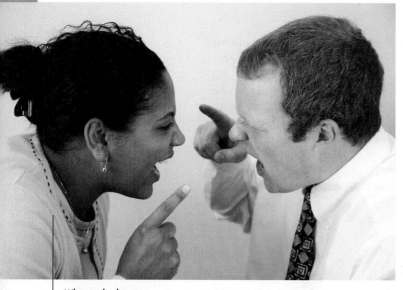

What is the biggest ideological difference you have had with someone on campus?

You may very well work with an older person from the "Traditional" generation, who is very focused on a team approach and less focused on the individual. In the same group, you will have a "Boomer," who believes strongly in visibility or face time at the office and equates that as time spent working. Your team might include a member of "Generation X," who believes that his time is as important as money and that it doesn't matter if he works overtime as long as he does the job and does it well. Members of your own generation—if you are a traditional-age, first-year student—might be focused on technology and finding a job that makes them happy.

Geographic Region Diversity

As strange as it may seem, there are some who are prejudiced against people from certain geographic regions in this country. It is true that there are people in all parts of our country who have ideas that are very different from those of the masses; however, we should not label an entire section of the country based on the actions of a few from that part of the country. In the case of geographic regions, as in all cases, one should determine the characteristics of an individual beyond her or his belonging to the group of those who live in a certain part of the country. You might find that a friend from California could open up all kinds of new ideas and thinking for you, or that a friend from the South could show you beautiful beaches and golf courses, or that a friend from New York could introduce you to Broadway or Central Park. As you expand your personal community of friends, make a special effort to get to know people from other regions of the country and learn to consider their unique characteristics rather than focus on where they come from.

> *"Everything we shut our eyes to, everything we run away from, everything we deny, denigrate or despise, serves to defeat us in the end. What seems nasty, painful, and evil, can become a source of beauty, joy, and strength, if faced with an open mind."*
>
> —Henry Miller

Physical, Mental, and Emotional Diversity

You will encounter a number of students who deal with physical, mental, and emotional challenges. They could be visually impaired or deaf or confined to a wheelchair. Quite a few college students suffer from depression and others battle bipolar disorders. Research shows that 49.2% of all students experience some kind of learning disability such as dyslexia. We tend to assume, for instance, that students who are labeled legally blind cannot see, when, in fact, 80% can read large- or regular-print books. They may have a problem in only one eye. Truthfully, these students are just like everyone else except that they have a physical problem that makes life a little more difficult. They have feelings just like the rest of us; they want to be included in social life and activities; and they don't want to be treated as disabled, different, and unable to participate. You might consider getting to know a physically, mentally, or emotionally challenged person and bringing this person into your social network.

Ideological Diversity

The fact that we all have different opinions and ideas that are rooted in our family backgrounds, socioeconomic status, religious beliefs, cultural experiences, political beliefs, educational levels, and travel experiences creates great diversity and can cause difficulties among individuals and groups of people. "Individuals tend to come to more extreme views if they deliberate a given issue with like-minded people" (Kallock, 2008). In other words, internal diversity among individuals tends to be squelched by the forces of group polarization. People tend to remain moderate when expressing their beliefs, until they are confident that they are among others who agree with them, and then they tend to become more extreme in their beliefs. These personal beliefs create diversity in thoughts, reasoning, ideas, and creativity. Political beliefs, for example, can be quite polarizing among individuals and groups. As an educated, enlightened individual, you will need to practice patience and understanding of other people's viewpoints and why they believe them even when you are diametrically opposed to those beliefs.

SEEING THE WORLD WITH CLEAR EYES

Why Is Having an Open Mind So Powerful?

As you seek to develop an open mind and become an educated citizen, you need to be aware of the terms *discrimination* and *prejudice*. If you discriminate against someone, you negatively judge that person on the basis of the group or class to which he or she belongs, rather than according to merit. For example, you might discriminate against a person who is highly qualified for a job, because he is of a certain race or religion, and ignore his qualifications. Prejudice, on the other hand, is an unreasonable opinion or feeling formed beforehand or without knowledge, thought, or reason; it is a preconceived opinion of a hostile nature regarding a racial, religious, or national group (Webster's College Dictionary, 1995).

If you discriminate against someone, it is because you are prejudiced against him or her due to preconceived ideas that are based on insufficient knowledge, irrational feelings, or inaccurate stereotypes. As you can see, prejudice is usually not based on reason or knowledge but on opinions most likely shaped by someone who influenced you or by a region of the country where you grew up. Finally, prejudice is not an illegal act, whereas discrimination in many cases is an illegal act. Discrimination is illegal in employment, housing, loans, and many other areas outlined in the Civil Rights Act of 1964.

To experience other people and to receive the benefits of knowing someone, you need to enter all relationships with an open mind. If you have a derogatory mind-set toward a race, an ethnic group, a sexual orientation, or a religion, for example, you have internal barriers that can keep you from getting to know who a person really is.

Distinguish between prejudice and discrimination by giving examples of each in the space below:

_____

_____

_____

_____

DID YOU KNOW

DITH PRAN was born in 1942 in Cambodia. He learned English and French and worked for the U.S. government as a translator, he also had jobs with a British film crew and as a hotel receptionist. In 1975, after meeting a *New York Times* reporter, he taught himself how to take photographs.

After U.S. forces left Cambodia, he stayed behind to cover the fall of Phnom Penh to the communist Khmer Rouge. Having stayed behind, he was forced to remain while foreign reporters were allowed to leave. From this point, Dith witnessed many atrocities and had to hide the fact that he was educated or knew some Americans. He pretended to be a taxicab driver.

Cambodians were forced to work in labor camps and Dith was not immune from this. He endured four years of starvation and torture before Vietnam overthrew the Khmer Rouge and he escaped the camp. He coined the term "The Killing Fields" because of the number of dead bodies he encountered during his escape. He later learned that his three brothers and 50 other members of his family had been killed during the genocide.

Dith escaped to Thailand in 1979, fearing for his life because of his association with Americans and his knowledge of what had happened in Cambodia. He moved to the United States in 1980. In 1984, the movie *The Killing Fields,* detailing the horrors and triumphs of his life, was released. He died of pancreatic cancer in 2008.

BLOOM LEVEL 4 QUESTION

CHANGING IDEAS TO *Reality*

REFLECTIONS ON DIVERSITY AND UNDERSTANDING

As a college student, you have an opportunity to make many new changes as you build a personal community of friends. You can have relationships with people from all over the world, people who espouse and embrace many ideas that are different from what you had been exposed to in the past. You can learn almost as much from this diverse population of students and peers as you learn from the lessons in the classroom. If you will open up your heart and mind to all of the possibilities, you will leave college a much more enlightened and interesting person than you were when you arrived. Perhaps this opportunity to experience such a great variety of people, ideas, and cultures is the most important aspect of a college education.

College will provide you an opportunity to expand your horizons and to change in many different ways. Here you will have classes with people from all over the world and from many regions of this country. Some of your fellow students will not only speak and dress differently; they will also most likely have different religions, beliefs, customs, values, and experiences. Instead of closing out those people who are different from you, embrace new and different cultures. While you don't have to be just like these new people, you are certain to learn to appreciate and benefit from the relationships.

Remember, we are motivated by what we value. As you continue on in the semester and work toward personal and professional growth and change, consider the following ideas:

▶ Examine your personal values and beliefs to determine if you need to make cultural adjustments.

▶ Listen to people and try to understand them before you form opinions about them.

▶ Stand up against intolerance and bigotry of any kind.

▶ Help others understand the importance of organizing against hate crimes.

▶ Develop relationships with people from a variety of backgrounds.

▶ Learn to appreciate and celebrate differences.

▶ Maintain close friendships with people who share your values and beliefs and with people who bring new and different ideas to the mix.

"To be nobody but yourself—in a world which is doing its best, night and day, to make you like everybody else—means to fight the hardest battle which any human being can fight, and never stop fighting."
—e. e. cummings

KNOWLEDGE *in* BLOOM

Cultural Research and Understanding Project

Each chapter-end assessment is based on *Bloom's Taxonomy of Learning*. See the inside front cover for a quick review.

UTILIZES LEVELS 1–6 OF THE TAXONOMY

Level 1 Question: Identify one culture, subculture, or religion that you are not a part of that you would like to research. You may use interviews, books, journals, the Internet, or newspapers as your resources.

The culture, subculture, or religion that I have chosen is: _____

I chose this topic because: _____

_____

_____

_____

Level 2 Question: What are the facts that you learned through researching this topic?

_____

_____

_____

_____

_____

What is one value that this culture or religion embraces?

_____

_____

_____

_____

_____

_____

_____

Level 3 Question: Prepare a statement that identifies one thing that people from this culture or religion believe that is different from what you have been taught.

_____

_____

_____

_____

_____

_____

Level 4 Question: Analyze the characteristics of the culture or religion you are researching and compare them to the characteristics of your own culture or religion.

_____

_____

_____

_____

_____

_____

_____

Level 5 Question: Determine what your opinions are of this religion or culture and justify your reasons for having these opinions.

_____

_____

_____

_____

_____

_____

Level 6 Question: After conducting your research, prepare a brief presentation with at least five positive points that you can share with your classmates about the religion or culture you studied. List the five points here.

_____

_____

_____

_____

_____

_____

_____

SQ3R *Mastery* STUDY SHEET

EXAMPLE QUESTION: *(from page 319)* Define ethnocentrism.	**ANSWER:**
EXAMPLE QUESTION: *(from pages 324–325)* What is the difference between age and generational diversity?	**ANSWER:**
AUTHOR QUESTION: *(from page 318)* What does globalization have to do with diversity appreciation?	**ANSWER:**
AUTHOR QUESTION: *(from page 322)* Identify and discuss three different cultural dimensions.	**ANSWER:**
AUTHOR QUESTION: *(from page 320)* Define xenocentrism	**ANSWER:**
AUTHOR QUESTION: *(from page 327)* What is the difference between discrimination and prejudice?	**ANSWER:**
AUTHOR QUESTION: *(from page 327)* Why is it important to have an open mind?	**ANSWER:**
YOUR QUESTION: *(from page ___)*	**ANSWER:**
YOUR QUESTION: *(from page ___)*	**ANSWER:**
YOUR QUESTION: *(from page ___)*	**ANSWER:**
YOUR QUESTION: *(from page ___)*	**ANSWER:**
YOUR QUESTION: *(from page ___)* Finally, after answering these questions, recite this chapter's major points in your mind. Consider the following general questions to help you master this material.	**ANSWER:**

► What was it about?
► What does it mean?
► What was the most important thing I learned? Why?
► What are the key points to remember?

CHAPTER 14
LIVE

DEVELOPING YOUR PLAN FOR WELLNESS AND PERSONAL RESPONSIBILITY

"The concept of total wellness recognizes that our every thought, word, and behavior affects our greater health and well-being."
—Greg Anderson

WHY READ THIS CHAPTER?

What's in it for me?

WHY will a chapter on developing a plan for wellness and personal responsibility help me while I'm in college? WHY do I need to know about healthy eating and exercise? WHY does learning about sexual transmitted diseases (STDs) affect me? WHY does my mind, body, and soul contribute to my making good grades this semester?

Why? Because you need to know about the powerful role that health plays in your educational process. This chapter introduces the body, mind, and soul connection so that you can begin to understand the importance of caring for yourself in all these aspects throughout your college career. We include this chapter to help you understand that it is difficult to concentrate on your studies when you are ill, facing a paramount emotional issue, or have just learned that you have an STD. Health—mental, physical, and spiritual—matters. Sometimes we place undue stress on ourselves and assume that our bodies will continue to take this abuse. We eat poorly and fail to exercise properly and then wonder why we don't feel good. This chapter will afford you the opportunities to review your own health status and to explore some areas where you might need to implement changes so that you can lead a healthier lifestyle. This chapter will introduce you to information that you may not currently possess about smoking, legal and illegal drugs, alcohol use, sexual behaviors, and the many ramifications these issues can have on your body, mind, and soul.

By carefully reading this chapter and taking the information provided seriously, you will be able to:

1. Understand holistic wellness and how to care for the body, mind, and soul.
2. Identify and understand the signs of depression and anxiety.
3. Understand the responsibility of eating well and tracking your food intake.
4. Understand the effects and dangers of alcohol and drug (legal, illegal, and prescription) use.
5. Identify and discuss the different types of birth control and their protection levels against pregnancy and STD transmission.

CHAPTER 14 / LIVE

"The greatest wealth is health."

—Virgil

334

NAME: Alyssa Bucchianeri
INSTITUTION: University of Nevada Las Vegas, Las Vegas, NV
MAJOR: Meetings and Events Management
AGE: 22

Some first-year students who are on their own for the first time tend not to take good care of themselves. Taking care of your mind, body, and soul is a very important part of college life. So I would recommend that you do everything possible to stay healthy by eating good food, working out, and making good choices. College is very stressful, so I learned to go to the gym and work out to manage my stress. I also found that just getting out of the dorm and going for a walk and having a change of scenery does wonders for my stress level and attitude.

You have heard of the dreaded "First-Year 15." Now, I think it might be the "First-Year 20." To avoid putting on 15–20 pounds, I recommend that you keep healthy snacks in your room. It is so easy to grab a bag of chips, especially in the middle of the day when you are rushed and hungry. Rather than eating empty calories, I always snack on fruit and healthy snacks.

So many first-year students are exposed to drinking, drugs, and smoking. I always tried—and still do try—to remember my parents' solid advice. They always told me to make smart choices and keep my wits about me. This is great advice for all college students. If I am going to a party or event where people are going to be drinking, I always go with a group of friends whom I trust to do the right thing and who will look out for each other. My group always has a designated driver who doesn't have anything to drink and who watches out for our group. If I choose to drink, I decide in advance how many drinks I will have, and I will not exceed that number. My safety and well-being are up to me! The best advice I can give you is to think about your future when making any choices, but especially choices about your physical and mental well-being.

Being a first-year student is exciting and challenging. Some days are very tough, but if you make healthy choices and build solid relationships, you will be fine. If I feel down, I surround myself with positive people, and I balance being with friends with taking time for just myself. Being alone gives me time to think about what I need to do and focus on making the right decisions. This chapter, "Live," can help you make positive choices too. Take the information to heart as I did, and you'll find out just how much it helps.

SCAN & QUESTION

In the preface of this book (page xix), you read about the **SQ3R Study Method**. Right now, take a few moments, **scan this chapter**, and on page 354, write **five questions** that you think will be important to your mastery of this material. In addition to the two questions below, you will find five questions from your authors. Use one of your "**Study for Quiz**" stickers to flag this page for easy reference.

EXAMPLES:

▶ **What does it mean to have a holistic approach to health?** (from page 336)

▶ **What effect does the mind have on wellness?** (from page 337)

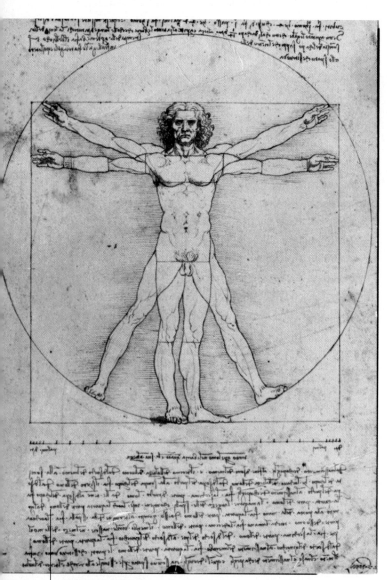

Have you noticed the wellness connection among the body, mind, and soul?

A HOLISTIC APPROACH TO WELLNESS

How Do I Care for the Mind, Soul, and Body?

By now, you have been a college student for several months and surely you are changing and growing in many ways including intellectually, emotionally, and physically. Now we will ask you to continue your pattern of change and growth and include practices that will make you healthy in all aspects of your life. In this chapter, you will find an overriding theme: You have to take care of yourself and you have the power to do so! This can mean everything from eating properly and getting enough exercise to avoiding binge drinking and taking illegal drugs to protecting yourself sexually. You will encounter situations on a daily basis where you have to make decisions. It is imperative to your health and academic success that you choose wisely!

"In many ancient systems of medicine (such as in China) treatment has been made with the view that mind, body, and soul are linked together as a whole and should not be seen as isolated from each other. Mind, body and soul healing focuses on the interactions between the brain, mind, body and the ways in which emotional, mental, social, spiritual, and behavioral factors affect us as a whole" (Tarkovsky, 2006). As far back as 400 BC, Hippocrates recognized the impact spiritual factors have on healing, so this idea that wellness is holistic is nothing new. But it does have some new spins to it.

WHAT IS MEANT BY "MIND"? If your mind is in balance with your body and soul, you will be using your mind's power to your best advantage, thinking clearly, and making good decisions. If your body is exhausted and your soul is depressed, your mind will not function well.

WHAT IS MEANT BY "SOUL"? In the context of wellness, the soul and spirituality are important to your ability to develop healthy relationships, to communicate well with diverse others, and to express yourself creatively.

WHAT IS MEANT BY "BODY"? For your body to be in balance with your mind and soul, you must exercise properly, get sufficient rest, engage in sports and other physical activity, and engage in good eating habits and nutrition to fuel your body. If your body is functioning poorly, your mind and soul will, too.

Maintaining a healthy body, mind, and soul can be one of the most exciting and challenging aspects of your college career, as well as of the rest of your life. If you achieve balance among all three of these important categories, you should feel optimistic, confident, and excited about what lies ahead in your future.

THE MIND'S EFFECT ON WELLNESS

How Do I Use the Hidden Powers of the Mind?

The mind is an incredibly complex organ. The health industry has not yet begun to tap into the awesome power the mind has over a person's physical health. Very basic studies have shown that the mind is a vital link to physical health. Your emotions and mental thoughts play a tremendous role in how you approach your overall wellness program. Your emotional well-being impacts all aspects of your general wellness and therefore is the platform for all health. People who are mentally healthy possess the following qualities. They:

How can having a positive attitude help you feel better and perform at your best?

► Have a positive sense of self-worth.
► Are determined to make an effort to be healthy.
► Can love and have meaningful relationships.
► Understand reality and the limitations placed on them.
► Have compassion for others.
► Understand that the world does not revolve around them.

SILENT PROBLEMS OF THE MIND

How Do I Control Depression and Anxiety Disorders?

Depression is a term used to describe emotions ranging from feeling blue to utter hopelessness. The use of "I'm depressed" to mean "I'm sad" or "I'm down" is a far cry from the illness of clinical depression. Depression is a sickness that can creep up on an individual and render that person helpless if it is not detected and properly treated.

ESSENTIAL CORNERSTONE

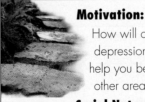

Motivation:
How will overcoming feelings of depression and helplessness help you become motivated in other areas of your life?

Social Networking Moment:
Share your response to this Essential Cornerstone with peers in your social network. Choose two responses from your peers and respond to their postings.

There are several major types of depressions. They include:

Situational Depression	Feelings of sadness due to disappointments, bad news, daily frustrations, or "people problems."
Clinical Depression	Clinical depression is major depression and is characterized by the inability to enjoy life, loss of interest in things you once loved doing, self-hatred, feelings of utter worthlessness, and suicidal thoughts. Clinical depression is diagnosed when these feelings last at least two weeks.
Dysthymia	Dysthymia is classified as mild to moderate depression and can last a long time—two years or more. There are times when the person can't remember not being depressed, and it is hard to enjoy life, family, or friends.
Seasonal Depression	Seasonal depression is caused by the weather or the changing seasons of the year. Some people are depressed by rain and others are depressed by a lack of sunshine.
Postpartum Depression	Postpartum depression, sometimes called "the baby blues," occurs after the birth of a child. It can be a very serious condition in which the mother avoids the child or even wants to cause harm to the child. It can occur up to a year or more after birth.

Some common signs of situational or mild depression include the following (Donatelle and Davis, 2002):

► Lingering sadness and unexplainable fatigue.

► Inability to find joy in pleasure-giving activities.

► Loss of interest in work, school, activities, and sex.

► Sleep disorders, including insomnia or early morning awakenings.

► Withdrawal from friends and family.

► Feelings of hopelessness and worthlessness, and a desire to die.

FIGURE **14.1**   *Are You Clinically Depressed?*

Sign and Symptoms

Feelings of helplessness and hopelessness	A bleak outlook—nothing will ever get better and there's nothing you can do to improve your situation.
Loss of interest in daily activities	No interest in or ability to enjoy former hobbies, pastimes, social activities, or intimacy.
Appetite or weight changes	Significant weight loss or weight gain—a change of more than 5% of body weight in a month.
Sleep changes	Either insomnia, especially waking in the early hours of the morning or oversleeping (also known as hypersomnia).
Psychomotor agitation or retardation	Either feeling "keyed up" and restless or sluggish and physically slowed down.
Loss of energy	Feeling fatigued and physically drained. Even small tasks are exhausting or take longer.
Self-loathing	Strong feelings of worthlessness or guilt. Harsh criticism of perceived faults and mistakes.
Concentration problems	Trouble focusing, making decisions, or remembering things.

(from HelpGuide.org)

Anxiety

According to the Anxiety Disorders Association of America, anxiety disorders are the most common mental illness in this country—with more than 13% of U.S. adults suffering from some form of anxiety disorder at any one time. Learning to cope with anxiety allows you to focus and maintain balance in your health and academic welfare. There are several ways to proactively approach dealing with anxiety: relaxation techniques such as yoga, music, dance therapy, and meditation; cognitive behavior therapy and other forms of therapy; and medication.

If you are feeling depressed or your anxiety has reached a level where you cannot control it, but your depression seems minor or situational, try some of these helpful hints for picking yourself up out of the blues:

What actions can you take TODAY to control your anxiety and depression if you feel them getting out of control?

- ▶ Get physical exercise because it causes the release of endorphins, which help to stimulate you and give you a personal high.

- ▶ Spend time talking with a good friend sharing your thoughts and feelings.

- ▶ Control your self-talk. If you're feeding yourself negative words, change to positive thoughts.

- ▶ Do something special for yourself: Take a long walk in the park, watch a favorite movie, listen to a special CD, or visit a friend.

- ▶ Nurture yourself by doing things you love and enjoy and that bring you peace.

- ▶ *Never* be afraid or ashamed to seek professional assistance.

THE SOUL'S EFFECT ON WELLNESS

Is Your Well Running Dry?

The world is a tough place to be at times. You read the newspapers and see all the bad things that are happening around us. You listen to the evening news and hear about murder, war, gas prices, negative politics, etc. You feel the pressures of working, struggling to pay bills, finding time to exercise and eat right, studying for difficult tests, writing papers, keeping relationships going, communicating with others—the list of stressors goes on and on. According to Housden (2007), "We are usually preoccupied with being useful—doing something with an outcome in mind, rather than being open to where we are at this moment."

But in the midst of all these worldly concerns, you need to take time to find peace and joy. For at least a few minutes every day, you need to turn loose all the pressures that weigh you down and cause you to feel defeated and overwhelmed. You need to nurture and feed your soul. The soul can be nurtured in many ways—solid, meaningful relationships; participating in something that gives you a creative outlet such as a play; talking to someone who makes you laugh and forget your problems, at least temporarily; watching an uplifting movie; or communicating with new and diverse types of people. Just as your body needs to be fed a healthy diet of good, nutritious food, your soul needs to be nourished with activities and thoughts that bring you joy, comfort, and peace.

> "The poorest man would not part with health for money, but the richest would gladly part with all their money for health."
> —Charles Caleb Colton

FIGURE **14.2** *Ways to Nourish Your Soul*

▶ Commune with nature by taking a hike.
▶ Sit outside in a park.
▶ Ride a bike on a beautiful fall day.
▶ Go for a drive in the country.
▶ Stop everything and giggle with a friend.
▶ Walk on the beach.
▶ Row in a river or lake.
▶ Have friends over who lift you up and make you feel good about yourself.
▶ Experiment with your creative side—write a poem, act in a play, learn to play an instrument.
▶ Roll on the grass with a little child and giggle like she does.
▶ Look around you and count your blessings.

THE BODY'S EFFECT ON WELLNESS

Can You Believe You Ate the Whole Thing?

How many times per week do you binge on junk food?

Eating has become Americans' favorite hobby. Rather than eating to live, many of us live to eat. We socialize around food—dinner and a movie, pizza and a beer with friends, and so on. Research has shown that after they've eaten, most people have no idea how much they ate, what it contained, how it was grown, or what effect the food will have on their health. Dr. Phil McGraw, a well-known talk show host, states, "Food is the most powerfully addictive substance in the world because you can't abstain from it." He goes on to say, "It's not chocolates or potato chips that sabotage diets (try fear, old attitudes, tempting environments)." What we eat and why we eat it is more complicated than it appears at first glance. For many first-year students, however, weight gain happens simply because they don't pay enough attention to what they are eating, they do not exercise, or they change their nutrition habits when they arrive on campus.

Some points that might be helpful as you work on changing your diet to maximize your overall health:

▶ Choose lean cuts of meat or baked or broiled poultry or fish.
▶ Eat a variety of foods, making sure you are getting the right variety and amount of nutrients.
▶ Choose whole-grain breads and cereals.
▶ Drink low-fat milk and eat low-fat cheese.
▶ Drink at least six glasses of water a day.
▶ Severely limit unhealthy foods, fast-food restaurants, and eating binges.
▶ Snack on fruits instead of potato chips. Apples, for example, have no fat.
▶ Stay away from supersize meals, unless you want a supersize body!

For three days write down everything you eat or drink—snacks, wine, meals—every bite and sip. Use the ***Three-Day Food Tracker*** sheet located at the end of this chapter. This sheet will assist you in keeping track of your food intake.

After you have a complete list of what you ate for three days, analyze your eating habits and determine what you are eating that you should stop eating or curtail. What is missing from your diet that you need in order to be healthy? Visit *www.mypyramid.gov* to assist you in this exercise.

Develop a five-point plan to ensure that your eating habits are improved based on your findings.

1. _____
2. _____
3. _____
4. _____
5. _____

BLOOM LEVELS 1 & 3 QUESTIONS

WHAT YOU DO TODAY MAY IMPACT YOU FOR YEARS TO COME

What Is Your Responsibility to Ensure Wellness?

The following section will simply provide you with information that you can study and, from there, make intelligent decisions about drinking, drug usage, smoking, and sexual behavior. The only thing we ask is that you consider carefully this fact: Everything you put into your body and do with and to your body has a direct effect, either positive or negative, on your overall wellness.

Drugs and Alcohol

First, you need to know that alcohol *is* a drug; it is addictive; and many college students get hooked. Although it is legal for people over 21, it is a drug just as cocaine and Ecstasy are drugs. Drugs can basically be divided into two categories—legal and illegal. It may sound strange, but drugs run the gamut from caffeine to crystal methamphetamine. The decision to use a drug, legal or illegal, is yours and it is personal. However, every drug—from tobacco to roofies—has ramifications and health consequences. If you choose to use certain drugs, you are literally gambling with your life. Figures 14.4 and 14.5 are provided to give you a better understanding of many legal, illegal, and prescription drugs.

Do you think it is OK to take prescription drugs for recreational use because a doctor prescribed them?

How Can Prescription Drugs Negatively Impact Your Health?

More Americans today are addicted to prescription drugs than are addicted to illegal drugs, and college campuses are only a microcosm of the country. Non-medical use of prescription drugs for either recreational purposes or purposes other than their prescribed intent

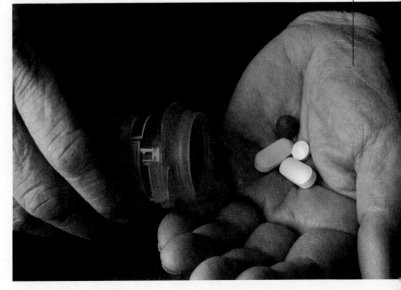

From Ordinary to Extraordinary

REAL PEOPLE | REAL LIVES | REAL CHANGE

MATTHEW L. KARRES
Motivational Speaker/Team Leader,
Weight Watchers® International

"FATSO!" The words still ring in my ears 40 years after she yelled them. When I was four years old and in pre-school, I rode a bus to school and I was the second person to be picked up. One student was already on the bus. When I climbed the steps and took my seat that first day, she yelled that word "Fatso" and thus began the years of verbal and emotional abuse.

I had always been big for my age. I had to have a larger desk than "normal" from kindergarten onward. By my eighth birthday, I weighed about 120 pounds and stood 5'9" tall. By the time I was in the sixth grade, I was 6'2" tall and even heavier. So there I was, tall, overweight, shy, and introverted. In junior high school, we had to weigh in for gym class and my classmates would run over to see how much I weighed. The scale read 225 pounds. In the ninth grade, my weight had

soared to 280 pounds and I wore a size 48 pants. This is when my mother took me to Overeaters Anonymous.

In the time period between the 9th and 10th grades, I lost 100 pounds by going on a very restricted diet from OA called "The Gray Sheet." By the time I'd begun the 10th grade, I was thin, people noticed me for something other than my weight, and I looked good for the first time that I could remember. I was happy—or so I thought. My happiness was short-lived, as my weight soon began rising again.

For the next eight years, I began to gain massive amounts of weight and the depression that followed was just as massive. My parents moved 3,000

miles away; college was not going well for me; and I was lonely, fat, depressed, and, to be truthful, suicidal. Food became my only friend—my best friend. In 10 years, I had gained over 250 pounds, reaching nearly 500 pounds and wearing size 62 pants. I developed sleep apnea, heart problems, and limb numbness.

I had to try something drastic, so I applied to become one of the first candidates for weight loss surgery. I had the surgery, but was given very inadequate warnings about the side effects: throwing up, gas, withdrawal, AND, that it was not a miracle cure. However, over three years, I lost 300 pounds and had two reconstructive surgeries. Things were good. Again, this was short-lived.

> I remember eating three Hostess Fruit Pies on the way to the Weight Watchers' meeting.

342

From Ordinary
to *Extraordinary*

REAL PEOPLE | REAL LIVES | REAL CHANGE

The problem with weight loss surgery is that it is NOT a miracle cure and you can still gain weight. I started gaining weight again and before I knew it, I was up almost 100 pounds. I was in horrible despair. Hopelessness was all I felt. My mother suggested that I join Weight Watchers®. I told her that I had tried Weight Watchers before, and then she said the words that changed my life forever.

"Matt," she stated, *"you have not tried Weight Watchers®. You tried their program YOUR way. You did not try their program THEIR way."* I decided to rejoin. I remember eating three Hostess Fruit Pies on the way to the Weight Watchers' meeting.

This time, I surrendered. I gave in to THEIR program. I did the mental and the physical work. Soon, I was losing weight again, this time in a healthy and lasting fashion. I dropped down to 190 pounds. By learning to eat properly, exercise, and think about everything that I put into my mouth, I have kept my weight steady for eight years and now I hold my "dream job" as a Motivational Leader for Weight Watchers®. It has NOT been easy and I fight every day, but I write this to say that if I can do this, you can too. There is no bigger food addict than me, but I learned that there is hope. Motivation and mental preparation can take you further than you ever imagined.

EXTRAORDINARY REFLECTIONS

Read the following statement and respond in your online journal or class notebook.

Matthew decided that he had to take a drastic step (surgery in his case) to make a positive change in his life. What drastic changes might you have to make in your life to bring about positive change in the areas of health and wellness?

14.3 *Commonly Used and Abused Legal Drugs*

NAME	USE	SOURCES	NEGATIVE EFFECTS
Caffeine	Alertness, pleasure, energy, reduce fatigue	Coffee, tea, chocolate, some soft drinks, medications	A stimulant, increased anxiety, highly addictive, increased urination, irregular heartbeat, indigestion
Alcohol	Relaxation, mood enhancer, overcome depression, overcome shyness, social acceptance, relieve tension, celebrate, bonding	Beer, wine, liquor, medications, some foods	Liver disease, memory loss, blackouts, false euphoria, depression, hangovers, birth defects, loss of balance, mental impairment, increased suicide rate, death
Tobacco	Stimulant, relaxation, social acceptance, curb appetite, increase alertness	Cigarettes, cigars, pipes, snuff, chewing tobacco	Highly addictive, increased heart and respiratory rate, increased blood pressure, increased risk of cancer, strokes, lung disease, gum disease, birth defects, strokes, cardiovascular disease
Over-the-counter drugs	Weight loss, alertness, sleeping, body building, depression, pain relief	Laxatives, diet medications, sleep enhancers, stimulants, herbal medications, nasal sprays, cough medications, pain relievers	Addiction, organ damage, nausea, vomiting, reduced absorption of vitamins and minerals, liver damage
Prescription drugs	Weight loss, alertness, sleeping, depression, pain relief, mood enhancers, muscle relaxers	Found in many forms, prescribed by medical professionals from every area of medical science	Addiction, impaired judgment, loss of memory, weight loss/gain, blackouts, death

has reached epidemic proportions. The three classes of prescription drugs most commonly abused are pain medications, antianxiety and sleep medications, and stimulants. All of these medications have a history of being overprescribed, and if students don't come to campus with pills or prescriptions from their homes, many acquire them through the Internet or other means. These drugs, because of their familiarity to the user, can be more dangerous and therefore more addictive. Casual use may unwittingly escalate into a full-blown, difficult-to-shake addiction.

Several drugs need to be discussed separately. These drugs are more commonly called "cocktail drugs" or "club drugs." They are called that because they are most commonly found in dance clubs, raves, and other places where people are interacting and inhibitions are low. Club drugs include Ecstasy, Sextasy, roofies, and crystal meth.

SEXTASY is a mixture of Ecstasy and Viagra. Ecstasy alters one's senses, but can hinder sexual functioning. To increase sexual functioning, many people have begun taking Viagra, whose real purpose is to treat impotence and assist prostate cancer patients. The mixture can cause serious problems! "Doctors warn that combining the two drugs can cause heart problems or erections that don't subside for more than four hours, possibly leading to anatomical damage" (Leinwand, 2002).

FIGURE

14.4   *Commonly Used Illegal Drugs and Dangerous Prescription Drugs*

SUBSTANCE	STREET NAME	ADMINISTRATION	THE EFECTS
MDMA	Ecstasy, E	Oral	Distortion of time and perception and enhanced enjoyment from tactile experiences
MDMA and Viagra*	Sextasy	Oral	Heightens sexual experience, rapid heart rate, increased blood pressure
Synthetic Heroin	Destiny, D	Oral	Drowsy, floating, without pain
Rohypnol	Roofies, date rape drug	Oral and in drinks	Sedation, muscle relaxation, reduction in anxiety with partial amnesia
Gamma Hydroxybutyrate	GHB	Oral and in drinks	Induces relaxation before sleep and eventual coma or death
Cocaine	Coke, crack, flake, rocks, snow	Injected, smoked, sniffed	Central nervous system stimulant, restlessness, irritability and anxiety
Amphetamines	Black beauties, crosses, hearts	Injected, oral, smoked, sniffed	Central nervous system stimulant but cause a crash effect when they wear off
Methamphetamine LSD	Crank, crystal, glass, ice, speed, acid, microdot	Injected, oral, smoked, sniffed	Central nervous system stimulant Heightened perception, hallucinations, confusion
Phencyclidine and Analogs	PCP, angel dust, boat hog, love boat	Injected, oral, smoked	Numbness, incoordination, distinct changes in body awareness similar to those associated with alcohol intoxication
Psilocybin	Magic mushroom, purple passion	Oral	Hallucinogen
Marijuana, Hashish	Blunt, grass, herb, pot, reefer, sinsemilla, smoke, weed, Mary Jane	Oral, smoked	Euphoria, mellowness, distortion in perception of time
Hashish	Hash	Oral, smoked	Euphoria and a sense of well-being, altered perception of distance and time
Anabolic Steroids	Testosterone, nandrolone	Oral, injected	Increase lean body mass, strength, and aggressiveness; cause hair loss, unexplained rage; body stops producing testosterone; testicles shrink; severe acne, depression; thoughts of suicide in some cases; tumors (liver in particular)
Heroin	Horse, smack	Injected, smoked, sniffed	Depression of the central nervous system, sense of euphoria
Opium	Dover's powder	Oral, smoked	Calm feeling, free of pain, irregular heartbeat
Barbiturates	Barbs	Injected, oral	Slurred speech, shallow breathing, sluggishness, fatigue, disorientation
OxyContin Lortab Vicodin	Oxy, OC, Tabs	Oral	Feeling of floating, being detached; HIGHLY addictive, can be deadly if overused or crushed to inhale; deadly when mixed with alcohol or other drugs
Glue	Sniff, whippets, Popper, rush	Inhaled	A temporary high that can result in brain damage, heart failure, and serious problems with the liver, lungs, and kidneys

*Viagra alone is NOT an illegal drug. Adapted from the National Institute of Drug Abuse.

ROOFIES AND GHB are very common in the club scene and can be slipped into a drink (alcoholic or not) with little trouble. Because they are usually odorless and colorless and have a very quick effect on the body, they rapidly alter your alertness and ability to function. We thus encourage you to guard your drink carefully if you are at a party or club. Letting your guard down may be a serious mistake!

CRYSTAL METH is one of the fastest-spreading drugs in this country—and one of THE most addictive and dangerous. It is used as a stimulant and can be smoked, sniffed, or injected. Some of the MANY effects include seizures, hallucinations, high blood pressure, depression, anxiety, heart attacks, rotting teeth, and malnutrition.

How much care do you actually take to protect yourself when you are out with friends?

Binge Drinking

It's common knowledge that many college students drink way too much. Although some control their drinking and use good judgment, many totally lose control. One young woman commented, "I got totally wasted and couldn't remember getting home. The taxi could have taken me anywhere" (Steinke, 2007). *Binge drinking* is classified as having three to five drinks within a three to four hour period. Many people say, "I only drink once a week." However, if that one drinking spell includes drink after drink after drink, it can be extremely detrimental to your liver, your memory, your digestive system, and your health in general, not to mention your grades and academic career.

"One of five women between the ages of 18 and 44 is said to be a binger, which is particularly disturbing because health experts are finding that alcohol takes a harsher toll on women than men; even relatively small amounts can cause damage. Women cannot drink as much as men because their bodies are smaller and their bodies have more fat and less water content. Water dilutes alcohol, and fat retains it so a martini stays in a woman's body far longer than in a man's" (Steinke, 2007). This fact, of course, doesn't mean that men can be careless about how much alcohol they consume.

In their breakthrough work *Dying to Drink,* Harvard researcher Henry Wechsler and science writer Bernice Wuethrich explore the problem of binge drinking. They state, "Two out of every five college students regularly binge drink resulting in approximately 1,400 student deaths, a distressing number of assaults and rapes, a shameful amount of vandalism, and countless cases of academic suicide" (Wechsler and Wuethrich, 2002). Many college students say they drink because it makes them relax, become better conversationalists, or act funnier than they typically are. Excessive drinking and all the ramifications and consequences are a heavy price to pay to be funnier, however. If you are participating in binge drinking, this is one activity you need to change before it brings serious consequences.

Tips for Personal Success

Consider the following tips for protecting yourself when drinking any beverage in public:

▶ Be suspicious of accepting drinks from anyone you do not know or have not known and trusted for a long time.

▶ Accept only unopened canned and/or bottled drinks when possible.

▶ Do not leave any beverage unattended while dancing or socializing. If you do, get another drink upon your return.

Now, it is your turn. Name three more tips that you would suggest to your friends so that they can protect themselves from predators.

1. _____

2. _____

3. _____

THINKING *for* CHANGE: An Activity for Critical Reflection

One of your new friends, Miriam Forsythe, has been going to a club in a popular area of town. College students hang out there after games, concerts, and campus events. Party Night, as it is known on campus, is Thursday, and you and Miriam plan to attend. Miriam had many dating restrictions when she was growing up, and is very inexperienced in taking care of herself, but she is enjoying her newfound freedom. In fact, you are somewhat worried about Miriam because she seems to be ignoring her classes and focusing only on having fun. She slept in this Thursday morning and cut classes so that she would be rested for Party Night.

Miriam has "flipped out" over Max, a senior who spent time with her at the club last Thursday night, and she is hoping that she will see him there tonight. You have heard that Max has quite a reputation as a "ladies' man," and you aren't sure that Miriam can take care of herself. When you try to talk to her about it, she brushes you off, and in so many words, tells you to mind your own business. When the two of you arrive at the club, she immediately hooks up with Max and ignores you for the rest of the evening. You look for her but are never able to locate her. Around midnight you go home with a group of friends. You look around for Miriam but she is nowhere to be found. At 3:30 a.m., Miriam staggers into your room, disheveled, drunk, and crying. She tells you that Max raped her in his apartment.

Describe the steps that you would take to help your friend.

1. _____

2. _____

3. _____

SMOKING CESSATION AND HOW TO DO IT

Is It Really Good to Be a Quitter?

Cigarette smoking is one of the most prevalent health problems in the world today. Nicotine is one of THE most addictive substances known to man, and according to the American Heart Association, it has historically been one of the hardest addictions to break. Smoking affects your brain and the more you smoke, the more you need to smoke. Many who have tried to quit state that stopping smoking is the single hardest thing they have ever tried to do; BUT, it can be done. It will take much effort and perhaps longer than you hoped, but it is possible. Consider the benefits of stopping as outlined by 1 on 1 Health in Figure 14.5.

How Addicted Are You?

Consider the following questions (adapted from 1 on 1 Health, 2006). Answer them carefully and honestly to determine the level of your addiction.

Check the statements that apply to you:

☐ Do you tend to smoke within a half hour after you wake up?
☐ Do you find it hard not to smoke where smoking is not allowed?
☐ Do you smoke 10 or more cigarettes a day?

FIGURE **14.5**   *The Effect of Stopping Smoking on the Body*

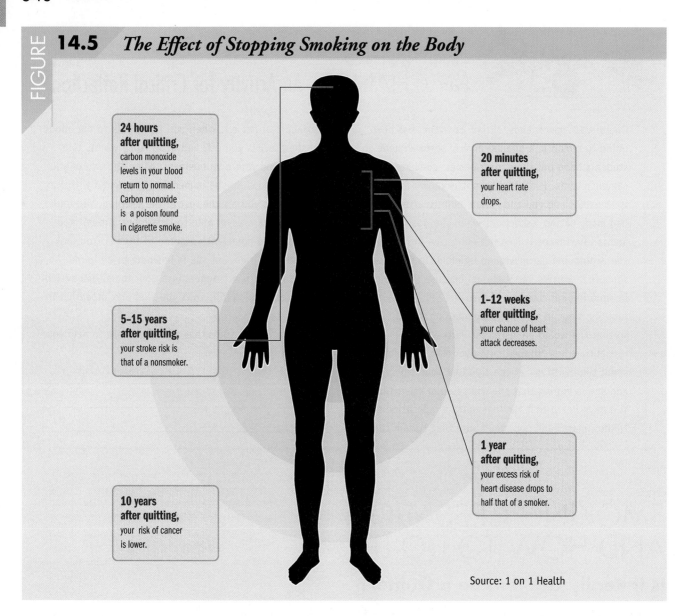

24 hours after quitting, carbon monoxide levels in your blood return to normal. Carbon monoxide is a poison found in cigarette smoke.

20 minutes after quitting, your heart rate drops.

5–15 years after quitting, your stroke risk is that of a nonsmoker.

1–12 weeks after quitting, your chance of heart attack decreases.

10 years after quitting, your risk of cancer is lower.

1 year after quitting, your excess risk of heart disease drops to half that of a smoker.

Source: 1 on 1 Health

☐ Do you smoke 25 or more cigarettes a day?
☐ Do you smoke more during the morning than during the rest of the day?
☐ Do you smoke when you're sick?
☐ Do you smoke when engaged in social activities such as parties, dinners, and when drinking?
☐ Do you associate smoking with certain places and activities?
☐ Do you want to smoke when you see others smoking?
☐ Does your mood change when you smoke or are not allowed to smoke?
☐ Have you tried to stop smoking in the past but failed?

The more checkmarks you have, the more you rely on nicotine. Even if you did not check any statements, it will still take hard work to quit smoking.

You Can Stop!

As you begin to prepare to stop smoking, you may need a plan. Some people can quit "cold turkey," but others need to develop a step-by-step plan to guide them along. Consider these tips from the U.S. Surgeon General's Office.

▶ Pay attention to WHY you smoke and think about your reasons for quitting.

▶ Tell your friends and family that you're planning to quit; ask for their help and support.

▶ Stop buying cigarettes.

▶ Think about what you'll do with the extra money when you stop buying cigarettes.

▶ Make a list of people to reach out to when you need help.

▶ Buy a stop-smoking aid; some people need them.

SEXUALLY TRANSMITTED DISEASES

Can It Happen to You?

Sexually transmitted diseases (STDs) are diseases that are generally transmitted through vaginal or anal intercourse or oral sex. Although they are most commonly spread through sexual contact, some can be transmitted through related nonsexual activities. (For example, human immunodeficiency virus—HIV—can be contracted by using contaminated needles, and crabs can be contracted through contact with contaminated bed linens or towels.)

Have you or someone you know tried to stop smoking? Was it easy or difficult? Did they need medical help to stop?

FIGURE 14.6 *Sexually Transmitted Diseases*

STD	TRANSMISSION	SYMPTOMS	DIAGNOSIS	CONSEQUENCES
AIDS/HIV	Sexual contact (vaginal, oral, and anal) Infusion with contaminated blood (sharing needles, etc.) From mother to fetus Breast feeding	People may go years without symptoms. When symptoms appear they may include flu-like symptoms, fever, weight loss, fatigue, diarrhea, and cancer.	Bodily fluids such as blood, urine, or saliva reveal HIV antibodies. Two tests include the Western Blot and the ELISA. A new "20 Minute Test" is now available at many doctors' offices.	Transmission to sexual partners, many health-related issues such as heart problems, gastroenterological issues, and death.
CHLAMYDIA	Sexual contact (vaginal, oral, and anal) By touching one's eye after touching infected genitals From mother to child	Women: Sometimes no symptoms; painful urination, occasional vaginal discharge, bleeding between periods Men: Discharge from penis, painful urination	A cervical smear for women Extract of fluid from the penis for men	Rapid progression if undiagnosed or untreated Cancer Pneumonia Death
GONORRHEA	Sexual contact (vaginal, oral, and anal) From mother to child	Women: Vaginal discharge, painful urination, bleeding between periods Men: Discharge from penis, painful urination	Medical examination from discharge or culture	Transmission to sexual partners, Various inflammations Possible sterility in men and women

(continued)

14.6 *Sexually Transmitted Diseases (continued)*

STD	TRANSMISSION	SYMPTOMS	DIAGNOSIS	CONSEQUENCES
GENITAL WARTS	Sexual contact (vaginal, oral, and anal) Other types of contact such as infected towels or clothing	Women: Single or multiple soft, fleshy growths around anus, vulva, vagina, or urethra; itching or burning sensation around sexual organs Men: Burning around sexual organs; single or multiple soft, fleshy growths around anus or penis	Medical examination	Transmission to sexual and nonsexual partners Precancerous conditions Cannot be cured
HERPES (SIMPLEX VIRUS TYPES I AND II)	Sexual contact (vaginal, oral, and anal) Touching Kissing Sharing towels, toilet seats	Single or multiple blisters or sores on genitals; generally painful, but disappear without scarring, reappear	Medical examination Culture and fluid inspections	Transmission to sexual and nonsexual partners Cannot be cured
HEPATITIS (VIRAL A, B, C, AND D TYPES)	Sexual contact, especially involving the anus Contact with infected fecal matter Transfusion of contaminated blood Severe alcoholism Exposure to toxic materials	Can be asymptomatic; mild flu-like symptoms, fever, abdominal pain, vomiting, and yellowish skin or eyes; loss of appetite; whitish bowel movements; brown urine	Medical examination of blood for hepatitis antibody; liver biopsy	Transmission to sexual and nonsexual partners Severe liver problems or failure Cancer of the liver Death
SYPHILIS	Sexual contact (vaginal, oral, and anal) Touching an infected chancre	Four stages: (1) painless red spots later forming a sore; (2) skin rash or mucous patches; (3) latent stage, no symptoms; (4) complications leading to possible death	Primary stages by medical examination of fluid from a chancre Secondary stage by blood test, VDRL	Transmission to sexual and nonsexual partners Death (although seldom advances this far today)

Adapted from *Sex on Your Terms* by Elizabeth Powell, Allyn and Bacon, 1996, and *Access to Health,* 7th ed., by Rebecca J. Donatelle and Lorraine G. Davis, Allyn and Bacon, 2002.

STDS AND BIRTH CONTROL

Do You Know What You Need to Know?

Figure 14.7 is provided to give you information about other serious sexually transmitted diseases and the most common birth control methods.

FIGURE **14.7** *Birth Control and STD Protection*

TYPE	USAGE	PREVENTION OF STDS		
		YES*	NO	NOT NECESSARILY
Abstinence	Refraining from *all sexual activity*, vaginal, anal, oral, and outercourse. One hundred percent effective.	X		
Outercourse	Oral genital sex and mutual masturbation.			X
The Pill	Also called oral contraceptive. The most widely used form of birth control.		X	
The Male Pill	Also called oral contraceptive. Newly developed for male usage.		X	
The Patch	Called the Ortho-Evra patch, it is a transdermal method of dispensing similar medicine as in the Pill. The patch lasts for one week.		X	
The NuvaRing	A clear, flexible vaginal ring that is self-inserted in the vagina and releases a low dose of hormones. It lasts for a month.		X	
Diaphragm	Round, flexible disk inserted into the vagina to cover the cervix.		X	
IUD	Also called intrauterine device. Must be inserted into the uterus by a physician.		X	
Male Condom	A sheath, generally latex, worn over the penis to prevent sperm from entering the vagina.	X		
Female Condom	A loose-fitting sheath inserted into the vagina to prevent sperm from entering the uterus.	X		
Spermicides	Inserted into the vagina to kill sperm. Comes in foams, jellies, suppositories, and creams.		X	
Withdrawal	Also called coitus interruptus. The penis is withdrawn from the vagina before ejaculation.		X	
Rhythm Method	Abstaining from sexual intercourse during the menstrual cycle when ovulation occurs.		X	
Norplant	Silicone tubes surgically embedded in a woman's upper arm to suppress fertilization.		X	
Sterilization	Male and female surgery. Male version is called vasectomy, and female versions are called tubal sterilization, tubal ligation, and hysterectomy.		X	
Cervical Cap	Much like the diaphragm, it is fitted into the vagina by a doctor. It is meant to be used with a spermicide and can provide up to 48 hours of protection.		X	

*Only total abstinence is 100% effective in preventing sexually transmitted diseases.

CHANGING IDEAS TO *Reality*

Your understanding of wellness and the gift that a healthy body is to you during your college education and beyond is a wonderful beginning to a bright future. During this chapter you have been given the opportunity to think about the roles the mind, body, and soul have in your overall approach to wellness. You've gotten to look at the importance of personal responsibility in your approach to relationships, alcohol, and drugs. College is a time when you have an opportunity to reflect on the great questions in life and enjoy wonderful relationships and conviviality, but this can take place only if your body, mind, and soul are healthy.

Remember these tips as you plan for your future of living well:

▶ Take time to be with friends or family.
▶ Use the power of positive thinking.
▶ Keep yourself healthy with exercise.
▶ Take care of your spiritual health.
▶ Think before you drink or take drugs.
▶ Develop a way to decompress after school or work.
▶ Understand that your choices have consequences.
▶ Eat a balanced and regular diet.
▶ Surround yourself with positive people.
▶ Protect yourself at clubs and parties.
▶ Be careful around new people until you know you can trust them.

Our wish for you is that you carefully develop your wellness plan and take personal responsibility for your total health. We urge you to make wise decisions since some choices have very bad consequences. No matter what you may have done in the past, there is always an opportunity to change, mature, and become more responsible for your own well-being.

DID YOU KNOW ?

GREG LOUGANIS was born in 1960, adopted by his Greek-American parents, and raised in California. In 1976 at the age of 16 he placed second in the Summer Olympics in Montreal, Canada. In 1982, he won two world diving titles and in 1984, he won two gold medals at the Los Angeles Olympic Games. In 1988, he won two more gold medals at the Seoul, Korea, Olympic Games even though he suffered a concussion after hitting his head on the springboard. This feat earned him ABC's *Wide World of Sports* title of "Athlete of the Year" for 1988.

In 1994, Louganis announced that he was gay and in 1995 he published an autobiography revealing that his partner had abused and raped him for years and that he was HIV positive. He received much criticism for not revealing his HIV status after his diving accident in 1988. He was advised by an HIV expert that his minor bleeding posed no danger to other athletes. Regardless, after his disclosure, he lost every major company endorsement except for Speedo®.

Today, Greg Louganis is a gay-rights activist, TV commentator, and actor. In 1997, Mario Lopez portrayed him in the movie *Breaking the Surface: The Greg Louganis Story*.

"Live with intention. Walk to the edge. Listen hard. Practice wellness. Play with abandon. Laugh. Choose with no regret. Appreciate your friends. Continue to learn. Do what you love. Live as if this is all there is."

—Mary Anne Radmacher

KNOWLEDGE in BLOOM

Bringing Positive Change in Your Life

Each chapter-end assessment is based on *Bloom's Taxonomy of Learning*. See the inside front cover for a quick review.

UTILIZES LEVELS 1–6 OF THE TAXONOMY

Throughout this chapter, we have tried to give you information that will be useful to you as you think about your overall wellness. The following activity will ask you to look at your life in more detail. You will be asked to identify one area of wellness in the mind, soul, or body that you would like to improve.

The area of wellness I want to improve is _____

Using the Change Implementation Model from Chapter 1, design a plan to bring this change in wellness into your life.

LEVEL 1—REMEMBERING Identify what you need or want to change about your wellness and why.	
LEVEL 2—UNDERSTANDING Research your options for making the desired change and seek advice and assistance from a variety of sources.	
LEVEL 3—APPLYING Demonstrate how these sources would be helpful.	
LEVEL 4—ANALYZING What conclusions could be drawn about your life if these changes are not made?	
LEVEL 5—EVALUATING Predict how your wellness will be enhanced by employing this change in your life.	
LEVEL 6—CREATING Design a plan to bring about this wellness change in your life. Consider using one of the goal-setting charts from Chapter 1.	

SQ3R *Mastery* Study Sheet

EXAMPLE QUESTION: *(from page 336)* What does it mean to have a holistic approach to health?	**ANSWER:**
EXAMPLE QUESTION: *(from page 337)* What effect does the mind have on wellness?	**ANSWER:**
AUTHOR QUESTION: *(from page 344)* Why are prescription drugs as dangerous as nonprescription drugs?	**ANSWER:**
AUTHOR QUESTION: *from page 346)* What are some of the residual damages from binge drinking?	**ANSWER:**
AUTHOR QUESTION: *(from page 336)* How do the body, mind, and soul affect wellness?	**ANSWER:**
AUTHOR QUESTION: *(from page 337)* What is depression and how can you take steps to improve depression if you have it?	**ANSWER:**
AUTHOR QUESTION: *(from page 351)* Discuss at least three birth control methods.	**ANSWER:**
YOUR QUESTION: *(from page ___)*	**ANSWER:**
YOUR QUESTION: *(from page ___)*	**ANSWER:**
YOUR QUESTION: *(from page ___)*	**ANSWER:**
YOUR QUESTION: *(from page ___)*	**ANSWER:**
YOUR QUESTION: *(from page ___)*	**ANSWER:**

Finally, after answering these questions, recite this chapter's major points in your mind. Consider the following general questions to help you master this material.

▶ What was it about?
▶ What does it mean?
▶ What was the most important thing I learned? Why?
▶ What were the key points to remember?

Three-Day Food Tracker

For the next **three days**, track *everything you consume through your mouth*: nutritious food, junk food, water, alcohol, carbonated drinks, fruits, chewing gum, etc. . . . After you have "tracked" your food, return to page 341 and complete the questions regarding your food intake.

DAY ONE	DAY TWO	DAY THREE

CHAPTER 15
PLAN

FOCUSING
ON YOUR
PROFESSIONAL
CAREER AND
LIVING WELL

"No one can tell you what your life's work is, but it is important that you find it. There is a part of you that already knows; affirm that part."

—Willis
 W. Harman

WHY READ THIS CHAPTER?

What's in it for me?

Why? Because the world has changed dramatically over the past few years, making a great deal of previous information about careers obsolete. In fact, change has caused many jobs and careers that had long been staples of the U.S. economy to disappear. This means that many people don't exactly know how to advise you because they may be working from information and experiences that were good for them and their time but are not necessarily good for you and this time. So you have to take control of your life and your destiny and plan for a successful and rewarding future and career. This chapter should help guide you in making key decisions and in planning for the future.

WHY do I have to know how to write a resume and cover letter when I have no idea what I really want to do when I get out of college? WHY will a chapter on career planning help me at all? WHY is interviewing such an important part of the job search process? WHY do I need to plan for the future when I can hardly keep my head above water now?

By carefully reading this chapter and taking the information provided seriously, you will be able to:

1. Identify the Ten Steps to preparing for the future.
2. Develop a career plan based on comprehensice self-study questions.
3. Use the D.O.C.T.O.R. system to write a powerful cover letter and resume.
4. Write a compelling thank you note.
5. Use the R.E.W.A.R.D.S. system to prepare for an interview.

CHAPTER 15 / PLAN

"The driving force of a career must come from the individual. Remember: jobs are owned by the company; you own your career."

—Earl Nightingale

NAME: Kendra Hernandez
INSTITUTION: University of Arizona, Tucson, AZ
MAJOR: Nursing
AGE: 20

I am the first in my family to attend college so I have to overcome the barriers that have held others in my family back. I've had to deal with change and face new challenges on my own because my family had no experience with college. My parents were worried about my going away from home. My grandparents were very afraid because I was going so far away—but it is actually only two hours away. They were all proud that I could have this experience and do what they did not have the opportunity to accomplish. I want to succeed for them as well as for myself.

I have had to learn to deal with the fact that I am different from other students in some ways. Even though I was born in this country and am an American citizen, I get lots of questions such as, "Were you born in Mexico?" Because I am Hispanic, I sometimes feel different, but that's just something I have to deal with. I'm sure everyone feels different in some ways. Universities and colleges have people attending from all over the world and many different nationalities represented by students who are American citizens. I advise all students to get to know people from different backgrounds and customs because it will be part of your growth. Be open to meeting new people who have different backgrounds from you. There are great people from all races and nationalities.

Choosing a major is a very important decision, so I advise students to take their time and explore a variety of possibilities before locking into a final choice. I joined a club that had a variety of medical professionals speak, and this helped me sort out my direction. I thought I wanted to be a doctor but after shadowing several nurses in a hospital and asking lots of questions, I realized that I really want to be a nurse. I love taking care of people and having the one-on-one contact. I am a "people person" so nursing fits my personal makeup much better than being a doctor. These nurses are now my mentors and part of my network. They serve as great references for me and open many doors for me because they know I am dedicated to becoming an outstanding nurse. Follow your heart, but pay attention to where your heart is taking you!

SCAN & QUESTION

In the preface of this book (page xix), you read about the **SQ3R Study Method**. Right now, take a few moments, **scan this chapter**, and on page 380, write **five questions** that you think will be important to your mastery of this material. In addition to the two questions below, you will find five questions from your authors. Use one of your **"Study for Quiz"** stickers to flag this page for easy reference.

EXAMPLES:

▶ **Why is it important to write an excellent resume?** (from page 372)

▶ **What does R.E.W.A.R.D.S. stand for?** (from page 374)

PLANNING FOR THE FUTURE

What's Change Got to Do with It?

Change has got everything to do with it! One of the things that human beings have the most difficulty handling is change. Yet, never before in the history of the world have people been bombarded with so many changes—and they are not likely to slow down anytime soon. If you look at technology, for example, you know that you hardly learn to use one version of a cell phone or computer before a newer and greater version is on the market. Because change is going to be a watchword for your generation, your authors have interwoven one central theme—**change**—throughout your text, and nowhere does it apply more powerfully than in planning for a career and your future.

The very first chapter of this book focused on change, which shows you how important change is to your future. The entire book is based on the changes you may need to make as you move through your college career, as well as the multitude of changes that are coming your way in every aspect of your life. We have focused so much attention on change because it is real, now, and in your face.

WHAT AM I GOING TO DO FOR THE REST OF MY LIFE?

How Do I Make Such an Awesome Decision?

"What am I going to do for the rest of my life?" is an overwhelming question for anyone, much less a beginning college student, especially in a dramatically changing global environment. What was true last year—and sometimes even last week—is no longer true. Your generation has a wonderful opportunity to be the first generation that truly functions in a world economy; at the same time, you have the concern of having few guidelines to follow.

While many things that worked for your parents and grandparents are still important and relevant today—things like ethics, integrity, hard work, education, honesty, teamwork—many practices that were true in their time are no longer valid. Your grandfather may have gone to work for a company and stayed there all his life. Back then, employers were loyal to employees, and employees were loyal to the company. Work stayed pretty much the same from one year to the next. All that has changed. You will have many different jobs during your lifetime—you will most likely have three or four different careers, and what constitutes your work will be constantly changing.

What changes do you foresee coming in your chosen career field in the next five years?

What Is the Difference Between a Career and a Job?

A job is just a place you go to earn a paycheck or a task that an employer assigns to you. It could be making hamburgers at a fast-food restaurant. A career could be owning a chain of fast-food restaurants, which allows you to be the entrepreneur you always wanted to become. A career is something you own. Employers will be looking for people who can fill a job; you should be looking for a career that enhances your life. You need to use jobs to progress within your career choice. You might use your current or future job to move forward in a career progression, applying skills, experience, and knowledge to advance. The ideal career will provide internal rewards as well as monetary satisfaction.

What unique interests, skills, and talents do you possess to give you that "cutting edge" in today's workforce?

10 BABY STEPS THAT WILL BECOME GIANT SUCCESSES TOMORROW

What Strategies Can I Use to Successfully Prepare for My Future?

You might consider what you are doing today and the rest of your college career as baby steps that will lead to giant steps in being prepared for the future. The following strategies will help you as you move toward your goals.

1. **Master the material and make good grades.** Grades do matter! While not everyone can graduate with a 4.0 GPA, you need to be one of those people who earns a respectable GPA. Not only do good grades show that you have gained knowledge in certain areas, they also indicate the work ethic and sense of responsibility that employers are seeking.

2. **Come to grips with your abilities, interests, values, and personal characteristics.** You might be telling people that you want to be a corporate attorney or a businesswoman. Do you really know what these careers entail? How many years of education are required? What kind of GPA does it take to get into a really good business school?

Specifically, what do you want to do? Where will the jobs be? What kind of preparation does it take? Do you have the ability and perseverance to become what you dream about becoming?

3. **Fine-tune your computer skills.** Most first-year students today have good computer skills, but these skills need to be very strong. Your skills need to include the ability to work with spreadsheets, databases, and PowerPoint. Some careers will require knowledge and expertise of industry software—you need to be an expert if this is true in the field you want to work in. Learn to develop Web pages, and create your own Web site that reflects a professional, career-oriented person.

4. **Hone your communication (speaking and writing) skills.** By now, you are tired of hearing this, but it's true. Enroll in classes that are writing and speaking intensive, even if you hate the thought of doing so, because many recruiters point out the weaknesses of applicants' writing and speaking skills. Good communications skills could be a major asset to you in a job search in the future. You have to pay the price to become a good writer and speaker!

"A study has shown that first and second year students spend more time deciding on a movie to watch than on what they might want for a career, even though a movie lasts two hours and a career lasts a lifetime."
—Bob Orndorff

From Ordinary to Extraordinary

REAL PEOPLE | REAL LIVES | REAL CHANGE

MARK JONES
SCANA Senior Customer Service Trainer
Columbia, SC

My proudest moment? Finally coming to the realization that I am a functional member of a highly dysfunctional family. *"I know. I know. Many people say they have a dysfunctional family,"* but in my case, it is the raw, inescapable truth. My realization may not sound like much to an outsider, but when you finally realize that you do not have to be a victim of your family or your past, it is a proud moment! I can confidently say, ***"I am not like them."***

I don't have any memories of a time when my family was "normal." My mother, who has been clinically depressed my entire life, attempted suicide when I was four years old. I have never known a day when she was not heavily medicated. My father had the first of four heart attacks when I was six. My parents divorced when I was 11 and I went to live with my father. My mother remarried when I was 13. When I was 15—my father died, leaving us very little. Even the mobile home in which we lived was repossessed.

My new stepfather was legally blind and has never driven a car. My mother did not drive either. They never wanted me to get my permit or drive and fought my attempts to do so for years. They thought walking everywhere was perfectly normal. My stepfather did not have any children of his own and did not have any parenting skills. I was treated more as a tenant than a son or stepson. As a matter of fact, I had to pay rent to live with him and my own mother. Due to my father's death, I drew a small Social Security check until I graduated from high school. Every month, much of that money had to be turned over to my stepfather. I even had to buy my own bed to sleep in. Of course, we had our share of good times, too. But I knew this situation was far from "normal"—whatever that was.

When I was in my early twenties, I begged a dear friend, Stella, to let me use her car so I could try for my driver's license. I had practically no driving experience, but somehow, I passed the test. I paid $200 for my first car in two installments of $100 each. It was a 1973 Buick LeSabre that was wrecked down one entire side and had been used in demolition donut field races. But, it was much better than walking everywhere. This was a turning point in my life. I was in my early twenties and working in a local grocery store. I had enrolled in the university right after high school, but I

> I paid $200 for my first car ... a 1973 Buick LeSabre that was wrecked down one entire side and had been used in demolition donut field races.

From Ordinary to Extraordinary

REAL PEOPLE | REAL LIVES | REAL CHANGE

had to drop out because I could not get a grant and did not make enough money to pay tuition. I later enrolled in the local community college but after one semester, I realized I could not afford this either.

Basically, I had to make a hard, life-altering decision. I did not want to live my life in debt as my father had, so I made up my mind that I would have to take a few steps back to eventually go forward. I began to look for a job that offered educational benefits. I scanned the phone book for hospitals, utility companies, banks, and government agencies that offered this benefit. Every Monday night, their job lines would be updated and I would call, fill out an application, and wait. Nothing!

Finally, I learned how to properly fill out an application. I would call the job lines many times and write down every word in their advertisements. Then, I would craft my application and letter based on *their needs,*

not *my experiences.* I had to learn to apply for a job as if I already had it. After two years and many attempts to secure a suitable position, a utility company hired me—AND they had educational benefits. Finally, I could go back to school and get another car! I began working toward my degree and after six long, hard years, I graduated with a Bachelor of Science in business management. It was not easy, as I am sure you know. I had to take some courses online, and I was in class every Friday night for years and years.

During my time in college, I worked my way up in the company and today, 17 years later, I am a senior trainer for SCANA, an $11 billion Fortune 500 utility holding company founded in 1846. I design training programs and development materials for new hires, system enhancements, and employee upgrades.

I look back on my childhood and early adulthood and I am proud of the

fact that I did not let my past or my family dictate my future. I survived. I refused to succumb to their life. I knew that I had to have my own life with my own fate. You can have this too. Never let your past or your family tell you what you're capable of doing. Take chances. Take risks. And, if you have to take a step backward to go forward, never be ashamed to do that, too.

EXTRAORDINARY REFLECTION

Read the following statement and respond in your online journal or class notebook.

Mr. Jones came from a family that did not support him financially, emotionally, or educationally. What advice would you give to someone who might be experiencing the same type of environment? Does your family have to play a role in your life for you to be successful?

ESSENTIAL CORNERSTONE

Accountability:
How will being accountable help you in making plans for your future?

Social Networking Moment:
Share your response to this Essential Cornerstone with peers in your social network. Choose two responses from your peers and respond to their postings.

5. Actively engage in exploring career options. Your career—and variations of it—will last a lifetime. Doesn't that fact make it evident that you need to spend some time "trying on" careers to see if one might be a good fit? Read about careers in professional journals in your library, go to the career counseling center, talk to people who are in the career that interests you, and attend career fairs and job expos.

6. Get involved and stay active. Job recruiters are looking for people who are leaders, who understand teamwork, and who have shown by their involvement that they can manage time and make things happen. Select one or two activities or organizations and become actively engaged. Work your way to the top. You'll learn valuable skills, and it will look great on your resume! Go to job interviews with excellent experiences on your resume.

7. Give back to your community. Here again, recruiters consider community service a great asset. Many times students look at community service as just another task, but after it's over, they realize how many benefits they derived from helping others. Many careers have been jump-started by an outstanding community service project that showcased a person's talents. You'll get more than you give by participating in community service.

8. Spend your summers working in internships, preferably ones that carry college credit. Once you have decided on a direction that interests you, explore the field by actually working in it. If you begin as a first-year student working for a company that interests you, perform well, and go back every summer, the chances are good that a job will be waiting for you when you graduate from college.

9. Expand your diversity and your cultural and international knowledge. This is a great time to learn everything you can about people from different backgrounds. Make friends with people from international backgrounds, explore different cultures, and learn to appreciate and celebrate diversity.

10. Take advantage of your campus career center. Few students really take full advantage of their college's career center. The counselors there may not have all the answers, but they can start you in the right direction. Check out the center on your campus—and soon!

(Adapted from "Top Ten Career Strategies for Freshmen and Sophomores" [Orndorff, 2008].)

DEVELOPING YOUR CAREER SELF-STUDY PLAN

What Do You Want to Be When You "Grow Up"?

More people than you would imagine have trouble deciding what they want to be when they "grow up." Studies indicate that more than 20% of all first-year college students do not know what their majors will be. That's all right for the time being, but before long you will need to make a decision, as this choice affects your selection of classes, cocurricular activities, and possible internships.

The questions that follow are designed to help you decide what you want to do with the rest of your life—your career.

What Is Your Personality Type?

You can best answer this question by taking a personality inventory, such as the Myers-Briggs Type Indicator®. (An inventory based on the MBTI is located in Chapter 7 of this book.) This question is important, because your personality may very well indicate the type of work in which you will be successful and happy. If you are a "people person", you probably will not be very happy, for example, in a job with minimal human contact and interaction.

Describe your personality type. _____
_____

How will your personality type affect your career path? _____
_____

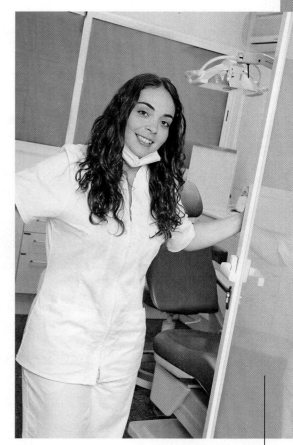

What Are Your Interests?

Understanding your specific interests may help you decide on a career. If you love working on cars, you might consider becoming a mechanical engineer. If you love to draw or build things, you might be interested in architecture or sculpting.

What are your major interests? _____
_____

How can these interests be transferred to a career choice? _____
_____

Do You Enjoy Physical or Mental Work?

Many people would go crazy if they had to spend even one hour per day in an office. Others would be unhappy if they had to work in the sun all day or use a great deal of physical strength. The answer to this question will greatly narrow your list of potential career choices. For example, if you are an outdoors person who loves being outside in all kinds of weather, then you should probably avoid careers that are limited to indoor work. You should also consider whether you have any physical limitations that might affect your career choice.

Do your interests and passion match your chosen major and/or career path?

Do you enjoy physical or mental work or both? Why? _____
_____

What does this mean to your career path? _____
_____

What Is Most Important? Money? Service? Independence? Or a Combination?

Most people, if asked, "Why do you work?" would respond, "For the money." There is nothing wrong with wanting to make money in your profession, but not all professions, regardless of their worth, pay well. Some of the hardest and most rewarding work pays the least. You have to decide whether to go for the money or to do something that is personally challenging and rewarding to you. Many times, you can find a career with both!

Tips for Personal Success

Consider the following tips for preparing to be successful in your future career:

▶ Read about a variety of careers that interest you.

▶ Study several Web sites that provide information about career planning.

▶ Identify jobs and careers that appear to be "rising" and not "setting."

Now it's your turn. Create a list of three tips about steps to take today to prepare for the right career in the future that you would offer to your fellow classmates.

1. _____
2. _____
3. _____

Would it bother you (or would you love it) to travel two to four days per week for your career?

Is your major goal in choosing a profession money or something else? What? _____

_____

What does your goal mean to your career path?

_____

_____

Where Do You Want to Live?

Although this question may sound strange, many careers are limited by geography. If you are interested in oceanography, you would be hard-pressed to live in Iowa; if you love farming, New York City would be an improbable place for you to live. If you like small towns, you might not be happy in Atlanta. Some people simply prefer certain parts of the United States (or the world) to others. You need to ask yourself, "What climate do I really enjoy?" "Where would I be the happiest?" "Do I want to live near my family or away from them?"

Where do you eventually want to live? Why? _____

_____

What does your preference mean for your career path? _____

_____

Do You Want to Travel?

Some jobs require travel; some people love to travel, some hate it. Ask yourself whether you want to be away from your home and family four nights per week, or whether you want a job that does not require any travel.

Do you enjoy travel? Do you want to do a lot of traveling? _____

_____

What does this mean for your career path? _____

_____

What Motivates You and What Do You Value?

Do you value relationships, possessions, money? Are you motivated by love, security, challenges, or power? Once you have identified what you value and what motivates you, you can identify careers that closely match your personal value system and eliminate careers that don't motivate you. If you have to constantly compromise your values just to get a paycheck, you may be unhappy, and motivation will be hard to find on a daily basis.

What do you truly value in your life and what motivates you? _____

_____

How might these two things affect your career decisions? _____

_____

What Are Your Skills?

Are you especially good at one or two things? Are you good with computers, a good manager of money, a good carpenter, a good communicator? Employers still stress the importance of three basic skills: writing, speaking, and listening. If you have these skills, you are ahead of the pack. If not, you need to enroll in a class that will help you become better at all three.

What are your skills? What do you do well? _____

_____

How could your strongest skills help you make a career decision? _____

_____

Do You Like Routine?

The answer to this question will narrow down your choices tremendously. If you like routine, you will want a career that is conducive to routine and provides structure. If you do not like routine and enjoy doing different things each day, certain careers will be unrealistic for you.

Do you like routine or do you prefer variety? Why? _____

_____

How does this affect your career path? _____

_____

DREAM JOB

Using the answers you provided to the previous questions and a variety of additional resources such as Web sites, shadowing, and interviews, write a description of your dream job—the job you would have if you could do anything you want to do.

_____

_____

_____

_____

_____

BLOOM LEVEL 5 QUESTION

HELP ME: I'M UNDECLARED

Is It Awful that I Don't Know What I Want to Do?

No, it is not. And being undeclared is not a fatal disease. It is not a disgrace or a weakness. It is a temporary state of mind, and the best way to deal with it is to stop and think. You should not declare a major because you are ashamed to be undeclared, and you shouldn't allow yourself to be pressured into declaring a major. Instead, you can take measures to work toward declaring a major and being satisfied with your decision. It is better to be undeclared than to spend several semesters in a field that is wrong for you, wasting hours that won't count toward a degree. On the other hand, the sooner you declare a major, the less likely you will be to take courses that do not count toward your eventual decision. While you do need to take your time and make a good decision, you don't have forever!

THINKING for CHANGE: An Activity for Critical Reflection

LaKeisha has been trying to plan for her future, but she really has no idea what she would like to do with her life. Her grades are excellent, and she loves college, but she doesn't have a clue of what she wants to declare as a major. She has read her textbooks carefully, listened to her most forward-thinking professors, and talked to her parents, but so far she has come up with a blank slate. Her parents didn't go to college, so LaKeisha can get very little guidance at home.

LaKeisha knows that she needs to declare a major—and that means she has to have some idea of what she wants to do with her life. Her biology professor, Dr. Margaret Palmer, has made quite an impression on her. In fact, she has suggested to LaKeisha that she consider majoring in biology, with plans of becoming a medical researcher or doctor. Her words to LaKeisha were, "You are a very bright young woman. Students don't come along every day who can grasp science and

math concepts like you can. I could help you apply for scholarships if you are interested."

LaKeisha is interested in finding out more from Dr. Palmer. She thinks she might love being a doctor or a researcher, but she believes that she needs to know more before going down that path. How can LaKeisha go about getting Dr. Palmer to become her mentor? How might she get Dr. Palmer to let her work with her as an assistant so she can get some hands-on experience?

_____

_____

What kinds of long-term plans will LaKeisha need to make if she decides to pursue a career as a doctor or medical researcher?

_____

_____

10 Steps To Career Decision Making

STEP 1—DREAM! If money were not a problem or concern, what would you do for the rest of your life? If you could do anything in the world, what would you do? Where would you do it? These are the types of questions you must ask yourself as you try to select a major and a career. Go outside, lie on the grass, and look up at the sky; think silently for a little while. Let your mind wander, and let the sky be the limit. Write your dreams down. These dreams may be closer to reality than you think.

STEP 2—GO WHERE THE PUCK IS GOING! Sound crazy? The great hockey champ Wayne Gretzky made the comment that _this **ONE STEP**_ had been his key to success. What does it mean? He said that when he was playing hockey, he did not skate to where the puck was at the moment, he skated to where the puck was GOING. He anticipated the direction of where it was going to be hit, and when it came his way, he was already there—ready to play. Think of your career in this light. Go to where the future will be bright, not necessarily where the present is bright at this moment. Look ahead and try to determine what is going to be "hot" in the future, not what is hot right now. Plan ahead. Look at trends. Read. Ask questions. Think in the future, not the moment.

STEP 3—TALK TO YOUR ADVISOR. Academic advisors are there to help you. But don't be surprised if their doors are sometimes closed. They teach, conduct research, perform community service, and sometimes advise hundreds of students. Always call in advance; make an appointment to see your advisor. When you have that appointment, make your advisor work for you. Take your college catalog and ask questions, hard questions. Your advisor will not make a career decision for you, but if you ask the proper questions, he or she can be of monumental help to you and your career decisions.

Use students in your program as advisors, too. They will be invaluable to you as you work your way through the daily routine of college. Experienced students can assist you in making decisions about your classes, electives, and work-study programs. They can even help you join and become an active member of a preprofessional program.

STEP 4—USE ELECTIVES. The accreditation agency that works with your school requires that you be allowed at least one free elective in your degree program. Some programs allow many more. Use your electives wisely! Do not take courses just to get the hours. The wisest students use their electives to delve into new areas of interest or take a block of courses in an area that might enhance their career opportunities.

STEP 5—GO TO THE CAREER CENTER. Even the smallest colleges have some type of career center or a career counselor. Use them! Campus career centers usually provide free services. The same types of services in the community could cost from $200 to $2,000. The professionals in the career center can provide you information on a variety of careers and fields, and they can administer interest and personality inventories that can help you make career and other major decisions.

STEP 6—READ, READ, READ! Nothing will help you more than reading about careers and majors. Ask your advisor or counselor to help you locate information on your areas of interest. Gather information from colleges, agencies, associations, and places of employment. Then read it!

STEP 7—SHADOW. Shadowing describes the process of following someone around on the job. If you are wondering what engineers do on the job, try calling an engineering office to see whether you can sit with several of their engineers for a day over spring break. Shadowing is the very best way to get firsthand, honest information regarding a profession in which you might be interested.

STEP 8—JOIN PREPROFESSIONAL ORGANIZATIONS. One of the most important steps you can take as a college student is to become involved in campus organizations and clubs that offer educational opportunities, social interaction, and hands-on experience in your chosen field. Preprofessional organizations can open doors that will help you make a career decision, grow in your field, meet professionals already working in your field, and, eventually, get a job.

STEP 9—GET A PART-TIME JOB. Work in an area that you may be interested in pursuing as a career. Get a part-time job while you are in school or work in a related field in the summer.

STEP 10—TRY TO GET A SUMMER PRACTICUM OR INTERNSHIP. Work in your field of interest to gain practical experience and see if it really suits you. Some programs require a practicum or internship, and this experience often leads to your first full-time job.

By working through this 10-step plan, you will come closer to finding what you really want and need in your life's work. Take your time, study, read, ask questions, shadow others, and most importantly, make your own decisions. Yes, you may change majors or even careers along the way, but that is a part of life's journey.

> "It's a sad day when you find out that it's not an accident—or time—or fortune, but just YOURSELF that kept things from you."
> —Lilian Hellman

WORKIN' 9 TO 5—OR TRYING TO

Is It Really Possible to Sell Yourself Through a Cover Letter and Resume?

Remember the old saying, "You are what you eat"? When searching for any position, you could change that to read, ***"You are what you write."*** Your resume and cover letter are your first marketing tools and in many cases must stand alone when a recruiter is determining whether or not to interview you. Just as a well-designed and well-written resume and cover letter can be a wonderful first step, a poorly designed and poorly written resume and cover letter can doom you before you even leave your house. A good thing to remember is this: A resume and cover letter get you the interview; the interview gets you the job.

A cover letter is basically an expansion of your resume. A cover letter gives you the chance to link your resume, skills, and experience together with your interest in *a specific company's* position and their advertising. You will need to write many cover letters to make this link work properly; in other words, you will most likely need to write a cover letter designed for each position for which you apply. Your cover letter will often be the stepping stone to get an employer to even look at your resume. Consider it "a teaser," if you will, of all of your talents and experience. Just as you would never send someone a greeting card and not sign it, you would never send a resume and not tell the person or committee *why* you sent it. Your cover letter tells why.

WRITE A POWERFUL AND CONCISE COVER LETTER

How Do You Get Your Foot in the Door?

The most important part of the job search process is the preparation that must be done *prior to starting* the interview process. A carefully crafted letter and resume communicate your past history (education, skills, and experience) that makes you the ideal candidate for the position. They are the first marketing pieces a recruiter sees when determining whether or not to interview you. Consider the general tips outlined in Figure 15.1

Figure 15.2 provides a sample cover letter and indicates the correct format and spacing to the left of the letter's content.

FIGURE

15.1 *General Tips for the Cover Letter and Resume*

- ▶ Both your resume and cover letter *MUST be typed*. There are no exceptions to this rule. Ever! Seriously, EVER!
- ▶ Your cover letter and resume must be printed on the same *type and color* of *fine-quality paper*. Cheap paper sends the message that you don't care. This is not the place or time to pinch pennies; buy excellent quality, 100% cotton stock, resume-quality paper.
- ▶ Check your printer and be sure that the print quality is impeccable. Never send a cover letter or resume with smudges, ink smears, or poor print quality.
- ▶ When you print your cover letter and resume, be certain that the watermark on the paper is turned in the correct direction. Hold it up to the light and you will see the watermark embedded in the paper. This may sound silly and picky, but people notice attention to detail.
- ▶ Do not fold your cover letter or resume. Purchase a packet of 9 x 13 envelopes in which to send your materials.
- ▶ Do not handwrite the address on the envelope. Use a label or type the address directly on the envelope. Remember, first impressions are important.
- ▶ Never send a generic photocopy of a cover letter or resume, even on the finest paper.
- ▶ Layout, design, font, spacing and color must be considered in the building of your cover letter and resume.
- ▶ Unless you are specifically asked to do so, NEVER discuss money or salary history in either your cover letter or resume. This could work against you. When asked for a salary history, use ranges.
- ▶ Your resume and cover letter MUST be error-free. That's right, not one single error is acceptable including grammar, spelling, punctuation, layout/spacing, dates, or content.
- ▶ Each cover letter must be signed in black or blue ink.

FIGURE

15.2   *Sample Cover Letter with Formatting Information*

Your name and address on high-quality paper. Your name should be larger and/or in a different font to call attention. ⟶

The date (then double space) ⟶

The specific person, title, and address to whom you are writing (then double space) ⟶

The formal salutation followed by a colon (then double space) ⟶

Paragraph 1 (then double space) ⟶

Paragraph 2 (then double space) ⟶

Paragraph 3 (then double space) ⟶

Final paragraph or closing (then double space) ⟶

The complementary close (then four spaces) ⟶

Your handwritten signature in black or blue ink within the four spaces ⟶

Your typed name ⟶

Enclosure contents ⟶

CARSON SCOTT

1234 Lake Shadow Drive,   (123) 555-1234
Maple City, PA 12345   Scott@bl.com

January 3, 2011

Mr. James Pixler, RN, CAN
Director of Placement and Advancement
Grace Care Center
123 Sizemore Street, Suite 444
Philadelphia, PA 12345

Dear Mr. Pixler:

Seven years ago, my mother was under the treatment of two incredible nurses at Grace Care Center in Philadelphia. My family and I agree that the care she was given was extraordinary. When I saw your ad in today's *Philadelphia Carrier,* I was extremely pleased to know that I now have the qualifications to be a part of the Grace Care Team as a Medical Assistant.

Next month, I will graduate with an Occupational Associate's Degree from Victory College of Health and Technology as a certified Medical Assistant. My resume indicates that I was fortunate to do my internship at Mercy Family Care Practice in Harrisburg. During this time, I was directly involved in patient care, records documentation, and family outreach.

As a part of my degree from Victory, I received a 4.0 in the following classes:

✓ Management Communications
✓ Microsoft Office (Word, Excel, Outlook, PowerPoint)
✓ Business Communications I, II, III
✓ Anatomy and Physiology I, II, III
✓ Medical Coding I, II
✓ Principles of Pharmacology
✓ Immunology I, II, III, IV
✓ Urinalysis and Body Fluids
✓ Clinical Practicum I, II, III

This, along with my past certificate in Medical Transcription and my immense respect for Grace Care Center, makes me the perfect candidate for your position.

I have detailed all of my experience on the enclosed resume. I will call you on Monday, January 24 at 11:30 a.m. to discuss how my education and experiences can help streamline operations and continue superior patient care at Grace. In the meantime, please feel free to contact me at the number above.

Sincerely,

carson scott

CARSON SCOTT

Enclosure: Resume

UNDERSTAND THE DO'S AND DON'T'S OF MEMORABLE RESUMES

How Do You Sell Yourself?

"Eight seconds." That is all you have to gain the attention of your potential employer, according to Susan Ireland, author and consultant (2003). *"In eight seconds, an employer scans your resume and decides whether she will invest more time to consider you as a job candidate. The secret to passing the eight-second test is to make your resume look inviting and quick to read"* (p. 14).

A resume is the blueprint that details what you have accomplished regarding your education, experience, skills acquisition, workplace successes, and progressive responsibility and/or leadership. It is a painting (that YOU are able to "paint") of how your professional life looks. It is the ultimate advertisement of YOU! Your resume must create interest and hopefully a *desire* to find out more about you! Just as your cover letter should be tailored to specific positions, your resume should be, too.

As you begin to build your resume, remember to "call in the **DOCTOR.**"

D Visual **design** and format are imperative to a successful resume. You need to think about the font that you plan to use; whether color is appropriate (usually, it is not); the use of bullets, lines, or shading; and where you are going to put information. You also need to pay attention to the text balance on the page (centered left/right, top/bottom). The visual aspect of your resume will be the first impression. "Make it pretty" (Britton-Whitcomb, 2003).

O Writing a clear and specific **objective** can help get your foot in the door. The reader, usually your potential employer, needs to be able to scan your resume and gather as much detail as possible as quickly as possible. A job-specific objective can help. Consider the following two objectives:

Before: **Objective:** To get a job as an elementary school teacher in the Dallas Area School District

After: **Objective:** To secure an elementary teaching position that will enable me to use my 14 years of creative teaching experience, curriculum development abilities, supervisory skills, and commitment to superior instruction in a team environment.

C **Clarity** is of paramount importance, especially when including your past responsibilities, education, and job responsibilities. Be certain that you let the reader know exactly what you have done, what specific education you have gained, and what progress you have made. Being vague and unclear can cost you an interview.

T When writing your resume, you may be tempted to fudge a little bit here and there to make your resume look better. Perhaps you were out of work for a few months and you think it would look bad to have this gap in your chronological history. Avoid the urge to fudge. Telling the absolute **truth** on a resume is essential. A lie, even a small one, can (and usually will) come back to haunt you.

O Before you begin your resume, think about the **organization** of your data. You will be provided a model resume in this chapter; however, there are several other formats you might select. It is most important that you present your information in an attractive, easy-to-read, comprehensive format.

R **Reviewing** your resume and cover letter is important, but having someone else review them for clarity, accuracy, spelling, grammar, placement, and overall content can be one of the best things you can do for your job search.

The following basic tips will help you as you begin building a dynamic resume.

GENERAL TIPS

- ▶ Do not date-stamp or record the preparation date of your resume in any place.
- ▶ Limit your resume (and cover letter) to one page each (a two-page resume is appropriate if you have more than 10 years' experience).
- ▶ Use standard resume paper colors such as white, cream, gray, or beige.
- ▶ Use bullets (such as these) to help profile lists.
- ▶ Avoid fancy or hard-to-read fonts such as *curlz* or **CURLZ**.
- ▶ Use a standard font size between 10 and 14 points.
- ▶ Do not staple anything to your resume (or cover letter).
- ▶ Try to avoid the use of "I" or "me" or "my" in your resume (if you must use them, do so sparingly).
- ▶ Avoid contractions such as "don't," and do not use abbreviations.
- ▶ Use action verbs such as "designed," "managed," "created," "recruited," "simplified," and/or "built."
- ▶ Avoid the use of full sentences; fragments are fine on a resume, but not in a cover letter.
- ▶ Use the correct verb tense. You will use past tense (such as "recruited") except when talking about your current job.
- ▶ Do not include information that does not pertain to this particular job.
- ▶ Choose a format that puts your "best foot" or greatest assets forward.

Remember, the job market is highly competitive. Your job is to write a resume that is solid, appealing, comprehensive, and brief. The idea is to get someone to read it and make that person want to know more about you.

There are different types of resumes, but primarily they can be classified as chronological resumes, functional resumes, accomplishment resumes, or a combination of each.

- ▶ A **chronological resume** (Figure 15.3) organizes education and work experiences in a reverse chronological order (i.e., your last or present job is listed first).
- ▶ A **functional resume** organizes your work and experiences around specific skills and duties.
- ▶ An **accomplishment resume** allows you to place your past accomplishments into categories that are not necessarily associated with the job you are applying for but show your track record of "getting the job done."

In the past, what preparations have served you best in getting ready for an interview?

THE BIG DAY IS HERE

How Do You Make the Impression of a Lifetime?

Remember the ***"eight seconds rule"*** for making an impression. Consider this: During the interview process, you have even less time. A judgment is made immediately about you: your dress, your grooming, your stance, your handshake, and your overall visual impression. Right or wrong, the interviewer will form an immediate first impression of you—just as you will form an immediate first impression of your interviewer.

15.3 *Chronological Resume*

CARSON SCOTT
1234 Lake Shadow Drive, Maple City, PA 12345   (123) 555-1234
Scott@bl.com

OBJECTIVE: To work as a medical assistant in an atmosphere that uses my organizational skills, compassion for people, desire to make a difference, and impeccable work ethic.

PROFESSIONAL EXPERIENCE:

January 2007–Present   Medical Assistant Intern
                                 Mercy Family Care Practice, Harrisburg, PA
                                 ▶ Responsible for completing patient charts
                                 ▶ Took patient's vitals
                                 ▶ Assisted with medical coding

February 2003–December 2006   Medical Transcriptionist
                                 The Office of Brenda Wilson, MD, Lancaster, PA
                                 ▶ Interpreted and typed medical reports
                                 ▶ Worked with insurance documentation
                                 ▶ Assisted with medical coding
                                 ▶ Served as Office Manager (1/05–12/06)

March 1998–February 2003   Ward Orderly
                                 Wallace Hospital, Lancaster, PA
                                 ▶ Assisted nurses with patient care
                                 ▶ Cleaned patient rooms
                                 ▶ Served patient meals

August 1995–March 1998   Administrative Assistant
                                 Ellen Abbot Nursing Care Facility
                                 ▶ Typed office reports
                                 ▶ Organized patient files

EDUCATION:
Occupational Associate's Degree—Medical Assistant
Victory Health Institute, Harrisburg, PA
May 2008 (with honors)

Certificate of Completion—Medical Transcription
Philadelphia Technical Institute
December 2002

Vocational High School Diploma—Health Sciences
Philadelphia Vocational High School
August 1995

As you begin to prepare for your interview, consider the following mnemonic. If you confidently *carry* **R E W A R D S** with you to an interview, you will most likely *get* rewards after the interview such as a job offer, benefits, and a career in which you can grow and prosper.

R = **Rapport**

Rapport is basically your "relationship" (intended or unintended) with another person— the emotional alliance you establish with someone. Consider how you come across to others. Rapport involves your verbal and nonverbal communication efforts. You should strive to establish a positive relationship with potential employers and future colleagues.

E = Education and Training

Be confident about what you know and eloquently promote your abilities, skills, and talents to the interviewer. Remember, if you don't promote yourself, it is unlikely that anyone else will.

W = Willingness

Project a sense of willingness to learn new things, to become a team member, to assist the company with growth and new projects, and to keep up with advancements and changes in the modern world of work. Potential employers enjoy seeing an attitude of willingness and engagement.

A = Appearance

Dress for success. Pay close attention to your grooming, your hygiene, your hair, your clothing, and, yes, even your shoes and socks (or hosiery). It all matters—and it is all noticed. Never make the mistake of thinking that appearance is not important.

R = Response

Project positivity and optimism in your responses to the questions asked in the interview. Even if you have to talk about your weaknesses or past experiences of conflict and turmoil, put a positive spin on them. Let the interviewer know that you have learned from adversity.

D = Demeanor

Project a quality of confidence (not cockiness), intelligence, professionalism, and positivity. Carrying yourself with confidence during the interview will not go unnoticed. Pay attention to your handshake, your eye contact, your posture, your mannerisms, and your facial expressions.

S = Sincerity

No one likes phony people, especially a potential employer. Be yourself and strive to be sincere in your answers, your emotions, and your passion.

WIN, LOSE, OR DRAW, *ALWAYS* SAY "THANK YOU" IN WRITING

Do I Have to Say "Thank You" Even If I Don't Get the Job?

Indeed, it is safe to say that sending a thank you note is ***"the most overlooked step in the entire job search process"*** (Bolles, 2008). Yes, this is a mandatory step for every interview, and it is also mandatory that you send one to every person who interviewed you. Period. In today's world of high-tech and run, run, run, this one act will set you apart from the thousands who interview on a daily basis. And yes, you must send a thank you note even if you DO NOT get the job. "When do I send the thank you note?" you might ask. ***Immediately after the interview.***

Sending a simple thank you note does many things. It lets the employer know that you have good manners, that you respect other people's time and efforts, that you are considerate, that you really do care about the position, and that you have positive people and communication skills. Yes, all of that from a card and a stamp that can cost less than $2.

In Figures 15.4 and 15.5, you will find examples of two thank you notes. Review them and consider using them as templates to build your own notes.

FIGURE 15.4 *Thank-You Note: After the Interview*

CARSON SCOTT
1234 Lake Shadow Drive
Maple City, PA 12345
Scott@bl.com

January 20, 2011

Mr. James Pixler, RN
Director of Placement
Grace Care Center
123 Sizemore Street
Philadelphia, PA 12345

Dear Mr. Pixler,

I wanted to thank you for the wonderful opportunity to meet with you and the team at Grace Care Center on Monday. Your facilities are amazing, and the new wing is going to be a remarkable addition to your center.

I enjoyed learning more about the new position in Medical Assisting, and I think that my qualifications and experiences have prepared me for this challenging opportunity. I would consider it an honor to answer any further questions that you might have or to meet with you again if you consider it necessary.

I look forward to hearing from you at your convenience. If you need any additional information, you can reach me at 123-555-3454.

Thank you,

carson scott

CARSON SCOTT

FIGURE 15.5 *Thank-Your Note: After a Position Rejection*

CARSON SCOTT
1234 Lake Shadow Drive
Maple City, PA 12345
Scott@bl.com

January 20, 2011

Mr. James Pixler, RN
Director of Placement
Grace Care Center
123 Sizemore Street
Philadelphia, PA 12345

Dear Mr. Pixler,

I wanted to thank you for the opportunity to meet with you and the team at Grace Care Center on Monday. I enjoyed learning more about your center and the planned addition.

While I was not offered the position, I did want to let you know that I appreciate your time and I would like for you to contact me if you have any future openings where you feel my qualifications and experiences would match your needs. Grace is an incredible facility, and I would consider it an honor to hold a position there.

If you need to contact me in the future, you can reach me at 123-555-3454.

Thank you for your time and assistance and good luck to you and your colleagues.

Sincerely,

carson scott

CARSON SCOTT

CHANGING IDEAS TO *reality*

REFLECTIONS ON CAREER AND LIFE DEVELOPMENT

Making a decision about your major or career can be difficult, but, fortunately, you still have a few months before you have to make this choice. Use this time to explore all avenues that will expose you to different possibilities. This is a growing time for you and you might discover new interests and directions that you had never considered before. Follow your heart, and pursue your dreams. If there is something you have always wanted to do or be, chances are your desires will not change even after you study other options.

This is your one lifetime! You need to prepare to do something you love. No matter how much money you make, you won't be happy unless you are doing something that matters to you, something that allows you to keep learning and becoming, something that provides you opportunities to give back—perhaps the best gift of all.

As you reflect on this chapter, keep the following pointers in mind:

▶ Identify the assets you can offer a company.

▶ Learn to promote and sell yourself in an interview.

▶ Discover your personality type and make it work for you.

▶ *Shadow* and do volunteer work to learn as much as you can about the profession.

▶ Realize that life is *more* than money.

▶ Know your own *value* system and what motivates you.

"If you follow your bliss, doors will open for you that wouldn't have opened for anyone else."

—Joseph Campbell

KNOWLEDGE *in* BLOOM

DEVELOPING SKILLS and Knowledge to Make Wise Career Decisions

Each chapter-end assessment is based on *Bloom's Taxonomy of Learning*. See the inside front cover for a quick review.

UTILIZES LEVEL 4 OF THE TAXONOMY

Applying the 10 Essential Cornerstones

On page 8 in Chapter 1, "Change," you will find a list of **10 ESSENTIAL CORNERSTONES**. These cornerstones are the foundation for a successful life and career. Although you are a first-year student and have time to make decisions about your career, ways you plan to change, and how you want to live your life, now is a good time to start thinking about these heavy decisions. You have one life . . . this is not a trial run!

After researching several Web sites about a career you might be interested in and talking with people who are pursuing this career, apply the 10 Cornerstones to this possible choice to see if it meets the criteria for a lasting, rewarding career.

Passion

How does this career possibility make you feel when you think about going to work and doing this every day for many years? How would this choice enable you to give back to others and feel rewarded?

_____

_____

_____

_____

Motivation

How does this career choice relate to goals and objectives you might have already set for yourself? Will this career help you keep growing and learning? Will it help you further develop your inner strengths? Discuss your responses in the space below.

_____

_____

_____

_____

Knowledge

Will you be able to master the knowledge that is required to be successful in the field that you are exploring? How will this field require you to keep learning and growing? Will the knowledge you have to master be challenging and exhilarating to you?

_____

_____

_____

_____

Resourcefulness

Is this a field that will allow you to be resourceful? Will this field challenge you to seek new and different opportunities? Will you need to be a problem solver?

_____

_____

_____

_____

Creativity

Will this career allow you to be creative? Will you be able to implement innovative ideas? Will you have an opportunity to grow in ways that allow you to solve complex problems?

_____

_____

_____

_____

Adaptability

Will you be required to use adaptive techniques? Will you be able to grow by constantly reinventing yourself?

_____

_____

_____

_____

Open-Mindedness

Will this career give you an opportunity to work in a diverse work community? Will you be required to learn to appreciate differences in cultures? Would learning a new language be valued, appreciated, and useful?

_____

_____

_____

_____

Communication

Will you work in an environment that supports networking among colleagues and clients? Will this career enable you to develop mentors and to become a mentor yourself?

_____

_____

_____

_____

Accountability

Will this career enable you to be accountable for the overall development of your well-being? Will it provide opportunities to develop solid relationships? Will it offer you resources to learn more about financial development and responsibility?

_____

_____

_____

_____

Vision

Will this career provide opportunities to continue growing as the global economy keeps bringing about major changes to the workplace? Will the company's management be visionary in their approach to keeping up with competition?

_____

_____

_____

_____

SQ3R *Mastery* STUDY SHEET

EXAMPLE QUESTION: *(from page 374)* What does R.E.W.A.R.D. stand for?		**ANSWER:**
EXAMPLE QUESTION: *(from page 372)* Why is it important to write an excellent resume?		**ANSWER:**
AUTHOR QUESTION: *(from page 361)* Discuss the differences between a career and a job.		**ANSWER:**
AUTHOR QUESTION: *(from page 364)* Why does personality type matter when deciding on a major or a job?		**ANSWER:**
AUTHOR QUESTION: *(from page 368)* Discuss three of the steps to declaring a major.		**ANSWER:**
AUTHOR QUESTION: *(from page 370)* Why is it important to write a compelling cover letter to accompany your resume or application?		**ANSWER:**
AUTHOR QUESTION: *(from page 375)* Why do you need to write a thank you note even if you do not get the position?		**ANSWER:**
YOUR QUESTION: *(from page ___)*		**ANSWER:**
YOUR QUESTION: *(from page ___)*		**ANSWER:**
YOUR QUESTION: *(from page ___)*		**ANSWER:**
YOUR QUESTION: *(from page ___)*		**ANSWER:**
YOUR QUESTION: *(from page ___)*		**ANSWER:**

Finally, after answering these questions, recite this chapter's major points in your mind. Consider the following general questions to help you master this material.

- ▶ What was it about?
- ▶ What does it mean?
- ▶ What was the most important thing I learned? Why?
- ▶ What were the key points to remember?

REFERENCES

Adler, R., Rosenfeld, L., & Towne, N. (2006). *Interplay. The Process of Interpersonal Communication* (2nd ed.). New York: Holt, Rinehart and Winston.

Altman, I., & Taylor, D. (1973). *Social Penetration: The Development of Interpersonal Relationships.* New York: Holt.

American Library Association. (1989). *Presidential Committee on Information Literacy. Final Report.* Chicago: American Library Association.

American Psychological Association. (2008). *For a Better Understanding of Sexual Orientation and Homosexuality.* Retrieved August 12, 2008, from http://www.apa.org/topics/orientation.html.

Anderson, L., & Bolt, S. (2008). *Professionalism: Real Skills for Workplace Success.* Upper Saddle River, NJ: Pearson Prentice Hall.

Bach, D. (2003). *The Finish Rich Notebook.* New York: Broadway Books.

Barrett, D. (2008). *Average Student Loans Top $19,000.* Retrieved September 2, 2008, from http://encarta.msn.com/encnet/departments/financialaid/?article=averagestudentloans.

Beebe, S., Beebe, S., & Redmond, M. (2008). *Interpersonal Communication: Relating to Others* (5th ed.). Boston: Allyn and Bacon.

Block, S. (February 22, 2006). Students Suffocate Under Tens of Thousands in Loans. *USA Today.*

Bolles, R. N. (2008). *What Color Is Your Parachute? A Practical Manual for Job-Hunters and Career-Changers, 2008 Edition.* Berkeley, CA: Ten Speed Press.

Bosack, J. *Fallacies.* Dubuque, IA: Educulture Publishers, 1978.

Britton-Whitcomb, S. (2003). *Resume Magic: Trade Secrets of a Professional Resume Writer.* Indianapolis, IN: JIST Works Publishing, Inc.

Broderick, C. (2003). *Why Care About Your Credit Score?* InCharge Education Foundation, Inc.

Bureau of Labor Statistics. (2006). *How Americans Spend Time.* Washington, DC: Department of the Census. Retrieved February 9, 2009, from www.bls.gov.

Chronicle of Higher Education. (August 29, 2008). *Almanac Edition, 2008–2009, 55*(1), 18.

Cojonet (City of Jacksonville, FL). (2003). *Consumer Affairs Gets New Tough Law on Car Title Businesses.* Accessed from www.coj.net/Departments/Regulatory+and+Environmental+Services/Consumer+Affairs/TITLE+LOANS.htm.

Collegeboard. (2008). *College Prices Increase in Step with Inflation: Financial Aid Grows but Fewer Private Loans Even Before Credit Crisis.* Accessed at http://www.collegeboard.com/press/releases/201194.html.

Consumer Response Center. (2003). *Identity Theft and Fraud,* 2003; *ConsumerReport, Money Advisor,* 2008; *The State* Newspaper, August 31, 2008.

Consumer Reports. (September 2008). *Protect Yourself Online: The Biggest Threats and the Best Solutions.*

Consumer Reports. Money Advisor. (September 2008). *Protecting Your Identity.*

Cooper-Arnold, A. L. (2006). *Credit Card Debt: A Survival Guide for Students.* www.youngmoney.com/credit_debt/credit_basics/050804-02.

Daly, J., & Engleberg, I. (2006). *Presentations in Everyday Life: Strategies for Effective Speaking.* Upper Saddle River, NJ: Allyn and Bacon.

Department of the Census, Department of Labor. (2008). *Education and Training Pay.* Washington, DC: U.S. Government Printing Office.

DeVito, J. A. (2007). *Interpersonal Messages: Communication and Relationship Skills.* Boston: Pearson Education.

The Digerati Life. (2008). *Lost Money: How Money Drains Add Up to $175,000 in 10 Years.* Retrieved September 5, 2008, from http://www.thedigeratilife.com/blog.index.php/2008/07/31/lost-money-how-money-drains-.

Donatelle, R., & Davis, L. (2002). *Health: The Basics.* Upper Saddle River, NJ: Prentice Hall.

Drugs of Abuse: National Institute on Drug Abuse website, accessed at http://www.nida.nih.gov/.

Dunn, R., & Griggs, S. (2000). *Practical Approaches to Using Learning Styles in Higher Education.* New York: Bergin & Garvey.

Feagin, J. R., & Feagin, C. B. (2008). *Racial and Ethnic Relations.* Upper Saddle River, NJ: Pearson/Prentice Hall.

Gamble, T., and Gamble, M. (1978). *Public Speaking in the Age of Diversity.* Upper Saddle River, NJ: Prentice Hall.

Gardner, H. (1983). *Frames of Mind: The Theory of Multiple Intelligence.* New York: Basic Books.

Get More Done. (2009). Retrieved January 3, 2009, from www.getmoredone.com.

Girando, D., Dusek, D., & Everly, G. (2009). *Controlling Stress and Tension* (8th ed.). Boston: Benjamin Cummings.

Glenn, J. M. L. (October 2007). Generations at Work: The New Diversity. *Business Education Forum, 62*(1).

The Goddess Path. (2009). *Mnemosyne, the Goddess of Memory.* Accessed from www.goddessgift.com.

Goleman, D. (2006). *Emotional Intelligence: Why It Can Matter More than IQ* (10th Anniv. Ed.). New York: Bantam.

Gordon, E. E. (2005). *The 2010 Meltdown: Solving the Impending Jobs Crisis.* Westport, CT: Praeger.

Hall, E. (1966). *The Hidden Dimension.* Garden City, NY: Doubleday.

Housden, R. (2007). Taking a Chance on Joy. *O's Guide to Life: The Best of the Oprah Magazine.* Birmingham, AL: Oxmoor House.

Ireland, S. (2003). *The Complete Idiot's Guide to the Perfect Resume.* Indianapolis, IN: Alpha Publishing Company.

Jung, C. (1921). *Psychology Types.* In *Collected Works of C.G. Jung* (Volume 6; R. Hull, Translator). Princeton, NJ: Princeton University Press, 1976.

Kallock, A. (April 16, 2009). Sunstein: Lack of Ideological Diversity Leads to Extremism. *The Harvard Law Review.*

Kiewra, K., & Fletcher, H. (1984). The Relationship Between Note Taking Variables and Achievement Measure. *Human Learning, 3,* 273–280.

Kirszner, L., & Mandell, S. (1995). *The Holt Handbook.* Orlando, FL: Harcourt Brace College Publishers.

Konowalow, S. (2003). *Planning Your Future: Keys to Financial Freedom.* Columbus, OH: Prentice Hall.

Lane, H. (1976). *The Wild Boy of Aveyron.* Cambridge, MA: Harvard University Press.

Lane, S. (2008). *Interpersonal Communication: Competence and Contexts.* Boston: Pearson/Allyn and Bacon.

Leinwood, D. (September 23, 2002). Ecstasy-Viagra Mix Alarms Doctors. *USA Today.*

Light, R. (2001). *Making the Most of College: Students Speak Their Minds.* Cambridge, MA: Harvard University Press.

Maslow, A. (1943). A Theory of Human Motivation. *Psychological Review. 50,* 370–396.

McCornack, S. (2007). *Reflect and Relate: An Introduction to Interpersonal Communication.* Boston: Bedford-St. Martin's Press.

National Leadership Council for Liberal Education and America's Promise. (2008). *College Learning for the New Global Century.* Washington, DC.

Nellie Mae Study. (2005). *Credit Cards 101,* p. 1.

Nelson, D., & Low, G. (2003). *Emotional Intelligence: Achieving Academic and Career Excellence.* Upper Saddle River, NJ: Prentice Hall.

1 on 1 health. (2006). *You Can Stop Smoking: Tips to Help You Quit for Good.* GlaxoSmithKline Group.

Ormondroyd, J., Engle, M., & Cosgrave, T. (2001). *How to Critically Analyze Information Sources.* Cornell University Libraries, www.library.cornell.edu.

Orndorff, Bob. (2008). "Top Ten Career Strategies for Freshmen and Sophomores." Retrieved on November 18, 2008, from http://www.jobweb.com/parents.aspx?id=50.

Payday Loan: Consumer Information. (2008). Retrieved February 12, 2009, from www.paydayloaninfo.org.

Pauk, W. (2005). *How to Study in College* (8th ed.). New York: Houghton Mifflin.

Paul, R., & Elder, L. (2006). *A Miniature Guide to Critical Thinking: Concepts and Tools.* Dillon Beach, CA: Foundation for Critical Thinking.

Personality Type Portraits. Retrieved December 2, 2008, from www.personalitypage.com.

Potter, J. (2005). *Becoming a Strategic Thinker: Developing Skills for Success.* Upper Saddle River, NJ: Pearson/Prentice.

Rosato, D. (July 2008). Life Without Plastic. *Money,* pp. 91–95.

Russell, N. S. (2003). *Words, Words, Words.* Retrieved October 7, 2008, from http://www.careerknowhow.com/improvement/words.htm.

Sapir-Whorf Hypothesis. (1956). In Whorf, B. *Language, Thought, and Reality.* Cambridge, MA: MIT Press.

Schmalleger, R. (2006). *Criminal Justice: A Brief Introduction* (6th ed.). Upper Saddle River, NJ: Prentice Hall.

Seyler, D. (2003). *Steps to College Reading* (2nd ed.). Boston: Allyn & Bacon.

Shattuck, R. (1980). *The Forbidden Experiment: The Story of the Wild Boy of Aveyron.* New York: Farrar, Straus & Giroux.

Sherfield, R. (2004). *The Everything Self-Esteem Book.* Avon, MA: Adams Media.

Sherfield, R., & Moody, P. (2009). *Solving the Professional Development Puzzle: 101 Solutions for Career and Life Planning.* Upper Saddle River, NJ: Pearson.

Slavin, R. E. (2009). *Education Psychology: Theory and Practice.* Upper Saddle River, NJ: Pearson Education.

Smilksten, R. (2003). *We're Born to Learn: Using the Brain's Natural Learning Process to Create Today's Curriculum.* Thousand Oaks, CA: Corwin Press.

Smith, B. (2007). *Breaking Through: College Reading* (8th ed.). Upper Saddle River, NJ: Pearson Education.

Snyder, C. R. (2000). Hope Theory: Rainbows of the Mind. *Psychology Inquiry, 13,* 249–275.

Snyder, C. R., & Lopez, S. (2007). *Positive Psychology: The Scientific and Practical Explorations of Human Strength.* Thousand Oaks, CA: Sage Publications.

The *State* Newspaper. (August 31, 2008). *Protecting Your Identity.*

Steinke, R. (2007). Women on the Rocks. *O's Guide to Life: The Best of the Oprah Magazine.* Birmingham, AL: Oxmoor House.

Tarkovsky, S. (2006). *Mind, Body, and Soul: The Key to Overall Wellness and Health.* Ezine articles.com. Retrieved September 11, 2006, from http://ezinearticles.com/?Mind,-Body,-and-Soul—-The-Key-To-Overall-Wellness-and-Health.

Texas A&M University. *Improve Your Memory.* Retrieved January 5, 2009, from www.scs.tamu.edu/selfhelp/elibrary/memory.asp.

Tidwell, L., & Walther, J. (July 2002). Computer-Mediated Communication Effects on Disclosure, Impressions, and Interpersonal Evaluations: Getting to Know One Another a Bit at a Time. *Human Communication Research, 28,* 317–348.

Tieger, P., & Barron-Tieger, B. (2001). *Do What You Are: Discover the Perfect Career for You Through the Secrets of Personality Type* (3rd ed.). Boston: Little, Brown.

Turnitin.com. Accessed September 30, 2008, from http://www.turnitin.com/static/home.html.

21 Facts About the Internet. (2008). Retrieved January 24, 2009, from http://www.bizwaremagic.com/quick_internet_history.htm.

UC Berkeley—Teaching Library Internet Workshop. (2005). *Evaluating Web Pages: Techniques to Apply and Questions to Ask.* www.lib.berkeley.edu/TeachingLib/Guides/Internet/Evaluate.htr. Copyright by the Regents of the University of California.

U.S. Bank. (2002). *Paying for College: A Guide to Financial Aid.* Minneapolis, MN.

U.S. Bureau of Labor Statistics. (2007). *U.S. Census. Education and Training Pay.* Washington, DC: U.S. Government Printing Office.

U.S. Department of Education. (2008). *Newsblade.* http://newsblaze.com/story/20070912020000800001.mwir/topstory.html.

U.S. Department of Education. (2008–2009). *The Student Guide: Financial Aid from the U.S. Department of Education.* Washington, DC: U.S. Dept. of Education.

U.S. Equal Opportunity Commission. (1990). *American's with Disability Act of 1990,* Titles I and V. http://www.eeoc.gov/policy/ada.html.

Waitley, D. (1997). *Psychology of Success: Developing Your Self-Esteem.* Boston: Irwin Career Education Division.

Wallechinsky, D., & Wallace, A. (2005). *The New Book of Lists: The Original Compendium of Curious Information.* Edinburgh, Scotland: Conongate Books.

Walther, J., & Burgoon, J. (1992). Relational Communication in Computer-Mediated Interaction. *Human Communication Research, 19,* 50–88.

Webster's College Dictionary. (1995). New York: Random House.

Wechsler, H., & Wuethrich, B. (2002). *Dying to Drink: Confronting Binge Drinking on College Campuses.* New York: Rodale Press.

Wetmore, D. (2008). *Time Management Facts and Figures.* Accessed December 1, 2008, from www.balancetime.com.

Williams, E. (June 26, 2008). *Students need help combating credit card debt.* Testimony before the House Financial Services Subcommittee on Financial Institutions and Consumer Credit. Retrieved September 2, 2008, from http://www.americanprogress.org/issues/2008/06/williams_testimony.html.

Woolfolk, A. (2006). *Educational Psychology* (10th ed.). Boston: Allyn and Bacon.

Yip, P. (August 31, 2008). College Campuses Are Ripe for the Picking. *The State* newspaper.

Zarefsky, D. (2001). *Public Speaking: Strategies for Success* (3rd ed.). Boston: Pearson/Allyn & Bacon.

Zen Habits. (2008). *Simple Living Manifesto: 72 Ways to Simplify Your Life.* Accessed from http://zenhabits.net.

INDEX